A farewell to arms?

From 'long war' to long peace in Northern Ireland

EDITED BY
MICHAEL COX, ADRIAN GUELKE
AND FIONA STEPHEN

Manchester University Press

MANCHESTER AND NEW YORK

distributed exclusively in the USA by St. Martin's Press

Published by Manchester University Press
Oxford Road, Manchester MI3 9NR, UK
http://www.manchesteruniversitypress.co.uk

Distributed exclusively in the USA by
St. Martin's Press, Inc., 175 Fifth Avenue, New York,
NY 10010, USA

Distributed exclusively in Canada by
UBC Press, University of British Columbia, 2029 West Mall,
Vancouver, BC, Canada V6T 1Z2

British Library Cataloguing-in-Publication Data
A catalogue record for this book is avalaible from the British Library

Library of Congress Cataloging-in-Publication Data applied for

ISBN 0 7190 5796 5 *hardback*
     0 7190 5797 3 *paperback*

First published 2000

07 06 05 04 03 02 01 00   10 9 8 7 6 5 4 3 2 1

Typeset in Caslon and Frutiger Condensed
by Koinonia Ltd, Manchester
Printed in Great Britain
by Bell & Bain Limited, Glasgow

Contents

APPENDICES

List of tables and figures

Tables

Figure

List of contributors

Arthur Aughey teaches politics in the University of Ulster and is the author of several works on Northern Ireland, including *Under Siege: Ulster Unionism and the Anglo-Irish Agreement* and (with Duncan Morrow), *Northern Ireland Politics*.

Paul Bew is Professor of Irish Politics at the Queen's University of Belfast and has published several books on the politics and history of Ireland and Northern Ireland including *Ideology and the Irish Question* (with Peter Gibbon and Henry Patterson), *Northern Ireland 1921–1996* and (with Henry Patterson) *The British State and the Ulster Crisis*.

Michael Cox is Professor of International Relations in the Department of International Politics in the University of Wales, Aberystwyth. He taught at the Queen's University of Belfast between 1972 and 1995. He has also been editor of *Irish Studies of International Affairs* since 1995, and is the author of several books on international politics, including *US Foreign Policy after the Cold War: Superpower without a Mission?* and *Rethinking the Soviet Collapse*.

John Darby was formerly director of INCORE (Institute for Conflict Resolution) at the University of Ulster, Coleraine. He is the author of several books on the North – the most recent being *Managing Difference* and *Scorpions in a Bottle*.

Brice Dixon has taught at both the Queen's University of Belfast and Ulster University where he is Professor of Law. He is currently Chief Commissioner for the Northern Ireland Human Rights Commission.

John Dumbrell teaches American Studies at the University of Keele and has a long-standing interest in Northern Ireland. His books include *American Foreign Policy: Carter to Clinton* and *The Making of American Foreign Policy*.

Sean Farren was elected for the constituency of North Antrim at Assembly and Forum elections in 1982, 1996 and 1998. During the 1996–1998 negotiations he was one of the SDLP's Senior Negotiators. He was appointed Minister for Higher Education in the Northern Ireland Executive established in December 1999.

Kate Fearon is an adviser to the Northern Ireland Women's Coalition and the author of *Women's Work: The Story of the Northern Ireland Women's Coalition*.

Paul Gillespie is both Foreign Editor of *The Irish Times* and project leader of the UK Group in the Institute of European Affairs, Dublin. He has written extensively on Irish international relations, including *Britain's European Question: the Issues for Ireland* and *Blair's Britain, England, Europe: A View from Ireland*.

Adrian Guelke is a native of South Africa who has lived and taught in Northern Ireland for over twenty years. He is currently Professor of Comparative Politics and Director of the Centre for the Study of Ethnic Conflict at the Queen's University of Belfast. His publications include *Northern Ireland: the International Perspective*, *The Age of Terrorism and the International Political System: 1967–1994* and *South Africa in Transition: the Misunderstood Miracle*.

Fred Halliday is Professor of International Relations at the London School of Economics. A close student of the conflict since the early days of the Troubles, he has published over ten books on world politics, including *The Making of the Second Cold War*, and more recently *Revolution and World Politics*.

Caroline Kennedy-Pipe teaches at the University of Durham and is editor of the journal *Civil Wars*. She has written widely on the Cold War and is also the author of *The Origins of the Present Troubles in Northern Ireland*.

Francesco Letamendia is Professor of Political Science at the University of the Basque Country at Bilbao. He has published extensively on the Basque question and has played a key role in the Basque peace process.

John Loughlin is Professor of European Politics at the University of Wales, Cardiff. The author of several works on ethnicity and nationalism, he was academic adviser to the European Centre for Minority Issues, Flensburg, Germany which organised a conference involving Corsican political groups held on the Aaland Islands, Finland in August 1998.

Martin Mansergh is Head of Research for Fianna Fail and adviser to the taoiseach. Viewed by many as one of the key players in the Irish peace process.

Colin McInnes is professor of international relations at the University of Wales, Aberystwyth who has written widely on the security situation in Northern Ireland. He is the author of several studies on strategy and warfare including *Hot War: Cold War – A History of the British Army*.

Elizabeth Meehan is Jean Monnet Professor at the Queen's University of Belfast. She has written extensively on citizenship and Europe, her more recent books being *Equality, Politics and Gender* and *Citizenship and the European Community*.

Mike Morrissey works in the Urban Institute, a University of Ulster research centre. He researches and publishes mainly in the fields of urban regeneration, local development and the impact of the Troubles on the region.

Marie Smyth is Director of the 'Cost of the Troubles' project based in Belfast. She is the author (with Mike Morrisey and Marie-Therese Fay) of *Northern Ireland's Troubles: the Human Costs*.

Fiona Stephen was Director of the Northern Ireland Council for Integrated Education 1989–1994. She is now a Research Fellow in the Department of International Politics at the University of Wales, Aberystwyth. She is currently completing a study on the politics of integrated education in Northern Ireland.

Michael von Tangen Page is currently a Research Fellow at the Centre for Defence Studies, King's College, London and the author of *Prisons, Peace and Terrorism*.

Preface and acknowledgements

This book began life as an idea in 1998 when it was becoming increasingly obvious to all three of the editors that the peace process in Northern Ireland was rapidly taking shape – and that therefore it would be a most useful exercise to bring together a number of experts to see how they viewed the unexpected end of the Troubles and the possibility of a lasting peace. Though the majority are academics who have lived and worked in Ireland and Northern Ireland through bad times and now (hopefully) good, we thought it absolutely vital to include amongst our list of contributors those who had also been at the coalface of politics. Two at least - Martin Mansergh and Sean Farren – have been key actors in the peace process itself, while a third – Paul Bew – has played what many see as a critical role in the modernisation of Ulster unionism. Others too have been more than just disinterested academic observers: Brice Dixon, for example, is currently Chief Commissioner for the Northern Ireland Human Rights Commission; Kate Fearon an adviser to the Northern Ireland Women's Coalition; and Paul Gillespie foreign editor for the *The Irish Times*. However, we not only tried to mix the intellectual brew, but also attempted to ensure that all facets of the peace process – domestic and international – were given their proper due. No doubt there will be those who will think that eight chapters on the international and comparative dimensions of the peace process is something of a luxury. We disagree strongly, indeed would insist that only by bringing in the wider world can we really begin to make sense of the Irish peace process. We will leave it up to the reader to judge whether or not we have got the balance right.

In putting this volume together we have accumulated quite a few debts. First, we would like to thank the many writers who have contributed to the project – for their expertise and for their speed in responding to queries from the editors. Another big vote of thanks must also go to the readers and anonymous referees who made such useful comments on earlier versions of the book. At Manchester University Press, Nicola Viinikka was her normally enthusiastic and shrewd self.

We would also like to thank Pippa Kenyon, Tony Mason and the production team at Manchester for carrying the project forward to completion. Finally, a special word to our six children all of whom were born in Northern Ireland while the Troubles were still in full flood. In their own different ways they were all affected by the conflict, but have come out the other end all the stronger for having lived through interesting and tragic times. To them we would like to dedicate this study in love and hope.

June 2000   Michael Cox, Adrian Guelke and Fiona Stephen
                                                              Belfast and Aberystwyth

Glossary and abbreviations

ANC   African National Congress

Anglo-Irish Agreement   Signed by Irish and British governments, November 1985

ANIA   Americans for a New Irish Agenda

Ard Fheis   Conference of Irish political parties

Articles 2 and 3   Articles in the Constitution of the Irish republic which laid claim to the six counties of Northern Ireland

Belfast Agreement   Otherwise known as the Good Friday Agreement, signed in April 1998

Bloomfield Report   May 1998 report by Sir Kenneth Bloomfield into the victims of the Troubles

CAP   Common Agricultural Policy

CCMS   Council for Catholic Maintained Schools

CEAC   Curriculum Examination and Assessment Council

CIRA   Continuity IRA – small splinter group opposed to the peace process

CLMC   Combined Loyalist Military Command; loyalist paramilitary coordinating body formed in 1991 comprising: UDA, UFF, UVF and Red Hand Commando

CRC   Community Relations Council

CRE   Commission for Racial Equality

Dail   Lower house of the Irish parliament

DED   Department of Economic Development

DENI   Department of Education, Northern Ireland

Direct Rule   Introduced in 1972 following the proroguing of Stormont

Downing Street Declaration   Key document of the peace process published jointly
    by the UK and Irish governments, December 1993

DPPB   District Policing Partnership Board

DUP   Democratic Unionist Party, led by Revd Ian Paisley

EC/EU   European Community/European Union

ECHR   European Convention on Human Rights

ECWG   Equality Commission Working Group

EEC   European Economic Community

EOCNI   Equal Opportunities Commission Northern Ireland

ETA   Euskadi ta Askatasuna, Basque for 'Homeland and Freedom'

FAIR   Families Acting for Innocent Relatives

FAIT   Families Against Intimidation and Terror

FEC   Fair Employment Commission

Fianna Fáil   Constitutional nationalist party in the Irish republic

Fine Gael   One of the two main parties in the Irish Republic

FLNC   National Liberation Front of Corsica (Front de Liberation nationale de
    la Corse)

Framework Document   Published in February 1995 by Irish and British
    governments with purpose of bringing about an agreed settlement in
    Ireland

George Mitchell   President's Clinton's special envoy to Northern Ireland

GNP   Gross National Product

HB   Herri Batasuna, political wing of ETA (means Popular Unity in Basque)

HURT   Homes United by Republican Terror, later Homes United by Recurring
    Terror

IEF   Integrated Education Fund

INCORE   Institute for Conflict Resolution

INLA   Irish National Liberation Army; republican paramilitary group formed in
    1974 as a breakaway from the Official IRA

INTERREG   1989 EU initiative to foster economic cooperation between
    contiguous territories of different EU countries

IRA   Irish Republican Army, also referred to as Provisional IRA; formed in late
    1969 after a split with the Official IRA

JSA   Jobseekers Allowance

LVF   Loyalist Volunteer Force

Mitchell Report   Published February 1996 laying down six conditions for inclusive political discussions, including the renunciation of force and no resort to anything other than democratic and peaceful means

NICE   Northern Ireland Centre in Europe

NICIE   Northern Ireland Council for Integrated Education

NIO   Northern Ireland Office, British government department

NITVT   Northern Ireland Terrorist Victims Together

NIWC   Northern Ireland Women's Coalition

Northern Ireland Forum   Public initiative in the Irish republic taken in 1983 to explore different possible 'solutions' to the 'Irish Question'

Omagh   Town in Northern Ireland where twenty-eight were killed in 1998 by bomb after the signing of the Good Friday Agreement

PAFT   Policy Appraisal and Fair Treatment

Patten Report   1999 commission report drafted by Chris Patten advocating reform of RUC

PLO   Palestine Liberation Organisation

PMVD   Politically motivated violent offenders

PNV   Partido Nacionalista Vasco

PR(STV)   proportional representation (single transferable vote)

PUP   Progressive Unionist Party, loyalist party closest to the UVF.

Real IRA (RIRA)   Splinter group opposed to peace process

RIR   Royal Irish Regiment (formerly UDR)

RTE   Radio Telefis Eireann, radio and TV network in the Irish Republic

RUC   Royal Ulster Constabulary, Northern Ireland police force

SACHR   Standing Advisory Committee on Human Rights

SAS   Special Air Services, elite regiment of the British Army

SDLP   Social Democratic and Labour Party, largest nationalist party in Northern Ireland led by John Hume

Sinn Féin   Political wing of the IRA

SSPR   Special Support Programme for Peace and Reconciliation initiated in Northern Ireland after 1994 ceasefires

Sunningdale   Location in UK where agreement was reached that led to the formation of a power sharing executive in 1974

SWAPO   South West African People's Organisation

Tanaiste   Official title of the deputy prime minister of the Irish republic

Taoiseach   Official title of the prime minister of the Irish Republic

TD   Member of the Dail

TSN   Targeting Social Need

UDA   Ulster Defence Association, largest loyalist paramilitary organisation

UDP   Ulster Democratic Party

UDR   Ulster Defence Regiment, locally recruited and based regiment of the
         British Army (renamed Royal Irish Regiment in 1992)

UFF   Ulster Freedom Fighters, proscribed loyalist paramilitary organisation

UKUP   United Kingdom Unionist Party, led by Bob McCartney and opposed to
           the Good Friday Agreement

UTU   Ulster Teachers' Union

UUP   Ulster Unionist Party

UVF   Ulster Volunteer Force, proscribed loyalist paramilitary organisation

UWC   Ulster Worker's Council, loyalist committee that planned the collapse of
           the power sharing agreement of 1974

Washington 3   The three conditions laid down by the British government in
           March 1993 for Sinn Fein joining all-party talks, which included 'actual
           decommissioning of some arms as a tangible confidence-building
           measure'

Introduction: a farewell to arms? From long war to uncertain peace in Northern Ireland

MICHAEL COX, ADRIAN GUELKE

AND FIONA STEPHEN

All wars, we are told, must one day come to an end. However, the pace at which they do so may be agonisingly slow, especially when there is no obvious winner or loser, and particularly so in a society as deeply divided as Northern Ireland where the quarrel, to paraphrase Winston Churchill, appears to have lost none of its original integrity. And there has been no peace process so long in gestation as the one in Northern Ireland. Indeed, so tentative has the process been at times, that the more cynical might conclude that many within the North either did not care for the peace or had become so used to the conflict that they preferred its certainties to the uncertainty of the new world order awaiting them round the corner. This might seem unfair, and no doubt some of those on the ground would argue that the real obstacle to peace was not the people of Ireland but certain politicians and parties at Westminster. There is some truth in this, but there is still something we should never forget about the struggle for peace in the North: it happened not because the different protagonists were necessarily convinced that harmony was preferable to conflict, but rather because they were finally impelled to the rather unpalatable conclusion that they could no longer go on pursuing their mutually incompatible objectives by means of armed violence or by repeating the time-honoured slogan of 'no surrender'. It would be comforting to report that there had been a meeting of minds; that peace was the natural result of a rapid growth of that most valuable piece of scarce political real estate – the middle ground. But it did not happen like that and it would be dishonest to assume that it did. There was no Road to Damascus conversion to the other side's point of view, no sudden outbreak of moderation, but a long and very painful, and as yet incomplete, recognition that the old means of achieving desired ends either would not work or were no longer acceptable to those upon whom the opposing camps depended for support. This is why the various parts of jigsaw puzzle called the Irish peace process have taken so long to fit into place, and why many still feel that the process itself is either an illusion or a mere interlude – an inter-war period if you like – that will one day give way to yet another cycle of hostilities until one of the two sides finally triumphs and the other concedes defeat.

This rather tough-minded assessment will no doubt shock liberal sensibilities and those who feel that peace is somehow more natural than war, discussion more productive than the threat of violence, and intransigence less likely to achieve one's aims and objectives than accommodation. However, the Irish Question has never been one with which liberal moderates have ever felt particularly comfortable, or to which they have ever provided particularly insightful answers – or at least answers to which the different peoples of Ireland have ever listened with very much interest or enthusiasm. This is no criticism of the people or even of liberals. It is simply a statement of the obvious, and a recognition that when peace did finally come to Ireland it did so for perhaps the least idealistic of motives. Moreover, when it came, it surprised nearly all of the so-called experts. In fact, most seasoned observers of the Irish scene believed there would never be a peace process in the first place, not because it was wrong in principle, but because there was little if any chance of it happening. It is easy to forget now, but we do need to remind ourselves, that back in the early 1990s the wise money was not on peace but a on a continuation of what the IRA had come to term the 'long war'. The idea that within a few years there would be a cessation of serious military violence, that some time on there would be an agreed settlement, and that within eighteen months of that Unionists might even contemplate the idea of sitting around the same table with republicans, would have been regarded as mere fantasy. That there remained obstacles to peace was obvious: but we should not forget how far the process has come and how few had earlier anticipated it.

The editors of this book can claim no special wisdom, and like many people living in Northern Ireland in the early 1990s could not see any particular grounds for optimism either. True, John Hume had already opened up a dialogue with senior figures in the republican movement. And in 1992, the republicans themselves began to start revising some of their more cherished ideas about the centrality of the armed struggle. But on the ground the killing went on. Thus it was logical to conclude that what some referred to as this most manageable of conflicts, which caused enough pain to hurt, but not sufficient pain to hurt badly enough, would continue. Yet we were prepared to learn, and possibly accepted earlier than most that changes both inside and outside Ireland as a whole – the ending of the Cold War, European integration, regional settlements in places like the Middle East and South Africa – were beginning to redefine the political landscape in the North and therefore made possible that which would have once seemed inconceivable. This was not always a comfortable or fashionable thing to say in public, as at least two of the editors discovered to their cost when they spoke to a large, distinguished, though mainly British audience at a meeting hosted by Chatham House in London a few weeks before the Good Friday Agreement. The response to our argument that the world was changing and along with it the situation in Northern Ireland provoked scepticism at best, hostility at worst. One rather well-known editor of a progressive political magazine attacked us most forcefully for being so naïve. To be sceptical about the possibility of peace in Ireland, John Lloyd insisted, was no sin but rather a sign of good judgement; and to assume that there had been any change in republican thinking was plainly absurd. An equally eminent personage not known for his progressive views at all was even more scathing. What we were saying was plain nonsense, according to Lord Beloff. There could be no agreement between Ulster unionism and Irish nationalism: they were just too incompatible to make any sort of deal a real possibility. Judging by the number of nodding heads in the room most of the audience seemed to agree with him, and indeed with most of the many speakers from the floor who attacked us for deigning to suggest that for the first time in a very long time, some form of inclusive settlement was feasible and that hostility to such a settlement within the British establishment could easily prevent it taking place.

We make these observations not to prove how wise we were (and how unwise our critics) but to emphasise that the Irish peace process has generated as much hostile comment as it has enthusiasm, and as much suspicion as it has good will on both sides of the Irish sea. In some ways it still does. Nor could it have been otherwise given the length of the 'Troubles', the human costs involved and the retrograde impact the conflict has had on the politics of the two islands of Ireland and Great Britain. There has been too much blood shed, too many lives destroyed and too little to look forward to politically for too long for people to welcome the peace process with open arms, especially those who have lost relatives, who have seen their aspirations come to nothing, or who simply feel that peace has been purchased at too heavy a price. Only the politically irresponsible or the perverse would want to wind back the clock of history. But critics of the peace process – from both sides – do have a point. After all, the process has involved one side effectively abandoning the cause for which it had been fighting for the better part of thirty years and another having to negotiate with people they had previously vilified as terrorists. Moreover, peace could only have happened if those same 'men of violence' had been given a seat at the political table – the same men whom only a few years previously had been denounced as murderers and killers, and with whom therefore it would simply be immoral to negotiate. To reach the point we have today, a lot of words have had to be swallowed and many an assumption jettisoned, to make the peace process possible.

But how did we arrive at our present and most unexpected position? The full story has yet to be told, and no doubt different authors will have their own different tales to tell about the war that finally came in from the cold. Some of the answers, however, are provided by one of the key players in the peace process itself: Dr Martin Mansergh. The son of one of Ireland's most distinguished historians, Dr Mansergh from his critical position within the taoiseach's office (at different times he has acted as advisor to Charles Haughey, Albert Reynolds and Bertie Ahern) affords us a privileged insight into the way in which the building blocks of the peace process were painfully put in place. As he makes clear, there was no sudden breakthrough, only a long and hard process of negotiations which finally culminated in the Good Friday Agreement: and even then, there was still much to do. This is a view which Caroline Kennedy-Pipe endorses in her historical reconstruction of the long road that led from war to peace. The Good Friday Agreement of 1998, she notes, 'signalled a profound transformation in the politics of Northern Ireland'. Yet, she adds, we should not forget what has not changed as a result. Ireland remains partitioned, there is still a disaffected nationalist minority in the North and many Unionists remain deeply suspicious about the peace process. A return to war is most unlikely: on the other hand, the structures supporting a long-term peace still have to be built from the bottom up. We might have a framework for a solution to the Irish Question, but we still have not solved it.

The next three essays go on to discuss the new arrangements in some detail. The first is by the well-known commentator Paul Bew who provides a typically trenchant analysis of the meaning of the Good Friday Agreement. Though Bew warns against false optimism, he still feels that Northern Ireland is on the verge of completing a transition from being what he calls an ethnic democracy to becoming a liberal political entity. Sean Farren (a minister in the first Northern Ireland government) would appear to agree. In the process, he provides additional insights into the peace process by looking at the major role played by his own party, the SDLP, and their efforts to persuade Sinn Féin to abandon old positions. As Farren notes, critical to the whole success of the peace process was Sinn Féin's willingness 'to accept or at least acquiesce in arrangements that fell far short of its declared goal' of a united Ireland. But it was not just republicans who had to rethink old positions; so too did a large number of Unionists, as Arthur Aughey explains. But it has been at a price to the unity of the 'Unionist family'. Moreover, while David Trimble may have managed to win the support of the majority of his own party in November 1999, thus triggering the formation of the first executive, he was, according to Aughey taking an enormous gamble – and whether he could keep the show on the road would in the end depend as much, if not more, on how far those in the republican movement were prepared to go in facing down their own hardliners. Only time would tell.

This brings us logically to the next three issues that all form part and parcel of the process but all the time threaten to arrest its progress: the decommissioning of weapons, prisoner release and police reform. Each is dealt with in turn by Colin McInnes, Michael von Tangen Page and Brice Dickson (at the time of writing, Chief Commissioner of the Northern Ireland Human Rights Commission). McInnes is clear: while the absence of weapons decommissioning did not prevent the peace process from moving forward, it did slow it down considerably. It also has the capacity to prevent the process going very much further unless and until it is seriously addressed. To a lesser extent, the same might be said about the prisoner issue, according to Tangen Page. Without prisoner support there would have been no peace process in the first place. However, the release of prisoners back into society still evokes the most painful of memories, especially among their numerous victims, and unless the question is handled with great sensitivity by all concerned it could easily poison the atmosphere. Even more controversial is the problem of who polices Northern Ireland and how; and as Brice Dickson points out, this particular issue continues to divide people in the North probably more than any other. So divisive was it in fact that the politicians decided to hand it over to an independent commission – the Patten Commission. However, far from calming frayed nerves the Patten Report only set them on edge even more. Yet until the question of legitimate policing and human rights is tackled, says Dickson, there will never be a serious settlement in the North.

In the next section we move our attention away from high politics to the situation on the ground: and perhaps there is no issue more poignant or difficult to deal with than the unheard voices in Northern Ireland – the 3,601 'lost lives' of the 'Troubles'. In a telling account, Marie Smyth both assesses the costs and reminds us all that it was the poorest who suffered most but whose families are still receiving what she calls 'paltry' support and compensation in the new Northern Ireland. It is essential, she says, that they are not forgotten. Mike Morrissey then turns the spotlight from the deeply personal to the economic, and in a detailed discussion suggests that the notion that there was ever an economy of war in the North is quite misleading. No doubt there will be some form of peace dividend. On the other hand, other more global forces are just as likely to shape the economic future of Northern Ireland as the cessation of paramilitary violence. But who wins or who loses economically will also depend on the role played by women in the new Northern Ireland, once a bastion of traditionalism, now changing very rapidly indeed on all fronts. And as Kate Fearon explains, it is not just the men who made the peace but the women too, and from her position within the Northern Ireland Women's Coalition – for whom she continues to work as a political adviser – she provides us with yet another fascinating perspective on how the Good Friday Agreement was constructed. Fiona Stephen tells an equally important story about the role of education in general and integrated education in particular. The tale is a complex one. A divided education system was more symptom of Northern Ireland's problems than cause. On the other hand, integrated education had and continues to have a useful role to play in the formation of the new Northern Ireland

Last, but by no means least, we turn our attention to the international dimensions of the peace process. We begin with a detailed investigation of the changing character of Anglo-Irish relations written by the well-known Irish journalist, Paul Gillespie. Having alienated the two countries for the best part of sixty years, Northern Ireland ultimately forced Dublin and London together in order to be able to manage the Troubles more effectively. But what began as management in the 1980s, he notes, laid the foundation for the final set of agreements that constituted the basis of the peace process a few years later. Another set of changing relations that have also contributed to the peace in the North is that between Europe and Ireland. As Elizabeth Meehan observes, while peace may have occurred without a Europeanisation of the Irish Question, the fact that Ireland became a serious European player at the same time as Europe itself was redefining the contours of the nation state, made an enormous difference to what occurred in Northern Ireland. Even more direct was the American role. The US, it is now accepted, was the critical 'third' actor in the peace process. How and why it became so heavily involved, and with what consequences for the so-called 'special relationship' between the UK and the US, is discussed by John Dumbrell. This is followed by two other essays on four other conflicts: one by Adrian Guelke on the impact of the difficult transitions in South Africa and the Middle East on Northern Ireland; and the other by Francesco Letamendia and John Loughlin on the fascinating parallels and differences between the situation in the North and those in the Basque Country and Corsica. Michael Cox continues the international theme with an assessment of how the end of the Cold War helped facilitate the peace process. While agreeing that there were many reasons for the peace, he insists that what happened in the wider world after 1989 did play its part in helping bring the IRA war to an end. His perhaps more upbeat note is countered by John Darby who looks at the ways in which violence can also corrupt peace processes. An astute observer of Northern Ireland, Darby reminds us that although all 'ceasefires' are to be welcome, in themselves they do not always bring an end to violence in deeply divided societies. Finally, in a wide-ranging discussion of peace processes in the late twentieth century, Fred Halliday emphasises yet again the importance, indeed the necessity, of looking at Northern Ireland from a wider international perspective. It may be reassuring for some to think of the Irish Question as being unique. However, this is not just intellectually parochial but means we cannot learn from the experience of others. Ireland is certainly different: but it is not so different – or so 'singular', to use Halliday's term – as to make useful comparison impossible.

But can we now talk of an end to one particular phase in Irish history and the opening up of another one? This is a question the editors return to in their conclusion, followed by a chronology of the key events and extracts from some of the most important documents to do with the peace process. Though careful to avoid any grand claims – Northern Ireland after all has been the graveyard of many a false dawn – the editors believe that the Good Friday Agreement does offer some real hope for the future. Indeed, in one very important sense there would seem to be no viable alternative to that Agreement. Of course, it does not give everybody what they want; nor does it mean there will not be more setbacks along the road. However, it does give the key actors enough to make the final settlement legitimate in the eyes of most of the people in the North and the overwhelming majority of the citizen of the Irish republic. A few years ago this would have been inconceivable: whether it marks a 'closure' to the Irish Question or merely another way of asking it, we shall have to wait and see.

PART I
The context for the peace process

1

The background to the Irish peace process[1]

MARTIN MANSERGH

When the 'Troubles' finally broke out in Derry in August 1969, I was with my family in County Cork. Nightly, with other guests and locals, we crowded around the hotel's television. My brother and I discussed the significance of what was happening with my father, who had grown up in Tipperary during the War of Independence and who was convinced that sooner or later the IRA would re-emerge and dominate events. Having been in college during the time of student unrest and familiar with the international culture of protest of the 1960s, we argued strongly that this was about civil rights, and was completely different from old-style nationalism. With the typical critical, but not self-critical, assurance of youth, we felt that my father, who was a historian, understood the Ireland of the 1920s much better than the Ireland of the late 1960s. We all know who was right and who was wrong!

The tension between old and new was summarised by J. Bowyer Bell in the conclusion to his monumental book on the Irish Troubles, where he noted that, by the end of the 1960s, the newly emerging values had not had sufficient time to permeate :

> In the end the Troubles came because Ireland was improperly synchronised; it was no one's fault and not easy to predict. The old values had not eroded and the new opportunities had not attracted ... The traditional rites and rituals seemed so natural, so easy. These ways offered great benefits, Orange and Green, often unavowed, often psychological, not economic or political, often to those denied elsewhere by the existing organisation of society and the island. So there were always new and frantic believers suddenly converted to the past as the means into the future. Those who sought to act on events, to make history to history's patterns, had the legitimisation of the past as authority.[2]

The peace process has to resolve much more than the Troubles of the past twenty-five years. It has to address the whole legacy of history and the many unresolved problems inherited from the past. Those festering problems have contributed to the length and virulence of the Troubles, which cost well over 3,000 lives and claimed many times more victims in terms of injuries or personal grief and trauma.

All of us must ask ourselves, as historians will ask, whether the Troubles had to go on for so long? What could have prevented them from breaking out in the beginning? Could they have been channelled into more peaceful political methods? Could they have been brought to an end sooner with less loss of life? No definitive conclusions can be drawn. Nevertheless, I shall try to give my own answers and personal reflections on them.

In the period 1886–1918, the battle for Home Rule was fought, won and lost. The demand itself was a compromise, but deferring its implementation and conceding an indefinite derogation to six of the Ulster counties was more than it was able to bear.

Whether a firmer attitude by the British government, less reckless opportunism by the Conservative opposition or a more accommodating attitude to specific concerns of Ulster unionists on the part of nationalists would have made a decisive difference is difficult to say. Nationalists from the day of Parnell tended simply to see the *reactionary* elements, what A. T. Q. Stewart in 1967 called 'the last ditch stand of the Ascendancy'.[3] They were little conscious of genuine differences in political and cultural identity or of differences in economic interests between the more industrialised north-east and the rest of the island, and were dismissive of religious fears. What eventually emerged was the result not of democratic debate but of relationships of power. Lloyd George himself told Arthur Griffith during the Treaty negotiations that in the pre-war years, led by the instinct of trained politicians, the whole force of the opposition concentrated on Ulster: 'Ulster was arming and would fight. We were powerless. The politician who thinks he can deal out abstract justice without reference to forces around him cannot govern.'[4]

The new compromise that emerged from the crucible of conflict allowed Ulster unionists and the bulk of Irish nationalists to go their separate ways. From 1916 on, full independence and sovereignty took precedence over a unity that appeared remote, while preservation of the Union in the area where unionists were most concentrated superseded the Union as a whole, and included three of Ulster's nine counties being 'written off'.

Sir Alfred Cope, Sinn Féin's chief contact in Dublin Castle, made a fascinating proposal on 3 September 1921 (recorded in Tom Jones's diary) that Lloyd George should do one of two things: either tell the north-east publicly that they must come in or lose Fermanagh and Tyrone, and then the South would give up independence [meaning full republican status], or offer the Dail acceptance of the republic, on condition that they met other British interests.[5] In 1947, speaking in Chatham House at a time when India was on everyone's mind, my father argued that the British government had made a mistake in not accepting the external association formula in 1921.[6] Cope felt that if the Dail were offered independence, they might give up unity, or that if they were given unity, they would give up independence. It was a question of symbolism. The tragedy of the 1921 settlement was that it did not at the time clearly offer one or the other. It brought civil war in the South and sporadic violence leading to civil war in the North after a delay of fifty years. One can sometimes speculate whether, if the present consequences of the resistance to Home Rule could have been foreseen, Ulster unionists would have chosen to act any differently. I conclude, a little sadly, that the answer, with one or two exceptions, would have been 'No'.

The backdrop to the war of independence had been the doctrine of national self-determination proclaimed by President Woodrow Wilson. Ireland's right to self-determination was never explicitly recognised or accepted by the British at that time. Indeed, as late as 1941, Churchill was maintaining that 'juridically, we have never recognised that southern Ireland is an independent sovereign State'.[7] The legitimacy of Irish neutrality during the Second World War was not fully accepted. Until both countries became members of the European Community and had to treat with each other in a multilateral setting as partners, a psychology of mutual resentment lingered in Anglo-Irish relations. Nevertheless, when the dust settled, the 1921 settlement appeared to give southern nationalists and northern unionists broadly what they wanted. Southern unionists and Protestants for a time enjoyed special representation in the Free State Senate and a fair degree of toleration, even if society was not pluralist in the modern sense. For another three or four decades, they still owned a lot of such wealth as there was.

The unequivocal losers were northern nationalists. Eamon Phoenix has described the disastrous divisions among northern nationalists, as they faced acute political dilemmas.[8] Republican separatism in the South left them with 'little or no influence' in the North. Southern policy towards the North was inconsistent and ineffective. The Belfast boycott was a disaster, breaking the economic unity of the country with no benefit to show. Michael Collins tried to exert some counter-productive physical leverage, but the civil war removed all serious political pressure on the North. The four safeguards in the Government of Ireland Act 1920 and the 1921 Treaty – proportional representation, the Council of Ireland, the non-discrimination clause and the Boundary Commission – were all dismantled or ignored.

In 1925, given a choice between negotiating an emancipation of the minority (and Kevin O'Higgins stated in negotiations with Baldwin, the British prime minister, and in the presence of Craig, that 'it was not just rhetoric to say that the Catholic nationalists are living in conditions of Catholics prior to Catholic emancipation'), or abolishing some of the financial obligations on the Free State under the Treaty, the Cosgrave government eagerly grasped the latter. Craig offered occasional meetings, which never took place, instead of the Council of Ireland, and gave as evidence that there was no real problem in inter-community relations, that Lady Craig had recently been invited to a bridge evening with Catholics and that a Protestant doctor had been invited to open a Catholic bazaar![9]

A few liberal unionists, like General Hugh Montgomery, founder of the Irish Association, had serious doubts about the treatment of the minority by the unionist majority. After a long period of political estrangement, which probably reached its height during the counterproductive anti-partition campaign, the tentative rapprochement between Lemass (and later Lynch) and O'Neill touched on possibilities of North–South co-operation between northern unionism and the southern nationalist state, without directly addressing issues of discrimination, such as the siting of the new university at Coleraine rather than Derry, which remained rampant in unionist government decisions during the 1960s. In the state of the world before the 1960s, with the upheavals of the Second World War in Europe, the communist blanket over Eastern Europe, and the continued existence of colonial empires, the situation of northern nationalists did not particularly stick out.

The IRA campaigns of 1939 and 1956–62 were remarkably ineffective. Why was the experience post-1970 so different? How did the civil rights campaign give way so quickly to a campaign of terror like that which followed the French Revolution? I believe two events in 1970, one in Britain, one in Ireland, had a great influence. Whatever the later merits of imposing direct rule and of Sunningdale, the change of government in Britain from Labour to Conservative replaced the initial reformist approach and sensitivity with a determination to restore order and to give clear backing to the Stormont régime, most clearly shown a year later with the introduction of internment followed by Bloody Sunday, when fourteen unarmed civilians were shot dead in Derry in an apparently premeditated way.

In 1922 the British Government had withdrawn politically and psychologically from Ireland and its problems, and there was enormous reluctance in the late 1960s to become directly involved again. In the end, the unrest was so great – and following Jack Lynch's August 1969 broadcast there was the risk from the British point of view that, if they did not intervene, others might be forced to do so – that the British Army was sent in.

Initially, the hope was to resolve the problem with some limited reforms and to withdraw again. The prospect that unionist hegemony would be propped up and that for most purposes nationalists would remain second-class citizens, despite the obvious failure of the unionist state, was enough to cause a section of the nationalist population to decide that democratic protest was ineffectual, and that it was time for the traditional recourse to arms, a solution that had never been systematically tried in the North before but that would complete the task begun in 1916–21.

There was little analysis of the differences between the situation in the North and the situation in the rest of the country fifty years earlier, differences that had given most of the leaders of the independence struggle pause for thought and that had led them to agree, with varying degrees of conviction, that, whatever the rights of the situation, coercion of the North was not practicable. Eamon de Valera's 1957 Ard Fheis speech was particularly lucid. In it he said that a forced unity, even if it could be brought about, would ruin national life for generations.

The other catalyst, I believe, was the arms crisis in the South. That was when the Irish government recoiling from giving any assistance for self-defence for fear of misuse lost all restraining political influence over militant republicanism in the North, a situation that would continue for almost twenty years. Post-1970, notwithstanding some critical moments when public emotions ran high, the South may have been secured and stabilised, but militant nationalists regarded themselves as on their own. It has taken twenty-four years to find the way back to conditions of peace.

While the British twice held discussions with republicans, in 1972 and 1975, and thereafter maintained some limited covert channel, there was no direct line of political communication on the Irish government side, as far as I am aware, apart from limited, mostly indirect, contacts at the time of the hunger strikes. The prevailing orthodoxy, based on a combination of the arms crisis experience and concern about the effects of the failed British attempts to negotiate bilaterally, was that there should be no contact of any kind between governments and spokespersons for paramilitaries for fear of giving them the impression that they were winning, and also as a means of demonstrating moral distance and indeed repugnance. As late as two weeks before the IRA ceasefire in mid-August 1994, Dr Garret FitzGerald, the principal guardian of this orthodoxy, said that he was disturbed by reports that I was in direct contact with republicans.[10] All of this presupposed that the paramilitaries could be militarily defeated or forced to stop by political developments or by public political exhortation from a distance.

John Hume showed great political courage in engaging in dialogue, publicly and privately, from the second half of the 1980s. The pressures that were placed upon him took a severe toll at the time, especially in 1993 and 1994. Even though Albert Reynolds only met Gerry Adams for the first time on 6 September 1994, it was the culmination of a willingness to take enormous political risks for the sake of peace, taking up the initiative begun a few years earlier by Charles Haughey. It is difficult to make omelettes without breaking eggs. All of us were conscious that in politics the dividing line between success and débâcle is often a very thin one and that we had to be ready, if necessary, to sacrifice our jobs and perhaps even put ourselves at risk. To enable people to be willing to make critical strategic decisions for their movements – which carried far greater risks for them – a relationship of trust had to be created, and ultimately that was virtually impossible to do at a distance. In December 1993, when potentially actionable reports started to appear in the British tabloid press about meetings with IRA and UVF leaders north of the border, I recall going home at the weekend to Tipperary and being comforted to be told that, regardless of their truth or otherwise, everyone was behind me.

Let us consider all the factors that have contributed to the present situation. Attempts to defeat the IRA by military or security measures had failed, although there was some success in containing the violence, to the extent that, after the carnage of the early to mid-1970s, deaths from all sources settled to around eighty to one hundred a year, what was controversially called 'the acceptable level of violence'. Events like the Enniskillen bombing in 1987, the kidnapping and mutilation of a Dublin dentist, and the Eksund arms shipment facilitated the introduction of new extradition legislation and tough security measures.

Close security cooperation was necessary, both to protect the people of this state and to prevent as far as possible cross-border attacks that might invite retaliation. While the fortunes of war continually fluctuated, the overall situation was a prolonged military stalemate, with the risk after particular incidents and at times of high tension that the situation might get completely out of hand, causing large numbers of civilian casualties. A factor in the last few years was the increasing intensity of loyalist violence, which was beginning to outstrip republican violence.

A second factor was the initiatives designed to achieve a political settlement between mainstream unionists and nationalists. The only one to get off the ground, Sunningdale, had its democratic legitimacy fatally undermined by the *mal-à-propos* British election of February 1974, and failed to quell either republican or loyalist violence. It was brought down by the clearest exercise of the unionist veto since 1912–14. Inter-party talks, predicated on an internal settlement, went nowhere between 1975 and 1980. From 1980, the focus shifted to the Anglo-Irish framework promoted by the two governments, a shift resisted by unionists for well over a decade. The Anglo-Irish Agreement was partly intended to galvanise the Unionists into talks. The discussions between the parties, which began in 1991 under the auspices of Northern Ireland Secretary of State Peter Brooke and continued under Sir Patrick Mayhew, and the subsequent bilateral talks and preparation of the Framework Document, created the possibility that these would turn at some point into serious negotiations that would culminate in a political settlement, however remote the chances of this might at times have appeared.

Despite occasional appearances to the contrary, in 1993 and 1994 the peace process and the talks process were not in conflict or competition with each other. They were in fact complementary. Republicans felt they should be at any real negotiations on the political future of Ireland. Not only could the government not afford to admit defeat on the question of restarting talks, but they had to maintain their determination to secure such negotiations. In the spring of 1994, following a three-month pause after the Downing Street Declaration, they resumed their efforts, making it clear that they were not prepared to wait on Sinn Féin's decision on the Declaration. At the same time, Albert Reynolds felt that to wait for peace until some time after a political settlement between unionists and nationalists was arrived at, might involve waiting till kingdom come, with no guarantee that a settlement from which the direct parties to the conflict were excluded would necessarily or automatically bring an end to violence. Witness Sunningdale. Understandably, perhaps, unionists were not keen to negotiate while violence was going on, especially with no assurance that any concessions that they might make would be sufficient to bring peace.

A further factor was the power of opinion. In the North, the SDLP, with its advocacy of a purely peaceful approach, succeeded in retaining the support of a majority of nationalists, despite a strong electoral challenge from Sinn Féin following the hunger strikes, when they developed their twin 'armalite and ballot-box' strategy. The main churches, with a few individual clerical exceptions, set their face against paramilitary violence, and tried to foster better inter-community

relations with varying degrees of success. Other groups – permanent like the trade
unions, or transitory like the peace people and similar later bodies – worked strongly
for peace. In the South, despite its republican origins and aims, governments
turned their face firmly against the use of violence, and pursued to the best of their
ability, in difficult circumstances, policies of compromise and conciliation. By and
large, writers and broadcasters encouraged a better understanding of the past,
including the recognition of different traditions. Sometimes, though, revisionism
went overboard. In consequence, there was a risk (a) of making a present of past
freedom struggles to the IRA and treating them as the true successors of the
founders of this state, thus in a sense delegitimising the state; and (b) of under-
writing the credibility of the threat of loyalist paramilitary resistance not just to imposed constitutional change but to all forms of reasonable democratic compromise.

One prominent Fianna Fáil deputy, who subsequently went on to play an
important role in improving Anglo-Irish and North–South relations, told me that
the turning point for him was watching the invasion of Cyprus in August 1974,
which instead of ending partition cemented it. My impression is that a certain and
understandable ambivalence at the beginning among a section of the population in
the South gave way over time to a more decided rejection of methods of violence.
Paramilitary-associated parties were unable to win any significant electoral support,
apart briefly from the period of the hunger strikes. Even those most directly
involved were horrified by some of the things that took place either accidentally or
by way of retaliation. The truth – that in war many people not in any way involved
are killed – was hammered home relentlessly by events.

The physical and material ability to carry on the long war almost indefinitely
was not in doubt. But the moral capacity to do so, without any realistic prospect of
a military or political breakthrough, with the gradual realisation that political aims
cannot be advanced in this way and may even go backwards rather than forwards,
and with a sense of responsibility towards those involved, was also something that
had to be assessed. Paramilitary violence on both sides represented a form of
political veto. While it was capable of prolonging the stalemate and frustrating
political initiatives, it could advance little. As Gerry Adams has acknowledged,
republicans could not achieve their aims on their own.

Apartheid and communism collapsed not so much through material default
but through a loss of conviction. The value of continued struggle in the face of a
gradually intensifying public hostility was open to question. I believe that, had the
violence continued much longer, some of the parties in this state would have
become increasingly reluctant to sit round the table under any conditions with
those they held responsible – a trend in opinion that had to be taken into account.
There are some dangerous myths around, accepted not only by those involved but
by many independent commentators. While I do not agree that violence has never
had any political effect, I see absolutely no evidence from our dealings with the
British government, or indeed its dealings with anyone else, that it was materially
swayed by bombs in the City of London. The Downing Street Declaration came

about for quite other political reasons; left to themselves, the British government was set to go in a different direction. The bombs at Heathrow airport in March 1994, which failed to explode and to which Albert Reynolds reacted very strongly, showed a serious failure in psychological understanding. *A fortiori*, anyone tempted to believe that some future political impasse could be broken by a renewed bombing campaign in the City of London would be disastrously mistaken. I also believe that, if the loyalists had bombed Dublin in 1994, far from weakening the resolve of the government and the people to achieve an equitable peace, it would have caused intense anger and increased determination. Democratic governments have no choice but to show firm resolve in the face of attempts to intimidate them by violence, and by and large over the past twenty years in Europe and round the world they have successfully done so. In this regard there is a solidarity among democratic governments today that bars the path for organisations using terrorist methods.

I now turn to the building blocks of the peace process: they go back a very long way and were slowly and painfully put together. Jack Lynch in the early 1970s accepted, on a *de facto* basis at least, that unity should only come about by agreement and consent. Although the Sunningdale Agreement, with its twin principles of power-sharing and an Irish dimension, collapsed after a few months, it nevertheless defined the basic ingredients of a political settlement – even though these might be described differently today. Nationalists had to accept that unity would not come in a single step.

In the late 1970s, the Irish embassy in Washington, together with John Hume, helped to develop an active interest in democratic political progress, both at the level of president and administration and in Congress. This came to fruition in 1985 with   the creation of the International Fund for Ireland. Charles Haughey as Taoiseach adjusted this policy on the basis that it was better to try to unite Irish-American opinion behind the policy of the Irish government than to excommunicate those who sympathised in varying degrees with armed struggle in the North. There was a historical precedent for this, about which he occasionally spoke, in the 'New Departure' of 1878 of Devoy, Parnell and Davitt.

Another element was the putting in place of the Anglo-Irish Framework in two stages, in 1980 and 1985. At first, it was oriented more on an East–West axis, with constructive ambiguity as to whether the totality of relationships covered constitutional or merely institutional issues. Both the Downing Street Declaration and the Framework Document were also joint initiatives by the two governments.

An interesting question is how much the Anglo-Irish Agreement concluded by Dr Garret FitzGerald and Margaret Thatcher contributed to the peace process. At one level, its political purpose was about intensifying the political marginalisation of Sinn Féin which had challenged the SDLP for leadership of the nationalist community and whose growth was a particular preoccupation of Garret FitzGerald. For Margaret Thatcher, it meant intensified cooperation against the IRA, but it also institutionalised the Irish government's right to be heard in relation to the nationalist community. It reaffirmed that, if a majority in Northern Ireland voted clearly for a united Ireland, Britain would legislate to bring it about. While this was merely a re-statement of what had been the British position since 1920-21 and was the opposite side of the coin of the famous British guarantee of 1949, it was an important affirmation, coming from so unionist and strategically minded a prime minister as Margaret Thatcher. What constituted 'clearly' voting for a united Ireland, and whether it meant something more than a simple majority, was left constructively ambiguous.

The Anglo-Irish Agreement was opposed at the time by three groups, the Unionists, Sinn Féin and Fianna Fáil. Despite massive protests, unionists were for the first time not in a position to pull the Agreement down, but for many years they would not begin any talks in its shadow or under its auspices. Sinn Féin felt that the gains were not commensurate with the costs to nationalists in terms of increased vulnerability to loyalist attacks, and the Agreement cut little ice in their heartlands. Fianna Fáil mistook Article 1 of the Agreement as constituting *de jure* recognition of Northern Ireland and therefore incompatible with Articles 2 and 3 of the South's Constitution. The Supreme Court in 1990 took a different view. But there was little problem about embracing and working the institutional mechanisms of the Anglo-Irish Conference, either in opposition or on return to office.

That opposition may have been costly in domestic political terms, but it created opportunities from 1988, first of all vis-à-vis unionists, in trying to interest them in negotiations on a new agreement that would replace or transcend the Anglo-Irish Agreement, and secondly vis-à-vis Sinn Féin, with whom, leaving aside the use of violence, some political and ideological common ground was shared. Particularly from the time of the hunger strikes, which cost Fianna Fáil two seats and the election of June 1981, Fianna Fáil in the early to mid-1980s, either working in opposition or in government in 1982, reverted under Charles Haughey to its republican roots, in a way not seen since Eamon de Valera. This happened not just because of the leader's northern nationalist background and his own instincts, which were in tune with much of the party's grassroots, but also because of a determination to hold the republican ground and not cede it to anyone else. In the early 1980s both Fianna Fáil and Sinn Féin moved away from federalism towards the unitary state. The reason was simple: northern nationalists were no longer willing to accept a restored majority-rule Stormont, even in the context of a loosely federal or confederal Ireland. It was during that period that many of the elements of the ideological bridge, which would be of crucial importance in the peace process right up to the ceasefire, were built.

In 1987, a Redemptorist priest from the north was in contact with the then Taoiseach, Charles Haughey, trying to establish dialogue with a view to finding a basis for bringing violence to an end. Only the two governments were seen as being able to break the impasse. There was a sense of responsibility, to be found in all of the three main churches, that they had a role in bringing shameful acts of violence to an end, putting their moral integrity to the service of that aim. As is known, a dialogue took place in 1988 between the SDLP and Sinn Féin on the principles underlying resolution of the conflict. They were unable to agree, however, on British neutrality, following the Anglo-Irish Agreement. The government *per se* was not involved, but the party of government was. The Fianna Fáil attitude in their two secret meetings with Sinn Féin in 1988 was more agnostic on the question of British neutrality, but would have been concerned to emphasise the unacceptability of violence, which divided and therefore weakened nationalists in the North and divided North from South, as well as opinion in America. Both the SDLP and Fianna Fáil formed the view separately that northern republicans were not then ready to end their campaign and that their primary aim in any continuing dialogue with constitutional parties was to end their political isolation and build a broad front. Under the conditions existing at the time, neither Fianna Fáil nor the SDLP could accept that outcome. This particular phase was followed by the abortive Duisburg talks in 1989, which involved all constitutional parties in the North and a Redemptorist proxy for Sinn Féin.

In 1989, another element fell into place when Charles Haughey announced at his party's Ard Fheis that, if violence were to cease, he would be prepared to reconvene the Forum. The New Ireland Forum, the first purely Irish initiative in response to the Prior Assembly back in 1983, had left a report that provided a valuable modern consensus formulation of the constitutional nationalist position, North and South, which northern republicans also increasingly came to appreciate.

Peter Brooke was an exceptional Northern Secretary, the most distinguished since William Whitelaw. His Anglo-Irish background had left him with a warm love of Ireland – he once proudly told me that a distant relation, the eighteenth-century poet Charlotte Brooke, had been the first to use the word Fenian in the English language. His analogy with Cyprus, and his prediction that governments sooner or later end up talking to those they regarded as terrorists, whetted interest. His subsequent statement, made in the context of the end of the Cold War, that Britain had no selfish, strategic or economic interest was to be a foundation block around which some of the first drafts of a Joint Declaration were built.

This began to take recognisable shape in the autumn of 1991, under the direction of the Taoiseach, Mr Haughey, with the help of John Hume and with some input from the Redemptorist priest whose idea a Joint Declaration was. The possibility of an initiative was mentioned at the first of the series of regular meetings from December 1991 between the new British prime minister, John Major, and the Taoiseach. But it was not possible to obtain, through intermediaries, any firm republican endorsement of the strategy or the draft, before Mr Haughey was replaced as Taoiseach by Mr Reynolds in February 1992.

Mr Reynolds and Mr Major had a warm personal relationship. The fortnight before Mr Reynolds took office was characterised by an upsurge in violence. He brought to his office a sense of affronted decency that such things were continuing. He was determined to go for peace as an end in itself, independent of any other political agenda, pursuing an even-handed and balanced approach to issues. He picked up the threads of the proposed initiative, and pushed it with vigour. It took from April 1992 to June 1993 to finalise what he called 'a formula for peace'. There were difficulties with the republican desire for a definite timescale for agreement; with reaching a common understanding of the application of the principle of self-determination and its relationship to consent; and with the political realism of casting the British in the role of persuaders for unity. The Irish government was determined not to subscribe to anything that would be clearly at variance with its international obligations, principally the Anglo-Irish Agreement. Even so, the initial draft went to the outer limits of what was acceptable. Even when difficulties of communications were partially overcome – and in the circumstances they were difficult enough just among republicans themselves – the whole initiative was understandably treated with extreme caution on both sides. John Hume was kept informed and of course had his own dialogue and relationship with Gerry Adams, which became public in April 1993. The public Hume-Adams statements were parallel and complementary to some of the elements in the Declaration but differently expressed in a helpful and constructive manner. The attacks on them from some quarters were totally unwarranted.

In June 1993, not without much soul-searching on the republican side, the draft was handed over to the British government by the Taoiseach. To say that they handled it with kid gloves would be something of an understatement. They were prepared to discuss but not negotiate it, and on several occasions in the autumn of 1993 many of them would have preferred to put it aside. But an initiative that might bring peace was always going to be more important than attempts to restart inter-party talks or even early discussions of the Framework Document. Some progress was being made towards an understanding. Then the stakes were raised dramatically when John Hume and Gerry Adams announced that they had finished their discussions and were putting their conclusions to the Irish government. But the perception that the northern nationalist leaders were seeking to lay down conditions for peace raised tensions and wild rumours in the North. The government opened a channel to the Loyalist paramilitaries through the Revd Roy Magee to reassure them that the government was seeking peace for its own sake and not seeking to impose joint authority or any other solution. Magee gave the government a set of political principles addressing loyalist concerns, which it subsequently incorporated in the Draft Declaration.

At the Brussels summit meeting at the end of October, the Taoiseach agreed to create some public distance from Hume and Adams, arguing that both he and the prime minister had a broader canvas to take into account, but it was on the firm understanding that the Draft Declaration would be pursued, an understanding that turned out not to be solid. There followed an extraordinary series of diplomatic crises behind the scenes. The Taoiseach resisted enormous pressure to drop the initiative, making it clear that he would try to proceed with it in some shape or form – if necessary, recast as a purely Irish initiative. If the British government would not join him in the endeavour, he would not be prepared to present a collaborative front in America or elsewhere.

The principal obstacle was the Unionists, with whom the British Conservatives the previous summer had formed an informal parliamentary alliance. In the end – and this was a very healthy thing to happen – the Taoiseach approached Archbishop Eames, and communicated to him the government's ideas, and sought his advice. Dr Eames helped to draft paragraphs 6–8 of the Declaration which were essentially about creating greater trust between North and South, and he also briefed Downing Street on the desire among the majority population for peace, provided it did not involve a major concession of principle. The Alliance Party leader, Dr John Alderdice, was kept similarly informed, and was enthusiastic about the Declaration when it was published. Serious negotiations took place in the first fortnight of December, and the Declaration was announced on 15 December in Downing Street by John Major and Albert Reynolds. The British finally became convinced that they had to take hold of the peace initiative, if the moral high ground were not to be lost, regardless of whether it in fact brought peace, about which they were highly sceptical. Although credit is due to Margaret Thatcher for her part in upholding the Anglo-Irish Agreement, I was always fairly clear that there was little hope of an end to belligerence in Ireland while she remained British prime minister. John Major deserves great credit for his political courage in adopting the Declaration and indeed later the Framework Document, which put at risk the unionist alliance.

What began as an Irish peace initiative, addressing the fundamental concerns of republicans, ended up, mainly at the initiative of the Taoiseach and the Irish government, addressing the fundamental concerns of unionists in an even-handed way. As a result, it was acquiesced in by the Ulster unionists – Molyneaux said he did not want to be responsible for delaying peace by a single day – and the loyalist paramilitaries had no great difficulty with it either. It had unprecedented cross-party political support, except from Sinn Féin and the DUP.

In the end, it did turn out to be a catalyst for peace, though that hung in the balance for several months. Perhaps it should have been more explicit about nationalist rights within the North, which were being worked on in the Framework Document, rather than concentrating on just the core constitutional questions. The core of the Declaration, apart from the balancing of self-determination with consent given concurrently, was the achievement of agreement between the people of Ireland north and south. Many trusted but independent advisers, such as the Belfast solicitor, the late Paddy McGrory, could see the merit of rooting the legitimacy of any new settlement in the consent and self-determination of the people of Ireland on both sides of the border.

With the Declaration at last out in the open, there was an enormous task of persuasion to be undertaken. The Irish government had no problem with providing comprehensive clarification in public and private, but, no more than the British government, was not prepared to renegotiate it. In countless speeches and interviews at home and abroad, explaining and promoting the case for peace, Albert Reynolds was magnificent. Section 31 was lifted as a result of his alliance in government with the minister for arts, culture and the Gaeltacht, Michael D. Higgins, motivated as always by lofty libertarian principles. The Taoiseach strongly supported the Adams visa to enter America, granted by President Clinton, where the strong support for peace among leading Irish-Americans was made clear. It was the first of a number of occasions right up to the Washington Conference in May 1995, when President Clinton and the US Administration, represented here by Ambassador Jean Kennedy-Smith (in my view the most positively influential US Ambassador there has ever been in Dublin), made crucial interventions. When firmness was required of the Taoiseach, it was shown – for example in his repudiation of the Heathrow bombing and the rejection of the 48-hour ceasefire after Easter. Nor would he have entered into any formal pact with Sinn Féin and the SDLP, which could have been too easily represented as a pan-nationalist front. Discussions on the Framework Document were resumed.

The British government did later provide clarification to Sinn Féin, and the Irish government clarification to loyalists. I can trace no explicit suggestion on the part of the British government that decommissioning of weapons was an additional precondition for entering political dialogue and round-table talks. The only delay envisaged was to make sure the cessation was for real. By June 1994, scepticism was widespread about the ability of the republican movement to adopt in a united way an alternative peace strategy. There were strains in the SDLP. In July, the Taoiseach warned that by the end of the summer holidays he would be forced to draw conclusions, and he also made it clear that he would reject a limited ceasefire of, say, three months, which would not make it possible to enter political dialogue or participate in the Forum. By the time of Sinn Féin's Letterkenny meeting, at which the Downing Street Declaration was apparently rejected, he knew that a lasting ceasefire had effectively been decided upon. The word 'permanent' would not be used, for ideological reasons and, no doubt, because it was what the British were looking for. But the phrases in the ceasefire statement, 'a complete cessation of violence' and 'a definitive commitment to the success of the democratic peace process', complemented by Martin McGuinness's statement some days later that 'the ceasefire will hold in all circumstances', were meant at the time to add up to the same thing. It was a declaration very similar in effect to the ceasefire statement combined with the proclamation of Eamon de Valera on behalf of republicans in the twenty-six counties in 1923, which stated that, as the democratic alternative to force, 'the ultimate Court of Appeal for deciding disputed questions of national expediency and policy is the people of Ireland', and that 'the war, so far as we are concerned, is finished'. While some volunteers may have been persuaded that the ceasefire was only tactical, the firm intention at the time was that it would be permanent.

Within a few days, the famous meeting between Albert Reynolds, John Hume and Gerry Adams was held in Dublin at Government Buildings. Their joint statement said: 'We reiterate that we cannot resolve this problem without the participation and agreement of the unionist people.' The loyalist ceasefire followed six weeks later on 13 October. The Peace Forum was convened on 28 October. The only deal was the one laid out in paragraph 10 of the Downing Street Declaration, which stated that, if paramilitary violence ceased permanently, the electoral mandate of those associated with it would be recognised, and they would be treated like any other political party for purposes of political dialogue.

Plans were made for the release of political prisoners and for the symbolic lifting of the state of emergency, and legislation was drafted to implement the European Convention on the Transfer of Prisoners. The British scaled down daytime troop deployments, and undertook to reopen cross-border roads. Bertie Ahern, as Minister for Finance, played a large role in negotiating the EU package for the North and for the South's border counties. The negotiations on the Framework Document were heading towards a conclusion, including a balanced constitutional understanding that would involve changes in both the Government of Ireland Act, 1920, and in Articles 2 and 3 of the Constitution. Indeed, on 11 November 1994 I was co-chairing with Sir John Chilcot, permanent undersecretary at the Northern Ireland Office, a meeting on these matters, when the decision to push through the appointment of the president of the High Court, which precipitated the fall of the government, was taken. Mr Reynolds's partner in the peace process, Dick Spring, provided continuity in the new government under John Bruton, who was also fully briefed by the outgoing Fianna Fáil Taoiseach.

It would be appropriate in this setting to mention some of those, apart from government and party leaders and clerical intermediaries, who played a key role in the early stages of the peace process. Of the Irish civil servants, Seán Ó hUiginn, head of the Anglo-Irish division in the Department of Foreign Affairs, who also had oversight of the talks process and was a principal craftsman of the Framework Document, was a key person. He has enormous understanding of constitutional nationalism in the North. Though formally retired, Dermot Nally, because of his immense experience, continued to liaise with the British cabinet secretary in 1993. Both were on the team negotiating with the British on the Joint Declaration. Fergus Finlay was also a colleague who made an important input at different times. On the British side, Sir John Chilcot, head of the Northern Ireland Office, was far-sighted and imaginative, while his deputy, Quentin Thomas, was tough-minded but unfailingly courteous. Both were resourceful. On the republican side, Martin McGuinness, in effect Sinn Féin's chief negotiator, assisted by a colleague from Belfast, also played a key role in the development of the Irish peace initiative and in helping to create the conditions that brought about a complete cessation of violence in August 1994. Gusty Spence played a guiding role in the loyalist ceasefire and the very eloquent and courageous statement that accompanied it, which he read out in a room in Glencairn Community Centre in the Shankill.

Albert Reynolds, speaking in September 1994 at commemorations of 1798 at Oulart Hill and of Liam Lynch at Kilcrumper, said that the physical force tradition had come to an end because it could go no further. But far from being at the end of history, we were at the dawn of a new era, with the whole island poised to overcome the disadvantages that have belaboured it throughout its history, in new relationships with other countries. As Charles Haughey said on television in December 1994, the peace process was something infinitely precious; it was a time of great hope and opportunity, which must not be squandered. Provided no one tried to test, to the limit and beyond, what was the maximum strain that the peace process could bear, it would surely hold, as there could be no conceivable gain to anyone from going back, only a huge loss to both communities and to the whole island. Unlike 1968, there is today a much better understanding of the rights of a minority community in a divided society or country. The price that the South has to pay for peace is continuing engagement in the affairs of the whole island, with a particular regard to equality of treatment and parity of esteem, as well as the development of cooperation at the very least from the subnormal to the normal between neighbouring jurisdictions on the island. The Americans are seen as the ultimate guarantors of fair play, and to my mind it was no accident that the first Mayhew-Adams meeting should have taken place in Washington.

As the son of a historian, Nicholas Mansergh, from whom I learnt much of what I know about Irish history, Anglo-Irish relations and the Irish republican tradition, I have been privileged to witness and participate in history being made in this country, while in the service of three distinguished Taoisigh, Charles Haughey, Albert Reynolds and Bertie Ahern. In his last book, published in 1991, my late father wrote: 'The fashioning of a new relationship is for another time and another pen.'[11] That was the extremely difficult and formidable task ahead: to uphold and consolidate the peace, and to negotiate a political settlement that is, to use an evocative phrase adapted in our constitutional negotiations from the late John Kelly, 'a new dispensation'.[12]

Postscript (September 1999)

The optimism and enthusiasm began to drain away in the course of 1995, as the peace process faced increasing difficulties. Unionists rejected the Framework Document, and refused to enter negotiations without a start to decommissioning, a stance supported by the Major government. The Forum for Peace and Reconciliation in Dublin had useful hearings and discussions, but failed to reach consensus on crucial issues. Even American intervention failed to resolve the crisis. With evidence of further stalling, the IRA set off a bomb at Canary Wharf in February 1996 as part of a renewal of a sporadic campaign. Multi-party negotiations were organised in the following months, but without Sinn Féin, who feared they would face continual harassment on the decommissioning issue. It took changes of government in London and Dublin to reinstate the IRA ceasefire. In September 1997, the Ulster Unionist Party agreed to enter multi-party talks with Sinn Féin. To many people's surprise all the threads of decades of political initiatives and agitation over decades were brought together in the 1998 Good Friday Agreement, which contained a far-reaching constitutional accommodation, a balanced range of partnership institutions and a radical reforming agenda in areas of equality, human rights, policing and justice, with prisoners being released. The concept of mutual consent underlay the Agreement, which was overwhelmingly endorsed by the people of Ireland North and South in concurrent referendums. The terrible bombing at Omagh in August 1998, following violent deaths arising from the Orange Order's attempts to march down the Garvaghy Road from Drumcree Church, reinforced popular rejection of paramilitary violence, but unfortunately did not provide the impetus for decisive forward movement.'

At the time of writing, despite many government-led initiatives to break the deadlock, the will of the people remains to be implemented by the parties, with republicans reluctant to commit themselves in advance to decommissioning, and unionists reluctant to establish a government without it. While many aspects of the Agreement within the authority of the two governments are being implemented, they cannot force the hand of parties reluctant to implement this or that aspect, so that the new dispensation in the fullest sense of the term remains in suspense, and the political future uncertain, with former Senator George Mitchell conducting a review. The most positive recent development has been the Patten Report on policing, which provides the basis for a newly based police force acceptable to both communities, a vital building block in the process. It is sometimes overlooked that democracy is not only about an exclusive commitment to peaceful means. It is also about honouring and implementing, and not obstructing, the expressed will of the people. The democratic tradition in Northern Ireland in both regards is weak. The Good Friday Agreement seeks to strengthen it by providing a powerful supportive framework that combines fundamental reforms with durable institutions.

Notes

1 This chapter is based on an address delivered to the National Committee for the Study of International Affairs under the auspices of the Royal Irish Academy which was published in *Irish Studies in International Affairs,* vol. 6, 1995, pp. 145–58.
2 J. Bowyer Bell, *The Irish Troubles: A Generation of Violence 1967–1992* (Dublin, 1993), p. 829.
3 A. T. Q. Stewart, *The Ulster Crisis: Resistance to Home Rule, 1912–14* (London, 1967), p. 44.
4 Thomas Jones, *Whitehall Diary - Vol. 3: Ireland 1918–1925* (ed. Keith Middlemas), pp. 129–30 (14 October 1921).
5 Jones, *Whitehall Diary – Vol. 3,* pp. 105–6 (3 September 1921).
6 Nicholas Mansergh, 'The Implications of Eire's Relationship with the British Common-wealth of Nations', *International Affairs,* vol. 24, no. 1 (January 1948).
7 Paul Canning, *British Policy Towards Ireland 1921–1941* (Oxford, 1985), p. 306.
8 Eamon Phoenix, *Nationalist Politics, Partition and the Catholic Minority in Northern Ireland 1890–1940* (Belfast, 1994).
9 Jones, *Whitehall Diary – Vol. 3,* pp. 241–3 (1 December 1925).
10 'Sinn Féin must tow the line on pledging peace for talks', *The Irish Times,* 20 August 1994. However, Dr FitzGerald made the point in discussion after this address that the time for a shift in policy had been well chosen.
11 Nicholas Mansergh, *The Unresolved Question: The Anglo-Irish Settlement and its Undoing 1912–72* (New Haven and London, 1991), p. 4.
12 *The Irish Constitution* (Dublin, 2nd edn, 1984), p. 12.

2

From war to peace in Northern Ireland

CAROLINE KENNEDY-PIPE

The Good Friday Agreement of 1998 signalled a profound transformation in the politics of Northern Ireland. The stagnation that had long paralysed the politics of the region has broken up. Old certainties have been undermined and those engaged in Northern Ireland have acknowledged it. Against the backdrop of the end of the Cold War, Sinn Féin with the backing of the IRA (or some parts of the movement) has for nearly a decade been engaged in a series of attempts to negotiate new political structures: a process which has owed much to the ideas of constitutional nationalism long espoused by the SDLP. The new Labour government, following the example of the previous Conservative Government has engaged in dialogue with Sinn Féin/IRA and made public its readiness to rethink constitutional arrangements in Ireland to enable new institutions with broad cross-community support to emerge. Tony Blair has as British prime minister gone further than his Conservative predecessors and taken the unprecedented step of acknowledging and apologising for some of the painful aspects of the British legacy in Ireland. In this current climate the Unionists appear bewildered and lacking the cohesion which had once upon a time seemed to characterise the politics of unionism. A. T. Q. Stewart's observation made several years ago that a central question in Northern Irish politics has to be: does Protestant Ulster have a mind?[1] has never appeared so pertinent. Indeed, as Arthur Aughey shows in this volume, the fragmentation of unionism is one of the key developments of recent years.

It is therefore an important time to take stock of the situation in Ireland. There are of course many constants. The island of Ireland is still partitioned: in the North British troops and a large security infrastructure remain in place and the men of violence, as the Omagh bombing demonstrated so tragically, have not all laid down their arms. There is still a disaffected nationalist minority and a loyalist unionist majority. Yet these components too are in the process of adjustment. The British Government has in the years since the Anglo-Irish Agreement of 1985 conceded the centrality of Dublin to any future settlement and signalled its intention to restructure the security apparatus, most notably to redefine the composition of the Royal Ulster Constabulary. The politics of demography too are increasingly important: by 1997 Catholics comprised just over 40 per cent of the population of Northern Ireland.[2] Although it is difficult to predict future birth rates within the province, or indeed whether the Catholic population will at some future point outnumber the Protestant community, the apparent growth in Catholic numbers raises a number of issues. Not the least of these is that a shift towards a new majority/minority dichotomy will in the longer term undoubtedly affect the nature of political and policing structures within Northern Ireland and the relationships of the province with both Dublin and Westminster.

In this spirit of acknowledging both the changes which made both the ceasefires of 1994 and the subsequent Good Friday Agreement possible, but outlining the constants which render any peace problematic, this chapter identifies and explore the main factors which have given rise to a shift away from the long war to the current fragile peace.

Beginnings

The creation in 1920 of Northern Ireland was, in the words of Brendan O'Leary and John McGarry, a text-book example of 'state and nation building failure'.[3] The establishment of Northern Ireland marked the partial retreat of the British state in Ireland and was proof of the bankruptcy of trying to construct a British identity throughout Ireland. It was also evidence of a failure of Irish nationalism. Nationalists lacked the resources to inspire a revolution throughout the whole island. The inability of nationalists to coerce or persuade the Protestants in Ulster to join what might be termed the 'Free State' project sprang from several sources. The nationalists were weak militarily, especially in comparison with the forces of the British Crown,[4] but more importantly Irish nationalism came to define itself in terms of opposition to the British state, the English language and Protestant religions.[5] These features were not likely to conciliate the Protestant community to the notion of a united and nationalist Ireland.[6]

Northern Ireland was therefore the product of 'varying' political power. 'A 30 per cent minority in the island was able to prevent one area from seceding but this region in turn contained a 30 per cent minority in favour of secession of the whole of Ireland. One minority had far greater political resources than the other.'[7] Yet the development of the Northern Ireland 'problem' and the later troubles was not simply the outcome of this 'settlement' in Anglo-Irish affairs but also the product of later struggle over the legitimacy of political institutions in the North.

In the years from 1920 until the mid-1960s Northern Ireland was characterised by three features. The first was that sovereignty over the province was at least in theory contested by both the British and the southern Irish states. Yet Northern Ireland was not fully integrated into either and little influence was exercised by either Dublin or Westminster in the politics of the province. The South was excluded from participation in the life of the North and after 1921 Westminster withdrew from the exercise of state power, leaving Stormont to govern. The dominance of Protestants within the new northern government gave rise to the second feature of the regime: Northern Irish political institutions lacked broad support across the two communities. The Unionists who governed made few efforts to win nationalist support. Unionist power was dependent upon maintaining the cohesion of the Unionist bloc and there was little incentive to make concessions to a minority. As Richard Rose has argued elsewhere, it was Catholic compliance not Catholic consent that was sought.[8] The minority therefore had little stake in maintaining or contributing to this system and for almost fifty years, nationalist politicians refused to act as an official opposition, opting out of the business of government.

Yet the third feature of Northern Irish politics, that of a disgruntled and disenfranchised minority, did not, despite Protestant fears and a few outbreaks of street violence, unduly disturb the workings of the Stormont regime. That is, until the development of a civil rights culture in the 1960s. This change was brought about by a combination of both external and internal factors which galvanised a burgeoning Catholic middle class into challenging the workings of what Farrell characterised as the 'Orange state'.[9]

Northern Ireland was during the years of the 1960s influenced by the crosscurrents in Anglo-Irish relations which arose out of the drive for greater European integration. The ongoing programme of economic modernisation in the South under the Taoiseach, Sean Lemass, demanded an improvement in economic relations with the UK, the EEC and Northern Ireland. The Southern Irish desire for entry into the EEC not only inspired an improvement in Anglo-Irish relations but also made it increasingly difficult for Westminster, which itself was seeking entry to the Community, to resist the pressure from Dublin for reform of the minority position in Northern Ireland. For the first time then it is possible to argue that the southern Irish were able to exert influence, albeit of a limited kind, over events in the North.

Perhaps more importantly, there were in this period also social and economic shifts within the North as a result of the development of the post-war British state and the extension of a 'welfare state' culture into Northern Ireland. In particular the provision of sweeping welfare benefits and legislation for greater access to higher education effected a change in both Catholic income and expectations. The introduction of welfare made transparent the obvious disparities in living standards between the North and the South of the island and rendered minority enthusiasm for joining the South more muted. Thus far it might be imagined that the nationalist community would, as a result of its greater educational and economic opportunities, be increasingly reconciled to the Stormont regime. Indeed, Terence O'Neill, the Northern Irish prime minister explained the benefits of the introduction of welfare programme in the following manner: 'it is frightfully hard to explain to a Protestant that if you give Roman Catholics a good job and a good house they will live like Protestants because they will see neighbours with cars and TV sets ... and refuse to have eighteen children...'.[10] However, his comment proved rather wide of the mark. Instead of reconciliation to the regime, the Catholic community sought further reform. Rather than concentrate on the politics of partition, the nationalist party undergoing a period of 'revisionism' now aimed to improve the economic and social conditions of the minority *within* the existing framework. This posed significant problems for unionist dominance. The rejection of 'abstentionist' politics, the pleas for equal treatment and reform *not* abolition of Stormont in itself undermined the unionist rationale for the exclusion of the minority which could no longer be characterised simply as 'disloyal rebels'.[11]

There were other currents feeding social and political change within Northern Ireland. Although it is now fashionable to recognise the impact of international events such as the end of the Cold War on the politics of Ireland,[12] influence of a potent kind was exercised by the international civil rights agenda of the 1960s. In January 1967, inspired in part by civil rights movements in the United States, the Northern Ireland Civil Rights Association was founded and drew support across both communities to bring about the abolition of discriminatory practices in the province. The slogan of 'equal rights' drew international attention and proved exceptionally damaging to the reputation of the Stormont regime.

Brian Faulkner, under pressure from the civil rights movement, Westminster and the demands of an ailing economy,[13] instigated reforms which granted the minority a greater degree of equality in employment and housing legislation and proposed reconstruction of the security apparatus. Not surprisingly, reform met resistance from parts of the unionist community which saw livelihood and government now threatened by the demands of an increasingly restless and articulate minority.

The first bloody encounter of the troubles occurred in Londonderry/Derry on 5 October 1968 when civil rights marchers clashed with the police. The eruption of violence on the streets and the wholesale movement of populations in urban areas into separate communities of Protestant and Catholics led to the formation of local vigilantes which in turn contributed to the resurgence of paramilitary groups. The scale and intensity of the sectarian violence throughout the summer of 1969, plus the inability of the RUC to maintain order, resulted in a request from Stormont to the Labour government for the deployment of additional troops to support the police.

The Labour government, under pressure from Dublin, which itself threatened not to stand idly by, embarrassed by international media coverage and explicitly appealed to by a minority group which had hitherto refused to accept the authority of the British, had little option but to respond. Troops arrived on the streets of Belfast and Londonderry/Derry in the summer of 1969 after a period of intense deliberation by both the British military and politicians.[14] (During the spring, British soldiers had been deployed to protect important electricity installations because of fears of paramilitary attacks.) Initially, troops were welcomed by the

Catholic community which believed itself defenceless against sectarian attacks. Seven thousand refugees were reputed to have moved across the border into the Republic of Ireland. The Lynch government established camps for 'refugees' on the southern side of the border, called for a United Nations Peacekeeping Force to be deployed and objected to the emergency legislation invoked by Stormont.[15]

The Labour government wishing to keep its involvement in Ireland strictly limited, at this point eschewed the notion of taking direct control. The deployment of troops in numbers was not intended to be permanent.[16] Attempts were made to reassure those in both communities that what might be termed an improved status quo would prevail: the Union and Stormont would continue but action on discrimination would be taken. As a result of the findings of the Cameron Commission appointed in March 1969 to investigate the causes of the violence, public housing came under the control of the Northern Ireland Housing Executive and little political power was left in the hands of local councils, which were viewed by Westminster as the source of sectarianism.[17] Lord Hunt's recommendation that an independent police authority be set up, the RUC be disarmed, the USC disbanded and a new part time force, the Ulster Defence Regiment (UDR), be set up under the General Officer commanding the Army, was also implemented in attempts to render the institutions of the North acceptable to the minority community.[18]

Reform of this nature, however, did little to ameliorate either unionist or nationalist anxieties. Unionists resented the negative findings of the Cameron and Hunt Reports and this was compounded by suspicion of the Labour government which was regarded as sympathetic to the nationalist cause. Loyalist extremists threatened to take over the Unionist bloc and within the space of three years, three different prime ministers held power. In working-class areas, anger was reflected in the reinvigoration of paramilitary organisations. On the loyalist side most notable, or notorious, were the Ulster Volunteer Force (UVF) and the Ulster Defence Association (UDA), which, in response to republican paramilitary activity engaged in random attacks against Catholic civilians. The IRA, notable only by its absence in the early stages of the 'Troubles' (graffiti within Catholic areas had identified IRA with 'I ran away', noting its feebleness in protecting the minority areas) re-emerged in Catholic areas.[19]

IRA impotence reflected deep-seated tensions within the republican movement over a number of issues, but specifically that of electoral abstentionism. The subsequent split within Sinn Féin (the political wing of the organisation) and the IRA brought about the formation of the Provisionals in 1970. They launched a campaign of violence against the British. Stormont, backed by the newly elected Conservative government, invoked emergency legislation and, on 9 August 1971, introduced internment without trial. Special prisons were established and filled, at least initially, with Catholics. Rather than containing the violence, these actions along with the use of curfews and house searches, resonant of British military campaigns in the colonies, fuelled the conflict. Internment led to a campaign of civil disobedience, to prolonged street violence and to an escalation of support within Catholic communities for the paramilitaries.[20] The alienation of the minority community was completed in January 1972 when members of the Parachute regiment were held responsible for the deaths of fourteen Catholics engaged in a civil rights demonstration.[21] On 2 February, a crowd of thirty thousand marched to the British Embassy in Dublin and burnt it down: events in the North had the potential to invoke disorder throughout Ireland and the British Isles.

The initial years of crisis therefore gave rise to a bloody and multi-levelled confrontation between the British and the Provisionals and between the two communities within the North. Yet the emergence or re-emergence of the men of violence was not the whole story. New political initiatives were also brought about by the changed circumstances. Unionism itself split in the face of reform as the UUP fractured. In April 1970, those unionists opposed to violence and in favour of reconciliation left the (Official) Unionist Party and formed the Alliance Party. During 1971, Ian Paisley launched the Democratic Unionist Party (DUP) to represent those Protestants who were dissatisfied with Stormont's reform in an attempt to recreate what Paisley termed 'traditional Unionism'. In August 1970, a predominantly Catholic party, the Social and Democratic Labour Party (SDLP), was founded, which although it held the aspiration of a united Ireland, had a clear reformist stance for Northern Ireland itself and replaced the Nationalist Party as the voice of moderate Catholic opinion. In June 1971, Brian Faulkner offered the SDLP positions on the opposition parliamentary committees, thus permitting nationalists a modicum of influence on the making of legislation. But in July 1971 after the army had killed two men during riots in Londonderry/Derry and the demands of the party for a public inquiry had been refused, the SDLP withdrew from Stormont.[22]

On 30 March 1972 the Conservative prime minister Edward Heath signalled the end of British attempts to reform Stormont by introducing Direct Rule. The closing down of the only system of government which had ever operated in Northern Ireland signalled the beginning of a second phase during which the British government attempted to both contain the violence and find new ways of governing the region.

Direct Rule

Direct Rule did little to solve the problems of Northern Ireland. It was both a bid to 'isolate' the IRA from the Catholic community and an attempt to build a moderate political centre in Ireland drawn from the SDLP, the Alliance Party and more liberal unionists. The prorogation of Stormont did not, however, end the violence. During 1972, 103 soldiers, 41 police and UDR men and 323 civilians were killed. Neither did Direct Rule succeed in creating a moderate centre. Some of the initiatives taken by the Secretary of State for Northern Ireland, William Whitelaw, proved controversial. The revelation that Whitelaw had actually held talks with members of the Provisionals in London in July 1972 and his decision to include an

'Irish dimension' in any future settlement undermined the position of many within the unionist camp who had been prepared to share power with the SDLP.

Direct rule also raised the question of Westminster's objectives in Ireland: was it in fact seeking to extricate itself from Northern Ireland? This became for many within both the unionist and republican camps a key question. The consultative paper on The Future of Northern Ireland, published shortly after the advent of Direct Rule, stated that no UK government had any wish to impede the realisation of Irish unity, if it came about through consent.[23] This underlined the paradox at the heart of Westminster's strategy in Ireland: the British government had assumed responsibility for governing Northern Ireland, it was after 1972 engaged in a massive military campaign against the Provisional IRA, yet it still defined its right to rule as one of arbitration between two warring communities in which it hoped to create the conditions for some form of devolved power sharing.

In March 1973 a referendum was held to decide whether or not Northern Ireland should remain part of the UK. It was boycotted by Catholics: the verdict was decisively in favouring of the Union but attempts by Westminster continued to promote devolution within the North. A white paper was published proposing self-government for the region: Westminster attempted to establish a power sharing executive and a council of Ireland to promote North–South ties through functional cooperation. In December, tripartite discussions were held to broker what became known as the Sunningdale Agreement. The principal aim was to create the conditions for a sufficient and representative number of parties to engage in local government but a southern dimension was recognised through the creation of a Council of Ireland. While acknowledging that the majority of people in the province wished to remain within the UK, a commitment was made that if the majority of people in Northern Ireland wished to become part of a united Ireland, the British government would support that desire.

This initiative collapsed in the face of unionist opposition. The Ulster Workers Council Strike of 1974 paralysed the province and the power sharing executive of Brian Faulkner (with SDLP member Gerry Fitt as deputy chief executive) was brought down. Some unionists made clear their anger with certain aspects of the deal, especially the proposed Council of Ireland, perceived as a back road to Irish unity. Harold Wilson, in power for a second time, accused the unionists of 'sponging on Westminster' but did little to break the strike: indeed the Army advised against a confrontation with loyalists which it was feared might lead to a war on two fronts.[24] The SDLP, already angered by the failure of the British to end the process of internment, remained convinced that the strike could have been broken by resolute action.

Normalisation and Ulsterisation

The collapse of power sharing led to a period of political stalemate during which few constitutional initiatives were attempted in Ireland. Indeed, from 1975 onwards,

Britain, first under a Labour government and then under the Conservative government of Mrs Thatcher, implemented policies designed to redefine the problem of
Northern Ireland as one of criminal activity, not political or constitutional struggle.
Ulsterisation or normalisation was, in many ways a logical outcome of the stated
British position in Ireland. Successive British governments had refused to declare a
war against the IRA and, unlike in colonial struggles in Northern Ireland there had
been no open declaration of a state of emergency.[25] Ulsterisation was designed to
place the security emphasis upon local forces such as the RUC and the UDR and to
allow a reduction in the number of British troops. This exercise was underlined by
the formula made infamous by Reginald Maudling that 'an acceptable level of
violence' had been attained in the conflict with the Provisional IRA. British
politicians associated with Northern Ireland in the late 1970s and 1980s were
reluctant to concede the use of the term 'war' or even 'civil war' to describe events in
the region lest the very use of the word conferred a degree of legitimacy on the IRA.

The movement away from the tacit recognition of the IRA as a legitimate
opponent was evidenced by the withdrawal of special category status from paramilitary prisoners which ended the distinction within prisons of ordinary and
political crimes. After March 1976, prisoners convicted of terrorist offences were
categorised as criminals. Up until this point, 'political' prisoners had been permitted certain concessions: they had been allowed to wear their own clothes and
had the freedom to associate with other political prisoners.[26]

It was primarily, but not only, republican prisoners, however, who challenged
the government on the issue of status.[27] Some refused to wear prison uniform and
dressed in blankets. The dispute escalated from a 'blanket' protest, through a 'dirty'
protest and finally in October 1980 into a 'hunger' strike. Bobby Sands, the leader of
IRA prisoners in the H-block and a hunger striker, was elected as an MP for
Fermanagh and South Tyrone. (The SDLP refused to stand a candidate against
Sands.) During a second hunger strike, the Thatcher government refused to make
concessions and ten strikers, including Sands himself, died. These hunger strikes
were a turning point in internal, European and international perceptions of the
British position in Ireland. For Sinn Féin, the election of Sands confirmed the
viability of entering candidates for election. Two other hunger strikers were also
elected to the Dail.

The management of the hunger strikes by the Thatcher government was widely
condemned. The European Commission of Human Rights criticised the British
and in February 1983 the European Parliament established an inquiry into the
economic and social problems of Northern Ireland. The American government too
expressed its concern over the handling of the issue. Indeed, the Irish Question
began to occupy an increasingly important place in the American political process
from the 1970s onwards. While scholars disagree over the reasons for the increasing
attention paid to Ireland by American politicians, and here of course the issue of
the Irish Diaspora is of note, there is also the question of the changing nature of the
Anglo-American relationship in which throughout the 1980s Britain was arguably

of diminishing importance to American foreign policy.[28] Hence, the troublesome issue of British rule in Ireland was allowed a higher visibility in Washington.

While the influence of the US would become increasingly important in Ireland in the aftermath of the hunger strikes, it was the emergence of Sinn Féin as a political force which was striking. At its Party Conference in 1981 Sinn Féin decided to adopt the approach of the 'ballot paper in this hand and an armalite in this hand'. This decision to contest elections within Northern Ireland meant that Sinn Féin would be competing against the SDLP which itself had, as a result of the hunger strikes, adopted a more militant stance. In the 1983 general election, Gerry Adams was returned as Sinn Féin MP for West Belfast, defeating the sitting SDLP member, Gerry Fitt. Republicans polled 13.4 per cent of the total vote compared to 17.9 per cent for the SDLP.[29] This level of support raised the possibility of Sinn Féin supplanting the SDLP as the voice of nationalism.

The Anglo-Irish Agreement

John Hume's response to the surge in support for Sinn Féin was to arrange the New Ireland Forum – a meeting of all the Irish democratic parties: under this rubric Sinn Féin was not invited. The Forum took a year to agree a framework through which a new Ireland might emerge. Three specific options were offered: a unitary state, a federal system and joint Anglo-Irish authority. This initiative served as a catalyst for thinking about political arrangements. Although the three options were openly rejected by Mrs Thatcher in her now famous declaration of 'out, out, out' to each,[30] cabinet committees were actually discussing how to move forward. From December 1984 senior civil servants on both sides of the Irish sea began exploratory talks which led to the Anglo-Irish Agreement of 1985.

John Major in his recent memoirs has denied that the Anglo-Irish Agreement of 1985 represented a turning point and argues that little was achieved.[31] This is a rather churlish assessment, not least because for many engaged in the Anglo-Irish process the Agreement provided the groundwork for the view that the 'Troubles' were the business of both Dublin and London. The Agreement established a consultative forum through which British and Irish ministers could discuss Northern Irish affairs and agreed closer Anglo-Irish collaboration on security issues. For the British government the inclusion of the southern dimension was an attempt to stem and reverse the growth of Sinn Féin and to stabilise support for the SDLP, as well as trying to encourage those within the UUP who supported devolution. The Agreement was opposed by the two main unionist parties and by Sinn Féin.

The aftermath of the Anglo-Irish Agreement, however, exposed unionism as having over the previous decade lost some of its influence with the British government. Although many methods, such as mass demonstrations and a boycott of public bodies, were attempted to disrupt the Agreement, these failed to have the impact achieved against Sunningdale. Most notably, public servants remained loyal to government. Weakness was also attributable to the relative decline in the economic position of the unionists: industrial output had fallen since 1974 and a number of crises had beset the economic base of the region. By the mid 1980s Northern Ireland was sustained by the huge subvention from Britain which provided 25-30 per cent of the Northern Ireland population's disposable income.[32] Threats that unionism might take an independent route were far less believable than ten years before: there was nowhere else to go. Indeed, what constituted unionism was itself in question as a political battle waged between the DUP and the UUP. Although an alliance had been forged between Ian Paisley and James Molyneaux in response to Hillsborough, in the years after both engaged in a struggle for what Paul Arthur has characterised as a battle for dominance of the unionist electorate.[33]

Yet if the aftermath of the Anglo-Irish Agreement revealed chinks in the unionist armour there were also sombre consequences for Sinn Féin. The popularity of the agreement in the South[34]signalled that within the 'island of Ireland', partition had been accepted. What appeared to be the acquiescence in British rule in Northern Ireland raised the question of how strongly the people of the republic sought reunification. The prolonged period of 'trouble' had brought home the probable consequences of unity: of these, unionist intransigence, the threat from the paramilitaries and the assumption of an economic burden were formidable disincentives. As Tom Garvin noted in 1988: 'If an offer of a united Ireland were to be seriously and publicly made by the British government ... it would have devastating and possibly destabilising effects on the Republic ...'[35]

There was also for Sinn Féin the problem of the 'long war'. The Anglo-Irish Agreement had improved security collaboration between North and South and raised the question of exactly how successful the IRA campaign had been. The results by the late 1980s were mixed. IRA violence had played a part in persuading the British to dismantle the Stormont regime, it had kept the issue of Irish unity on the political agenda souring Anglo-Irish relations for well over a generation, and it had arguably strengthened the position of the SDLP. But the campaign of violence had also proved counterproductive. It had led to an increase in paramilitary violence by loyalists who increasingly targeted working class Catholic areas, it had alienated moderate nationalist opinion (surveys demonstrated that Catholics in the North would be prepared to settle for a solution short of a united Ireland, such as power sharing) and had done little to dent British resolve. Although opinion polls demonstrated clearly that the majority of the British electorate would be glad to relinquish any claim to Northern Ireland, successive British governments had made clear that they would not and could not give way to 'terrorism'.

The Thatcher government proved resolute in pursuing a counter-insurgency campaign. Although doubts 'must assail anyone trying to evaluate the record of the British security forces in Ireland' during the 1980s[36] – the alleged 'shoot to kill' policy operated by the SAS, the supergrass trials, the strange affair of the Stalker inquiry and the subsequent refusal to prosecute anyone in the wake of the Sampson inquiry on the grounds of national security left serious question marks over the behaviour of some segments of the army and RUC – there is little question that by the late 1980s the IRA was doubtful of its ability to push the British out of Ireland. This situation of what we might term military stalemate further compounded the process of revisionism within parts of the republican movement and by 1988 Sinn Féin leaders were already engaged in separate negotiations with both John Hume and through a special negotiator, Martin Mansergh, with the government in Dublin – the so-called 'back channel'.

Towards peace

Adams signalled in discussions with Hume the turn towards the ideas of constitutional nationalism. He appealed for a national consensus on Irish reunification and appealed to Fianna Fáil in the South as well as the SDLP in the North. This shift was clearly articulated at the 1992 Ard Fheis when the movement adopted the document 'Towards a Lasting Peace'. In this Adams accepted that the issue of national self-determination was a complex one and that the British might act as the persuaders of unionism and once again opened a dialogue with Hume that culminated in the 1993 peace process.

This conversation with Hume had implications for the armed struggle. There was an inherent tension, recognised all along by Adams, that armed struggle and the seeking of electoral victory were incompatible. The explosion of the massive bomb in the city of London on the day in April 1993 that the Hume–Adams talks became public gave the impression that the two strategies were running in tandem. The perceived need to continue to defend the Catholic community in the North against loyalist attack made it difficult for the IRA to give up its struggle, let alone its arms. Sinn Féin have long claimed that for peace to work in Ireland, all sides including the British military and the RUC and the paramilitary groups must decommission weapons and oversee a complete demilitarisation of the region.[37] (It is this issue of the decommissioning of weapons which remains a sticking point.)

'Success' by the IRA during the 1990s, such as the bombings of the financial quarter of the city in London in 1992, was also being overtaken by disasters such as the killing of the two small boys in the town of Warrington in the spring of 1993 and the Shankhill bombing in the autumn. The problem for the Provisional IRA was that the political path being pursued by Sinn Féin deprived the bombing campaign of any sort of rationality. Continued violence begged the question of what was, or could be, the logic of the bombing campaign once Sinn Féin no longer sought to 'drive the British out' but rather sought to achieve recognition within the constitutional system?

The government of John Major had made clear both through Secretary of State Peter Brooke and his successor Patrick Mayhew that Britain, although neutral on the issue of Ireland, held that a renunciation of violence by the IRA was a necessary precondition for admission to the constitutional talks initiated by Brooke. Indeed, the aim of the secret contacts opened by the British government

after 1989 was to convince the Provisional IRA to end its armed campaign. These
talks marked a departure for the republican movement. The very fact that the
Provisionals were engaged with the British government underlined the fact that
they accepted Hume's analysis of the British position that it was willing to
withdraw from Ireland (or act as persuaders to the unionist population) if the right
conditions could be achieved.

Hume and the SDLP's influence was therefore considerable. Not only had
Hume acted as a key influence on Adams but his long expressed view that there
were three strands to the Irish problem: the relationship between Catholics and
Protestants, the relationship between Dublin and Belfast and the relationship
between Ireland and Britain, was accepted not only by Brooke but all those involved
as the key components to any settlement.

All of this signalled a watershed in republican thinking and in August 1994 the
first IRA ceasefire occurred followed by a loyalist cessation of violence in October.
The role of Adams and Martin McGuinness in persuading the IRA that abandoning the long war did not mean a sell-out was considerable. It was a difficult task
made harder by unionist intransigence, the hardliners within the IRA and the
increasingly problematic position of John Major's government. Within the Conservative Party there were many who had opposed the peace process and as Major's
parliamentary majority decreased he became increasingly dependent on the votes of
Unionists to sustain his policy on Europe. In part this and the reluctance of the
IRA to accept the decommissioning of weapons accounted for the renewal of the
IRA campaign in early 1997.

The election of a new Labour government in the spring of 1997 marked a
significant break with the past. Tony Blair and his 'new' Labour government had
taken power with a determination to modernise Britain – this included a general
commitment to devolution and to finding a settlement to the Irish 'Troubles'. Blair,
unlike more traditional members of the Labour Party, had no affinity to the idea of
Irish unity and made clear his support for the Union. However, he also recognised
that Sinn Féin was vital to peace.[38]

Blair also marked a departure from the British past in Ireland in further ways.
The first was in his recognition that the history of the 'Troubles' impacted in
complex ways upon the peace. The reopening of an inquiry into the events of
Bloody Sunday, the establishment of both the Bloomfield Commission and the
Patten Commission[39] plus Blair's willingness to openly address the tragedies of
Anglo-Irish relations demonstrated an awareness that the peace process should
address some of the outstanding issues which had long prevented nationalists from
establishing a positive view of successive British governments.[40] The second
departure made by Blair was a more pragmatic one: he actively embraced outside
intervention in the affairs of Northern Ireland. Previous prime ministers had been
sensitive to keeping the management of the region a domestic affair. Blair,
however, actively enlisted the help of the Democratic American President Bill
Clinton in bringing about peace. Clinton had of course been much engaged in the

affairs of Ireland since the early 1990s. Indeed, much to the fury of the Major government, he had ensured Adams was granted a visa to visit America.[41]

Clinton appointed the former senator George Mitchell as Special Envoy to Northern Ireland to coordinate the US economic programme under Major: but it was in conjunction with Blair that Clinton played a decisive role persuading both Adams and David Trimble, the leader of the Ulster unionists, as well as Bertie Ahern, the Irish leader, to accept the latest experiment in power sharing for the region – the Good Friday Agreement of 1998. This understanding has established a new assembly built on cross-community support, including Sinn Féin representatives, a North–South Council to develop co-operation within Ireland and a British–Irish Council to promote relations between all parts of the British Isles.

Endgames

John Hume remarked of the 1985 Anglo-Irish Agreement that it provided 'a framework for a solution, not the solution itself'. The same can be said of the constitutional frameworks suggested during the 1990s. They are designed to facilitate, not guarantee, peace in Northern Ireland. Myriad problems remain. These include: the decommissioning of paramilitary weapons, the attitude of hardline paramilitaries to peace (the Omagh outrage of August 1998 proved that not all republican paramilitary groups approved of negotiation) and the longer term strategy of a British government which is now openly committed to the success of the new devolved assembly at Stormont. At a local level, punishment attacks and loyalist paramilitary violence against Catholics demonstrate that peace is not total. Most crucial of all though is the question of whether the Unionists, who after all do constitute the majority (for now) of those within the province, will continue to accept power sharing arrangements with Sinn Féin in the new assembly.

Yet, there is concrete evidence that the last ten years or so have marked a break with the past in the 'thirty years crisis'. Republicans have accepted both a *constitutional* route to change in the North and that the violent tactics of old are quite simply counterproductive in a new and modernising Ireland. The southern Irish too, appeared content to relinquish claims to the 'six counties' and support British governments in the project of devolution and self-government in the North. The Unionists, although divided amongst themselves over the future, are prepared to accept change, even if they are fearful that they no longer have the power to bring down an elected assembly which does enjoy popular support across both communities. Indeed, this could be the crucial dimension – the fact that after thirty years, few wish to see the violence continue.

Notes

1   Stewart argued that this was not meant as an offensive question but as a deadly serious one. See A. T. Q. Stewart, 'The Mind of Protestant Ulster' in David Watts (ed.), *The Constitution of Northern Ireland: Problems and Prospects* Studies in Public Policy 4 (National Institute of Economic and Social Research, Policy Studies Institute, Royal Institute of International Affairs, London: Heinemann, 1981)

2   See John McGarry and Brendan O'Leary, *Policing Northern Ireland Proposals for a New Start* (Belfast: The Blackstaff Press, 1999), p. 8. See also Marie-Therese Fay, Mike Morrissey and Marie Smyth, *Northern Ireland's Troubles: The Human Costs* (London: Pluto, 1999) pp. 98, 113, 134.

3   Brendan O'Leary and John McGarry, *The Politics of Antagonism: Understanding Northern Ireland.* (London and Atlantic Highlands N.J.: The Athlone Press, 1993). p. 106.

4   David Fitzpatrick, 'Militarism in Ireland 1990–122', in Thomas Bartlett and Keith Jeffrey (eds), *A Military History of Ireland* (Cambridge: Cambridge University Press, 1996), pp. 379–406.

5   Paul Bew has argued that there was perhaps less distinction between the 'people of Ireland' and the 'people of Britain' than this formulation allows for. See Paul Bew, *Ideology and the Irish Question Ulster Unionism and Irish Nationalism 1912-1916* (Oxford: Oxford University Press, 1994), p. 160.

6   O'Leary and McGarry, *Politics of Antagonism* , pp. 107–47.

7   *Ibid.*

8   Richard Rose, *Governing Without Consensus: An Irish Perspective* (London: Faber and Faber, 1971).

9   Michael Farrell, *Northern Ireland: The Orange State*, 1st edn (London: Pluto, 1976).

10 Quoted in Patrick Buckland, *A History of Northern Ireland* (Dublin: Gill and Macmillan, 1981), p. 112

11 Paul Bew, Peter Gibbon and Henry Patterson, *The State in Northern Ireland, 1921–1972: Political Forces and Social Classes* (Manchester: Manchester University Press, 1979).

12 Michael Cox, 'The War That Came in from the Cold', *World Policy Journal*, Vol. XVI, no. 1, Spring 1999, pp. 59–67.

13 Terence O'Neill, *The Autobiography of Terence O'Neill, Prime Minister of Northern Ireland 1963–1969* (London: Rupert Hart-Davis, 1972).

14 Harold Wilson, *The Labour Government, 1964–70* (London: Harmonsdworth, 1971).

15 *Dail Eireann*, Vol. 241, 22 October 1969, Col. 1402.

16 James Callaghan, *A House Divided: The Dilemma of Northern Ireland* (London: Collins, 1973).

17 Cameron Report, *Disturbances in Northern Ireland*: Report of the Cameron Commission Appointed by the Governor of Northern Ireland (Belfast: HMSO, Cmnd. 532).

18 Hunt Committee, Report of the Advisory Committee on Police in Northern Ireland (Belfast,: HMSO, Cmnd. 535, 1969).

19 J. Bowyer Bell, *The Irish Troubles A Generation of Violence, 1967–1992* (Dublin: Gill and Macmillan, 1993), p. 113.

20 Paddy Hillyard, 'Law and Order', in John Darby (ed.), *Northern Ireland: The Background to the Conflict* (New York: Appletree Press, 1983), pp. 32–60.

21 On Bloody Sunday, thirteen civilians were shot dead by the British Army and a fourteenth civilian died later from his injuries.

22 J. J. Lee, *Ireland 1912–1985 Politics and Society* (Cambridge: Cambridge University Press, 1989), p. 436.

23 John Whyte, *Interpreting Northern Ireland* (Oxford: Clarendon Press, 1990), p. 143.

24 Robert Fisk, *The Point of No Return. The Strike which broke the British in Ulster* (London: André Deutsch, 1975).

25 R.Weitzer, 'Contested Order: The Struggle over British Security Policy in Northern Ireland', *Comparative Politics*, Vol. 19 (1987), pp. 293–5.

26 Michael von Tangen Page, *Prisons, Peace and Terrorism: Penal Policy in the Reduction of*

Political Violence in Northern Ireland, Italy and the Spanish Basque Country, 1968-97 (London: Macmillan, 1998), pp. 62–3.

27 *Ibid.*

28 Paul Arthur, 'The Anglo-Irish Agreement: A Device for Territorial Management?' in Dermot Keogh and Michael H. Haltzel (eds), *Northern Ireland and the Politics of Reconciliation* (Cambridge: Woodrow Wilson Center Press and Cambridge University Press, 1993), pp. 208–25.

29 J. J. Lee, *Ireland 1912–1985*, p. 455.

30 Margaret Thatcher, *The Downing Street Years* (London: Harper Collins,1993), p. 400.

31 John Major, *The Autobiography* (London: Harper Collins, 1999), p. 433.

32 On the economics of Northern Ireland see, P. Shirlow, 'The Economics of the Peace Process' in C. Gilligan and J. Tonge (eds), *Peace or War? Understanding the Peace Process in Northern Ireland* (London: Avebury, Aldershot, 1997), pp. 97-127.

33 Arthur, 'The Anglo-Irish Agreement', pp. 208–25.

34 An MRBI poll conducted a week after the Hillsborough Agreement revealed that 59 percent of the Irish electorate approved of it; by February 1986 some 69 per cent approved of it. See *Irish Political Studies*, 1986, 1. 144, 1987.

35 Tom Garvin, 'The North and the Rest: The Politics of the Republic of Ireland' in Charles Townshend (ed.), *Consensus in Ireland: Approaches in Ireland: Approaches and Recessions* (Oxford: Oxford University Press, 1988), p. 109.

36 This sentiment is that expressed by Charles Townshend in Townshend, 'The Supreme Law: Public Safety and State Security in Northern Ireland' in Keogh and Haltzel, *Northern Ireland*, p. 98.

37 See *An Phoblacht*, 5 September 1996 and John Major, *The Autobiography*, pp. 455–8.

38 See Michael Cox, 'Bringing in the International: The IRA Cease-fire and the End of the Cold War', *International Affairs*, Vol. 73 (October 1997).

39 *A New Beginning: Policing in Northern Ireland*. The Report of the Independent Commission on Policing for Northern Ireland (London: HMSO, 1999).

40 *Belfast Telegraph*, 22 June 1999.

41 Joseph O'Grady, 'An Irish Policy Born in the USA: Clinton's Break with the Past', *Foreign Affairs*, Vol. 75.3, May–June 1996, pp. 2–8.

PART II
Good Friday and beyond

3

The Belfast Agreement of 1998: from ethnic democracy to a multicultural consociational settlement?

PAUL BEW

What is the Belfast Agreement of 10 April 1998, which was supported by 71 per cent of those voting in the referendum in Northern Ireland on 22 May 1998, and how did it come about?[1] One recent interpretation by Professor Brendan O'Leary stresses that the Agreement is in conformity with the essential principles of Arend Lijphart's concept of consociationalism: it also draws attention to the long-term academic interest of the Secretary of State for Northern Ireland, Dr Mo Mowlam, in such a theory, as well as the fact that 'at least one of her advisors has had an abiding interest in the subject'.[2] The same article concedes, however, that politicians under the pressure of events are capable of coming up with similar arrangements without any necessary recourse to an elaborate theoretical backdrop. The analysis of the Agreement presented here will follow this latter approach; not least because earlier research has demonstrated that the conceptualisation of a previous attempt at a settlement, the Anglo-Irish Agreement of 1985, as 'coercive consociationalism' was flawed.[3] This has also been the approach of writers advocating the type of settlement actually attempted in 1998.[4]

The top line of 'Heads of Agreement' of January 1998 which heralded the Stormont Agreement document was 'balanced constitutional change'.[5] Now that the Belfast Agreement is completed we can see exactly what was meant by that phrase. There will be, it is clear, significant changes both to British legislation and to the Irish Constitution of 1937. The British government has decided to repeal the Government of Ireland Act of 1920. Some republicans profess to think this is very significant in a positive way, while some unionists are alarmed by the suggestion that in some way Northern Ireland's position within the UK is being weakened.

The nature of the constitutional deal

The Government of Ireland Act has been seen as Britain making a one-sided claim to supremacy over Northern Ireland regardless of the views of the people living there. It sits uneasily with later solemn declarations by Britain that the union is dependent upon, and arises solely from, majority support in the province – declarations given by the British government at the time of the Sunningdale Agreement in December 1973 and the Anglo-Irish Agreement of November 1985 and the Joint Declaration of December 1993.[6] In other words, one might say that the Government of Ireland Act represented an old-fashioned imperialist mindset and should be got rid of.

But there is another side to this matter. As David Trimble pointed out in an article in 1994, the controversial part of the Government of Ireland Act (section 75) is merely a 'saving clause' designed to assert Westminster's residual authority over a devolved Belfast parliament.[7] The purpose is not to make an imperialist British claim over Northern Ireland against the wish of a majority of its citizens. The key legislation establishing the union is anyway the Act of Union of 1800: this Act, as Trimble has stressed, remains in force.

The fact that David Trimble has long taken a relatively relaxed view of the significance of the Government of Ireland Act of 1920 has always carried with it the implication that he might trade it as part of a deal bringing changes to the Irish Constitution of 1937 – even though during the negotiation he often took a publicly rigid strand as, for example, when he published in March 1999 an article in the *Sunday Independent* apparently, but not actually, exhibiting a reluctance to accept change in this area.

Under the new situation it will be a matter of British legislation that Northern Ireland remains part of the UK for so long as the majority there supports the Union. Thus in Annex A, Section 1, paragraph 1 of the Agreement the following is affirmed:

> It is hereby declared that Northern Ireland in its entirety remains part of the United Kingdom and shall not cease to be so without the consent of a majority of the people of Northern Ireland voting in a poll held for the purposes of this section in accordance with Schedule 1.[8]

This is, in short, a continuation of the present reality as most people in Northern Ireland understand it. The Belfast Agreement (Strand 1, para 33) contains a formal and explicit reiteration of British sovereignty. But what about the changes which, as part of the deal, are to be made to the Irish constitution? At present these state:

> Article 2: The national territory consists of the whole island of Ireland, its islands and territorial seas.
> Article 3: Pending the re-integration of the national territory, and without prejudice to the right of the Parliament and Government established by this Constitution to exercise jurisdiction over the whole of that territory, the laws enacted by that Parliament shall have the like area and extent of applications as the laws of Saorstat Eireann (the Irish state).

Increasingly, in private discussions between the two governments the British began to challenge these Articles – and increasingly so after March 1990.

The McGimpsey case

In that month, Mr Justice Finlay ruled in the Irish Supreme Court in the celebrated McGimpsey case that the words: 'The national territory consists of the whole island of Ireland, its islands and territorial seas', constituted a declaration of the extent of the national territory 'as a claim of legal right'. This unanimous ruling grounded the territorial claim and the 'constitutional imperative' towards Irish unity in Article 2; in retrospect, however, it is now clear that the McGimpsey ruling sounded the death knell for Article 2.

At the margins of the European Union Summit in Corfu in June 1994 John Major pressed Albert Reynolds on two points: was the Irish government prepared to amend their constitution to the point where they would say their territorial claim over the North had been removed, and would they in public recognise the legitimacy of British rule in Northern Ireland for so long as it reflected the consent of the majority? This became known as the 'Corfu test'.

Reynolds endeavoured to reassure Major as to his good intentions, but even on the eve of the Framework Document's publication, the then Fianna Fáil Taoiseach was unwilling to change Article 2 though he was prepared to change Article 3 in a way which stressed both the consent principle and the existence of two jurisdictions in the island.[9] This represented progress of a sort but the problem remained – the Supreme Court ruling in the McGimpsey case had been based on Article 2 which remained unchanged. This is why David Trimble and his negotiators insisted so loudly that any change to the Irish Constitution had to be 'judge proof', in other words, Article 2 and not just Article 3 had to be revised.

In the new Stormont Agreement, Mr Ahern indicated that he was prepared to go further than Mr Reynolds to meet unionist concerns – and unionist concern about this matter was one of the major irritations in the framework controversy. Interestingly, the opposition to Bertie Ahern on this matter – centred on the *Sunday Business Post* and some Fianna Fáil TDs – appears to have collapsed in the wave of euphoria following the Good Friday Agreement, though clearly Sinn Féin still have difficulties on this point.

The new Article 2 will now read:

> It is the entitlement and birthright of every person born in the island of Ireland, which includes its islands and seas, to be part of the Irish nation. This is also the entitlement of all persons otherwise qualified in accordance with law to be citizens of Ireland. Furthermore the Irish nation cherishes its special affinity with people of Irish ancestry living abroad who share its cultural identity and heritage.[10]

From a nationalist point of view, the 'Irishness' of northern nationalists is in no way diminished by these new arrangements. Some say that Ireland is thus giving up its case in international law but in truth Ireland has never had a case in international law anyway – as the Irish Foreign Affairs Department officials admitted privately in 1969, Dublin recognised Northern Ireland in 1925 as part of the UK and states cannot undo such recognition by changing their internal constitutions at a later date.

Under this Agreement, the days of Paddy Hillery disputing the legitimacy of British rule in the North at the UN, or of Dick Spring stating as he did in 1985 that the Irish claim to juridical sovereignty remained intact, are gone forever. Instead, the principle of consent, which is at the core of so much recent intergovernmental policy, is further enhanced. In particular, it is possible to interpret the outcome of the referendum in the Republic of Ireland, in which an overwhelming majority of voters endorsed the changes to Articles 2 and 3 as part of the Good Friday Agreement, as implicitly a devastating rebuke against the IRA's campaign to create a united Ireland by coercion.

But, of course, consent is a two-way street, and the Good Friday Agreement contains much that is designed to win nationalist support for a new dispensation in the North. It is in these areas where the main difficulty for unionists lies, but as far as balanced constitutional change is concerned unionists can now contemplate for the first time since 1925 a new international agreement which fully recognises 'Northern Ireland's status as part of the United Kingdom' and which is not gainsaid by anything in the Irish Constitution.[11] In its structural aspects the Agreement is three-stranded, and it is to these strands that we now turn.

Strand 1: the local Assembly

The Stormont Agreement provides for a new Northern Ireland Assembly of 108 members, 48 more than were proposed for Wales and just 21 fewer than the Scottish parliament. It will have a substantial change of domestic policy freedom but foreign policy stays at Westminster. The Assembly was elected by PR (STV) using the eighteen Westminster parliamentary constituencies each returning six members. A similar system had been used for elections to the Northern Ireland Forum in 1996, when five seats had been allocated to each constituency. However, the top-up system used for the Northern Ireland Forum elections permitting minor parties unable to secure representation in five-member constituencies to get representation in the Forum was dropped.

At face value, it appears that the method of election received little attention in the negotiations. The arrangements did encounter some criticism, particularly from the Northern Ireland Women's Coalition and smaller parties to the talks, as offending the principle of inclusivity. They wanted to retain a top-up element to the system, similar in principle to that used in the 1996 Forum election, or the additional member element proposed for Scotland and Wales. Some of their proposals involved combining constituencies to give a lower threshold for election. As it was, the effect of increasing from five to six the number of members elected per constituency reduced the threshold for election from 16.7 per cent to 14.3 per cent.

It is provided in the Agreement that the Executive authority of the Assembly is to be discharged by a first minister and deputy first minister, elected jointly by the Assembly on a cross-community basis. On 1 July 1998, David Trimble, leader of the Ulster Unionist Party (UUP), and Seamus Mallon, deputy leader of the Social

Democratic and Labour Party (SDLP), were elected by the Assembly to the positions of first minister-designate and deputy first minister-designate respectively. This is reminiscent of the 1973 executive with Brian Faulkner (Ulster Unionist) and Gerry Fitt (SDLP) in the top two positions.

The Agreement provided for up to ten ministers with departmental responsibilities, allocated using the d'Hondt system on the basis of the seats won in the Assembly. Following the June 1998 elections this meant that there would be three Ulster Unionist ministers, three SDLP, two DUP and two Sinn Féin if the Executive was formed without a boycott by any of the parties or the exclusion of any of the parties. This is the site of our current and unresolved crisis around the issue of decommissioning.

Strand 2: North–South cooperation

Since the publication of the Stormont Agreement, Strand 2 – or the cross-border cooperation issue – has been the dog that has not barked in the night. When the Framework Document was published in February 1995[12] the Ulster unionists were very upset by proposals in this area – calling them an embryonic all Ireland government – but now they seem relatively relaxed on the issue and even rejectionist unionist critics have kept their main fire on other issues such as prisoners, policing and decommissioning.

As compared to the Framework Document, the Stormont Agreement lays much more formal stress on the accountability of the North South Ministerial Council. Indeed, it is made clear that the successful working of the North–South body is dependent on the successful working of the Assembly. Instead of the remit of the North–South Ministerial Council being established simply by legislation in the Dail and Westminster, it now emerges – and this is a totally new concept marking a radical break with part of the Framework Document – that a 'shadow' Northern Irish Assembly could throughout the summer of 1998 designate the functions of a new body from a list which 'may include' animal and plant health, social welfare, fraud control on a cross-border basis, agriculture and marine matters, etc. On the face of it, this rather confirms the view of Mr Trimble's supporters that it would be possible to negotiate a 'cross-borderism' which was both accountable to northern opinion – after all, John Hume has always enthusiastically supported this principle – and limited to areas no more sensitive than those currently going on and bound to continue and expand, agreement or no agreement.

In short, the new North–South body is not 'free standing', which is hardly surprising because at no time have the Irish government or the SDLP supported the 'free standing' concept. But what about the other big unionist problem – the section of the Anglo-Irish Agreement which called for North–South institutions with clear identity and purpose to enable representatives of democratic institutions, North and South, to enter into new, cooperative and constructive relationships to carry out delegated executive, harmonising and consultative functions?

Under the terms of the Framework Document, this body was to have a 'dynamic', albeit an 'agreed dynamic'. Unionists in 1995 were outraged: they ignored the significance of agreement or consent – and anathematised words like 'executive', 'harmonising' and 'dynamic' insofar as they characterised the powers of a North–South body. These concepts are now absent in this new Agreement. At the Lancaster House talks session, when Jeffrey Donaldson amused and astonished the world's media by tearing up the Framework Document, David Trimble quietly pointed out the way things were going in this respect. Will there be more or less cross-border activity five or ten years from now if the Stormont Agreement is ratified? It is genuinely difficult to tell. The manifold areas of policy which might be areas of cross-border cooperation reflect the list-making capacity of the civil services, North and South; there is nothing noted in the Lancaster House paper which might not be carried out under the Anglo-Irish Agreement of 1985.

What then is the philosophy of the two governments on the cross-border issue? British thinking is practical and pragmatic: it notes the existence of hundreds of cross-border voluntary bodies already in the sporting, religious and social fields – many of them with strong unionist participation – working harmoniously on the basis of a practical consent principle.[13] It hopes that an extension of this North–South activity might reduce nationalist alienation. Irish thinking is more visionary and more influenced by the notion of an 'island economy' in a European Union context. They would – the Framework Document is explicit on this point – like to see harmonisation reflecting the growing integration of the two economies within Europe. British officials tend to be a little sceptical about the island economy notion; they point out not just the still relevant different economic histories of the two parts of the island but the massive impact in the North of the huge multi-billion pound subvention from London.

Anyway, Ireland will join European Monetary Union in the first wave while Britain will not, thus slowing in some respects the integration of the two economies. But both sides meet in the belief that internal solution for the Northern Ireland problem is simply not available and that a North–South dimension is essential to any compromise. But where does all this leave us? The unionists in 1995 objected to the Framework Document on the grounds that it was allegedly an embryonic all-Ireland government.

Perhaps unionists overstated their case then. After all, the Framework Document came from the Major cabinet, which included in a pivotal position the strongly pro-unionist Lord Cranborne – whom Gerry Adams, according to press reports, believed was the greatest enemy of the peace process – and from the Irish government of John Bruton, known to the republicans as 'John Unionist'. Mr P. de Rossa, a cabinet minister close to Mr Bruton on the North, insisted at the time that a transitional arrangement would not provide stability.

Whatever the past, the unionists have now removed those terms which led them, and some hopeful republicans, to the assessment that the Framework was inherently transitional to a united Ireland. Nevertheless, there is no escaping the fact that unionists have had to concede cross-border institutions – now described in more neutral and pragmatic terms – as the price of a deal. It is an outcome that was perhaps obvious from the first day of the talks. It is perhaps worth adding that, quite regardless of the nit-picking detail, the regular cooperation between Belfast and Dublin which will ensue has the capacity to end the internal Irish cold war which has dogged the relationship between Northern Ireland and the Republic since 1921. Indeed, a better relationship between the two political entities on the island is perhaps a more certain outcome of this deal than a better relationship between the two communities in Northern Ireland.

Strand 3: East–West cooperation

When the Framework Document was published in 1995 even some of those intimately connected with its authorship were disappointed by the rather brief and unimaginative section on East–West relations or Strand 3. Little was proposed in this area that was really new, but here again the Stormont Agreement marks a difference: a totally novel institutional structure is proposed, a British–Irish Council which will comprise representatives of the British and Irish governments plus devolved institutions in Northern Ireland, Scotland and Wales.

The new body has, above all, symbolic importance for unionists. It establishes a new political link with the rest of the UK – implicitly challenging the nationalist tendency to define the problem simply as an island of Ireland problem. It links Northern Ireland to the UK-wide process of constitutional reform sponsored by the Blair government. As battles ensue, for example, over the allocation of regional public expenditure the British–Irish Council will give the involved assemblies a forum from which to defend their material interests.

The Belfast Agreement tells us that the Anglo-Irish Agreement of 1985 is to be replaced. But what is the significance of this? Here, there is a row between the UUP and the DUP. The UUP claims credit for getting rid of the Agreement – the culmination of a long campaign – while the DUP points out that the new Stormont Agreement makes provision for a new British–Irish Agreement dealing with the totality of relations which obviously bears a certain resemblance to the Hillsborough Accord structures. Are we really witnessing the delayed triumph of the anti-agreement campaign of the 1980s? Or, so far as unionists objected to the Anglo-Irish Agreement of 1985 on the grounds that it gave Dublin a role in the North in the 'secretive' Maryfield Secretariat without even the abandonment of the territorial claim – and this was a significant part of the rhetoric of the time – then the unionist case has been, in effect, conceded and as a potent symbol, the Maryfield operation is to be closed down.

Nevertheless, a close relationship between the British and Irish governments has been formed over the past thirteen years. The relationship is going to continue to be a significant feature of the Northern Irish scene even if, as it were, the Irish diplomatic presence here is regularised and put on a more, 'normal' basis as between two friendly states. This Anglo-Irish relationship is not as unproblematic as excluded unionists have tended to assume – there are often sharp disagreements. Some British officials are wryly inclined to say that Senator Mitchell's team, in a couple of years, achieved more real understanding of the local political scene than the Irish team over thirteen years.

Nevertheless, the Anglo-Irish intergovernmental and diplomatic relationship is part of the furniture and it has survived all Ian Paisley's rhetoric as well as his prediction that it could be smashed by popular resistance. This relationship will continue under the new British–Irish Intergovernmental Conference, but, at least, matters will be more open and democratic and local politicians will be involved in its working. But perhaps the greatest change here is not institutional at all but psychological. Although the Anglo-Irish Agreement of 1985 made reference to devolution, this was, in the view of senior British officials at the time, a mere 'lip service'. The agreement was imposed and the Dublin government given a voice in the North as a substitute for, not an incentive to, a power sharing deal which unionists at that time refused.

Gradually, and especially under John Major, the British moved back towards a policy of re-engaging the alienated unionists in the political system; this was related to general British perception – explicitly stated in Mrs Thatcher's memoirs – that the agreement had been less than a success.[14] The new Strand 3 deal protects nationalist interests by preserving a role for the Irish government in the North but it also protects unionist interest by healing the unionist rift with the British government and polity.

There are, of course, other controversial aspects to the Stormont Agreement – policing, prisoners, the equality/Irish language agenda – some of which generate more understandable emotion than the actual three strands which were negotiated in the main, it has to be said, by the unionists, SDLP, Alliance, and the two governments. Some of these are not as novel as they appear. In 1921, Sir James Craig (first Stormont prime minister) promised a police service which would be fully representative of the Catholic community.[15] After previous IRA campaigns failed, unionist governments were relatively liberal in their prisoner release programmes.

As long ago as the 1930s, the Stormont education minister Lord Charlemont instructed his ministry to recognise the Irish language in order to 'disarm criticism on the part of anti-British elements'.

Finally, commissions have been established to deal with equality, policing and human rights. The Agreement has been underpinned by a radical, if controversial, programme of release of paramilitary prisoners. But the complex process of multi-layered deal-making that produced the Good Friday Agreement does not preclude the characterisation of the outcome in terms employed by political scientists. Thus, according to Brendan O'Leary, this Agreement meets all four of the criteria for a consociational agreement laid out by Lijphart. That is:

1   cross-community executive power sharing;
2   proportionality rules applied throughout the relevant governmental and public
     sectors;
3   community self-government (or autonomy) and equality in cultural life; and
4   veto rights for minorities.[16]

Further, if the terminology developed by Sammy Smooha and Theo Hanf to describe modes of conflict regulation is used,[17] it might be said that Northern Ireland is on the verge of completing a transition from being an ethnic democracy (though not, I think, a state) in the 1921–72 period to being a liberal, multicultural, consociational-type political entity. That, of course, presumes that the great and unresolved issue – that of the decommissioning of paramilitary arms – does not bring the whole system tumbling down.

Notes

1   The terms, 'Stormont Agreement', 'Belfast Agreement' and 'Good Friday Agreement' are used interchangeably in this text to describe the one Agreement reached at Stormont Castle Grounds in Belfast on 10 April 1998.
2   Brendan O'Leary, 'The Nature of the Agreement', *Fordham International Law Journal*, Vol. 22, No. 4, 1999, p. 1630n.
3   See Paul Bew, Peter Gibbon and Henry Patterson, *Northern Ireland 1921–1996: Political Forces and Social Classes* (2nd edn), Serif, London, 1996, Chapter 6, especially pp. 213–17.
4   See Paul Bew, Henry Patterson and Paul Teague, *Between War and Peace: The Political Future of Northern Ireland*, Lawrence and Wishart, London, 1997, pp. 203–16.
5   For the text of the 'Heads of Agreement' document, see Appendix 12.
6   For the text of the Joint Declaration, see Appendix 4.
7   *Parliamentary Brief*, Summer 1994.
8   For full text of Annex A, see Appendix 2.
9   For text of Framework Document, see Appendix 9.
10 For text of the new Article 3, see Appendix 2.
11 See on this point Brigid Hadfield, 'The Belfast Agreement, Sovereignty and the State of the Union', *Public Law*, Winter 1998, pp. 599–616.
12 For the text of the Framework Document, see Appendix 9.
13 For an account of cross-border activity by non-governmental organisations, see John Whyte, 'The Permeability of the United Kingdom-Irish Border: A Preliminary Reconnaissance', *Administration*, Vol. 31, No. 3, 1983, pp. 300–15.
14 Margaret Thatcher, *The Downing Street Years*, Harper Collins, London, 1995 (paperback edn), pp. 402–6.
15 Paul Bew, 'The Political History of Northern Ireland: The Prospects for North–South Co-operation' in Anthony F. Heath, Richard Breen and Christopher T. Whelan (eds), *Ireland North and South: Perspectives from Social Science* (Proceedings of the British Academy, Vol. 98), Oxford, Oxford University Press for the British Academy, 1999, pp. 409–10.
16 O'Leary, 'The Nature of the Agreement', pp. 1631–41.
17 Sammy Smooha and Theo Hanf, 'The Diverse Modes of Conflict-Regulation in Deeply Divided Societies' in Anthony D. Smith (ed.), *Ethnicity and Nationalism*, Leiden and New York, E. J. Brill, 1992, pp. 27–34.

4

The SDLP and the roots of the Good Friday Agreement

SEAN FARREN

Introduction: from power sharing to the Anglo-Irish Agreement

The failure of the 1974 power sharing and Council of Ireland arrangements underlined several key determinants of political relationships in Northern Ireland at the time. First, unionist opposition to involvement with the South together with their very reluctant engagement with the nationalist community in Northern Ireland itself. To a considerable extent, both were motivated by fear and, consequently, by the need for protection and security. Unionist domination of political life in Northern Ireland prior to 1972 had been regarded as necessary to protect its community against the possibility of being overwhelmed by nationalists where the latter were in the majority in Northern Ireland and to ensure a united front against perceived threats from the nationalist majority in the rest of Ireland.

For nationalists, on the other hand, the very existence of Northern Ireland continued to be regarded at best an injustice to be tolerated, at worst a situation to be ended by force. Until the 1960s nationalists had assumed a sullen lack of cooperation with public life, if not outright opposition. Retreating into their own community they kept themselves apart from the general affairs of Northern Ireland through separate Catholic schools, their own sports and other socio-cultural activities. The civil rights movement, followed by the political upheavals of the late 1960s and early 1970s from which emerged the power sharing and Council of Ireland agreements, had offered a powerfully creative opportunity to break free from this condition with dignity and self-respect. The recently formed SDLP had strongly advocated both, arguing that a solution to political division required not domination by one community over the other, but a new partnership between both, as well as a new basis for relationships with the South.

Failure to achieve these objectives in 1974, reinforced by the failure of later initiatives in 1976 and 1980,[1] convinced the SDLP that a solution would not be found on the narrow ground of Northern Ireland alone. At its annual conference in

1979 the SDLP had already signalled the need for a shift in direction by calling on the British and Irish governments 'to promote a joint … process of political, social and economic development within which the representatives of the two traditions in Northern Ireland would work in partnership'.[2] A year later the SDLP strengthened this call, asking the two governments to hold a constitutional conference to consider possible structures for developing Anglo-Irish relations within which relationships between unionists and nationalists in Northern Ireland would be addressed.[3] The first call would be answered almost immediately. It would take more than a decade for the second to be heeded, but when it was it would lead to the Good Friday Agreement.

Following changes of government in Dublin and London in 1979 similar thinking began to inform Anglo-Irish relations. As a result a new twin-track approach emerged, one track of which was to dominate. This track involved increasingly closer intergovernmental cooperation. As it evolved, the SDLP was to become the northern voice of greatest influence on the process. The second track reflected the belief still held in some quarters, notably the Northern Ireland Office, that political institutions should first be established in Northern Ireland. Like previous initiatives it was to result in failure.

Initially, the first track was motivated by British needs for much greater security cooperation with the South to combat IRA violence. However, since no Irish government would cooperate on security alone, the British indicated a willingness to explore relationships on a wider basis. Two summit meetings in 1980 between prime minister Margaret Thatcher and taoiseach Charles Haughey formalised this strategy which commenced with a series of joint studies into possible areas for social, economic and cultural cooperation. Political initiatives, delayed by the downturn in Anglo-Irish relations during the hunger strikes and the Falklands war, did not regain momentum until 1984–85.

Meantime, attention focused on the second track launched by Secretary of State James Prior in 1982. Enthusiasm amongst the political parties for a proposed new assembly varied considerably. Only the DUP and Alliance expressed much enthusiasm, the UUP was lukewarm while the SDLP and Sinn Féin were hostile. SDLP hostility derived from continuing unionist opposition to power sharing and to any institutionalised relations with the South, as well as from bitter memories of previous failures. With its new policy emphasis on an Anglo-Irish framework, the SDLP also argued that nationalist opinion in Ireland should clarify its attitudes and relationships with the North and devise a common strategy for negotiations with both the unionists and the British.

Consequently, the SDLP entered the 1982 assembly elections seeking a mandate for an all-Ireland council in which constitutional nationalist parties would devise that strategy.[4] Following consultation with the government and parties in the South, the Forum for a New Ireland was established in 1983. Its remit was to take evidence on and to determine the most effective measures to achieve reconciliation between the divided sections of the Irish people.

The Forum's report in 1984 outlined key principles for reconciliation and new political structures within Northern Ireland and between both parts of Ireland.[5] These included a firm commitment to a constitutional approach and opposition to the use of violence; a recognition of the legitimacy of both the unionist and nationalist traditions; and a recommendation that the Irish and British governments proceed jointly to resolve the crisis. The Forum also proposed possible structural solutions: a unitary Irish state, a federal or confederal state and joint authority. Since none of these proposals was likely to attract unionists, at SDLP's insistence it was also indicated that consideration would be given to any other proposal that might win widespread support. Prime minister Thatcher's blunt rejection of the structural proposals underlined the wisdom of this more open-ended approach. So, notwithstanding her rejections, twelve months later, in November 1985, Mrs Thatcher signed the Anglo-Irish Agreement granting the Irish government a formal consultative role in the affairs of Northern Ireland. The first major political step in the SDLP's 1980 strategy had been taken.

1985 and beyond

Very significantly, for the majority of nationalists the New Ireland Forum marked the formal end to a territorial perspective on the partition of Ireland. Hitherto regarded as the territorial dismembering of Ireland, partition was henceforward to be primarily regarded as the product of dismembered relationships. While it remained the case, as the Forum's report indicates, that nationalists still aspired to Irish unity, their willingness to consider other options which might also obtain the endorsement of unionists was a significant political move. In essence, this amounted to a formal acknowledgement of the principle of consent, long central to SDLP principles. In other words, changes to the status of Northern Ireland required the agreement of the people living there and, conversely, stability in the North also required the agreement of both its communities.

Nationalist attention as represented by the parties in the Forum was now on working towards a settlement which would give due recognition to unionist as well as to nationalist rights and which would produce a political and constitutional framework for both parts of the country, most especially for Northern Ireland. The means to that end lay in developing British–Irish cooperation using the principles underlying the Anglo-Irish Agreement and the mechanisms established by it. The centrality of the principle of consent to the Anglo-Irish Agreement meant that for the first time the British government was able to formally accept the possibility of a united Ireland. This implied that Britain's role in the North was based simply on the will of the majority there and not on any strategic interest of its own. The significance of this was not lost on the SDLP. The party now had a powerful argument with which to develop the next phase of its strategy of achieving a comprehensive settlement. British acceptance of the possibility of a united Ireland meant that the onus lay on those who wanted Irish unity to persuade those opposed of its merits. This was a challenge to Sinn Féin and the IRA for whom the British presence was still that of a colonial occupier, the only response to which was to seek by whatever means possible a declaration to withdraw. By the mid-1980s those means were the combined use of the 'ballot box and the armalite'. Politically and militarily it was a forlorn strategy with no prospect of success. Politically Sinn Féin remained second to the SDLP in terms of electoral support within the nationalist community in the North, while in the South it enjoyed minimal support. Militarily there was absolutely no prospect of any kind of victory for the IRA. However, efforts to end the violence by counter-terrorist measures had not offered any signs of early success either and a kind of military stalemate had been reached. A new strategy was required if Sinn Féin and the IRA were not to condemn the people of Northern Ireland to the effects of a futile and endless campaign of violence.

In this situation approaches in 1987 to the SDLP to engage in talks with Sinn Féin were met with a willing response. These talks commenced in 1988 and lasted for some nine months, ending without any clear-cut results at the time. From Sinn Féin's perspective the talks were aimed at building a nationalist consensus within Ireland and in Irish circles abroad to achieve by diplomatic means a British withdrawal. However, since a consensus around very different objectives had already been achieved in the New Ireland Forum and a significant advance towards them recorded in the Anglo-Irish Agreement, such an aim had no prospect of gaining SDLP support. What the SDLP hoped to achieve was to convince Sinn Féin that progress could only be made by persuading the unionist community, the real opponents of Irish unity, of the attractions of change. Britain, in the SDLP's view, had become officially neutral on the question of unity. In addition, the SDLP also argued that persuading unionists would never be successful if pursued at the point of a gun. Hence the need to bring an end to violence and to work towards the establishment of conditions in which genuine negotiations could take place.

Failure to persuade Sinn Féin of its case did not deter the SDLP from pursuing its strategy. However, as long as IRA violence continued it was clear that Sinn Féin could not be admitted to any formal negotiations. This meant Sinn Féin's exclusion from the next major initiative at negotiating new institutions taken by secretary of state Brooke in 1991. In these negotiations the SDLP focused attention on developing a three-stranded agenda upon which it believed a successful settlement would ultimately have to be built. So, in the words of secretary of state Peter Brooke the talks would 'focus on three main relationships: those within Northern Ireland ... among the people of the island of Ireland; and between the two Governments'.[6] Dogged by procedural wrangles and interrupted by elections, the talks ended without any positive outcome. However, in the light of the negotiations that eventually led directly to the Good Friday Agreement, they were not without significance.

In its main submission the SDLP stressed a number of 'realities' which it believed had to be accepted in the search for a new political framework.[7] These included acceptance of the political process and the rejection of violence for political ends, a reiteration of the key points made to Sinn Féin. Secondly, the SDLP argued the need to accept the three central relationships, i.e. those between the people of Northern Ireland itself, those between the people of the North and the South, those between the people of Ireland and Britain as the basis for a settlement. Thirdly, the party argued that the Anglo-Irish Agreement represented an irreversible 'breakthrough in understanding and tackling the underlying causes of Anglo-Irish conflict'. Finally, the SDLP pointed to the growing significance of membership of the EC and the lessons that could be learnt from the manner in which the EC's founders had deliberately created a framework of cooperation to ensure that the centuries-old conflicts in Europe would be consigned to the past. The pooling of sovereignty which membership of the EC entailed was an example of particular pertinence to the Northern Ireland situation. The fact that both Britain and Ireland's membership of the EC required some pooling of sovereignty meant there was no principle precluding the same in the Irish situation. To a very limited degree the Anglo-Irish Agreement exemplified such pooling.

The proposals tabled during these talks are only of interest insofar as they revealed significant gaps between the SDLP and the Irish government, on the one hand, and, on the other, the two unionist parties and Alliance. The essential difference lay in the SDLP's insistence on a power sharing executive for Northern Ireland in which ministers would exercise responsibility for government departments while the other parties proposed that assembly departmental commmittees exercise this responsibility. On North–South relations unionist demands, supported by the British and Alliance, that Articles 2 and 3 of the Republic's Constitution be amended became very contentious and effectively logjammed talks on this area of the agenda. The Irish, with SDLP support, refused to make any firm commitment to constitutional change until other issues had been progressed. Proposals for North–South political institutions also revealed extremely wide gaps. The SDLP and the Irish government argued for a council with decision-making powers, whereas the unionists favoured a purely consultative body. While neither issue was resolved, it was evident that changes to Articles 2 and 3 had not been ruled out and that unionists were willing to discuss some form of a North–South political institution, probably with some decision-making powers. As to the form of new institutions in the North, it was clear that considerable movement would be required if agreement was to be reached.

From Hume–Adams to 1994 ceasefire

Termination of these talks coincided with renewed efforts to convince Sinn Féin of the need to end IRA violence. By then, as later evidence was to demonstrate, not only had the SDLP become involved again, but so also had both governments.[8] A major drive was under way to persuade Sinn Féin and the IRA that the latter's campaign should end as a prelude to Sinn Féin's entry into negotiations.

The SDLP's role became public in April 1993 when it was announced that party leader John Hume had renewed talks with Sinn Féin leader Gerry Adams.[9] Both declared they were engaged in 'a political dialogue aimed at investigating the possibility of developing an overall political strategy to establish peace and justice in Ireland'.[10] The statement's significance lay essentially in the oblique shift signalled in Sinn Féin's stand on the key question of consent. The traditional Sinn Féin view was that unionists could enjoy no right to override the will of the majority of the 'Irish people' in expressing their right to self-determination. Instead, the Hume–Adams statement argued that a settlement would be 'only achievable and viable if it can earn and enjoy the allegiance of the different traditions on this island, by accommodating diversity and providing for national reconciliation'.[11] By accepting the need for 'the allegiance of the different traditions', Sinn Féin seemed to be acknowledging the need for unionist consent, not just that of a (nationalist) majority in Ireland as a whole. If this was the case, Sinn Féin was moving towards the SDLP's position and also to that of both governments in the Anglo-Irish Agreement.

The Joint Declaration issued on 15 December 1993 by prime minister John Major and taoiseach Albert Reynolds was the governments' considered response to the apparent shift in Sinn Féin's position.[12] The Declaration dealt with the 'right to self-determination' of the people living in Ireland; the conditions under which the status of Northern Ireland might change; and the terms by which those political parties currently supporting the use of violence for political ends would be admitted to negotiations on the search for new political institutions. These were the issues upon which Sinn Féin had claimed, in its contacts with the SDLP and both governments, it needed clarification and reassurance so that it might present the IRA with a convincing case for a ceasefire.

The Joint Declaration had its roots firmly in the Anglo-Irish Agreement, repeating as it did key commitments of that Agreement, especially those on consent and the possibility of Irish unity. To meet Sinn Féin's arguments the Declaration added an explicit reference to an *all-Ireland* framework to a solution. The British prime minister did so by pledging 'to uphold the democratic wish of a greater number of the people of Northern Ireland on the issue of whether they prefer to support the Union or a sovereign united Ireland' but also 'to work together with the Irish government to achieve such an agreement, which will embrace the totality of relationships. The role of the British Government will be to encourage, facilitate and enable the achievement of such agreement … They accept that such an agreement may, as of right, take the form of a united Ireland achieved by peaceful means.'[13] Placed alongside another statement that the British government had 'no selfish strategic or economic interest in Northern Ireland', it was difficult to interpret this commitment other than as the British declaring no opposition to the possibility of Irish unity. Creating that possibility had to be left to those who believed unity to be in the best interests of the Irish people. Meantime, the British committed themselves to *encouraging* and *facilitating* agreement between the people of Ireland. If, in seeking agreement, the Irish people decided to unite, it was clear from the Declaration that this wish would be respected and, as the Anglo-Irish

Agreement had stated, both governments would 'introduce and support in their respective Parliaments legislation to give effect to that wish'.[14]

For its part, the Irish government reiterated its previous acceptance, in the Anglo-Irish Agreement, of the principle of consent to constitutional change by stating that 'it would be wrong to impose a united Ireland, in the absence of the freely given consent of a majority of the people of Northern Ireland' and 'that the democratic right of self-determination by the people of Ireland as a whole must be achieved and exercised with and subject to the agreement and consent of a majority of the people of Northern Ireland'.[15]

Furthermore, the Irish government indicated a willingness to examine 'any elements in the democratic life and organisation of the Irish State that can be represented to the Irish Government ... as a real and substantial threat to their [the Unionist] way of life and ethos, or that can be represented as not being fully consistent with a modern democratic and pluralist society, and undertakes to examine any possible ways of removing such obstacles'.[16] As a contribution to the dialogue of reconciliation, the Irish government undertook to set up a Forum for Peace and Reconciliation 'to make recommendations on ways in which agreement and trust between both traditions can be promoted and established'.[17]

The Declaration also dealt with the pressing need for political dialogue involving all parties in the North together with the two governments with the objective 'to create institutions and structures which, while respecting the diversity of the people of Ireland, would enable them to work together in all areas of common interest'. Such structures were regarded as essential in building the trust necessary to end past divisions, leading to an agreed and peaceful future. They would 'include institutional recognition of the special links that exist between the peoples of Ireland as part of the totality of relationships, while taking account of newly forged links with the rest of Europe'.[18] In effect, this was an endorsement of the agenda set for the 1991–92 talks. The governments indicated that if Sinn Féin accepted the terms of the declaration and the IRA ceased its campaign of violence, the former would be 'free to participate fully in democratic politics and join in dialogue in due course between the Governments and the political parties on the way ahead'.[19]

With so much groundwork laid for the kind of comprehensive approach to a settlement advocated by the SDLP in 1980, pressure now intensified to persuade the republican movement that the circumstances existed enabling Sinn Féin participate in negotiations. So, after considerable internal debate on 31 August 1994 the IRA announced 'a complete cessation of military operations ... to enhance the democratic process'.[20] A month later the main loyalist paramilitaries also announced a ceasefire. Anxious to consolidate this development, Albert Reynolds very publicly received Gerry Adams, in the company of John Hume, in Dublin and all three declared themselves to be 'totally and absolutely committed to democratic and peaceful methods of resolving our political problems'.[21] Reynolds also moved to establish the promised forum.

Settlement or impasse?

Of most significance in the Forum's deliberations were further signs of shifts in Sinn Féin's approaches to a number of key issues, most notably those relating to the principle of consent and to possible political structures in Northern Ireland as part of an overall agreement. While the party formally opposed the principle of consent as enunciated in the Joint Declaration, i.e. in a manner which would allow for a distinct voice to the northern electorate on the question of any constitutional change, it became clear that Sinn Féin was gradually moving towards the compromise hinted at in the April 1993 Hume–Adams statement. References by Sinn Féin delegates to a willingness to consider 'interim' (i.e. interim to a united Ireland) political structures for Northern Ireland were among those hints.

The publication by both governments of a set of consultative documents on possible political arrangements in March 1995 added to the expectation that important developments were likely. Entitled *Frameworks for the Future*, the documents outlined the shape that new structures might take.[22] Firstly, such structures would have to enable representatives from all sections of society to cooperate in governing Northern Ireland. This meant building into the fabric of government requirements for power sharing between nationalists and unionists together with mechanisms for safeguarding human and civil rights. The precise nature of such arrangements as well as the powers which they would exercise would be matters for negotiation. Nonetheless, it was clear that future institutions could include a parliamentary-type body and a politically controlled administration in which representatives from both communities would be involved.

Secondly, to address North–South relationships, new structures involving representatives from both parts of the island would have to be established. These structures would 'help heal the divisions among the communities on the island of Ireland; provide a forum for acknowledging the respective identities and requirements of the two major traditions … and promote understanding and agreement among the people and institutions in both parts of the island'.[23]

The SDLP was the northern party most anxious to see such structures in place.[24] As it proposed to the Forum for Peace and Reconciliation, ministers from both North and South would meet in council to discuss and agree matters of mutual concern while a parliamentary-type body could provide a broad political and consultative base for such matters. North–South structures could also have a special role on EU matters, many of which had a cross-border and all-Ireland remit.

Thirdly, in recognition of the historic and geo-political framework of the problems to be resolved, the establishment of British–Irish structures was also proposed. In this respect the Anglo-Irish Agreement had already set up the Inter-Governmental Ministerial Council and the Inter-Parliamentary Body. Further development of such structures to include representation from Northern Ireland, especially from unionists who were boycotting both, was not seen to be problematic.

As the broad principles upon which a settlement could be based were becoming clearer, the stumbling blocks along the road to that settlement became more process related. In other words, the crises which followed the ceasefires in 1994, derived from a failure to agree such matters as the timing and nature of negotiations, who should be present and by what means they should be empowered to participate.

The essence of this impasse lay primarily in unionist attitudes to Sinn Féin and the IRA and in the attitudes of the latter towards the British government. Both of the main unionist parties, with some support from the British government, insisted that Sinn Féin, because of its association with the IRA, had to clearly demonstrate its commitment to democracy before they would agree to enter negotiations with that party. This would be made evident by decommissioning IRA arms and by Sinn Féin receiving a fresh, post-ceasefire electoral mandate. Sinn Féin regarded such demands as unacceptable and suspected the British government was deliberately trying to undermine its position. The resultant logjam prevented the immediate opening of all-party negotiations and produced a protracted process of pre-negotiation talks between Sinn Féin and the British government.

Meantime the increasingly significant role of the US government, a role which the SDLP, through John Hume, had long cultivated and encouraged, was now more evident than ever. The most practical expression of this role was the invitation extended by both governments to Senator George Mitchell to examine how paramilitary arms might be decommissioned and on the linkage between this issue and the commencement of all-party talks. In its report the Mitchell commission recommended that all parties sign a set of six principles termed 'Principles for Democracy and Non-Violence' as a test of their *bona fides* before entering such talks and that the disarmament of paramilitary forces take place in parallel with negotiations.[25] While some parties declared their willingness to accept these principles, the unionist parties insisted that IRA disarmament should commence prior to Sinn Féin's entry to negotiations. Sinn Féin, while not rejecting the Mitchell principles, appeared to equivocate and made it clear that, in its view, the IRA would not consent to any disarmament until an agreement had been reached.

The negotiations which commenced on 10 June 1996 were intended to be as inclusive as was possible and practicable. However, with Sinn Féin excluded until a new IRA ceasefire, the negotiations started in the absence of the party around which much of process had been woven. With procedural wrangling absorbing a great deal of debate the talks made no substantial progress during their first year. Following the British general election of May 1997 at which Sinn Féin significantly increased its vote, the new Labour government indicated that entry to negotiations could follow as soon as six weeks after a renewed ceasefire. On 19 July the IRA announced that it would restore its ceasefire.

Despite the signs of compromise in Sinn Féin's approach to a solution, the party presented a very traditional republican case at the negotiations. In its view the case for 'a sovereign, united and independent Irish state' was simply self-evident.

Being so self-evidently right and just, achieving Irish unity merely required a British initiative. In Sinn Féin's analysis, it was British sovereignty over Northern Ireland that remained the essential barrier to unity, not unionist opposition. It followed that how unionists might become involved in persuading the British to move to such a position did not require immediate consideration. Britain had to move first on the question of sovereignty after which an accommodation and agreement with unionists could be determined.

With no support for its analysis from any of the other participants, nor for the proposals based on it, the Sinn Féin case was simply heard and noted. Given the analysis and the approach which had been argued for and accepted since the New Ireland Forum in 1984 and, even more significantly, since the Anglo-Irish Agreement, neither the Irish government nor the SDLP offered any support. The practical consequences of Sinn Féin's approach together with no progress on IRA decommissioning, was that the UUP simply refused to engage directly with its delegation. Sinn Féin's failure to accept the principle of consent allowed the UUP to claim that the Sinn Féin approach simply had nothing relevant to offer.

Notwithstanding Sinn Féin's fundamentalist position there was evidence suggesting a willingness to accept, or at least acquiesce, in arrangements that would fall far short of its declared goal. The party's very presence at the negotiations was part of that evidence. Violence was no longer instrumental. Furthermore, in a negotiating process where its approach was not shared by either the SDLP or the Irish government, it must have been clear to Sinn Féin that its goal of a united Ireland was not an immediately viable objective. Perhaps anticipating this, Sinn Féin highlighted issues on which progress could be made separately. These were the so-called 'equality agenda', issues like fair employment, greater recognition and support for the Irish language and the treatment of prisoners. While many of these issues were already being positively addressed, further progress could be represented as advances which Sinn Féin had helped to achieve, the case for Irish unity notwithstanding. With respect to the broader political agenda, Sinn Féin's stress on no 'internal settlement' and its reference to the need for a 'democratic accommodation of the differing views of the two main traditions, which takes full account of the conflicting identities',[26] contained hints that the party was prepared to be more flexible than its formal submission at first suggested.

The SDLP emphasised the New Ireland Forum's position on the rights of both unionists and nationalists 'to effective political, symbolic and administrative expression of their identity, ethos and way of life' as 'key to the success of the negotiations'.[27] This position meant that the negotiations would have to 'be focused within the framework which embraces and addresses the key political, social, economic and cultural relationships between the communities within the North, between communities North and South and, thirdly, on relationships between Ireland and Britain'.[28] Given the structure and agenda for the negotiations, this focus had already been adopted and no longer had to be argued for in any essential manner.

Both governments stressed the three-fold set of relationships outlined by the SDLP and placed considerable emphasis on the principles of consent and self-determination as expressed in the Joint Declaration.[29] With their common concerns about paramilitaries, they reminded participants in the talks of the commitments in the Mitchell Principles to abide by any agreement reached and to use only democratic means in pursuit of any changes which they might subsequently want to achieve to an agreement. Decommissioning paramilitary weapons and disbanding paramilitary organisations had not gone away as issues.

Breakthrough

Momentum gathered early in 1998 when a set of joint propositions were tabled by both governments derived, in part, 'from views of all parties on the various issues which arise in the talks' and because they represented their 'best guess at what could be a generally acceptable outcome'.[30] Not surprisingly, the kind of outcome foreseen was one which would include: a new northern assembly and administration; a North–South Ministerial Council; a British–Irish Council; provisions to safeguard human, social, economic and cultural rights; and constitutional change based on the principle of consent.

The atmosphere surrounding the talks was once again heavy with accusations and fears of betrayal. Divisions in unionist ranks increased and intensified. Within the UUP's own negotiating team, differences emerged threatening the party's continued presence in the negotiations.[31] Sinn Féin, which had submitted no proposals of its own for new northern institutions, accused the SDLP of opening the way, as a result of its acceptance of a Northern Ireland assembly, to the creation of a pre-1972 type regime. How a North–South council could function without an elected administration in the North from which to draw its northern membership, nor how trust might be developed between unionists and nationalists without a partnership institution, Sinn Féin did not explain.

Since the two governments had already set a May 1998 deadline for the negotiations, pressure mounted for an earlier conclusion to allow for referenda, North and South, on any agreement before the summer. In the event of a positive outcome to the referenda, it was planned that assembly elections also be held within the same period. With these considerations in mind, Senator Mitchell announced that the talks would close, with or without agreement, on 9 April.[32]

Institutionally the Good Friday Agreement was a realisation of what the three-stranded agenda and the relationships analysis underlying it, had long predicted. Other than failure, there never had been any prospect of an alternative outcome. Within the negotiations it had been more a question of parties attempting to strengthen or weaken proposals for its different aspects, than of seriously expecting a different outcome. Unionists were fully aware that North–South arrangements would have to entail a least some decision-making capacity if the SDLP was to be satisfied. Conversely, the SDLP was fully aware that such arrangements would have to include accountability by the northern members of a North–South council to an assembly in Belfast if the council was to be acceptable to unionists. Given that Irish unity was not a likely outcome, Sinn Féin's main aims were to ensure provisions for the early release of prisoners and for police reform, together with commitments on human, cultural and civil rights. The Agreement did contain such provisions, notably a review of the sentences of those held for terrorist offences and associated with paramilitary groups on ceasefire, with the intention of securing releases within two years. A special commission would examine policing. Other provisions included commitments to enhance the status of the Irish language and to reinforce provisions aimed at guaranteeing fair employment and an end to discrimination.

Constitutional changes included a declaration on the Irish government's part to amend Articles 2 and 3 of the Republic's Constitution, first, to remove the section implying a territorial claim on Northern Ireland and, second, to include the principle of consent as the only basis upon which Irish unity could be achieved. On the British government's part, it was agreed that the Government of Ireland Act (1920) would be repealed in its entirety and subsequent legislation would include the principle of consent. Finally, upon entering into force the Good Friday Agreement would mean that the 1985 Anglo-Irish Agreement would be replaced by a new British–Irish Agreement. The catalyst for all of the political developments over the intervening twelve and a half years would be replaced by its more comprehensive and far-reaching successor.

Notes

1 The Constitutional Convention, 1975–76, and the secretary of state's conference in 1980, aimed primarily at achieving agreement on political institutions for Northern Ireland.
2 SDLP, *Towards a New Ireland*, annual conference, 1979.
3 SDLP, *Northern Ireland – A Strategy for Peace*, annual conference, 1980.
4 SDLP, *Election Manifesto*, Assembly Elections, 1982.
5 *New Ireland Forum, Final Report*, Dublin: Stationery Office, 1984.
6 Statement by secretary of state Brooke to the House of Commons, 26 March 1991: *The Irish Times*, 27 March 1991.
7 SDLP paper to inter-party talks, 1991.
8 Eamonn Mallie, and David McKittrick, *The Fight for Peace*, London: Heinemann, 1996, chapters 6–8.
9 *Ibid.*, p. 171.
10 *The Irish Times*, 26 April 1993.
11 *Ibid.*
12 *The Joint Declaration of the Taoiseach, Mr Reynolds and the British Prime Minister, Mr John Major*, 15 December 1993.
13 *Ibid.*, para 4.
14 Anglo-Irish Agreement, Article 1(c).
15 *Joint Declaration*, para 5.
16 *Ibid.*, para 6.
17 *Ibid.*, para 11
18 *Ibid.*, para 9.

19 *Ibid.*, para 10.
20 *The Irish Times*, 1 September 1994.
21 *Ibid.*
22 *A New Framework for Agreement (Joint Framework Document)*, February 1994.
23 *Ibid.*, para 38.
24 SDLP, Submission on North–South structures to the Forum for Peace and Reconciliation, 1995.
25 *Report of the International Body*, January 1996.
26 *Ibid.*
27 SDLP, Submission to the multi-party talks, 13 October 1997.
28 *Ibid.*
29 Submissions by the British and Irish governments to the multi-party talks, 10 October 1997.
30 Joint Statement by the British and Irish Governments, 12 January 1998.
31 UUP MP Jeffrey Donaldson called for his party to reconsider participation in the talks, *Irish News*, 20 December 1997.
32 *The Irish Times*, 31 March 1998.

5

The 1998 Agreement: Unionist responses

ARTHUR AUGHEY

Introduction

Nationalist commentators, with eyes fixed on fifty years of unionist government in Northern Ireland after 1921, used to talk of the unionist 'monolith'. It is surprising how such notions survive long after whatever justification they once had is gone. Writing in July 1999, thirty years after the outbreak of the Troubles, even the political editor of *The Irish Times* had to remind his readers that those 'who had been inclined to lump all of unionism together' had, since the signing of the Belfast Agreement in April 1998, 'been made aware of the complexity – and the ferocity – of the competition' within it.[1] Not to have noticed this complexity and ferocity in the last quarter of a century was either a sign of severe inattentiveness or of ideological blindness. The end of unionist government in 1972 had removed the main institutional focus of political unity for Ulster Protestants. This both consolidated and encouraged unionism's organisational and political fragmentation.

An expression which emerged in the 1970s to take the place of the now redundant 'unionist monolith' was 'the unionist family'. This expression implied that though there might be party competition, differences of personal ambition and tactical disagreements between them, unionists together shared a common set of interests which transcended such divisions. Indeed, a consistent response at times of crisis has been the call for unionist (family) unity. The implication is questionable and the call, so far, has not been realised. Nonetheless, there is sufficient evidence to show that both are not pure fantasy. Despite a serious challenge by the Democratic Unionist Party (DUP) in the early 1980s to replace the Ulster Unionist Party (UUP) as the largest party, both cooperated to oppose the Anglo-Irish Agreement of 1985. Relations between the parties remained reasonably good under James (now Lord) Molyneaux's leadership of the UUP.

Interestingly, one of the stated aims of David Trimble when he became leader of the UUP in 1995 was to create the conditions for his party to become the party of

unionist unity. This now seems rather ironic. There has been even greater fragmentation within unionism since then. The so-called fringe loyalist parties, the
Progressive Unionist Party (close to the Ulster Volunteer Force) and the Ulster
Democratic Party (close to the Ulster Defence Association), have established
themselves in the electoral market. Robert McCartney's United Kingdom Unionist
Party (UKUP) emerged explicitly to challenge the direction of Trimble's policy,
only itself to split in 1999. McCartney's four Assembly colleagues have reconsti-
tuted themselves as the Northern Ireland Unionist Party, only to see one of their
colleagues defect when the executive was established in November 1999. Four
independent, anti-Trimble, unionists were also elected to the Assembly in 1998.
More significantly, the UUP itself has shown deep fissiparous tendencies since the
signing of the Belfast Agreement. The Ulster Unionist Council, the UUP's
governing body, is evenly divided over the wisdom of Trimble's strategy.

Therefore, to understand the responses of unionist parties to, and the splits
within unionism as a consequence of, the Belfast Agreement of 10 April 1998 it is
necessary to appreciate the commitments and objectives by which that Agreement
was assessed. In addition, the responses to its content cannot be divorced from the
conditions of its negotiation. The decision by the Ulster unionists to stay in the
negotiations after the summer of 1997 determined much of its attitude to the
outcome of those negotiations on Good Friday, 1998. Similarly, the decision by the
DUP and the UKUP to leave the negotiations also pre-determined their rejection
of its provisions. In this there were two key reference points for all unionists.

Objectives and dangers

The first was the joint unionist manifesto for the general election of 1987, agreed by
Molyneaux of the UUP and Ian Paisley of the DUP. That manifesto had committed unionists to seek 'an alternative to and a replacement of' the Anglo-Irish
Agreement of 15 November 1985. The practical politics of this commitment meant,
as the formula agreed for the Brooke/Mayhew Talks of 1991–92 revealed, negotiating within a three-stranded format. This involved the parties negotiating internal
arrangements for governing Northern Ireland; arrangements for cross-border
cooperation between Northern Ireland and the Republic of Ireland; and arrangements for continued intergovernmental cooperation between the UK and the
Republic of Ireland. Although differences had emerged during the Brooke/Mayhew
talks about the details of cross-border cooperation, a minimalist approach was
adopted by both the UUP and the DUP. The purpose of Strand One had been to
establish Northern Ireland's status as a part of the UK. In Strand Two, unionists
rejected a self-standing Council of Ireland with an executive remit. In Strand Three
the UUP and DUP both demanded an end to the Anglo-Irish Agreement.

The second reference point was the common rejection of the Framework
Document of February 1995. The Framework Document represented, according to
the two governments, the 'best assessment of where broad agreement might be

found' between unionists and nationalists. In terms of the disagreements of 1991 and 1992, official policy appeared to have resolved many of the disputed points in favour of the nationalist position. The formula of the Framework Document, however, was really the old formula of Irish unity by consent. Its meaning was not self-evident. If one were to accept that the principle of consent governs the principle of unity then, to all intents and purposes, the Union would be 'safe' (the very interpretation which loyalist paramilitaries advanced at the time of their ceasefire in October 1994). If, on the other hand, the bias is reversed then it is not consent to unity which is being sought but merely acquiesence in a political (peace) process designed to promote that end.

The UUP and the DUP read the Framework Document to mean that the principle of unity did indeed govern the principle of consent. The UUP response paper stated forcefully that the proposals were 'designed to trick the Ulster people into themselves ending the Union and their British identity. These papers cannot be considered as a basis for discussion, only rejected in their entirety'.[2] Paisley argued that it was a 'one-way street with only one proposal – the achievement of the republican, IRA/Sinn Féin, Dublin, SDLP agenda'.[3] For Robert McCartney, the Framework Document confirmed 'what many have suspected: Britain has resolved to leave Northern Ireland'. Furthermore, 'it is difficult to be a unionist and negotiate within its terms'.[4]

The Framework Document, then, set the outer limits of immediate nationalist ambition (which unionists rejected). The UUP/DUP proposals of 1991–92 set the optimum unionist outcome (which nationalists rejected). It was within these political boundaries that unionists were required to manoeuvre when the new talks got under way in June 1996. Carrying them through to a successful conclusion could only mean unionists accepting cross-border institutions and some sort of refashioned Anglo-Irish arrangement. This was, of course, the same agenda as in 1991–92. So the real political question was this. Given the constraints of this negotiating position could something be delivered with which the unionist parties could live and which they could sell to their electorate?

Judgement of the talks

The DUP and the UKUP thought it was impossible. The need to include militant republicanism in the process meant that unionist objectives would be discounted. For McCartney, the talks would be 'limited entirely within the four walls of the Framework Document'. It was a fantasy to believe that the minimalist unionist project of 1991–92 would be considered seriously. 'How can the Ulster Unionist Party contemplate participating in the present Talks when the parameters of those Talks are confined, in real terms, to the Framework Document which they have rejected entirely as a basis for discussion?'[5] The UKUP argued against touching the Talks 'Tar Baby'. The only outcome would be getting stuck fast to a process, designed by Sinn Féin with the collusion of the British and Irish governments, to destroy the Union. 'Without doubt', argued McCartney, 'the whole purpose of these talks is to wring further concessions from the majority that would both undermine the strength of the Union and the quality and nature of their British citizenship and identity.' If unionists negotiated on this territory they would be entering the political killing fields.[6] It was a view also held strongly by the DUP. Its objective, along with the UKUP, was to prevent substantive negotiations taking place on an agenda which would, as one DUP statement put it with usual under-statement, lead to 'the annexation of Northern Ireland by Dublin'.[7]

By contrast, the position of the new leader of the UUP, David Trimble, was to try to see the talks through to a positive conclusion. It was a delicately balanced decision and its practical outworking Trimble later admitted to have been 'a white knuckle ride'. The reason is clear. There is a fine line between testing the good faith of other negotiators in order to secure one's own long-term interests – Trimble's justification for his policy – and being seen to be either weak, a collaborator with injustice, the lackey of the British and Irish governments or, indeed, the dupe of republicans – the claims made by Trimble's opponents. This balance applied even more so after the Agreement was signed. A key test of nerve was the change of policy by the new Labour government which permitted the entry of Sinn Féin to the talks without prior disarmament. This provided the opportunity for the DUP and the UKUP to withdraw after the summer adjournment of July 1997. Ironically, as the talks chairman, George Mitchell, observed of this tactic: 'if their objective was, as they repeatedly insisted, to end this process, then their walkout was a fateful error'. He went on: 'No one can ever know for certain what might have been, but I believe that had Paisley and McCartney stayed and fought from within, there would have been no agreement. Their absence freed the UUP from daily attacks at the negotiating table, and gave the party room to negotiate that it might not otherwise have had.'[8]

This dispute within unionism about the very nature of the negotiations might be called the Anglo-Irish Agreement Syndrome. The signing of the Anglo-Irish Agreement in 1985 had been a tremendous shock to the unionist community. But its legacy had been an ambivalent one. On the one hand, there remained a deep-seated suspicion of the motives and objectives of the British government. Unionists had denounced the Agreement of 1985 as a great betrayal, a diktat and a sell-out. It was difficult for the unionist electorate now to believe that the intentions of the British and Irish governments were any less malevolent. In short, that was the judgement of the DUP and UKUP and in their own absolutist terms they had every justification. On the other hand, the lesson of the Anglo-Irish Agreement also appeared to be that unionists could not afford to be on the outside of a process which would determine their future. The fear of exclusion was also deeply imprinted on unionist minds. Unionists might be pessimistic about the trend of events and feel that the bias of political forces was still ranged against them. But it was better to be in than to be out. That was the judgement of the UUP and also, it appeared, the mood of the electorate. As serious negotiations got under way, the ambivalence of the Syndrome was captured in an interview which David Trimble gave to Paul Bew in November 1997.

Bew suggested to Trimble that most unionists were pessimistic about the talks and suspected that the Paisley/McCartney analysis had some substance. At the same time, they did not think that Paisley and McCartney had an effective strategy to achieve anything positive for unionists. Trimble admitted that there was indeed deep concern among unionists and conceded that pessimism was widespread. However, it was his view that there was support for the UUP's decision to stay in the talks precisely because of public concern. He went on: 'I do know that the people here appreciate the effort that we are making, know that it is the only hope of progress, and that the Paisley/McCartney line offers no hope to anybody.'[9] As Trimble had put it in a statement on 17 September before entering Castle Buildings to talks which now included Sinn Féin: 'Unionism will not be marginalised. Those who walk out leave the Union undefended.' That was one part of the Syndrome. The other was the observation that without a unionist presence the Union would be left 'to the tender mercies of the British and Irish Governments'.[10] That was the other part and it was hardly a vote of confidence in favour of the 'joint sponsors' of the talks or of the process itself.

If Trimble were to sign up to an agreement then the criteria by which he would be judged were well established. To what extent did the agreement attain the objectives laid down in the joint unionist manifesto of 1987? Were the proposed institutions predicated on the project of unity or was consent the governing principle? Were the institutions to be stable within the Union or were they designed to be transitional to an all-Ireland state? Was the influence of Dublin in the affairs of Northern Ireland to be diminished or significantly increased? Of course, the judgement of Trimble's opponents had been made already by their exit from the talks.

Judgement of the Belfast Agreement

Few unionists expected that there would be a deal at all. The initial polls, which revealed almost 45 per cent of unionist voters undecided about the merits of the Agreement, were simply registering that surprise. Indeed, attention was concentrated on what even fewer of them expected to find in the Agreement, namely the provisions for the early release of terrorist prisoners and reform of the Royal Ulster Constabulary (RUC). Also in evidence was that understandable suspicion which takes as its measure the rule of thumb that nothing which is proposed jointly by the British and Irish governments and is, moreover, acceptable to the SDLP and, apparently, Sinn Féin, could ever be good for unionists. Yet there were potential benefits which would accrue in an acceptable deal. The most important would be the opportunity to affect the course of events through the exercise of political influence. One of the demoralising aspects of unionist politics and a strong element in its prevailing pessimism has been the sense of being on the fringe of strategic decisions. Every now and then unionists might score a heckler's veto over Anglo-Irish policy. But that did not change the condition of being a heckler and potentially a very marginal heckler at that. From the time of the Anglo-Irish Agreement it has sometimes seemed that unionists would always share the same fate which A. J. P. Taylor attributed to central European politicians under the Habsburg Monarchy – endless, futile opposition. With an acceptable deal that might change and change for the better. First, though, unionist voters had to be reminded why the Agreement had taken the distinctive shape it had done.

Anticipating criticism from the DUP and UKUP about the betrayal of promises, Ken Maginnis reminded unionists of the historical constraints under which the UUP had had to operate. Of course the outcome might have looked very different if the negotiations had taken place at a different time 'unshackled by 26 years of unaccountable Direct Rule, unburdened by the secretive 1985 Anglo-Irish Agreement and free of the Irish Republic's irredentist territorial claim'. But this, argued Maginnis, was the politics of 'if only' and just as far removed from reality as Sinn Féin's fantasy that negotiations could ignore the fact of the Union and popular support for it. The deal had secured the key unionist objectives. But unionists must swallow some unpalatable concessions. In a delicate reference to the emotionally charged issue of prisoner releases Maginnis claimed that 'when the essentials are attained, other elements fall into place'. That was a big claim and a contested one.[11]

Trimble went further. Defending his support for the Belfast Agreement, Trimble argued that it 'is as good and as fair as it gets'.[12] In a subsequent series of speeches and articles Trimble was compelled to justify this judgement not only against his critics outside the UUP but also against influential critics within, including most of his parliamentary party and the pressure group Union First whose leading personality, Jeffrey Donaldson MP, was seen by many as a leader-in-waiting. In a speech to the Northern Ireland Forum on 17 April 1998, Trimble claimed fidelity to long-standing unionist objectives. He argued that the Belfast Agreement represented 'the culmination of a process begun by the current leader of the DUP and my predecessor, Lord Molyneaux'. For Trimble, the Agreement had achieved the unionist goal 'proposed separately by the UUP and the DUP in the 1992 Talks' of placing Northern Ireland's future within a wider British–Irish context than the Agreement of 1985. In an aside on the Framework Document he noted that in order to reach a settlement 'the SDLP and the Irish Government have had to lower their horizons'. And he addressed the central conceptual issue of the priority of consent over unity: 'As both Governments and all the political parties at Stormont, with the exception of Sinn Féin, admitted, the settlement arising out of this process is a partitionist one based on the principle of consent.' Trimble's questionable assertion was that one key purpose of the 1991–92 talks had been now achieved. 'We have sought and secured a permanent settlement, not agreed to a temporary transitional arrangement.' He pointed to the Irish government's commitment to modify Articles 2 and 3 of its Constitution as evidence of this.[13]

The important judgement here was on the nature of cross-border cooperation. The North–South Ministerial Council was always going to prove difficult for a unionist leader. It was never a question of whether unionists could be brought to embrace the idea enthusiatically. It was always a question of whether it would appear sufficiently non-threatening for them to be able to accept it. How might non-threatening be defined? There were two important and interrelated elements. First, it was essential that cross-border cooperation should be based on practical considerations and not be driven ideologically by nationalist ambition. Second, it was important that accountability to the Northern Assembly should be clear and unambiguous, preventing the North–South Council developing a distinctive life of its own. The unionist key words were consent, practicality and accountability. For Trimble, the achievement on North–South cooperation was a clear endorsement of these principles. 'This is all for the good of Northern Ireland and no-one in the unionist community should fear it. It is practical and sensible. Crucially no projects can begin without the consent of the Northern Ireland Assembly. Unionists will always have a veto.'[14]

In a reflective address to the Irish Association in November 1998, Trimble implied that the Agreement had created a new situation in which old antagonistic strategies could be overcome. 'Economic co-operation, we trust, is no longer advanced as a strategy for creeping unification. After the Agreement there is no longer any need to engage in such tactical manoeuvres and a growth in co-operation is consequently possible.' Though there was a large measure of wishful thinking in that assessment, Trimble proposed a more fruitful approach. 'Is it not better to say: "This area has proven potential, let us see how we can build upon it", rather than, "This was on the agenda in 1965 and 1975 and the situation now demands more"?' The Trimble vision was thus one of practical co-operation to end the 'cold war' on the island.[15] This view of North–South matters complemented his vision for Northern Ireland set out in a speech to business and community leaders in Belfast a few months earlier. 'We can now get down to the historic and honourable task of this generation: to raise up a new Northern Ireland in which pluralist unionism and constitutional nationalism can speak to each other with the civility which is the foundation of freedom.'[16] As Trimble had put it earlier, with conscious reference to Lord Craigavon's famous assertion about a Protestant parliament and a Protestant state, 'new unionism' aspired to 'a pluralist parliament for a pluralist people'. These were fine and imaginative words. Their realisation, though, was not entirely in Trimble's gift. It depended on what had been impossible so far in Northern Ireland's history, a sense of mutual responsibility rather than a strategy of sectarian frustration. That objective of inter-communal trust was made all the more difficult by deep intra-unionist division.

The anti-Agreement unionists, Trimble argued, had no alternative. Addressing the AGM of the Ulster Unionist Council (UUC) in January 1999, Trimble demanded of his critics: 'Where is your alternative? You know that ever since our Government imposed the Diktat that it could only be removed by persuasion. Ever since then, you and we have been committed to a process of negotiation. So if you did not want to negotiate this year then when were you going to do it? When were you going to get a better chance?'[17] There was genuine – and not tactical – anger on the UUP side that their unionist opponents, knowing well that there was no credible alternative, would take the advantages of the Agreement (like Assembly salaries and ministerial posts) while shouldering none of the responsibility and taking none of the pressure.

Criticism of anti-Agreement unionists for having 'no alternative' met the initial response that the alternative to a bad deal is simply to say no. That disposition, of course, has a respectable historical lineage in unionist politics. It had been the collective response to the Anglo-Irish Agreement. During the referendum campaign the DUP deputy leader, Peter Robinson, claimed that 'talk about no alternative is but a conscience salving refuge of excuse for unionists willing to embrace the pan-nationalist agenda'. For Robinson, the alternative to releasing prisoners was to keep them in prison; to Sinn Féin in government was keeping them out; to not insisting on disarmament of terrorist weapons was demanding it; to a rigged assembly was a democratic one; to 'forced integration through All-Ireland executive bodies' was non-political cooperation.[18] For Robert McCartney the 'claim that "there is no alternative" does not mean that a better, more broadly acceptable alternative does not exist but that a violent terrorist minority will not allow it to be considered'. The proposition that there is no alternative was a means to divert attention from the weaknesses of the Agreement and from its nationalist bias. Implementing the Agreement would confirm the corruption of public life in Northern Ireland and 'set the seal upon an ongoing process of political warfare within an unworkable assembly and a permanently unstable society'.[19] These are respectable arguments and not to be lightly dismissed.

The main charge of the Agreement's opponents was that it was simply the Framework Document in a different guise. Its provisions did not represent a success for unionism, rather a capitulation to the demands of the nationalist project. In a reference loaded with meaning, the DUP took to calling the Agreement the 'Trimble–Adams deal'. Arrangements for the internal governance of Northern Ireland, along with the 'Sinn Féin' rights agenda, would it was believed transform the character of public life in a manner conducive to republican purpose, even 'hollow out' Northern Ireland's Britishness. And the establishment of cross-border institutions in the manner proposed would advance the integrative ambitions of the Irish state. As the chairman of the DUP, Nigel Dodds, put it: 'the Northern Ireland recognised in this document is a different one from the Northern Ireland that I knew prior to this agreement. This is a Northern Ireland in transition to a united Ireland.' He went on: 'Once you establish the principle of an all-Ireland authority you have undermined Northern Ireland's position as part of the United Kingdom in a very fundamental and radical way.'[20] In short, if you opposed the Anglo-Irish Agreement and if you opposed the Framework Document you could not possibly be in favour of the Belfast Agreement. You had sold out. Trimble had not found a satisfactory alternative to and a replacement of the Anglo-Irish Agreement. What he had signed up to was a reformulation which only made matters worse.

The big lie of pro-Agreement unionists, as the DUP's *Step by Step Guide of the Trimble/Adams Deal* (sic) argued, is that Dublin's influence in Northern Ireland will be reduced. It will not. The British–Irish Inter-Governmental Conference will take over from its Anglo-Irish predecessor. Maryfield (the location of the old secretariat) may go but its substance and symbolism remain. Its scope will be reduced because of the powers devolved to the Northern Assembly but that was provided for in the Anglo-Irish Agreement anyway. Devolution on these terms was rejected by unionists in 1985. Trimble had not only capitulated on that issue but had also accepted the bolt-ons of the North–South implementation bodies. Moreover, the Assembly's operative principle is not proportionality of party support which unionists considered fair in 1991/92, but parity. This 'means that no decision can be made unless it has the agreement of John Hume's SDLP and/or Gerry Adams' Sinn Féin'.[21]

Both explicitly and implicitly, the DUP literature highlighted what might be called the 'Quisling factor' (or, in its local expression, the Lundy factor). The meaning was clear. One consistent objective of British policymakers, it proposed, has been to find a tendency within unionism which would collaborate with a policy of disengagement. They had now in Trimble found their man, a man who would fulfil what was required of him. And what was required was sustenance for a process of moving inexorably towards Irish unity. The DUP still had faith that this 'process' would eventually be rejected by ordinary unionists who 'will not allow a conflicting principle of consent, whereby the Government sets in place a process to unite Ireland and then tells the people of Northern Ireland that they have no power to control it. If consent can be given, it can be withheld, and it can be withheld at every stage of the process and not simply after the Government has set it on course.'[22] Others thought that particular game no longer worth the candle.

Thus, a surprising but logical response to this inexorability of betrayal was that of McCartney's UKUP ally Conor Cruise O'Brien. In his *Memoir* O'Brien now advocated unionist 'inclusion in a united Ireland: an inclusion negotiated on terms which would safeguard the vital interests of the Protestant community'. He contended that 'in the conditions of the late 20th century, no other way to safeguard the vital interests of the Protestant community in Northern Ireland is available'.[23] His reasoning was simple. Doing a deal with southern nationalists was much to be preferred to arrangements with the SDLP and Sinn Féin. O'Brien's recommendation did display a distillation of the logic of some of McCartney's own statements. For if you think that the Belfast Agreement is a great betrayal of Ulster unionism, if you think that the British government is intent on destroying the Union, if you think that it is all a convenient way to appease the terrorists, if you think it a diet of daily aggravation and cumulative humiliation, then *any* British strategy is death by a thousand cuts. The embarrassment suffered by McCartney confirmed that there is little logic in politics.

Popular assessment

On the eve of the referendum the editor of the *Belfast Newsletter* believed that unionist uncertainty was a result of people 'trying to weigh up the obvious benefits that would materialise from a long period of stability' (the UUP message) against 'a gut instinct that tells them that what the agreement amounts to is rather more than a tampering with the edges of their society' (the DUP and UKUP message).[24] This uncertainty remains and unionists are still divided along the lines of that promise and that concern. It is an uncertainty, of course, compounded by the IRA's refusal to disarm and by its continued operations. The UKUP systematically played on the worry that the intimidation and punishment beatings, which are the lot of some in areas contolled by paramilitaries, would soon be visited on districts of middle class affluence. The comfortable and complacent who, for a quiet life, had voted 'yes' should watch out. Soon they may not need to enquire, argued McCartney, 'for whom the bell tolls in the ghettos, for by then it may also be tolling for both them and their children'.[25] The larger fear which this thought expressed is that the republican struggle will simply enter a new phase with the provisions of the Agreement now the focus of a campaign of destabilisation. The unionist electorate remains to be convinced that the culture of republicanism has changed and that Sinn Féin will not try to subvert good government in its 'long march through the institutions'. Unionists doubt if republicans will make an honest attempt to foster stability. The UKUP argument touched a moral nerve, a concern that what is being officially sanctioned is mafia politics. These paramilitary mafias will enjoy the civilities of a liberal society while denying them to everyone else. The controversy following the publication of the Patten Report on policing in September 1999 merely brought this concern to the centre of public debate.

Others believe that view to be unduly alarmist though they acknowledge its emotional significance for the unionist electorate. In Trimble's view, the difficulties for unionists were mainly short-term and emotional ones. The long term could now look after itself on the basis of consent. The academic view has tended to share that optimism. For instance, Paul Bew's assessment was that the Agreement was asking unionists 'to go a long way to meet the concerns of the nationalist minority. It does not necessarily follow that it is not in the interests of the unionists to do so'. He believed there was no need for the present level of unionist pessimism. The price of change was worth paying in order to end the IRA's campaign, to secure the legitimacy of Northern Ireland's status and to remove the republic's territorial claim.[26] Brigid Hadfield, in her important legal study of the Agreement, also favoured the positive, Trimble reading of its implications for the Union.[27] That assessment echoed that in the UUP's clarification paper *Understanding the Agreement*. It noted that many of those aspects of the Agreement which are objectionable could be introduced anyway by the secretary of state. 'Unionists must make a judgement as to whether or not the features that bring us considerable constitutional gains outweigh those elements of the Agreement that we all find objectionable.'[28] The burden of this political calculation was reflected in the fine balance of Protestant opinion in both the referendum and in the Assembly elections. Only a marginal percentage separated the pro- and anti-Agreement sides. Unionism has remained seriously divided.

Opinion surveys since then have revealed that unionist opinion continues to fluctuate around that even mean. A poll conducted for the *Belfast Telegraph* in February 1999 showed a drop in support for the Agreement with almost a quarter of UUP voters saying that they would change the way they had voted in the referendum.[29] Another poll carried out for *The Irish Times* in April 1999 showed a slight increase in unionist support.[30] However, a post-Patten Report poll in September 1999 revealed a significant drop in unionist support to around 39 per cent.[31] If there has been no great surge in support for the Agreement equally there has been no great surge in support of its rejection. For all the absence of enthusiasm there is also, as yet, no sufficient constituency for its destruction. The Agreement has become the devil unionists know. The thought that there might be something even more devilish in store if the Agreement collapses is widespread. This mood explains the tactics of DUP. It also helps to explain the split between Robert McCartney, who was prepared to walk out of the Assembly, and his Assembly colleagues, who were not.

In their election campaign the DUP denied that it was trying to wreck the Assembly. It proposed only to use the terms of the Agreement to protect the interests of the unionist community. Furthermore, the DUP was prepared to take up its two posts in the Executive although it would refuse to partner Sinn Féin in government. Secure in the knowledge that it could mobilise voters opposed to the Agreement, the DUP was making its pitch for the 'soft yes' unionist voter frustrated by IRA intransigence.[32] Yet for all its tactical cleverness and aptitude for intra-unionist manoeuvring the practical position of the DUP was now little different from that of the UUP. The DUP's acceptance of posts in the Executive in November 1999, irrespective of rhetoric, put it very much inside the process.

In the year since the signing of the Agreement Trimble has managed to secure the support of his own party. Crucial votes in the Unionist Council have consistently backed his strategy. The Assembly party has exhibited remarkable solidarity under pressure, suffering only one defection. Trimble's personal ratings have remained reasonably high, a fact which might suggest that unionists do *not* think there is an alternative to the Agreement (which does not mean that they love the Agreement they do have). Northern Ireland has its own equivalent of Weimar Germany's *Vernunftrepublikaner*. These unionists have made a rational wager on the future. And rather like Gustav Stresemann, who proposed that Weimar was an affair of reason and not of the heart, their support for the Agreement itself may also be viewed in this way. But reason can only take you so far. And the limit is decommissioning. Only when this is addressed satisfactorily can Trimble take unionism further. Without it, he is unlikely to retain his position as leader of the UUP.

Guns and government

Tony Blair's retreat from the position of the Hillsborough Declaration of 1 April 1999, which required the IRA to put some weapons 'beyond use' before power could be devolved and Sinn Féin could take up its posts in the Executive, damaged Trimble's credibility amongst unionists. It became necessary to address this question yet again in July 1999. The UUP position had been consistent. There can be no executive power for Sinn Féin until the IRA begins to decommission. The Sinn Féin position had been equally consistent. There can be no prospect of IRA decommissioning until republicans have their rightful share of executive power. In short, 'no guns, no government' versus 'no government, no guns'. The rational compromise – and one in the spirit of the Agreement – was movement in tandem. The UUP and Sinn Féin would both 'jump together'. Gerry Adams had used this expression when Sinn Féin was under pressure to deliver 'prior' decommissioning. When the pressure was taken off after Hillsborough Adams no longer felt obliged.

In the weeks preceding the July talks, David Trimble had put this idea of jumping together at the centre of his party's strategy. In essence though not in words he was proposing that republicans and unionists should set aside the objective of winning the ideological argument over guns and government. They should concentrate on sharing the political risks. Jumping together, risk management or what might be called the principle of 'simultaneity' could be understood as a way to avoid the politics of blame and to secure both leaderships from their critics. The IRA would begin handing over its weaponry and the Executive would be set up. Even simultaneity, though, posed serious problems for the UUP, for its critics could argue that it was, in effect, resiling from a principled position and capitulating yet again to political pressure. Republicans would retain a significant advantage. It would be this. The potential of returning to violence could be kept as a tactic *within* democratic politics. And this could be more effective than the actual use of violence had been as a strategy *outside* democratic politics. The broad unionist concern was that once Sinn Féin got into government there would be insufficient will to eject it if the IRA did not fulfil its part of the bargain. In other words, they feared further appeasement of republicanism. The UUP objective in the July talks was thus three-fold: to secure a commitment from Sinn Féin that the IRA would decommission; to establish a credible timetable for the disposal of illegal weapons; and to guarantee that there would be sanctions if the IRA did not deliver.

This idea of risk management ought to have been well received by New Labour since it is one of the central planks of its own 'third way' thinking. Yet the British and Irish government's proposal of 2 July, *The Way Forward*, fell far short of unionist expectations and left Trimble in an exceptionally difficult position. None of the three objectives of the talks had been met. The republican commitment to decommission remained aspirational and not categorical. There was no statement from the IRA that it had any intention to decommission and none from Gerry

Adams that Sinn Féin had any particular responsibility to bring it about. This was at odds with official spin about a 'seismic shift' in republican attitudes. The sanction for non-compliance, what *The Way Forward* called the 'failsafe' clause, meant the suspension of the Executive as a whole but no specific penalty for Sinn Féin. Moreover, the establishment of the Executive was to take effect by 18 July before any move on decommissioning. That the procedures for transferring power were eventually gone through without clear cross-community support in the Assembly (and in rather farcical circumstances) further damaged relations between unionists and the British government. *The Way Forward* may have been a very British proposal to satisfy mutually exclusive demands by way of compromise and reasonableness. Nevertheless, and with the best of intentions, it did pander to the requirements of terrorists.

Compromise is a virtue but the UUP concluded that compromise is not an absolute virtue. It refused to accept *The Way Forward*. The feeling was that the UUP was being asked to take all the risks and to suffer all the potential damage. The Assembly party refused to be the sacrificial lamb. To have agreed to go into government with Sinn Féin at that point would have lost Trimble the leadership of the party. And without Trimble's leadership the Agreement itself would likely collapse. His decision ensured some hope of future success and avoided the certainty of failure. Yet despite optimistic claims that he had now become the 'hegemonic, commanding voice in unionist politics', Trimble's vulnerability was plain.[33] The Patten Report on policing on 9 September, which proposed wide-ranging changes to the RUC, symbolic as well as substantial, called Trimble's judgement into question yet again. As Frank Millar put it in *The Irish Times*, unionists were angry about the Patten Report. 'But is it likely they will turn out to damn Mr Patten without turning their fire also on the man who (in the minds of many of them at least) handed the policing issue over to him.'[34] Trimble's unionist opponents could scent blood. They felt – as did his friends – that he could be thrown to the wolves.

Conclusion

In the summer of 1999 it was still in the balance within unionism whether, as Trimble believed, 'those with misgivings will see the future under the Agreement is much better than the last 27 years under direct rule'.[35] His critics were, after the Patten Report, consolidating their support. Those who spoke now of unionist unity were not Trimble's people but those who felt that the Agreement was dead in the water. Unity was proposed as a way to re-organise for the alternative to the Agreement.

Facing down this challenge, Trimble asserted at his Party Conference on 9 October, 1999 that 'the true glory lies not in a grand beginning, but in carrying it on until all is completed'.[36] The conference speech recommitted the party to the principles of the Agreement. His problem remained that of delivering a credible compromise on the devolution/decommissioning question. The pressure to compromise had shifted again onto Trimble's shoulders. In the sectarian dynamic of Northern Ireland politics this shift represented a victory for republicans and a defeat for unionists. And this posed serious problems for the UUP leadership. There did not appear to be sufficient evidence that if the UUP did take the risk of accepting republican *bona fides* there would be appropriate insurance for that risk. After July, few believed the assurances of the British government that, in the event of IRA default on decommissioning, Sinn Féin would carry the blame for the collapse of the Agreement.

Therefore, on 27 November 1999, Trimble took an enormous gamble in securing his party's consent, albeit marginally (58 per cent to 42 per cent), to trigger the establishment of the Executive and the devolution of power *before* IRA decommissioning. There was no doubt about the courage of the decision. There was no doubt either about the unease many unionists felt and continue to feel, about its wisdom. This may have been a concession too far, clarifying all too publicly the weakness of the unionist position. One commentator wrote that: 'The Unionist compromises are concluded in resigned anticipation of defeat, in the spirit of Abraham, who expected neither mercy nor return. The Irish problem, as historically defined, is not susceptible to a loserless ending.'[37] Unionists, he believed, were the obvious losers. Trimble has made a different calculation, that in the new dispensation of devolved government things will change, but also that the vital things will remain the same. Certainly, unionism's epitaph has been written many times before. And yet it survives. It remains Trimble's view that the weight of practical interest and the realities of politics will settle in favour of maintaining the Union. His supporters can only hope that he is right.

Notes

1 D. Walsh, 'Mitchell called to another tour of NI duty', *The Irish Times*, 17 July 1999.
2 Ulster Unionist Party, 'We reject the governments' 'frameworks' proposals as the basis for negotiations', February 1995.
3 I. Paisley, 'A one-way street to the Republic', *Northern Ireland Brief*, Spring (1995), 50.
4 R. McCartney, 'Seeing truth stood upon its head', *Parliamentary Brief*, 3:5, March 1995, 7–8.
5 R. McCartney, *The McCartney Report on Consent* (Belfast, 1997), p. 21.
6 R. McCartney, 'Talks that won't do the union any good', *Northern Ireland Brief*, December (1995), xiv.
7 DUP, 'Democracy – not Dublin rule', April 1997.
8 G. J. Mitchell, *Making Peace* (New York, Alfred A. Knopf, 1999), p. 110.
9 P. Bew, 'A not impossible task – interview with David Trimble MP', *Parliamentary Brief*, 5:3, January 1998, 51.
10 UUP, 'Statement by Rt. Hon. David Trimble MP on entering Castle Buildings', 17 September 1998.
11 K. Maginnis, 'Way forward for unionism is a yes vote', *Belfast Telegraph*, 5 May 1998.
12 D. Trimble, 'Platform', *The Belfast Newsletter*, 18 April 1998.
13 UUP, 'Speech by Rt. Hon. David Trimble MP to the Northern Ireland Forum', 17 April 1998.
14 D. Trimble, 'Platform', *The Belfast Newsletter*, 18 April 1998.

15 UUP, 'Speech by Rt. Hon. David Trimble MP, First Minister, to the Annual Conference of The Irish Association in Wicklow', 20 November 1998.

16 UUP, 'Speech by Rt. Hon. David Trimble MP to business and community leaders in Belfast', 22 June 1998.

17 UUP, 'Speech by Rt. Hon. David Trimble to the AGM of the Ulster Unionist Council', 9 March 1999.

18 P. Robinson, 'Trimble running away from manifesto', 7 May 1998.

19 R. McCartney, 'Yes there is an alternative', *Parliamentary Brief*, 5:6, May/June 1998, 16–17.

20 N. Dodds, 'Accept and we are on the road to a united Ireland', *Parliamentary Brief*, 5:6, May/June 1998, 21.

21 DUP, 'Step by step guide of the Trimble/Adams deal', May 1998.

22 P. Robinson, 'Belfast deal just pushes the same problems further down the track', *The Irish Times*, 12 June 1998.

23 C. C. O'Brien, *Memoir* (Dublin, Poolbeg Press, 1998) p. 440.

24 G. Martin, 'Wavering unionists fear havoc a strong no vote could cause', *The Irish Times*, 20 May 1998.

25 R. McCartney, 'North's hope of a bright future is fast becoming a nightmare', *The Irish Times*, 12 January 1999.

26 P. Bew, 'The unionists have won, they just don't know it', *The Sunday Times*, 17 May 1998.

27 B. Hadfield, 'The Belfast Agreement, sovereignty and the state of the union', *Public Law*, Winter 1998, 599–616.

28 UUP, 'Understanding the Agreement', May 1998.

29 See for details, *Belfast Telegraph*, 12 February 1999.

30 See for details, *The Irish Times*, 27 April 1999.

31 J. O'Malley, 'Mitchell must call shots with parties', *The Sunday Independent*, 19 September 1999.

32 For outline of this position, see DUP, 'Speech to party conference by Peter D. Robinson MP', 28 November 1998.

33 P. Bew, 'Spin doctors got it wrong', *Belfast Telegraph*, 15 July 1999.

34 F. Millar, 'Patten leads full circle to Belfast Agreement', *The Irish Times*, 10 September 1999.

35 UUP, 'Speech by Rt. Hon. David Trimble to the AGM of the Ulster Unionist Council', 9 March 1999.

36 As reported in *The Irish Times*, 11 October 1999.

37 S. Simon, 'Trimble: a Moses, not a Judas', *Daily Telegraph*, 29 November 1999.

Table 6.1   Decommissioning and the peace process

Beginnings	1990–Autumn 1994	Decommissioning present but a background issue; focus is on framework of talks and obtaining ceasefires.
The 'Washington Three'	Autumn 1994 –November 1995	London and unionists favour 'prior decommissioning' – i.e. participation in negotiations dependent on decommissioning; Sinn Féin and IRA see this as equivalent to surrender.
Twin Track Initiative and the Mitchell Report	November 1995 –February 1996	Decommissioning to take place in parallel with talks on 'strands'. Talks participants must agree to 'Mitchell Principles' of democracy and non-violence. Modalities of decommissioning outlined.
Breakdown	February 1996–May 1997	Elections to Forum, end of IRA ceasefire. Process moribund.
Renewal	May 1997–April 1998	New governments inject new life; second IRA ceasefire; Sinn Féin admitted to talks; decommissioning slips until after agreement; further work on modalities and establishment of Independent International Commission.
The Good Friday Agreement	April 1998–June 1999	Timetable to decommission; Drumcree and Omagh; linkage to other issues.
'Parking the car'	July 1999–May 2000	Good Friday Agreement 'frozen' over lack of decommissioning
'Starting up?'	June 2000–	Executive re-established after compromise on decommissioning

Loyalist Military Command. Throughout this initial period the issue of decommissioning was in the background. Priority for the two governments instead lay with obtaining paramilitary ceasefires (particularly an IRA ceasefire) and on discussions over the framework of negotiations. In contrast decommissioning received little public attention. Nevertheless the Irish government raised the issue with Sinn Féin prior to the IRA ceasefire, not least in the spring of 1993 'Steps Envisaged' document. Irish foreign minister Dick Spring also made it clear in press briefings on the Downing Street Declaration that a permanent cessation of violence had to involve the giving up of arms, although decommissioning was not mentioned in the Declaration itself. Finally the issue may also have been discussed in the secret 'back channel' which operated at this time between the British government and Sinn Féin. However, the linkage between decommissioning and participation in negotiations was left unclear in public pronouncements.

This began to change in the second stage of the process, running from the 1994 ceasefires to the establishment of the Mitchell Commission in late 1995. During this period two sets of talks emerged. The first – the so-called 'strands' – examined future political structures in Northern Ireland and its relationship to the Republic of Ireland and the UK; the second focused on decommissioning. Crucially, in the absence of IRA decommissioning Sinn Féin was excluded from the multi-party talks on the strands. This placed decommissioning at the heart of the peace process since, without it, Sinn Féin could not participate in negotiations on political structures, thereby rendering these talks marginal. The question of when to start decommissioning weapons proved central: should it follow a political agreement, or should it precede negotiations as an indication of serious intent and to prevent the threat of a return to violence being used as leverage in talks? The British government attempted to clarify its position on these issues when the Northern Ireland secretary, Sir Patrick Mayhew, visited Washington in March 1995. Its position (expressed in what became known as the 'Washington Three') was that for Sinn Féin to join the talks the IRA had not only to indicate its *willingness* to disarm but to actually *begin* decommissioning, thereby demonstrating its commitment to peaceful means and engaging in confidence building. The 'Washington Three', however, had the effect of hardening the British government's position and turning decommissioning into *the* issue of the peace process, since Sinn Féin's participation was now conditional upon prior decommissioning.

Although prior decommissioning broadly satisfied unionist concerns it was unacceptable to republicans. In particular the idea of the IRA handing over its weapons to British security forces before an agreement was in place smacked of surrender. The Irish government was also beginning to suspect that the decommissioning issue was being used by London to slow progress down. This was particularly so when London's hardline position on decommissioning was coupled to the time it took to make the 'working assumption' that the IRA ceasefire was permanent and the perceived reliance of the Major government on Unionist MPs for its Commons majority. Although the Bruton government in Dublin retained its own suspicions over the IRA, it was also convinced that the IRA would not accept prior decommissioning since this would be tantamount to surrender and that as a result Sinn Féin would remain barred from the talks. A way therefore had to be found around the decommissioning problem if progress was to be made in the negotiations on the strands.

To break the growing impasse on the issue of decommissioning, in November

1995 the two governments launched the Twin Track Initiative. The first track involved preparatory multi-party talks to establish a framework for substantive negotiations (what became known as 'talks about talks'); the second created an independent commission, chaired by former US Senator George Mitchell, to examine the decommissioning of paramilitary arms. Decommissioning was now very much centre-stage in the peace process and the issue of how to sequence decommissioning and all-party negotiations, the biggest stumbling block to progress. The Mitchell Commission reported in January 1996 and proposed its own solution to the key problem of when to decommission – that decommissioning should move in parallel with all-party negotiations rather than precede or follow them.[5] The Mitchell Report argued that although 'each side of this argument [on sequencing] reflects a core of reasonable concern',[6] what was required was a compromise with each understanding that the other had legitimate concerns. To Mitchell, holding talks and decommissioning in parallel represented such a compromise. The Report also introduced two other key developments. The first was the articulation of what became known as the 'Mitchell Principles' – six principles 'of democracy and non-violence' to which all parties involved in the negotiations should 'affirm their total and absolute commitment'.[7] Acceptance of – or 'signing up to' – the Mitchell Principles quickly became a further prerequisite for participation in the formal talks process. Second, the Mitchell Report for the first time publicly addressed how decommissioning might be undertaken. Despite the significance of decommissioning for much of 1995, no real thought had been paid to questions relating to the process of decommissioning. Technical issues such as the verification of terrorist arsenals, how to hand weapons in and the possibility of prosecutions arising from weapons handed in if they had been involved in terrorist acts had been largely ignored in favour of the more obviously political question of when decommissioning should occur. This suggests very strongly that decommissioning was more important for its political meaning than for its military significance. The Mitchell Commission was the first body publicly to provide detailed answers to the more technical questions and its recommendations formed the basis of legislation introduced in both the British and Irish parliaments later that year.

Parallel decommissioning, however, proved unpopular with the Unionists, who maintained their support for prior decommissioning. Nor was it embraced wholeheartedly by the Major government. In particular John Major's decision to call elections to an assembly which would in turn provide the basis for representation at the multi-party talks was seen in Dublin as an attempt by London to downplay the significance of Mitchell. More importantly the decision to call elections was the last straw for the IRA. From the Provisionals' perspective, the Major government had backtracked on its commitment in the Downing Street Declaration to allow Sinn Féin into negotiations on the sole proviso of an IRA ceasefire. With the ceasefire in place, Major had then insisted on decommissioning before Sinn Féin could participate in the talks; with the Mitchell compromise, Major had now asked for elections. This created deep distrust within the republican community over the British government's real intentions. On 9 February 1996 the IRA 'with great reluctance' broke its ceasefire and exploded a bomb in London's Docklands, beginning a campaign which later escalated to Northern Ireland. Loyalist paramilitaries formally kept to their ceasefires, though the Orange Order and Apprentice Boy marches in 1996 and 1997 created a series of crises which threatened to end the entire process. As with the period before the IRA ceasefire, so the return to violence trumped the issue of decommissioning. But the failure to resolve the decommissioning issue had been a key element in the IRA's decision to recommence its bombing campaign. Despite the movement by the British government from prior to parallel decommissioning, this still fell far short of the IRA's fear that to hand in weapons before an agreement would constitute surrender. In contrast Unionists were unhappy about talking to Sinn Féin prior to decommissioning and, given the Major government's weak parliamentary position, were seen as holding considerable influence over the British government. The issue of decommissioning therefore lay at the centre of events leading up to the IRA's return to violence.

In early 1996 the Dublin government worked hard both to get a new ceasefire and to secure a date for all-party talks to begin. On the former it failed, but on 28 February it agreed with the British government that all-party talks should begin on 10 June, thereby moving from 'talks about talks' to substantive negotiations on the strands. In reality, however, there appeared to be little difference between the two since the parties concerned and the issues involved remained much the same. Rather 'talks about talks' merged into multi-party talks on the strands, with Sinn Féin banned due to the IRA's renewed campaign. Throughout 1996 and early 1997 decommissioning was somewhat in the background, at least for the two govern-ments. The Mitchell Report had established the basis for the two governments' positions and their priority was now on obtaining a new IRA ceasefire not on further developing the decommissioning issue. But Sinn Féin was rapidly losing all confidence in the two governments and without concessions from them, parti-cularly on decommissioning, was unlikely to push the IRA for a new ceasefire. By late 1996 the process was moribund with no real progress being made. The Major government appeared to lose its enthusiasm for Northern Ireland, frustrated over the lack of progress. In particular the prime minister, who had been instrumental in the early 1990s in securing the political will in London to advance the peace process, had become enmeshed in internal Conservative Party politics. Northern Ireland offered no solution to his more immediate problems, being at best a distraction and at worst a second front for his right wing critics to attack him on.

In the summer of 1997, new governments in London and Dublin provided the necessary impetus to reinvigorate the peace process. On 3 June the multi-party talks which had been suspended for the election campaign recommenced, with the new Northern Ireland Secretary Mo Mowlam focusing on decommissioning as the most important and sensitive issue confronting the talks.[8] On 25 June the British and Irish governments produced joint proposals on decommissioning (including a set of 'possible conclusions' on methods of decommissioning),[9] which although criticised by the Unionists nevertheless indicated the two governments' intention to resolve the problem. The two governments were also discussing the establishment of an independent body to oversee decommissioning, as suggested by the Mitchell Report. On 26 August agreement was reached on the establishment of an Independent International Commission on Decommissioning,[10] with the former Canadian General and member of the Mitchell Commission John de Chastelaine its chair. The most important event of the summer, however, was the 19 July announcement of a second IRA ceasefire. It is clear that the ceasefire owed much to the change in attitudes of both governments, not least on decommissioning. Policy shifts, however, were relatively small. This was hardly surprising – in opposition Labour had maintained a bipartisan consensus over Northern Ireland, including support for the Mitchell Commission's proposals on decommissioning. But within this framework the new government appeared both intent on making progress and willing to be flexible where possible. Perhaps the key difference was that as far as Labour was concerned, once the IRA ceasefire had been re-established, the major stumbling block to Sinn Féin's participation in talks was removed. On 29 August Mo Mowlam announced her decision to allow Sinn Féin entry to the talks based on her assessment that the ceasefire was indeed genuine, and on the sole proviso that Sinn Féin formally sign up to the Mitchell Principles on democracy and non-violence. In other words, IRA decommissioning was no longer a prerequisite for Sinn Féin's participation in the talks, nor indeed for loyalist paramilitaries. All that was required was a ceasefire and acceptance of the Mitchell Principles. Sinn Féin signed up to the Mitchell Principles on 9 September at a plenary session of the multi-party talks, with the major Unionist parties notable by their absence. The Democratic Unionist Party (DUP) and UK Unionists in particular argued that the ceasefire was a 'sham' (or, less provocatively, 'tactical') and withdrew from the negotiations unless there was decommissioning of IRA arms. Although the more moderate and larger Ulster Unionist Party also maintained an emphasis upon decommissioning, it demonstrated a greater willingness to compromise under its leader David Trimble, and entered into negotiations with Sinn Féin without IRA decommissioning.

At the end of 1997 the assassination of Billy Wright, the leader of the loyalist paramilitary group the LVF (Loyalist Volunteer Force), by the Republican INLA (Irish National Liberation Army) in the Maze prison threatened to spark a series of 'tit-for-tat' killings between republican and loyalist paramilitaries, undermining the peace process. With David Trimble at times appearing isolated both within unionism and even within his own party, hopes for an agreement were not high. But with the direct intervention of the prime minister and the taoiseach, and the influence of the White House (not least through the continuing efforts of George Mitchell), an agreement was finally reached at Stormont on Good Friday 1998. A key move in securing republican support for the Agreement was London's willingness to downplay the decommissioning issue. Sinn Féin repeatedly expressed its concerns that for the IRA to hand in weapons before an Agreement would be seen as surrender and was politically impossible. London therefore moved from parallel decommissioning being a requirement of the negotiating process to its being 'aspirational'. This in turn required a considerable compromise by the Unionists who had already moved from their favoured position of prior decommissioning to one of negotiating with Sinn Féin while the IRA still possessed its full military capability. To enter into an Agreement without decommissioning was an even greater step and one which many Unionists were unwilling to take – even in David Trimble's more moderate UUP. Pressure from within Northern Ireland, from London and from Washington, a sense that this was the best that would be available and the commitment in the Agreement to decommissioning all helped to allay Unionist fears, though these fears were not removed.

Decommissioning formed a small[11] but – at least in Unionist eyes – significant element of the Good Friday Agreement. Much of what was agreed on decommissioning was presaged by the Mitchell Report and previous agreements, principally those in the second half of 1997 between the British and Irish governments. The only significant development was the inclusion of a timetable for the completion of decommissioning (within two years of successful referenda on the Agreement). Despite the successful referenda, progress on implementing the Agreement was slow, with neither the establishment of the Northern Ireland Executive nor decommissioning occurring. Instead the summer of 1998 was dominated by two events – the Orange Order march at Drumcree and the Real IRA's bomb at Omagh. The decision by the Parades Commission not to allow the Protestant Orange Order to march down the Catholic Garvaghy Road led to a violent standoff between marchers and the British army, which included shots being fired by protesters. It was widely believed that two loyalist terror groups, the UDA and UVF, were heavily involved in the violence while the UFF ceasefire appeared close to breaking point. Although the situation was controlled by the security forces, Drumcree was a reminder both of the continued volatility in the Province and the opposition by a large section of the Unionist community to the Good Friday Agreement. In particular the Orange Order had come out strongly against the Good Friday Agreement and saw Drumcree as the opportunity to demonstrate its strength. But linkage to specific issues in the peace process (such as decommissioning) was at best tenuous, while the Order's failure to force the issue at Drumcree suggested that a repeat of Sunningdale was not likely.[12]

Events at Drumcree, however, were overshadowed by the Real IRA's bomb at Omagh in which 28 people were killed and 200 wounded. Once the initial horror of the attack had passed, fear for the future of the peace process quickly followed. The fear was two-fold. First, that hardline Unionists would not make a distinction between the 'Real IRA' – which claimed responsibility for the bomb – and the Provisional IRA, and that they would see the bomb as revealing the 'tactical' nature of the Provisional IRA's ceasefire. Sufficient pressure might be applied such that David Trimble would not be able to sit at the same table as Gerry Adams. Second, that Omagh revealed splits in the IRA and that the campaign of terror might be continued by a splinter group, despite the Provisional IRA's ceasefire and Sinn Féin's signing up to the Mitchell Principles. In particular there were concerns that even if the IRA handed in its weapons, sufficient had been acquired by dissident republican paramilitaries (such as the Real IRA) that violence might continue.[13] In the event, neither happened. Rather the bomb at Omagh appeared to have shaken both communities into an awareness of the costs of the peace process failing. The Real IRA announced that it would suspend its military activities, the INLA and LVF announced permanent ceasefires, Gerry Adams announced that violence must be 'a thing of the past – over, done with and gone',[14] Martin McGuinness was named as the link between the IRA and the Independent Commission on Decommissioning and Adams and Trimble had their first one-on-one meeting. Despite this flurry of activity, however, there was still little sign of decommissioning.

By the spring of 1999 decommissioning was once again a major issue, with Unionists – including David Trimble – arguing that Sinn Féin could not be allowed a presence on the Executive without decommissioning, while Sinn Féin maintained that their presence would reflect a democratic mandate. The problem simmered on until Sinn Féin (with three smaller parties) rejected the Hillsborough Agreement which had been drawn up by the British and Irish premiers on 1 April 1999 as a way forward. This plunged the peace process into crisis with decommissioning centre-stage. The central problem was whether Sinn Féin should be admitted to the Northern Ireland Executive without IRA decommissioning. The crisis was dramatically escalated when Tony Blair indicated that if there was no agreement by 30 June, when power was supposed to be transferred from London to Belfast, then he would suspend the Good Friday Agreement – what became known as 'parking the car'. As the 30 June deadline approached so negotiations became even more frantic, with calls from the Northern Ireland First Minister elect, David Trimble, for the removal of Mo Mowlam, the Northern Ireland Secretary, and the direct involvement of the two premiers in intensive talks at Stormont. A last-minute proposal by Tony Blair that the Executive should be established and include Sinn Féin, but that IRA decommissioning should follow very shortly thereafter and be completed by May 2000 under penalty of the Executive being suspended, failed to satisfy the Unionists. The process was therefore put on hold in a state of crisis unmatched since the second IRA ceasefire. At the heart of this crisis was the decommissioning issue. For Unionists, republican words had to be matched by republican deeds: Sinn Féin's proclamation that violence was a thing of the past had to be matched by IRA decommissioning. Unhappy over first negotiating and then signing an Agreement with Sinn Féin without IRA decommissioning, to then allow them onto a ruling Executive was a step too far. For Sinn Féin, however, the IRA remained a separate body which they could not order to decommission, while a democratic mandate entitled them to be present on the Executive. Indeed Sinn Féin attempted to play down the decommissioning issue, arguing that once new political processes were established violence would slip from the agenda and decommissioning would be unnecessary. With Unionists still deeply sceptical of republican intentions, however, this argument was unlikely to hold much sway. As a result the failure to resolve the issue of decommissioning stalled the implementation of the Good Friday Agreement and plunged the process into crisis. With the exception of a clear return to violence by a major paramilitary group, it is difficult to see any other issue – RUC reform, the release of prisoners, the establishment of cross-border bodies – having this effect on the peace process. Almost ten years into the peace process and two years after the Good Friday Agreement, there has been no significant decommissioning and, critically, no decommissioning of IRA arms.

Issues

A number of issues have figured in the debate about decommissioning. Principal amongst these is that of when decommissioning should take place, but other issue include: linkage with other aspects of the peace process; how the decommissioning process should be conducted; whose weapons should be included; and what weapons should be included? This section examines each of these in turn.

When to decommission?

This has been the biggest problem for decommissioning. The Unionist position for much of the period prior to the Good Friday Agreement was that decommissioning should precede all-party talks. This was seen both as a signifier of the IRA's commitment to peace, and as a means of preventing negotiations from being held hostage to the threat of a return to violence.[15] All of the major Unionist parties initially rejected the Mitchell Report's compromise of decommissioning and talks proceeding in parallel. However, the position of the larger Ulster Unionist Party led by David Trimble shifted during 1997 towards accepting the Mitchell compromise and eventually to an agreement prior to decommissioning. In contrast Sinn Féin consistently pointed to the 1993 Downing Street Declaration as the basis for their participation in talks. In this the British and Irish governments appeared to state that the sole precondition for Sinn Féin's admission to talks about the political future of Northern Ireland was an IRA ceasefire – in other words that the decommissioning of weapons was unrelated to participation in political talks. The favoured republican position was to decommission arms once a political agreement had been reached, thus avoiding any sense of surrender.[16] The more moderate nationalist party, the SDLP, viewed the issue of decommissioning before talks as something of a red herring pursued by those parties unwilling to see progress. In particular there was suspicion that parties associated with loyalist paramilitaries were admitted to talks solely on the basis of the loyalist ceasefire (announced shortly after the IRA ceasefire in 1994), but that the IRA were being asked to decommission their weapons before Sinn Féin could be admitted.

The Major government's position moved from decommissioning not being a prerequisite to negotiation (as stated in the Downing Street Declaration), to it being an essential litmus test and confidence-building measure prior to talks (the government's position after the IRA ceasefire), to agreeing with the January 1996 Mitchell Report's compromise of parallel talks, to its later position that Sinn Féin need only to 'address' the decommissioning issue prior to all-party talks (providing an IRA ceasefire was in place).[17] There are a number of possible explanation for this shift in position: that the government was demonstrating flexibility and adapting its position as required; that it was vacillating under weak leadership; or that it was not serious about peace and, beholden to the Unionists for a Commons majority, it deliberately placed a series of stumbling blocks in the path of all-party talks. In opposition, the Labour Party had supported the Mitchell compromise that decommissioning should occur in parallel with talks about Northern Ireland's political future, with participation being subject to accepting the 'Mitchell Principles' of non-violence and democratic means – implicitly requiring a ceasefire. In office the Blair government demonstrated a determination to restart talks, initially retaining the Mitchell compromise as the basis for sequencing decommissioning and talks. Priority, however, lay with obtaining an agreement. Parallel decommissioning therefore became an 'aspiration', which was dropped for the greater goal of securing the Good Friday Agreement.

Linkage

During the peace process, and particularly in the wake of the Good Friday Agreement, a number of attempts have been made to link decommissioning with other issues. This is perhaps unsurprising – successful negotiations require a willingness to compromise, and compromise in one area may be traded against another's concessions elsewhere. Nevertheless this can be a dangerous tactic. Concessions can easily be portrayed as unequal, while points of principle may have to be abandoned for progress or tactical advantage, leading to disillusionment amongst those wedded to these principles. For this reason, linkage *between* issues has often been less successful than a willingness to compromise *within* an issue. The two most obvious attempts at linkage between decommissioning and other issues in the peace process concerned the early release of prisoners and participation in the Northern Ireland Executive, both following the Good Friday Agreement.

In order to gain Unionist support in the referendum on the Good Friday Agreement, Tony Blair linked the early release of prisoners to progress in decommissioning. The basis for this in the Agreement was slim, largely resting on the idea that it was a package that required progress on all issues. For short term political reasons the British government made what was at best an implicit linkage much more explicit and direct. With the referendum secure, the government backed away from this linkage. The IRA, however, pursued a reverse linkage – that the early release of prisoners was necessary as a confidence-building measure before decommissioning could begin – while in December 1998 the LVF handed in a small number of weapons for decommissioning in an attempt to secure the early release of some of its prisoners.[18]

The second major linkage concerned participation in the Executive. Unionists argued that Sinn Féin should not be allowed to participate in the Executive until the IRA had begun decommissioning its weapons. The Good Friday Agreement is unclear on this, while Sinn Féin argued that participation in the Executive should be on the basis of their democratic mandate rather than any linkage to progress in decommissioning.[19] This disagreement was the key element in the breakdown of the process in summer 1999. A final attempt at linkage was a somewhat half-hearted attempt made by Gerry Adams, who stated in 1998 that Sinn Féin would review its position on decommissioning after that summer's marches. Adams was clearly hoping for concessions over the Orange Order parades in return for progress on decommissioning.

The success of linkage has been varied. Linkage between decommissioning and the early release of prisoners may have helped secure Unionist support for the Agreement, though it is noteworthy that this has not been rigorously pursued beyond the referendum. The refusal of Unionists to sit on an Executive with Sinn Féin prior to decommissioning proved a major stumbling block, while in contrast there is no direct evidence that Gerry Adams' attempt at linkage with the work of the Parades Commission bore fruit.[20] What is perhaps most important to note however is that linkage has failed to deliver decommissioning, particularly by the IRA. The lack of decommissioning has tended to lead Unionists to pursue the tactic of linkage, without any noteworthy success.

How to decommission?

Although receiving less publicity than other questions, the method (or 'modalities') of decommissioning has received considerable attention. Somewhat surprisingly perhaps, there does not seem to have been any attempt to learn lessons from decommissioning after internal conflicts elsewhere. Most of the key principles were established by the Mitchell Report. Among these were that decommissioning should be supervised by an independent body (the Independent International Commission on Decommissioning). Illegal weapons will be handed (directly or indirectly) to the Commission, not to the security forces. Illegal weapons will be destroyed not stored, to prevent further illegal use but also to prevent forensic examination at a later stage. Weapons handed in for destruction will not be used as evidence in court nor be subject to forensic testing, in an attempt to ensure that more illegally held weapons are handed in. The decommissioning process must also be subject to satisfactory verification, particularly that the required quantity of weapons is disposed of. The Mitchell Report recommended that the RUC and Garda provide the International Commission with 'the relevant data' on the size and composition of terrorist arsenals. (This of course assumes that the intelligence agencies which generate that data have an accurate picture of illegal stockpiles and one which may withstand challenge.) Finally one element not addressed is that of phasing. Despite the different sizes and composition of illegal arsenals, no agreed mechanism has been devised which ensures equivalent rates of decommissioning between the various parties. Nor is one deemed necessary. There is no military 'balance' to be maintained; rather what is important is the process and the end result.

Whose weapons?

For most of the participants in the peace process, including both governments and the Mitchell Commission, the issue of whose weapons to decommission is unproblematic – namely 'illegal' weapons held both North and South of the border by terrorist organisations. Weapons legally held by the security forces, including the police, are exempt. But for Sinn Féin the security forces are very much part of the problem in Northern Ireland. The British Army is viewed as the army of an occupying power while an armed police force (especially one dominated by Protestants) contributes to tension in Northern Ireland. Sinn Féin have therefore argued that decommissioning must also involve disarming the RUC and removing the British Army from Northern Ireland.

What weapons?

Violence in Northern Ireland has been perpetrated using a wide range of weapons. Some have been commercially produced, including most of the small arms used and explosives such as Semtex; others have been largely or wholly home-made, with varying levels of sophistication. It is assumed that decommissioning will focus on commercially produced weapons held in stockpiles due to problems identifying home-made weapons: the latter are not generally stockpiled but are made on an ad hoc basis for a specific mission; the real 'weapon' is the skill and experience of those who made them, not the end-product; many of the more dangerous and sophisticated devices rely on some commercially produced element which can be addressed in the decommissioning process; and finally the home-made weapons are the result of fear, distrust and/or anger which would hopefully be satisfactorily addressed by the peace process as a whole.

Conclusion

More than ten years after the inception of the peace process, no significant weapons had been decommissioned. The lack of decommissioning did not prevent republicans and Unionists entering into direct negotiation leading to an agreement being reached at Stormont on Good Friday in 1998; nor in the end, did it prevent the formation of the Executive of late 1999 (though hung like a Damocles sword over the new arrangements). In contrast, republican and loyalist ceasefires were essential prerequisites for the Good Friday Agreement, and the IRA's resumption of violence in 1996 proved more threatening to the process than the series of crises over decommissioning. In the 'hierarchy of issues', therefore, decommissioning appears to rank somewhere below that of the ceasefires. Nevertheless the significance of decommissioning was demonstrated by the ability to stall the process, first in 1995 prior to the Mitchell Report, then in the summer of 1999, and again in early 2000. Although Unionists viewed – and continue to view – decommissioning as vital, this perspective is not shared by all parties. The Major government at times appeared to share the Unionist perspective, on the other hand, particularly at the time of the Washington Three. The Blair government has taken a slightly more relaxed view, emphasising the importance of decommissioning but not so much as to place the process at risk. The Irish government has also tended towards a more relaxed view, while the nationalist SDLP saw decommissioning as a red herring pursued for tactical reasons by the British government in the mid-1990s. Sinn Féin, however, consistently argued that progress on the strands should be decoupled from the decommissioning issue and that political representation should be on the basis of democratic mandates rather than weapons destroyed. They have also – unsuccessfully – attempted to link the issue of decommissioning with demilitarisation, particularly the removal of the British Army and the disarming of the RUC. Decommissioning has therefore been essentially a political issue, and its relative importance contested by the parties to the process. Nevertheless two further points should be made. First, although its importance may be contested, few would deny that it has at times dominated the process and that it remains an important issue – if only because the Unionist majority still see it as vital. Decommissioning is embedded in the Good Friday Agreement, and had to be to ensure Unionist support. Second, although decommissioning has (to date) been seen primarily as a political issue, there are technical issues which may prove problematic, most particularly the verification aspects and the fact that decommissioning will not eradicate the ability of terrorist groups to kill, maim and destroy, merely reduce – albeit significantly – that capacity.

Notes

1 In contrast to legal weapons, which include not only those held by the security forces but the large number held by private citizens with official approval (members of gun clubs etc.).

2 Report of the International Body, 22 January 1996, para 15. Available at: http://www.nio.gov.uk/mitchrpt.htm, August 1997. Hereafter referred to as the Mitchell Report or Mitchell. On the Mitchell Commission and its Report, see below.

3 This is not intended to provide a detailed narrative of the peace process. Still the best, though by now dated, account is Eamonn Mallie and David McKittrick, *The Fight for Peace: The Secret Story behind the Irish Peace Process* (London: Heinemann, 1996). Newspaper coverage of the peace process has, of course, been extensive. Excellent (if not necessarily neutral) news coverage is provided in Northern Ireland by the *Belfast Telegraph*, on the mainland by the *Daily Telegraph* and *The Independent* and in Dublin by *The Irish Times*. A reading of these has informed many of the arguments in this chapter. Most of the major political parties maintain websites with useful material, including policy statements. These can be accessed via the Northern Ireland Office's website which itself contains texts of most major statements. See http://www.nio.gov.uk. IRA statements often appear in *An Phoblacht/Republican News*, which is also a useful source for Sinn Féin statements and interviews.

4 For a more detailed account of the relationship between decommissioning and the peace process, see Colin McInnes, 'The decommissioning of terrorist weapons and the peace process in Northern Ireland', *Contemporary Security Policy*, vol. 18, no. 3 (December 1997)

pp. 83–103; Roger MacGinty, 'Issue hierarchies in peace processes: the decommissioning of paramilitary arms and the Northern Ireland peace process', *Journal of Civil Wars*, vol. 1, no. 3 (Autumn 1998) pp. 24–45. See also Michael von Tangen Page, 'Arms decommissioning and the Northern Ireland Peace Agreement', *Security Dialogue*, vol. 29, no. 4 (1998) pp. 219–30. Some of the arguments in this chapter first appeared in my 'The decommissioning of terrorist weapons and the peace process'. I am grateful to the editors and publishers of *Contemporary Security Policy* for permission to reproduce these here.

5 Mitchell Report, para 34.
6 Mitchell Report, para 29.
7 Mitchell Report, para 20.
8 Address by Secretary of State at Resumption of Multi-Party Negotiations, Northern Ireland Information Service, 3 June 1997. This was reiterated in the Joint Statement by the British and Irish Governments, 23 July 1997. Available at: http://www.nio.gov.uk/press/970723d.htm, August 1997.
9 Resolving the Address to Decommissioning, Northern Ireland Information Service 25 June 1997. See in particular the annex 'Possible Conclusions to Item 2 (a)–(c) of the Agenda for the Remainder of the Opening Plenary'. See also the 16 July explanatory comments made by Paul Murphy, Minister of State at the Northern Ireland Office. *Resolving Decommissioning: Speaking Notes Explaining the Two Governments' Positions*, Northern Ireland Information Service, 16 July 1997.
10 Agreement between the Government of the United Kingdom of Great Britain and Northern Ireland and the Government of the Republic of Ireland Establishing the Independent International Commission on Decommissioning, Northern Ireland Information Service, 26 August 1997.
11 Section 7 of the Agreement concerned decommissioning but was less than half a page in length and contained just six sentences. For the text of the Good Friday Agreement see Appendix 2. Many of the key documents are also available on the Northern Ireland office's homepage at: http://www.nio.org.uk.htm.
12 On the BBC radio programme *Today*, David McNally, a leading Orangeman, threatened that the Order would paralyse Ulster, drawing a parallel with the manner in which Unionist opposition to the 1973 Sunningdale Agreement on power sharing had led to its collapse. The arson attack on a Catholic family at the height of the 1998 Drumcree disturbances, killing three young children, led to a split in the Order with a number of senior figures arguing that the protest should be called off. As the Revd William Bingham, himself a senior Orangeman and a key figure in the 'proximity talks' over Drumcree stated, 'no road is worth a life'. See Toby Harnden, 'We can paralyse Ulster', *Electronic Telegraph*, 10 July 1998 and 'Murders fail to end stand-off', *Electronic Telegraph*, 13 July 1998. It is also worth noting that the Apprentice Boys' march in Londonderry later in the year – traditionally a potential flashpoint – passed off peacefully.
13 The Real IRA (RIRA) appears to have originated after a heated meeting of IRA leaders at Gweedore, Co. Donegal in October 1997, where objections were raised to republican involvement in the peace process. Significantly the IRA's Quarter Master General, who was responsible for its weapons explosives and ammunition, resigned at the meeting and appointed himself Chief of Staff for RIRA, leading to fears that he might use his knowledge of the IRA stockpile to help equip RIRA.
14 See Sean O'Neill and Jon Hibbs, 'Violence is over claims Adams', *Electronic Telegraph*, 2 September 1998.
15 See for example comments made by Ken Maginnis in *Hansard* (House of Commons), 16 January 1997, Cols 476–7.
16 See for example 'Doherty says democratic mandate is basis for talks entry', Sinn Féin press release, 29 August 1997; 'The Republican analysis will be at the negotiations', Sinn Féin press release, 29 August 1997.
17 This elaboration of the government's position appeared in the joint Anglo-Irish communiqué of 28 February 1996, the first meeting of the two premiers after the end of the

    IRA ceasefire. Anglo-Irish Communique for Summit on 28 February 1996, para 12. Press
    Notice, 10 Downing Street, 28 February 1996.
18 Under the terms of the Good Friday Agreement, LVF prisoners were not eligible for early
    release.
19 Toby Harnden, 'Trimble attacks Adams in arms row', *Electronic Telegraph*, 25 May 1998.
20 Although the critical 1998 Orange Order march at Drumcree was not allowed to pass down
    the Catholic Garvaghy Road, there is no evidence that this was related to the
    decommissioning issue.

7

A 'most difficult and unpalatable part' – the release of politically motivated violent offenders

MICHAEL VON TANGEN PAGE

Introduction

One of the more controversial issues in the peace process was the problem of what would happen to the large number of prisoners who were gaoled for scheduled (terrorist) crimes. Many people found the release of terrorist prisoners repugnant, yet to the paramilitaries the release of members was a vital, if not core, demand if they were to sign up to a peace deal. In September 1994 there were 1,429 prisoners held for scheduled crimes in Northern Ireland's prisons.[1] There were also smaller numbers of (largely republican) prisoners held in England, the Republic of Ireland, the US and continental Europe. In Northern Ireland the bulk of politically motivated violent offenders (PMVOs) were held in the male Maze Prison (also known as Long Kesh) south of Belfast. In this gaol prisoners were held in separate segregated wings according to paramilitary affiliation. There were also smaller numbers of prisoners who had chosen to leave their paramilitary organisation and live in an integrated wing of Maghaberry Prison. Maghaberry was also the site of Northern Ireland's women's prison although there were only very few female scheduled prisoners.

The basic problem that these prisoners presented was that like most aspects of the 'Troubles' the position in which they were regarded depended very much on the perspective of the two different communities. To many unionists scheduled prisoners were criminal terrorists while to republicans these prisoners were part of an army of resistance against British colonial rule. Yet it was clear from a very early stage that prisoners would have to be released if a negotiated settlement that included the paramilitaries was going to be reached.

The politicians allied to the paramilitaries have always made it clear that the issue of prisoners was central to the success of the peace process. On the eve of the Provisional Irish Republican Army's (IRA) first ceasefire in August 1995 Sinn Féin President Gerry Adams made a speech in which he demanded a number of concessions from the British and Irish governments. Prominent among these demands was the introduction of an amnesty. David Adams of the Ulster Democratic Party (UDP) emphasised that the release of prisoners was also important to loyalists in a television interview several years later. He said of the link between the position of the prisoners and the ongoing negotiation process, 'we aren't involved in some sort of benign political dialogue, what we are involved in is conflict resolution. And as part and parcel of conflict resolution political prisoners must be a central issue.'[2] However, there was considerable unease, especially within the unionist population, to the suggestion that people convicted of 'terrorist' crimes should be released. Even after a release programme was included in the 1998 Belfast Agreement many unionists have continued to oppose the release of prisoners. In its 1998 Northern Ireland Assembly Manifesto the Democratic Unionist Party (DUP), which opposed the Agreement, stated: 'All decent people recoil with moral contempt at the prospect of the mass release of those who have murdered and maimed the innocent, whilst the RUC is to be demoralised and disarmed.'[3]

Despite this level of polarisation over what should happen to conflict-related prisoners the release programme included in the Agreement has been one of the few parts of the Agreement which has been implemented on time and with relatively little difficulty. In order to understand the centrality of the prisoners it is important to look at the reason why conflict-related prisoners have become so central to the conflict, before assessing the impact which the prisoners have had on the peace process as a whole.

The importance of the prisons in the Northern Ireland conflict

Historically the republican movement has always seen the prisons as an important part of their conflict with the British. This was recognised by Billy McKee, a former Provisional IRA leader, in the early 1970s when he said: 'This war will be won in the prisons.'[4] At the start of the 'Troubles', republicans used the prisons to demonstrate their legitimacy as combatants and their status as victims of an imperialist oppressor. Over time the prisoners were also to become an important political think tank for the republican movement and ultimately in the early 1980s the prisons were to become the issue with which Sinn Féin was able to launch its political strategy.

In 1972 Billy McKee led a hunger strike in Belfast Prison which resulted in the granting of 'Special Category Status', a form of political recognition, to republican and loyalist prisoners in Northern Ireland. The prisoners were held in segregated compounds within the Maze Prison. Inside these compounds the individual paramilitary groups would impose their own discipline and regulate affairs in much the same way as prisoners of war. By 1977, however, the secretary of state for Northern Ireland, Merlyn Rees, decided on the recommendation of a report produced by Lord Gardener to abolish Special Category Status and attempted to class all prisoners in the region as normal prisoners. This resulted in opposition from both loyalist and republican prisoners and the republican protests that led to worldwide attention being directed at Northern Ireland's prisons.

Initially the republican prisoners refused to put on the prison uniform which they were expected to wear in a 'blanket' protest. When this failed to gain much attention outside of the prisons or any concessions from the British the next stage of the escalation was the 'dirty' protest when republicans refused to wash or use the prisons sanitary facilities – smearing excrement on the walls of their cells instead. By 1980 after some four years of protest the prisoners had grown impatient and decided to escalate the dispute through a hunger strike. This protest ended after it seemed that a compromise solution had been reached but when this failed to materialise a new strike began. The new strike consisted of a series of single fasts by prisoners over much of 1981 which resulted in the death of ten prisoners before its collapse. The refusal of the government to concede to the demands of the prisoners also led to widespread protests both within Northern Ireland and internationally. Once the protest collapsed, however, the British government introduced a number of concessions which allowed the prisoners to claim some success.

Sinn Féin used the prison issue to launch its election platform. Initially using the hunger striker Bobby Sands as an 'anti H-Block' candidate in the Fermanagh and South Tyrone Westminster by-election, republicans were able to prove that the prison dispute had significant levels of support from the wider nationalist electorate. The successful election of Sands and following his death that of a Sinn Féin activist, Owen Carron, was enough to give the Sinn Féin President Gerry Adams the ammunition he needed to launch what became know as the 'Armalite and Ballot Box Paper' strategy which combined active support for the Provisional IRA's armed campaign with a political strategy of contesting elections.[5]

While loyalists have not attached the same mystique to prisoners which republicans have they still remain a very important constituency. Like the republicans, the loyalists have been very keen to see themselves as prisoners of war and have also resisted the attempts by successive British governments to 'criminalise' them. The loyalist prisoners also became a form of think tank for their organisations outside the prisons and were a vital ideological force behind the increased politicisation of the loyalist paramilitaries in the late 1980s and early 1990s.

Many important paramilitary strategies originated from the prisons. Most importantly, the prisoners from both the loyalist and republican wings of the Maze Prison have been widely credited with having had an influential role in the peace process.[6] It was certainly the case that when Sinn Féin was considering how the republican movement should react to the Downing Street Declaration of December 1993, prisoners on home leave under the Christmas Parole Scheme played a leading role in debates. Similarly, during the process that led to the loyalist ceasefire in October 1994, the Combined Loyalist Military Command went into the Maze Prison to discuss the possibility of a ceasefire with their members inside the gaol.[7]

The role of the prisoners after the 1994 ceasefires

On 31 August and 13 October 1994 respectively the Provisional IRA and the Combined Loyalist Military Command (CLMC) announced ceasefires. Almost immediately after the two ceasefires had commenced, pressure began to grow on the authorities to reward the paramilitaries by starting to release prisoners. Leading loyalist and republican spokespersons called for the introduction of an amnesty for prisoners convicted of scheduled crimes. The Republic of Ireland was the first to announce its intention to release Provisional IRA members in late November 1994. There was, however, significant opposition to these releases from a number of police widows. The widows ensured that nobody convicted of the murder of a Garda Siochana officer was released from the republic's prisons at this stage. The first nine prisoners were released just before Christmas 1994.[8] The Irish government then announced a further series of early releases in 1995 which included most of the Provisional IRA prisoners not guilty of the murder of a Garda officer. The Irish government then started to place pressure on the British to also begin releasing prisoners. Prisoners allied to the republican splinter organisations the Continuity IRA or the Irish National Liberation Army (INLA), who were opposed to the peace process, were deliberately excluded from the release programme.

In Northern Ireland, the situation was not as clear cut as in the Irish republic. There was significant opposition to a lenient release policy from Unionist MPs and in at least one poll on early release, 54 per cent of respondents in Northern Ireland indicated their opposition compared to only 34 per cent of respondents who supported the early release of prisoners. The majority was substantially higher among Protestants, who opposed the policy by 72 per cent to 20 per cent support.[9] Given such levels of opposition within one section of the community and the opposition from Unionist politicians, it was inevitable that the UK authorities would proceed with extreme caution.

The Northern Ireland Office (NIO) found itself in a quandary, in that the paramilitaries demanded some recognition of the cessation of violence through penal policy while the politicians representing the Unionist parties were hostile to any release. Given the 'democratic deficit' which has existed in Northern Ireland since the imposition of Direct Rule, the government could have overruled the objections from unionists. It was, however, morally very difficult to defend ignoring the unionist community in this way on such a significant issue. Further, by the middle of 1995 the Conservative government in Westminster was facing real difficulty in passing legislation, as its majority had declined significantly since the previous general election and the right wing of the Conservative Party was in open rebellion against the prime minister, John Major, over European policy. This placed the two main Unionist parties in an extremely powerful position within the House of Commons, at times casting crucial votes for or against the government. To cloud the political situation further the previous prime minister, Margaret

Thatcher, through her political allies, was indicating her own opposition to the early release of any paramilitaries in Northern Ireland.[10]

The NIO had in the past made clear that the continuing political violence outside the prisons was a major barrier to releasing paramilitaries. In 1986 the minister of state, Nicholas Scott, told the House of Commons that:

> In coming to a conclusion as to whether a prisoner will or will not commit another offence outside, factors that must be taken into account are the organisation to which he or she has some allegiance and the level of violence outside the prison ... If the threat of violence were removed, that would affect our judgement of the likelihood of prisoners being caught up in a campaign of violence.[11]

This pledge made it clear that the authorities at least on one level recognised the importance that prison release could have for the possible ending of violence. Indeed it is interesting to note that according to the former taoiseach, Dr Garrett FitzGerald, the UK government had considered offering the early release of paramilitary prisoners if political violence came to an end as early as 1985, during the negotiations with Dublin that led to the Anglo-Irish Agreement.[12]

In October 1995, the government moved the Northern Ireland (Remission of Sentences) Bill that restored a form of 50 per cent remission to the 417 scheduled prisoners who had since 1989 only received remission of one-third of their sentences. While this would result in about 90 paramilitary prisoners being released in 1995, amounting to about a tenth of the approximately 900 paramilitary prisoners held in Northern Ireland at that time, the reaction of republicans was negative.[13] Sinn Féin's prison policy spokesperson, Pat McGeown, told *The Times* that 50 per cent remission would have 'little or no impact in terms of reducing the numbers of political prisoners in British gaols either in the next twelve months or indeed by the year 2000'.[14]

According to the secretary of state Sir Patrick Mayhew the decision to introduce the change in the remission procedure was made possible by the fact that the ceasefires had held for over a year and that the risk of further attacks by the paramilitaries had greatly decreased. He included an important safeguard in the policy – release on licence. Rather than simply change the remission rate back to 50 per cent, which would have resulted in automatic release of prisoners after half the sentence had been served, one-third remission was retained with the remainder of the period up to the 50 per cent level being a licence period. In this period, a person could be re-imprisoned if his or her behaviour had not been good. In the debate, Mayhew made clear that he interpreted this as meaning that if the prisoner re-offended (as with all prisoners released on remission) or he was convinced that they represented a danger to the public, then the prisoner would return to gaol.[15]

This concession resulted in the sceptical support of the Unionist parties for the policy. The Labour Party supported the move but some opposition MPs were worried about the nature of the licence and the role that this created for the secretary of state without some form of judicial procedure. The largest nationalist party, the Social Democratic and Labour Party (SDLP), was also unenthusiastic about the Bill but supported the idea of the release, even though it represented less than had existed between 1979 and 1989.[16]

The broad acceptance of the Bill meant that in November 1995 88 prisoners were released.[17] While the releases had been intended to help the peace process, the situation outside the prisons had deteriorated at that stage, due to the political difficulties in starting all-party talks. The delay in finding a compromise over the issue of the decommissioning of paramilitary arms prior to the commencement of talks caused considerable republican frustration. On 9 February 1996 a large bomb exploded in London's Docklands area.[18] This was followed by other Provisional IRA bombs in England and Germany and eventually the resumption of its campaign in Northern Ireland.

Outside Northern Ireland, the transfer of Irish prisoners in British gaols to the prison systems in Northern Ireland and the Irish republic was a cause of discontent. The issue was resolved by a change in policy at the Home Office. Over 40 prisoners were granted 'temporary extended' transfers to Northern Irish prisons in line with the recommendations of the 1992 'Ferrers Report'.[19] The Report argued that people should be transferred to prisons as close to their relatives as possible.[20] Temporary extended transfers gave the families better access but ensured that the prisoners were still under the control of the home secretary. However, there were complaints about the slow introduction of the new policy. The home secretary, Michael Howard, was accused of being unwilling to approve the transfers of the prisoners back to Ireland for political reasons.[21] However, according to *The Sunday Times*, the opposition also came from the former prime minister, Baroness Thatcher, whose personal intervention with her successor John Major had stopped the first planned transfers in February 1993.[22] Ultimately, however, after a dirty protest by some republican prisoners at Whitemoor Prison, the policy was implemented.

This still left the problem of those prisoners from the Irish republic who did not have links with Northern Ireland. This was resolved by the Irish republic's decision to ratify the European Convention of Prisoner Transfers in November 1995. The UK had incorporated the Convention into domestic law in 1984 so there is, in theory, little reason to prevent the transfer of prisoners to the republic. However, the British government showed signs of being wary of transferring people convicted of 'terrorist type' offences, and initially only Patrick Kelly, a Provisional IRA member with cancer, was transferred to the Irish republic. This attitude changed in the period after the Labour Party's general election victory of May 1997 and the resumption of the Provisional IRA ceasefire in July. The new home secretary, Jack Straw, allowed several more transfers to both the Irish republic and Northern Ireland and indicated that by the end of 1998 only one Irish prisoner convicted of a terrorist-related crime would remain in England.

The first impact of the resumption in violence on prison policy came in the Irish republic when on 10 February 1996 the government rescinded the release of nine republican prisoners who had been due to leave gaol later that day.[23] In

Northern Ireland the government did not make any change in penal policy but it was quite clear that further reforms were no longer on the cards. One reason why the British probably did not suspend the new remission policy was that the loyalist ceasefire was still holding and in the initial phase of the British response the maintenance of this ceasefire was of prime importance.

In June 1997 the former taoiseach, Albert Reynolds, called for further concessions by the British in the form of improved remission rates to convince the Provisional IRA that the newly elected Labour government was sincere in its commitment to include the republican movement in the talks process. While this did not occur, the new Secretary of State, Dr Marjorie Mowlam, did give the go-ahead for a series of meetings between a Sinn Féin delegation and civil servants. The meetings resulted on the 18 July 1997 in a statement from Sinn Féin's President, Gerry Adams, which called on the Provisional IRA to restore its ceasefire. In the statement Adams indicated that aside from understandings regarding the participation of Sinn Féin in political talks it was clear that 'negotiations would be enhanced by specific confidence building measures'. He then specifically mentioned the question of demilitarisation including the issue of prisoners as being of importance.[24] Adams' statement was rapidly followed by a new ceasefire on the 20 July 1997.

While the British government did not introduce any new initiatives in the prisons after the ceasefires it did start the process towards the inclusion of Sinn Féin in the all-party negotiations at Stormont. However, over Christmas 1997–98 the prisoners again became important in Northern Ireland. After the republican ceasefire, the Irish government began a series of confidence-building measures, including the release of Provisional IRA prisoners, while the British government speeded up the transfer of prisoners from England to Northern Ireland and the Irish republic. This caused considerable disaffection amongst loyalist prisoners who felt the republican movement was achieving too many concessions whilst loyalists were being ignored. Further, during the Christmas period the INLA murdered Billy Wright, the leader of the dissident loyalist group the Loyalist Volunteer Force (LVF), in the Maze Prison, resulting in a significant rise in sectarian tension. For a period the loyalist ceasefire hung in the balance but the secretary of state for Northern Ireland, Mo Mowlam, went into the Maze Prison and discussed the prisoners' grievances directly with them and persuaded them to reaffirm their support for the peace process.[25]

Dr Mowlam made clear in a written presentation to the prisoners, published immediately after her visit to the Maze, that the 'prison issue' was part of the wider peace process. 'We recognise that prisoner issues are important to parties on both sides. They too need to be resolved …'. However, she then went on to say, 'let me be clear, there will be no significant changes to release arrangements in any other context [except the success of the peace talks]'. In so doing she demonstrated that the release of prisoners would be considered but only as part of a wider political settlement of the conflict.[26]

The Belfast Agreement and its implementation

The release of all conflict-related prisoners in the UK and Republic of Ireland was an important part of the 'Good Friday' Belfast Peace Agreement of April 1998. While the bulk of the document covered the form of government for Northern Ireland, it also contained a number of confidence-building measures. Alongside arms decommissioning, which was essential for the unionist negotiators, there was also the inclusion of an early release scheme as a concession to the paramilitaries. The Belfast Agreement allowed for the release of all 500 conflict-related PMVOs in the UK and Ireland by 28 July 2000. An independent commission was established to review each case on an individual basis and assess if a prisoner qualified for release. This allowed for a phased and structured release programme over the two-year period that also reflected the seriousness of a prisoner's crime.[27] This was not, however, an amnesty. People who break their release conditions by becoming re-involved in political violence will be expected to serve out their sentences in full on top of any new sentence.

The Sentence Review Commission was established under the terms of the Northern Ireland (Sentences) Act 1998 to administer the release scheme.[28] The Commission was co-chaired by a South African human rights lawyer, Brian Currin, and a retired senior NIO civil servant, Sir John Blelloch.[29] In order to qualify for release a prisoner has to have been a member of one of the paramilitary organisations recognised by the Secretary of State to be supporting the Agreement and observing a ceasefire. The smooth running of the scheme meant that by 22 January 1999 some 238 prisoners had been released.[30] The release scheme was felt to have demonstrated its worth when two prominent rejectionist groups, the INLA and the LVF, both announced ceasefires in order to take advantage of the release scheme. Further, the only decommissioning to have taken place in the first twelve months of the agreement occurred when the LVF handed some weaponry over to be destroyed in December 1998. This perhaps underlines the widespread unionist perception that these two issues are linked despite the refusal of Sinn Féin to recognise this.

The continued refusal of the paramilitaries to decommission and the increase in punishment beatings resulted in increased hostility among pro-Agreement unionists and the Conservative Party. In January 1999 two prominent Labour back benchers, Harry Barnes and Frank Field, lodged an early day motion in the House of Commons calling for a slow down of the release scheme and the Conservative Party broke with the bi-partisan approach to the Belfast Agreement by calling for the suspension of the release programme until there was an end to punishment beatings and the start of decommissioning. This hostility was further increased when on 22 June 1999 Patrick Magee, the Brighton bomber, who had nearly killed the prime minister Margaret Thatcher was released after only serving one-third of the period of the time the judge had recommended when he was sentenced to life imprisonment. In response to this criticism, a Downing Street spokesman acknowledged that the 'most difficult and unpalatable part' of the Agreement was the release of prisoners, before going on to say, 'It is hard to swallow. In the end, though, we have to keep the process moving forward.'[31]

Public opinion in Northern Ireland, however, continued to harden against the release programme for a number of reasons. The refusal of the Irish government to release the Provisional IRA members who had been convicted of the murder of a Garda detective, Jerry McCabe, under the terms of the Agreement led to accusations of hypocrisy and double standards.[32] Further, the decision of the secretary of state, in August that while the Provisional IRA ceasefire was imperfect it was still intact also damaged many people's faith in the safeguards introduced. In September 1999 a *Belfast Telegraph* opinion poll saw a significant drop in public support for the release of prisoners. Only 12 per cent of the poll sample supported the release programme, indicating that even republican supporters now had serious doubts about the policy. This was despite the fact that by this stage, 290 people, over half the number of prisoners eligible for release, were now out of gaol.[33] These doubts deepened when the notorious UDA prison commander, Johnny Adair, was released on the 15 September 1999. Adair had served only four years of a sixteen-year sentence for 'directing terrorism' and had been accused of being responsible for the deaths of up to 30 Catholics.[34] The release of such individuals can only be very painful to victims of terrorism and have a potentially negative impact on the peace process.

The position of victims within Northern Ireland is perhaps the most sensitive issue that the release of prisoners brings into question. A number of factors were built into the Agreement in order to at least acknowledge the position of victims. A Commission was established, led by the former civil servant Sir Kenneth Bloomfield, to examine ways of addressing victims needs. Further, with special reference to the prisoners, a number of safeguards were built into the Agreement and the subsequent legislation. Firstly, the families of victims had the right to request for information on the release date of the person convicted of the relevant crime. Secondly, the releases were under licence rather than an amnesty. This means that in the future if a prisoner is suspected of becoming re-involved in political violence, or is re-convicted, during the time they would still have been serving their sentence in gaol then they will resume their original sentence. These were intended to demonstrate to victims that they were not being ignored even if the prisoners were being released. However, the failure to form an Executive over the summer of 1999 and the on-going refusal of the paramilitaries to even consider the possibility of arms decommissioning has had a strong negative impact on the public perception of the Belfast Agreement.[35] In a situation where low-level violence in the form of 'punishment beatings' and occasional assassinations have continued in many working class districts of Northern Ireland, the release of prisoners has become increasingly contentious and open to question.

Conclusion

The prisoners played an important, if secondary, role in the events that resulted in the 1998 Belfast Agreement. This role can be divided into three significant segments. Firstly, the prisons were vital in developing the political strategy of the paramilitaries in Northern Ireland. They were especially vital in making the paramilitaries realise that they had to negotiate and that a military victory was not possible. Secondly, they were an important confidence-building issue whilst simultaneously being a block on agreement as many of the democratic political parties did not wish to see the release of prisoners. Finally, they were a vital part of the negotiation process.

These three interlinked but separate roles were to impact significantly on the peace process. Whilst it was clear that the release of PMVOs would not guarantee a peace agreement in their own right it was also clear that the political parties allied to the paramilitaries could not sign up to any agreement that did not involve their release. The Unionist political parties, however, had grave doubts about the release of prisoners and while it is impossible to assess the impact that the inclusion of a prisoner release had on unionist voters' support for the Agreement, it undoubtedly played a role in fostering hostility. Similarly, the prisoners' endorsements of the political lines of those paramilitary parties taking part in the negotiations were important in aiding the 'doves' within both republican and loyalist organisations. It is difficult to see whether prominent politicians such as Gerry Adams or David Irvine could have supported the Agreement without the support given to them by the prisoners. Certainly it has been argued that the voice of ex-prisoners has been vital in maintaining support for the Belfast Agreement within hardline communities.[36] The inclusion of the prisoner release in the Agreement has also led to the decision of two previously rejectionist groups to support the peace process in order to achieve the release of their members from gaol. It has also arguably been a factor in maintaining the Ulster Defence Association's (UDA) ceasefire despite the failure of the UDP to get any members elected to the Assembly and the organisation's virtual collapse. Ultimately, however, it is doubtful that the prisons in themselves could make or break the peace process in the way that decommissioning has threatened to do. On the other hand they were a vital part of the package that persuaded the paramilitaries to sign up to an Agreement which fails to satisfy their principal political objectives completely.

Notes

1 Brian Gormally and Kieran McEvoy, *Release and Reintegration of Politically Motivated Prisoners in Northern Ireland* (Belfast: NIACRO, 1995) p. 64.
2 Interview with David Adams, BBC 2 *Newsnight*, 9 February 1998.
3 DUP, *Assembly Manifesto* (Belfast, 1998).
4 Quoted in T. P. Coogan, *On the Blanket* (Swords, Co. Dublin: Ward River Press, 1980) p. 73.
5 For a detailed examination of the hunger strike, see P. O'Malley, *Biting at the Grave* (Belfast: Blackstaff Press, 1990).

6   *Guardian*, 21 December 1993.
7   *The Irish Times*, 11 October 1994.
8   *The Irish Times*, 17 September 1994 and 23 December 1994.
9   *Irish Political Studies 1996*, Vol. 11 (PSAI Press, 1996) p. 274.
10 *The Independent*, 21 November 1993, and the *Sun*, 2 September 1994.
11 Cited in B. Rolston and M. Tomlinson, 'The Challenge Within. Prisons and Propaganda in Northern Ireland' in M. Tomlinson, T. Varley and C. McCullagh (eds), *Whose Law and Order?* (Belfast: Queens University, 1988) p. 185.
12 *The Independent*, 13 November 1994.
13 *Hansard* (House of Commons), 30 October 1995, Cols 23–4. Northern Ireland (Remission of Sentences) Bill (Second Reading) .
14 *The Times*, 27 October 1995.
15 *Hansard,* 30 October 1995, Col. 24.
16 *Ibid.,* Cols 35–45.
17 *The Times*, 13 November 1995.
18 *The Independent*, 11 February 1996.
19 *Civil Liberty Agenda* (London: National Council for Civil Liberties, Spring Issue 1993) p. 24.
20 'Report of the Interdepartmental Working Group's Review of the Provisions for the Transfer of Prisoners Between UK Jurisdictions' (Ferrers' Report), 1992 (unpublished typescript, copy in the House of Commons Library) pp. 25–6.
21 *An Phoblacht/ Republican News*, 16 December 1993.
22 *The Sunday Times*, 19 December 1993.
23 P. Bew and G. Gillespie, *The Northern Ireland Peace Process – A Chronology* (London: Serif, 1996) p. 164.
24 'Adams, McGuinness Urge IRA to Restore Cessation', Sinn Féin Press Release, 18 July 1997.
25 *The Independent*, 9 January 1998.
26 M. Mowlam, 'Text of the Message Delivered on 9 January 1998 to loyalist prisoners in HMP Maze, by the Secretary of State for Northern Ireland, Marjorie Mowlam', Northern Ireland Office press release, 9 January 1998.
27 'Prisoners', *The Agreement, Agreement reached in the multi-party negotiations*, 10 April 1998, paras 1–3.
28 Northern Ireland (Sentences) Act 1998, section 1(1).
29 'Mowlam Announces Appointment of Sentence Review Commissioners', *Northern Ireland Information Service*, 30 July 1998.
30 'Early Releases and Christmas Home Leave – the Facts', *Northern Ireland Information Service*, 22 January 1999.
31 *The Irish Independent*, 23 June 1999.
32 *The Irish Times*, 9 February 1999.
33 *Belfast Telegraph*, 7 September 1999.
34 *The Irish Times*, 15 September 1999.
35 Kirsten E. Schultze and M. L. R Smith, 'Arms Issue Plagues Ulster Peace Deal', *Jane's Intelligence Review*, September 1999.
36 See for example Tracy Davanna, 'Persuaders for Peace', *Fortnight*, February 1999.

8

Policing and human rights after the conflict

BRICE DICKSON

Introduction

When the two governments and the various political parties in Northern Ireland reached agreement on Good Friday 1998[1] there were some key issues which still so divided the participants that they were deliberately allocated a separate resolution process. Amongst these were the reforms required to the criminal justice system,[2] the content of a Bill of Rights[3] and, perhaps most importantly of all, the future of policing. The parties to the Agreement recognised that it provided an opportunity for a new beginning to policing but they went on to delegate responsibility for proposing what shape that new beginning should take to an independent commission. This Commission, under the chairmanship of Chris Patten, was established on 3 June 1998. It reported on 9 September 1999 and the British government issued its response to the report on 19 January 2000.[4]

Before setting out the terms of reference of the Patten commission it is worth stressing the Belfast Agreement's recognition that a new beginning to policing was required. Even though a new beginning does not necessarily imply that policing in Northern Ireland was in a condition in which it should not have been, the very acknowledgement that a fresh start was justified was a significant concession on the part of those parties, chiefly unionist, who, throughout the thirty years of troubles, viewed the Royal Ulster Constabulary (RUC) as their first line of defence against crime and disorder, and especially paramilitary violence. At the same time, the ambiguity in the phrase 'a new beginning' allowed observers to note that nationalists were not stipulating the complete replacement of the RUC as a precondition to any permanent reform in this area. Although both unionists and nationalists lost no time in descending into rhetoric to re-state their pre-Agreement stances on policing, epitomised on the unionist side by the Democratic Unionist Party's (DUP's) insistence that no changes at all should be made to the RUC and on the nationalist side by Sinn Féin's demand that the RUC should be disbanded, the path was left open for constructive and rational consideration to be given to desirable developments in policing which would render the service 'capable of attracting and sustaining support from the community as a whole'.

Indeed the participants in the Belfast Agreement had specified the features which policing structures and arrangements would need to display if support from the community as a whole were to be forthcoming:

> The participants believe it essential that policing structures and arrangements are such that the police service is professional, effective and efficient, fair and impartial, free from partisan control; accountable, both under the law for its actions and to the community it serves; representative of the society it polices, and operates within a coherent and cooperative criminal justice system which conforms with human rights norms. The participants also believe that these structures and arrangements must be capable of maintaining law and order including responding effectively to crime and to any terrorist threat and to public order problems … They believe that any such structures and arrangements should be capable of delivering a policing service, in constructive and inclusive partnerships with the community at all levels, and with the maximum delegation of authority and responsibility, consistent with the foregoing principles.

The Agreement then went on to stipulate the precise terms of reference of the commission of inquiry. By and large these flesh out the desiderata just listed. They add, in particular, that the Commission's proposals should include *means* of encouraging widespread community support for the new arrangements, and that those arrangements should include matters such as composition, recruitment, training, culture, ethos and symbols (and also the re-training, job placement and educational and professional development required during the transition to policing in a peaceful society). The proposals must also be designed to ensure that 'the legislative and constitutional framework requires the impartial discharge of policing functions and conforms with internationally accepted norms in relation to policing standards'.

Finally, the terms of reference say that the Commission's proposals should ensure that 'there are clearly established arrangements enabling local people, and their political representatives, to articulate their views and concerns about policing and to establish publicly policing priorities and influence policing policies, subject to safeguards to ensure police impartiality and freedom from partisan political control'.

Past 'abuses'

The terms of reference bear the hallmarks of a rushed job. Several parts of them overlap and in general they are very wordy. No doubt several phrases were added at the behest of specific political parties. Significantly, one whole area of policing controversy was deliberately excluded from the terms of reference, namely, responsibility for alleged past abuses by police officers. Consonant with the whole tenor of the Belfast Agreement, there was no mechanism created for investigating or remedying real or perceived grievances involving police (or indeed any other) actions. Somehow, this simple fact was not adequately conveyed to members of the public. Thus, after the Commission was established[5] and the opportunity arose for people to make submissions to it, or to meet with Commissioners, a great deal of the time was taken up in reciting the details of past incidents, only for the Commissioners to have to reply that it was not part of their function to deal with such matters. When the Commission's Report was published,[6] the only reference to these alleged former abuses was in para 1.6:

> we were not set up as a committee of inquiry with all the legal powers to call for papers and to interrogate witnesses. We were not charged with a quasi-legal investigation of the past. If there is a case for such inquiries, it is up to government to appoint them, not for us to rewrite our terms of reference. But we have naturally had to inform ourselves about past practice in order to propose future conduct.

Clearly the reason for raising such incidents with the Commission was to stress that, to those submitting, the RUC was a discredited force. Many went on to argue that the force should therefore be disbanded, although some simply used their stories (personally hurtful though they were) to highlight the need for radical reform. At other meetings and in other submissions, the relatives of police officers who had been killed or injured in the troubles told *their* stories, this time with a view to arguing that so many sacrifices had been made in the fight against terrorism that no changes at all should be made to the policing arrangements in Northern Ireland. For every call of 'Disband the RUC' there was at least one claiming that the RUC was the best police force in the world. The figure most frequently quoted, and one that bears constant repetition, is that 302 serving officers were killed during the thirty years of the Troubles.[7]

Somehow the Commission had to chart a course between these two positions. It did so, and rightly, by focusing on the future, not on the past. It tried to establish mechanisms for ensuring that, if abuses *had* occurred, they could not occur in the future. It relied also on the work already done by Dr Maurice Hayes in his report on 'A Police Ombudsman for Northern Ireland', which led to the inclusion in the Police (NI) Act 1998 of new provisions creating a completely independent system for investigating complaints against the police (the first of its kind in Europe).[8] And the Commission further laid the foundation for a less controversial future to policing by placing at the forefront of its recommendations a commitment to ensuring that the police in Northern Ireland adhere closely to human rights standards. In its response to the Patten Report the British government said that the Commission was right to place much emphasis on human rights, but the secretary of state stressed that the government's response was driven by respect for the sacrifices of the past as well as by the need to have a police service that was both representative and effective.

The human rights approach

Few human rights activists would have dared to predict that the Patten Report would give as much prominence as it did to human rights. Chapter 4 is devoted to the concept and makes seven recommendations designed to entrench a human rights culture in the proposed Northern Ireland Police Service. The Report calls for 'a comprehensive programme of action to focus policing in Northern Ireland on a human rights-based approach' (para 4.6); it says this should be the philosophy of policing and inspire everything that a police service does; it wants every officer to perceive his or her job in terms of the protection of human rights (para 4.13). The Report then becomes more specific by recommending that a fresh oath[9] should be taken by all new and existing police officers, one which expresses an explicit commitment to upholding human rights (para 4.7); it calls for a new Code of Ethics, integrating the European Convention on Human Rights (ECHR) into police practice (para 4.8); moreover, all codes of practice on aspects of policing should be strictly in accordance with the ECHR (para 4.8). All police officers, and police civilians, should be trained (and updated as required) in the fundamental principles and standards of human rights and the practical implications for policing, and the human rights dimension should be integrated into every module of police training (para 4.9). Awareness of human rights issues and respect for human rights in the performance of duty is to be an important element in the appraisal of police officers (para 4.10). At a more general level, Patten proposes that a human rights legal expert should be appointed to the staff of the police legal services (para 4.11) and that the performance of the police as a whole with regard to human rights should be closely monitored by the new Policing Board, which is to replace the largely discredited – because of its lack of powers – Police Authority (para 4.12).

Other chapters in the Report are peppered with references to human rights. The non-political members of the Policing Board should include someone from the field of human rights (para 6.12), new legislation on covert policing should comply with the ECHR (para 6.43) and *as a matter of priority* all members of the police service should be instructed in the implications of the Universal Declaration of Human Rights 1948 and of the Human Rights Act 1998, the Act which, from 2 October 2000, makes the ECHR part of the law throughout the UK (para 16.21).

The Government has accepted that all new police officers should take a new police oath (and is considering extending this to new officers throughout the UK) but is not proposing that already attested officers should have to do so – the secretary of state cites 'significant' (but unspecified) legal difficulties for this decision.[10] All officers are, however, to receive human rights training and will be required to behave in accordance with a statutory code of ethics. But much more important than the rhetoric of human rights is the practice thereof. In order to assess whether the Report, and the government's response to it, will ensure that the practice of policing adheres to appropriate human rights standards, we need to consider aspects of the Report in more detail. We will deal with three of these: eligibility for the new service, the accountability of the service and the legal powers of the service.

Eligibility

On eligibility, Patten notes that to date the RUC has had stricter criteria for admission than other police services; relatively minor police records have disqualified applicants. No actual figures, however, are provided on how many applicants are turned down on this basis. The Commission recommends that the admission criteria should be relaxed a little:

> We emphatically do not suggest that people with serious criminal or terrorist backgrounds should be considered for police service but we do recommend that young people should not be automatically disqualified for relatively minor criminal offences, particularly if they have since had a number of years without further transgressions, and that the criteria on this aspect of eligibility should be the same as those in the rest of the United Kingdom. We also recommend that there should be a procedure for appeal to the Police Ombudsman against disqualification of candidates (para 15.13).

Consistent with its stance on not making judgements about alleged human rights abuses perpetrated by police officers in the past, the Report makes no mention of whether any currently serving police officers should be disqualified from appointment to the new Police Service because of *their* personal histories. Obviously there should be no currently serving officers who have a serious criminal or terrorist background: any officers convicted of such offences would have been dismissed from the force. But there may be currently serving officers who have been tried and acquitted of such offences, or accused but not tried. On the one hand it can be argued that these officers should not be treated any less generously than non-police officers with such a background: if the latter can be eligible for the new Police Service then so should the former. The principle against double jeopardy would require no less.[11] On the other hand it can be said that the system for bringing serving police officers to justice for crimes they committed is so flawed, and the conviction rate – in cases where prosecutions or disciplinary charges *are* brought – so low, that like is not being compared with like. In support of this second position one can cite the facts that crimes alleged against the police have always been investigated by the police themselves, that case-hardening amongst judges is inclined to make them believe the word of a police officer over the word of an accuser of a police officer and that in police disciplinary hearings the standard of proof required is so high as to make it virtually impossible to uphold a complaint (quite apart from the fact that the persons adjudicating upon the complaint are, again, fellow police officers).

There does not seem to be an easy answer to this conundrum. Much may depend on the extent to which careful records have been maintained of police officers' career histories. If those files still show that officer X was accused of offence Y at some point during the Troubles, but was never formally charged or convicted, then it may be possible, and even desirable, provided the offence in question was a serious one involving death or more than a minor injury, for a specially convened panel to review the files and to consider whether there is anything there which demonstrates clearly (even if not beyond a reasonable doubt, the criminal standard of proof) that the officer may not have the requisite degree of commitment to human rights which Patten is now calling for. The position of officers whose actions have led to the Police Authority paying out sums of compensation to victims of those actions would be particularly vulnerable under this system: they may have escaped any disciplinary sanction before, or at the time of, the civil suit, because they were not proved to have breached the Code of Discipline, but they can still be said to have been responsible for the actions in question. Of course many compensatory sums are paid not because the Police Authority is admitting liability but because it wishes to settle to avoid further legal costs, the scandal of a court hearing or adverse publicity. In those cases the officer involved could usually *not* be shown to be legally responsible for what he or she did.

All in all, however, the chances of excluding from the new Police Service current officers who have in the past been aberrant, but not found guilty of, or liable for, any crime or breach of discipline, are slim. To be equitable, any screening process applied to such officers would also have to be applied to other potential recruits: the argument that they, unlike serving police officers, are not coming from an environment in which commitment to human rights should already have been a prerequisite for the job, holds no water because respect for human rights should be a *sine qua non* in every environment. Perhaps the best that can be hoped for is that all members of the new Police Service will be required not just to make an explicit declaration affirming their commitment to human rights but also to demonstrate at an interview, or in some form of psychometric test, how committed they are to the protection of human rights – including the human rights of *criminals*. The government, in its response to the Patten Report, stated categorically that 'there will be no question whatever of ex-terrorists joining the service',[12] but no mention was made of what should happen to those existing police officers who have a dubious past.

Another important aspect of the eligibility question is how to ensure that nationalists are proportionally represented in the new Police Service. There no longer seems to be any disagreement over the need for such proportional representation, the present 7 per cent ratio for Catholics being universally condemned as far too low. But there is considerable disagreement over how to rectify the imbalance. The Patten Report made the controversial recommendation that an equal number of Protestants and Catholics should be drawn from the pool of qualified candidates for the service:

> Our model envisages that 370 officer recruits will be taken each year on average ... 185 of these would be Catholic and 185 would be 'Protestant or undetermined' (the present categories used by the RUC) ... We believe that the ratio of recruits should be kept to 50:50, at least for ten years of the model. In the event that the level of

Catholic application does not initially produce enough qualified candidates ... it may be necessary to aggregate the numbers over two or three years.

The Patten Commission was aware that implementation of any such proposal would require an amendment to the fair employment legislation in Northern Ireland[13] but was advised that it would not be incompatible with European legislation. While this may be true at present, it may not be so for much longer. This is because there are proposals in circulation to add a Protocol 12 to the ECHR, and to issue Directives under Article 13 of the Treaty of Rome (as amended by the Treaty of European Union – the Amsterdam Treaty), to make religious discrimination unlawful. If the model of gender discrimination law is followed – and that is a highly developed model which is the pride and joy of European lawyers – then it is unlikely that the sort of exception which Patten is proposing would pass muster with the European courts.[14] Positive discrimination is not a concept which those courts have yet countenanced.[15] Nevertheless, the British government has signalled its intention to implement Patten on this point, albeit on a three-year pilot basis.[16]

One further dimension to membership of the new Police Service deserves discussion. Patten recommends that there should be no ban on officers being members of any legal organisation, provided it is clear that the officer's primary and overriding loyalty is to the values of that police service. The Commission adds, however, that all officers should be required to register their interests and associations and that the register should be held both by the police service and by the Police Ombudsman. There is not an explicit proposal that the register be available for public inspection, but it would surely make sense if that were so.

To many, this part of the Patten Report will not have gone far enough. In particular, they will argue that there is a fundamental inconsistency between simultaneous membership of the Loyal Orders and of the Northern Ireland Police Service. But such a stance is flawed on two counts. First, it is attributing to *all* members of the Loyal Orders the undoubted excesses which *some* reprobate members of those Orders have committed. It is suggesting that mere membership of such groups automatically means that one is unable to lead a blameless life. Second, it is confusing religious commitment with professional commitment, implying that if someone holds a religious belief which is avowedly anti-Catholic he or she will be professionally unable to police the Catholic population in an impartial way. That is like saying that a lawyer with such religious beliefs cannot properly represent a person with different beliefs, or that a teacher, doctor or social worker could not put his or her personal religious views out of mind when dealing with others in a professional capacity. To disqualify people from certain positions because of their religious beliefs is indeed a slippery slope and is a very difficult stance to defend in international human rights law. The government has not yet clarified its position regarding this aspect of the Patten Report.

Accountability

The Patten Report contains many proposals on improving arrangements for both the democratic and the legal accountability of the police. The former turn on the proposed Policing Board and the District Policing Partnership Boards (DPPBs), on which no fewer than thirty recommendations are pronounced. There is little to say about these from a human rights point of view except to commend them for being based on values such as transparency, representativeness and responsibility. The government has accepted these proposals, save for the idea that DPPBs should be empowered to purchase 'community safety services' on top of normal policing.[17] The one aspect of democratic accountability which is not so well analysed in the Report is that of the scope of the Chief Constable's so-called 'operational independence' (paras 6.19–6.23). The Patten Commission had been urged, by the Police Authority and the Committee on the Administration of Justice[18] amongst others, to suggest a statutory definition of operational independence, as a way of delimiting the Chief Constable's freedom of action. But the Commission preferred to redefine the problem rather than the concept. It stated that:

> The arguments involved in support of 'operational independence' – that it minimises the risk of political influence and that it properly imposes on the Chief Constable the burden of taking decisions on matters about which only he or she has all the facts and expertise needed – are powerful arguments, but they support a case not for 'independence' but for 'responsibility'. We strongly prefer the term 'operational responsibility' to the term 'operational independence'.

The problem with this approach is that it addresses the Chief Constable's accountability only *ex post facto*. It requires the Chief Constable's conduct of an operational matter to be susceptible to inquiry or review after the event (para 6.21), while leaving the Chief Constable free to decide in advance of an operation how exactly it should be conducted. Yet that is precisely where the difficulties have arisen in the past in Northern Ireland. Operational decisions have been taken with little or no external involvement and such scrutiny as has been allowed has been retrospective. In many instances, if independent voices had been allowed to have their say as to how the operation should be conducted, there would have been much less need for detailed scrutiny after the event. No one would seriously suggest that political majorities should be allowed to dictate to senior police officers how to conduct their business, but the range of perspectives represented, say, on the proposed Policing Board would surely be worth taking into account – so far as it is practicable to do so – before an important operational decision is taken.

As regards legal accountability, Patten makes great play of the office of the Police Ombudsman. He recommends, surely rightly, that that office needs to be fully staffed and resourced, that the Ombudsman should take the initiative as well as reacting to complaints, that the Ombudsman should compile data on trends and patterns in complaints against the police and should investigate police policies and practices even if the conduct of officers is not itself culpable, and that access should

be granted to all past reports on the RUC (including, presumably, the controversial Stalker-Sampson and Stevens Reports[19]). But Patten fails to mention two
other crucial aspects of this topic. One is that, unless the standard of proof
required for a finding of guilt in a disciplinary hearing is reduced from that of
'beyond a reasonable doubt' to something approaching 'on the balance of
probabilities', it will continue to be well nigh impossible to achieve such findings.
The appalling record as regards complaints made by persons arrested under the
emergency laws in Northern Ireland speaks for itself in this context (from 1995 to
1998 only two out of 466 complaints led to charges of any kind being laid against
police officers[20]). The other is that even when the provisions on the Police Ombudsman are fully in force there will continue to be cases where allegations against
police officers of criminal behaviour will be investigated by the police themselves
unless the Police Ombudsman calls in her independent investigators as a matter of
public interest.[21] These will be cases where the allegations arise otherwise than
through a complaint by a member of the public: they could range over matters
such as corruption, fraud, physical abuse, extortion, domestic violence, etc. There
is a strong argument for insisting that the responsibility for *all* criminal investiga-
tions against police officers is transferred automatically to completely independent
investigators.

Police powers

The controversy over how to formulate the legal accountability of the police in
Northern Ireland is perhaps best examined within the context of the exercise of two
contentious police powers – the power to use firearms and the power to use plastic
bullets.[22] Surprisingly, Patten says next to nothing about the use of firearms (paras
8.17–8.20), merely that there should be a periodic review of whether it is possible to
move towards a routinely unarmed police service. He does not point to the
apparent inconsistency between the law in Northern Ireland on when police
officers can use lethal force and the law as stated in the ECHR.[23] On plastic bullets
he concludes that they should not be immediately withdrawn but that better
controls should be placed on their use, that research should be conducted to find a
more acceptable alternative and that a range of other public order equipment
should be supplied to the police so that a commander has more options to choose
from. While there is room for arguing that, given the police's inadequate defences
to petrol bombs, plastic bullets must be retained as a weapon of last resort in such
situations, there is no defence for the omission in Patten of any reference to the
various international standards on the use of firearms. The UN's Basic Principles
on the Use of Force and Firearms by Law Enforcement Officials, adopted by the
UN Congress on the Prevention of Crime and the Treatment of Offenders in 1990,
is particularly apposite here, but also relevant are the UN's Principles on the
Effective Prevention and Investigation of Extra-Legal, Arbitrary and Summary
Executions, a set of recommendations issued by the Economic and Social Council
in 1989. Basic Principle 9 of the 1990 document, for example, specifies that 'inten-

tional lethal use of firearms may only be made when strictly unavoidable in order to protect life', while Principle 11 of the 1989 document states that:

> In cases in which the established investigative procedures are inadequate because of lack of expertise or impartiality, because of the importance of the matter or because of the apparent existence of a pattern of abuse, and in cases where there are complaints from the family of the victim about these inadequacies or other substantial reasons, Governments shall pursue investigations through an independent commission of inquiry or similar procedure.

This is an instance where, despite all the fine talk in the Patten Report about the need to commit the police service to human rights, there is a lack of detail as to what exactly this needs to entail in practice. The Commission might also have referred to recent decisions of the European Court of Human Rights which hold that states are obliged not just not to take life but also to thoroughly investigate the taking of life.[24] The people of Northern Ireland need to be reassured that the new Northern Ireland Police Service will comply fully with that obligation.

It is to be regretted that the Patten Report does not contain a deeper analysis of the impact of the emergency powers on policing practices in Northern Ireland.[25] Even without delving into alleged past abuses of those laws, the Commission could have examined the potential in the current emergency laws for abuse and for infection of the prevailing police culture. There is an undeniable link between perceptions of the RUC within the nationalist community and the fact that that community has been severely affected by the operation of the emergency laws through the police's powers to stop, search, arrest and detain. The unionist community has been affected also, but not to the same extent, either quantitatively or, arguably, qualitatively. Patten does recommend the closure of the holding centres in Northern Ireland, which have no statutory basis anyway (para 8.15),[26] and the keeping of records for all stops and searches and other such actions taken under emergency laws. It is unfortunate that the Report does not recommend the repeal, or at any rate the suspension, of the remainder of the emergency laws. To maintain them during a period of ceasefires, even ones as tenuous as those currently in place, is quite possibly a breach of Article 15 of the ECHR, which tolerates such laws only if there is 'a public emergency threatening the life of the nation'. Very regrettably, the government's Terrorism Bill, currently before Parliament at the time of writing, provides for the continuation of most of the emergency powers in Northern Ireland indefinitely. In its response to the Patten Report the government made no concessions in this regard; indeed it asserted that there would be no question of rushing forward with changes to the style of policing or the size of the service 'in the absence of a stable security environment' (as assessed by the Chief Constable).[27]

Conclusion

Policing remains just about the most crucial element in any permanent political settlement for Northern Ireland. If a new Police Service is to gain the kind of broad community support which the framers of the Belfast Agreement were hoping for, it must display not just a deep theoretical commitment to human rights but also an obvious practical one. It must at the same time be conscious of its role as one of the most important public authorities in Northern Ireland. All 'designated' public authorities are now statutorily obliged[28] to have due regard to the need to promote equality of opportunity between different sectors of society and to have regard to the desirability of promoting good relations between some of those sectors (those characterised by religion, race or politics). It is unfortunate that the Patten Commission makes no reference at all to these duties and that the Northern Ireland Act itself specifically excludes the RUC from the scope of them. The secretary of state should remove that exemption and the proposed international overseer of the implementation of the Patten recommendations should be given an extended remit to ensure that in all its activities the new Northern Ireland Police Service adheres to the spirit as well as to the letter of human rights *and* equality standards.

Brice Dickson is Chief Commissioner, Northern Ireland Human Rights Commission. The views expressed in this chapter are the author's alone; they should not necessarily be taken as representing the views of the Northern Ireland Human Rights Commission.

Notes

1   For a good explanation of how the Agreement was arrived at and a summary of what it says, see J. Ruane and J. Todd, 'The Belfast Agreement: Context, Content, Consequences' in J. Ruane and J. Todd (eds), *After the Good Friday Agreement: Analysing Political Change in Northern Ireland* (Dublin, University College Dublin Press, 1999).

2   This was referred to a Criminal Justice Review Panel, chaired by a Northern Ireland Office official but with external advisers attached to it. It was due to report in the autumn of 1999 but did not do so until early 2000.

3   A task allocated to the new Northern Ireland Human Rights Commission (Northern Ireland Act 1998, section 69(7)).

4   Through a statement to the House of Commons by the secretary of state for Northern Ireland, Peter Mandelson: HC Debates, 19 January 2000, Cols 845–8. The statement announced a new name for the RUC – 'The Police Service of Northern Ireland' – to be adopted from the autumn of 2001. Many Unionists have reacted angrily to this 'betrayal'.

5   The chair of the Commission was Mr Chris Patten, formerly Governor of Hong Kong and an ex-cabinet minister. The seven other members were Dr Maurice Hayes (a former Ombudsman for Northern Ireland), Dr Gerald Lynch (President of the John Jay College of Criminal Justice in New York), Mrs Kathleen O'Toole (a former Secretary for Public Safety in Massachusetts), Professor Clifford Shearing (Professor of Criminology and Sociology at the University of Toronto and also a Professor at the University of the Western Cape, South Africa), Sir John Smith (a former Inspector of Constabulary in the UK), Mr Peter Smith (a QC in Northern Ireland) and Mrs Lucy Woods (then Chief Executive of British Telecom in Northern Ireland).

6   *A New Beginning: Policing in Northern Ireland* (hereinafter the Patten Report).

7 The circumstances surrounding each of the deaths are vividly described by C. Ryder, *The RUC: A Force Under Fire*, 2nd edn (London, Methuen, 2000).

8 Sections 50–65. The Police Ombudsman – Mrs Nuala O'Loan – was appointed in October 1999. Her office does not officially start work until June 2000.

9 The Patten Report refers to an oath but in fact police officers make a declaration.

10 HC Debates, 19 January 2000, Col. 846.

11 One of the recommendations of the Macpherson Inquiry into the murder of Stephen Lawrence was that the principle of double jeopardy should be re-formulated so as to allow for second trials if new evidence is forthcoming which might have led to a finding of guilt at the first trial: Cmnd. 4262–I (1999), para 7.46. The Law Commission issued a Consultation Paper on the subject later in 1999 (No. 156) but provisionally recommended rejection of the Macpherson suggestion.

12 HC Debates, 19 January 2000, Col. 847.

13 Consolidated in the Fair Employment and Treatment (NI) Order 1998.

14 I.e. the European Court of Human Rights in Strasbourg and the European Court of Justice in Luxembourg.

15 The two vital decisions of the European Court of Justice are those in *Kalanke v. Freie Hansestadt Bremen* [1995] ECR I–3051 *and Marschall v. Land Nordrhein-Westfalen* [1997] ECR I–6363.

16 HC Debates, 19 January 2000, Col. 847.

17 *Ibid.*, Col. 846.

18 The Committee on the Administration of Justice is the most prominent and most expert independent civil liberties non-governmental organisation in Northern Ireland.

19 The Stalker-Sampson Reports concern allegations of a shoot-to-kill policy on the part of the RUC. The Stevens Report deals with allegations of collusion between the police and some loyalist paramilitary organisations.

20 Annual Reports of the Independent Commission for Police Complaints.

21 Police (NI) Act 1998, s. 55(6).

22 For a useful account of the relevant international standards relevant to this field see R. Crawshaw, B. Devlin and T. Williamson, *Human Rights and Policing* (The Hague, Kluwer Law International, 1998), especially chs 7 and 8.

23 See B. Dickson, 'Northern Ireland and the European Convention' in B. Dickson (ed.), *Human Rights and the European Convention* (London, Sweet & Maxwell, 1997).

24 See, e.g., *Kaya v. Turkey* (1999) 28 EHRR 1, *Güleç v. Turkey* (1999) 28 EHRR 121 and *Yasa v. Turkey* (1999) 28 EHRR 408.

25 These powers are conferred by the Prevention of Terrorism (Temporary Provisions) Act 1989 (mostly the power to arrest and detain) and the Northern Ireland (Emergency Provisions) Act 1996.

26 On 10 December 1999 the Chief Constable announced that Castlereagh Holding Centre would close in the near future.

27 HC Debates, 19 January 2000, Col. 847.

28 By section 75 of the Northern Ireland Act 1998.

PART IV
Society and the economy after the Troubles

9

The human consequences of armed conflict: constructing 'victimhood' in the context of Northern Ireland's Troubles

MARIE SMYTH

Until the beginning of the peace process of the 1990s, any comprehensive attempt at assessing the human impact of the Troubles was deemed premature, and such assessments were limited to statements about the total number of fatal casualties and the estimated damage to the economy. For the most part the society functioned on the basis of denial of the extent of the damage, so any examination of such damage whilst the conflict was ongoing was likely to underestimate it. Auditing the harm caused, it seems, is a task associated with the end of conflict, a task which cannot be embarked upon whilst the conflict is ongoing and survival is often the main goal.

It was only with the advent of the ceasefires of 1994 that an evaluation of the impact of the Troubles became more feasible. Even then, such an appraisal is fraught with difficulties. So divided is the society, and so complete the bifurcation of identity within Northern Ireland – and academics are not above these processes – that to arrive at a comprehensive overview of the humanitarian costs of the Troubles in Northern Ireland presents a challenge. The identifications of the assessor with one or other side of the conflict will tend to blind them to aspects of the total picture.

This chapter will provide an overview of the human consequences of the Troubles, using deaths due to the conflict as an indicator. For this reason, the assessment of the impact of the Troubles presented here uses the relatively unequivocal measure of death in the Troubles. Whilst there are some definitional issues[1] surrounding the use of death due to the Troubles, it is the least problematic in analytical terms. Death is also a reasonably good surrogate for other effects of the Troubles, such as injury,[2] and the death rate of a geographical area is correlated with reported exposure to Troubles-related violence and its psycho-social consequences.[3] An examination of the numbers of deaths each year compared with the number of injuries associated with the Troubles shows a correlation coefficient of 0.93. Injuries outnumber deaths by approximately ten to one but follow the same

Table 9.1   Distribution of deaths 1969–98

Year	Frequency of deaths	% of total
1969	18	0.5
1970	26	0.7
1971	186	5.2
1972	497	13.8
1973	274	7.6
1974	307	8.5
1975	265	7.4
1976	314	8.7
1977	117	3.2
1978	83	2.3
1979	124	3.4
1980	86	2.4
1981	115	3.2
1982	112	3.1
1983	88	2.4
1984	74	2.1
1985	61	1.7
1986	64	1.8
1987	103	2.9
1988	105	2.9
1989	81	2.2
1990	84	2.3
1991	101	2.8
1992	93	2.6
1993	90	2.5
1994	68	1.9
1995	9	0.2
1996	21	0.6
1997	23	0.6
1998	12	0.3
Total	3,601	100.0
Average no. of deaths per year	120	

patterns of distribution. Deaths and injuries together compose the primary human cost of the Troubles.

The second part of the chapter will provide a description of and commentary on the emergence of 'victim politics' and the construction of 'victim-hood' during the Northern Ireland peace process from 1994 until the review of the Good Friday Agreement of September 1999.

Analysis of deaths in the Troubles

The analysis that follows is of a comprehensive database of deaths due to the Troubles between 1969 and 1998. This database, compiled as part of 'The Cost of the Troubles' study, is described and analysed in greater detail elsewhere.[4]

Deaths over time

The early 1970s were the years that saw the highest death rates of any in the thirty years of the Troubles. Table 9.1 shows that 1972 was the year in which the largest number of people died. Subsequently, in the late 1970s, as a result of security policies and shifting military and paramilitary strategies, the Troubles settled into what became known as 'an acceptable level of violence', a steady, if high level of deaths that never again reached the peaks of the early 1970s.

Just over half of all deaths occurred in the period 1971–76. If the frequency of deaths can be regarded as a good indicator of the intensity of the conflict, then these five years stand out over the entire three decades. The key events were the introduction of internment in 1971, the proroguing of Stormont in 1972 and 1974, when the power sharing Executive was brought down by the Ulster Workers Council strike. After 1976, despite events such as the renewed loyalist strike in 1977 and the hunger strikes of the early 1980s, the number of deaths in any one year never again reached the same level and in only seven years was it greater than 100. Data on injuries confirms the concentration of violence in the 1970s, with almost a third of all injuries suffered between 1972 and 1977.

Just over half of all deaths due to the British Army (163 deaths or 51.6 per cent) occurred between 1971 and 1973 compared to 15.3 per cent of deaths (7 deaths) attributable to the RUC. Republican and loyalist paramilitaries were also responsible for large number of deaths during this time (502 and 216), although it was not their most active period. The years 1971–73 saw the most proactive security activity by the Army, indicated by the number and share of the total deaths due to them that occurred in the last five months in 1971 and all of 1972–73. Paramilitary peaks of activity came later, with 40 per cent of deaths (452 deaths) perpetrated by loyalist paramilitaries occurring between 1974 and 1976. In the case of republican paramilitaries, 47 per cent of all the deaths they have been responsible for occurred in the period 1971–76.

Cause of death

Overall, shooting was the main cause of death, followed by explosion. Nearly 91 per cent of victims died from these causes. Deaths caused by explosions were concentrated in the 1970s whereas deaths due to shooting were fairly evenly distributed across the entire period.

Table 9.2   Deaths by status of victims 1969–94

Year	Republicans	Loyalists	RUC	UDR/RIR	Army	Civilian	Civilian % of total
1969	2	1	1			14	78
1970	5		2		1	18	69
1971	24		10	5	46	97	53
1972	77	11	16	24	108	258	52
1973	39	13	13	10	59	135	50
1974	24	6	15	7	45	204	68
1975	24	26	12	7	15	178	68
1976	25	12	25	15	15	217	70
1977	15	5	15	14	15	49	43
1978	9	1	9	7	15	40	49
1979	16	1	14	10	38	39	33
1980	5	2	9	9	12	42	53
1981	21	2	21	14	10	42	38
1982	9	5	12	8	32	39	37
1983	9	2	18	10	6	37	45
1984	16	1	9	10	10	24	34
1985	8	1	23	4	2	21	36
1986	6	2	12	8	4	31	49
1987	24	5	16	8	3	43	43
1988	17	4	6	12	23	38	38
1989	6	2	8	2	26	34	44
1990	8	1	12	8	10	41	51
1991	14	2	7	7	5	60	63
1992	14	2	4	3	4	64	70
1993	5	1	6	2	6	65	76
1994	17	2	3	2	1	38	60
Total	439	110	298	206	511	1,868	
% of grand total	13	3	9	6	15	54	

Status of those killed

Table 9.2 shows deaths which occurred between 1969 and 1994 (the year of the first IRA ceasefire) according to the status of the individuals involved.

From Table 9.2 it emerges that civilians, rather than members of the security forces or republican or loyalist paramilitaries, form the largest category of deaths, accounting for over half of those killed. The percentages of civilian deaths decreased in the period 1972–73 during the post-internment violence and increased in 1974–76 with the proliferation of bombings and sectarian attacks. The

Table 9.3   Age distribution of those killed

Age	Frequency	Per cent
0–4	21	0.6
5–9	17	0.5
10–14	51	1.4
15–19	468	13.1
20–24	720	20.2
25–29	578	16.2
30–34	427	12.0
35–39	330	9.3
40–44	231	6.5
45–49	205	5.8
50–54	186	5.2
55–59	124	3.5
60–64	96	2.7
65–69	47	1.3
70–74	36	1.0
75+	23	0.6
Total	3,560	100.0

proportion of civilian deaths increased again in the 1990s, although this is partly due to relatively low levels of security casualties.

Overall, members of paramilitary organisations make up 16 per cent of total deaths and the total security force deaths make up a further 30 per cent. In other contemporary armed conflicts, the percentage of civilian casualties is often around 80 to 90 per cent. The pattern is similar for injuries, with the proportion of injured security force personnel at around 30 per cent.

Gender

Those killed in the Troubles have been overwhelmingly male (91.1 per cent) with more than nine out of ten of all fatal casualties men. Table 9.3 shows that the victims were skewed towards the younger age groups.

More than a third of victims were in their twenties, with over half in their twenties or thirties, and one in six victims were aged 19 or less. The death risk to the 20–24 age group was more than twice as high as any group over 40. Just under a quarter of all victims was aged 21 or less and another half was aged 22–39. Almost three-quarters of those who died were under the age of 40.

Religion or ethno-political category

The religious (or ethno-political) breakdown of deaths in the Troubles is one of the most sensitive sets of figures, since it denies or supports the claims to greater

Table 9.4   Distribution of deaths by religion

Religion	Frequency	Valid %
Don't know	333	9.2
Protestant	1,065	29.6
Catholic	1,548	43.0
NNI	655	18.2
Total	3601	100.0

Notes: NNI = Non Northern Ireland.

suffering by one or other community. This analysis is shown in Table 9.4. Religion was not recorded for victims from outside Northern Ireland (NNI). Furthermore, the data did not contain religious affiliation for a high proportion of deaths among Northern Ireland security forces, explaining the bulk of the 'not known' category.

An examination of the numbers of deaths shows that more Catholics than Protestants have died in the Troubles. Given the smaller proportion of Catholics in the general population, Catholics have a higher death risk than Protestants. We explore this further, as follows.

Since the local security forces are 92 per cent Protestant, this proportion was used to redistribute the 'not known' category in Table 9.4 between the two religious groups. These results are shown in Table 9.5. Changes in the relative size of the Catholic and Protestant populations of Northern Ireland were taken into account by calculating the rate from the base of either the 1991 Census of Population, or from an average of the 1971, 1981 and 1991 censuses.

Columns 1 and 2 of Table 9.5 show the death rates for Protestants and Catholics calculated from the base of the 1991 Census only. Columns 3 and 4 show the rate if it is calculated using a base of the average of the population figures in the three censuses, since the deaths occurred over a period in which there were changes in the religious balance of the population in Northern Ireland.

In the first row of Table 9.5, death rates for Catholic and Protestant civilians only are shown. Using the 1991 Census figures alone, the rate is 2.48 per thousand

Table 9.5   Death rates by religion (per 1,000 population)

	1991 Census		Average '71, '81 and '91	
	Catholic	Protestant	Catholic	Protestant
Civilians	2.48	1.46	3.01	1.26
Civilians and security	2.5	1.9	3.1	1.6
Excluding 'own' deaths	1.9	1.6	2.3	1.4

Table 9.6   Organisations responsible for deaths

Organisation responsible	Frequency	Valid %
Republican paramilitaries	2,001	55.7
Loyalist paramilitaries	983	27.4
British Army	318	8.9
UDR	11	0.3
RUC	53	1.5
Civilian	11	0.3
Other	216	6.0
Total	3,593	100.0

for Catholic compared with 1.46 per thousand for Protestants. Using the average of the three censuses, the rate becomes 3.01 per thousand for Catholics compared with 1.26 per thousand for Protestants.

However, to exclude security deaths omits a cohort of deaths that are largely Protestant. Since substantial numbers of security deaths had missing values for religion, we re-calculated the death ratios, attributing 'Protestant' to a proportion of security deaths in accordance with the known religious composition of the security forces. The second row in Table 9.5 shows that, using the 1991 Census figures alone, the rate then becomes is 2.5 per thousand for Catholic compared with 1.9 per thousand for Protestants. Using the average of the three censuses, the rate becomes 3.1 per thousand for Catholic compared with 1.6 per thousand for Protestants.

In the third row, all deaths that were attributable to perpetrators within the same community as the victim – all Catholics killed by republican paramilitaries and all Protestants killed by loyalist paramilitaries – were removed. This gives a new rate. Using the 1991 Census figures alone, the rate becomes 1.9 per thousand for Catholic compared with 1.6 per thousand for Protestants. Using the average of the three censuses, the rate becomes 2.3 per thousand for Catholic compared with 1.4 per thousand for Protestants.

The risk for the two groups varied substantially over time. Between 1969 and 1976 (using 1971 Census figures) the Catholic death risk was more than twice that of Protestants, whereas the converse appears to be true between 1977 and 1986. In the final period, the risk for Catholics was about 50 per cent greater. Overall, however, there have been more deaths in relative and absolute terms in the Catholic community in Northern Ireland than in the Protestant community.

Responsibility for deaths

Table 9.6 shows that paramilitary organisations were responsible for 80 per cent of all deaths and more than half of all deaths was the responsibility of republican paramilitaries. For each of their members who died, republican paramilitaries killed five and a half other individuals, whereas loyalist paramilitaries killed eight and a

Table 9.7   Deaths by religion by organisation responsible

Organisation responsible	Don't know	%	Protestant	%	Catholic	%	NNI	%
Republican paramilitaries	278	83.5	745	70.0	381	24.7	597	91.4
Loyalist paramilitaries	25	7.5	207	19.5	735	47.6	16	2.5
British Army	4	1.2	32	3.0	266	17.2	16	2.5
UDR			4	0.4	7	0.5		
RUC	1	0.3	7	0.7	43	2.8	2	0.3
Civilian			9	0.8	2	0.1		
Other	25	7.5	60	5.6	109	7.1	22	3.4
Total	333	100.0	1,064	100.0	1,543	100.0	653	100.0

Notes: NNI = Non Northern Ireland.

half people for each of their members who was killed. The figure for the British Army was just over half a person and for the RUC just less than a sixth of a person.

The categories of 'republican' and 'loyalist' paramilitaries each cover a number of different organisations. Within the republican grouping, the IRA (formerly the Provisional IRA) was responsible for the greatest number of deaths (1,684 or 85 per cent of those attributed to republican paramilitaries). Other republican organisations killed substantially fewer people, with the factions associated with the INLA killing 127 people. Due to limitations in the data, it was not possible to accurately attribute the deaths due to loyalist paramilitaries to the various loyalist organisations, so 449 deaths were simply attributed overall to loyalist organisations. Of these, 254 were attributable to the UVF and 177 to the UFF.

The conflict in Northern Ireland has given rise to much political rhetoric about defence of and opposition to the presence of the British State, and to perceptions about where the greatest threat to a community lies. Table 9.7 breaks down the deaths by religion according to organisation responsible.

Table 9.7 tends to support the perceptions of each of the two communities as to who constitutes the greatest threat to them. The largest share of Protestant deaths has been caused by republican organisations, which are responsible for 70 per cent of total Protestant deaths. If the 'not known' category is treated as before (that is, 92 per cent are regarded as Protestant) then republican paramilitaries have been responsible for over 80 per cent of all Protestant deaths in the Troubles. Conversely, almost half of Catholic deaths are due to loyalist paramilitary activity, and over a fifth of Catholic deaths are due to security force activity, with the British Army having played the most significant role.

The size of threat posed by paramilitaries to their own community is clarified in Table 9.7. Nearly a fifth of Protestant deaths are the responsibility of loyalist paramilitaries and over a quarter of all Catholics who died were killed by republican paramilitaries. This latter figure is partially due to the republican bombing campaign, during which city centre bombs caused random civilian casualties. The paramilitaries that claim to defend each community have in fact been a significant source of deaths within their own communities. Furthermore, republican paramilitaries have been the most significant cause of deaths of other republicans with feuds, with the execution of informers providing the rationale. The British Army has been responsible for just over 30 per cent of deaths among republican paramilitaries, whilst republican paramilitaries themselves have been responsible for almost all the deaths of security forces (1,070). Overall, for every organisation responsible for deaths in the Troubles, the biggest single category of victim has been civilians.

Local deaths and fatal incidents

Overall, Belfast has the highest death rate of any district council area in Northern Ireland. The fatal incident rate in Belfast (4.69 per thousand) compared with that in Ards (0.12 per thousand) illustrates the wide variation between areas in terms of their experience of the Troubles. The overall death rate for Northern Ireland is 2.2 per thousand. In terms of absolute number of incidents, Belfast, Newry & Mourne, Derry, Armagh, Dungannon and Craigavon stand out. In both absolute and relative terms the greatest intensity of violent deaths has occurred in Belfast, with the rates per 1,000 population almost twice as high as the next district, Armagh. In some other areas, for example, Castlereagh and North Down, the number of residents killed was greater than the number of fatal incidents. This is explained either by membership of the security forces or perhaps by residents killed in bombs in city centres.

Elsewhere,[5] further analysis of these data show that even within district council areas, not all communities have been equally affected. Death rates for postal districts show how particular parts of Belfast, Derry/Londonderry, South Armagh and 'Mid Ulster' have experienced high intensities of violence. In terms of postal districts, BT14, BT12, BT13, BT15 and BT11, all in North and West Belfast, have the highest number of resident victims, followed by BT47 and BT48 – Derry/Londonderry. BT34 and BT35 constitute Newry and South Armagh. Suffering has not been evenly distributed geographically, nor indeed according to gender, religion, status or age.

Victim culture in Northern Ireland

From the beginning of the peace process, and the announcement of the Combined Loyalist Military Command's ceasefire in which they express 'abject and true remorse' to 'the loved ones of all *innocent* victims' (my emphasis), the battle-lines on the issue of 'victims' were beginning to be drawn. The attempts to draw distinctions between categories of victims was to become more marked following the intensification of the activities of the anti-agreement lobby.

As the peace process progressed, the advisability of addressing the issues faced by those bereaved and injured in the Troubles was recognised first by the Irish government. Its Forum for Peace and Reconciliation devoted two hearings to the issue in November 1995 and early in 1996. However, the reluctance of some unionists to participate in this exercise limited its usefulness.

By March 1995, the British government had paid a total of £1,119,585,000 in compensation for the Troubles, £300,516,000 in damages to property and £814,219,000 in personal injuries. Expensive though this provision was, many did not qualify for compensation and there were obvious inequities in the compensation scheme. Nor did the scheme suffice in addressing the concerns of those that had been bereaved or injured, as the prospect of putting violence in the past became more substantial.

With all the complications of the peace process, the 1996 failure of the cease-fires, and their subsequent reinstatement, consistent demands for the release of prisoners were frequently voiced by both republican and loyalist parties with links to paramilitary organisations from early on in the peace process. Concessions to prisoners were seen as important confidence-building measures, and included the repatriation of Irish prisoners held in British jails in late 1997. Prisoners were a crucial part of the peace process, and their views were regularly consulted during negotiations. Indeed, the secretary of state, Mo Mowlam, herself met with prisoners in January 1998 in order to encourage their support for the peace process. On that occasion, she apologised to those bereaved and injured, justifying her actions by reference to support for the peace process. Nonetheless, television coverage of this occasion enraged many. Government anticipated that the sensitivities of those bereaved and injured would form obstacles to the acceptability of measures such as the early release of prisoners. Politicians in the early days of implementation made many such apologies to 'victims', referring to the larger goal of peace as justification for the measures they were implementing.

It was clear from an early stage that, if an agreement could be reached, concessions to prisoners would have to form part of that agreement. Indeed, the Irish government had already begun the process of early release by January 1995, and continued to release IRA prisoners from that date onwards. Within the voluntary sector, concern was being publicly expressed about the plight of those bereaved and injured, and voluntary groups offering services to this population were experiencing an unprecedented increase in demand for their services. The Social Services Inspectorate had already begun the first official examination of 'services to meet the psychological needs of individuals affected by civil unrest in Northern Ireland'[6] under the direction of John Park. His Report was to be published in March 1998, and was to find that, by and large, those affected by the Troubles did not avail of statutory services. The pressure was increasing on the government to 'manage' the unfolding peace process, and therefore to address the issue of those who had been bereaved and injured.

It has been argued that government policy in relation to victims of the

Troubles has been entirely driven by their need to offset the concessions to prisoners with gestures to those who have suffered at the hands of these same prisoners and others. However, there is also some evidence that Unionists pressed for the needs of certain sections of victims to be addressed, and that the secretary of state in particular had some humanitarian interest in the topic. Whatever the merits of that argument, in October 1997, the secretary of state appointed Sir Kenneth Bloomfield, former head of the Northern Ireland Civil Service and Governor of BBC Northern Ireland, to act as a one-man victims' commission. His brief was to investigate the situation of:

> those who had become victims in the last thirty years as a consequence of events in Northern Ireland, recognising that those events have had appalling repercussions for many people not living in Northern Ireland.[7]

Bloomfield, assisted by Mary Butcher, Lady Mayhew's former secretary, embarked on a series of public meetings and consultations. Significantly, Bloomfield adopted a neutral definition of the population with which he was to concern himself. This did not exclude by definition, for example, those bereaved or injured in state violence, or those with associations to paramilitary organisations. This was not to satisfy groups in the nationalist community such as Relatives for Justice, who saw Bloomfield's lack of explicit attention to state violence as problematic, and his inclusiveness as mere lip-service. Gaining the confidence of the nationalist community was always going to be a challenge for Bloomfield, coming as he did from a background in Stormont. However, nationalist mistrust notwithstanding, in hindsight it was arguably the backlash against his attempt at a neutral approach to 'victims' that provided the impetus to the later politicisation of the victims issue by unionists, mainly from the anti-Agreement camp. Nor did it reassure unionists when the new British Labour government were perceived by them to be giving further concessions to nationalists, such as its announcement in January 1998 of a new public inquiry into the events of Bloody Sunday in January 1972.

Meanwhile the violence continued albeit at a lower level, leading first the Ulster Democratic Party and then Sinn Féin to be temporarily excluded from the talks for breaches of the ceasefire. Sporadic violent incidents and deaths continued. By then, dissident loyalists and republicans – the Loyalist Volunteer Force and the Continuity IRA – had organised themselves militarily.

In the negotiations leading up to the signing of the Good Friday Agreement, signed on 10 April 1998, the Northern Ireland Women's Coalition tabled a section on victims of the Troubles. Paragraphs 11 and 12 on page 18 of the published Agreement show what survived the negotiations.[8]

In her speech on the Good Friday Agreement in the House of Commons the secretary of state welcomed the Agreement and again returned to the subject:

> It is important when we are talking about all these positive developments that we do not lose sight of the terrible price that has been paid by the victims of violence and their families. No amount of progress in the search for lasting peace will bring

back those loved ones who have been lost. But I hope that Ken Bloomfield's Victims' Commission will soon be in a position to provide us with some practical suggestions as to how we can best recognise the suffering endured by the victims of violence and their families. I cannot say better than the words in the agreement itself. 'The achievement of a peaceful and just society would be the true memorial to the victims of violence.'[9]

Bloomfield published his Report in May 1998. In his Introduction he wrote:

In more than twenty five years of public service I have never been asked to undertake a task of such human sensitivity. The letters I have read and the stories I have heard in carrying out the work of the Commission will be burned in my memory forever.[10]

The Report itself did not make firm recommendations on a Truth Commission for Northern Ireland, and made a series of exhortations to employers, social services and other agencies to improve their practices in relation to those bereaved and injured. Significantly, Bloomfield recommended that: 'victims must, at barest minimum, be as well served as former prisoners in terms of their rehabilitation, future employment, etc.'[11] Bloomfield also recommended a review of the Compensation Scheme. The Report launch was accompanied by an announcement of a £5m down-payment of funding by government for work with those bereaved and injured in the Troubles. The amount of money allocated was disappointingly low, but some comfort was taken that it was only a down-payment.

At the launch of the Bloomfield Report, the secretary of state also announced the appointment of Adam Ingram as Minister for Victims. However, Ingram already held the position of Minister for Security, and in his first months as Minister for Victims, his security role seemed to occupy his time almost exclusively. It was perhaps ill-conceived to give Ingram a second area of responsibility on top of the heavy responsibility of security. Whatever the official rationale, the appointment was interpreted in some quarters as yet another signal that the victims issue was not a high priority for the government.

On 20 May, the Minister for Justice and Law Reform in the Irish government, John O'Donoghue, appointed former tanaiste John Wilson to review services to those affected by the Troubles who were living in the Republic of Ireland. A Victims Commission was established in Dublin, and began work in the subsequent months.

Meanwhile, in the aftermath of the Good Friday Agreement, a referendum was conducted in which 71 per cent of voters supported the Agreement. The anti-Agreement forces – the Democratic Unionist Party and the Independent Unionist Party – seemed vanquished.

In June 1998, the Victims Liaison Unit at Stormont was established to 'take forward the process of identifying and prioritising a packages of measures to help victims, their families and support groups'. A small team of civil servants from various departments was deployed for the purpose.

By June 1998, an 'initial support package' of expenditure on victims was announced. The money was to go towards establishing a trauma unit for young people affected by the Troubles, and towards supporting local groups including Survivors of Trauma, WAVE and Families Against Intimidation and Terror (FAIT). The total expenditure came out of the initial £5m announced in May 1998. The allocation of money to FAIT, a group specialising not in service provision to victims, but in campaigning against punishment attacks by paramilitaries, drew the fury of one Sinn Féin assemblyman, who complained of its political nature. Anyway, the funding allocated to FAIT was subsequently withdrawn following disclosures of irregularities and conflict within the organisation.

Sporadic violence continued. Three young brothers were killed in July in a petrol bombing incident when their home in Ballymoney was attacked. Mo Mowlam wrote an article for the *Belfast Newsletter* on 14 July 1998 in which she addresses the tragedy of their deaths, but went on to the image of 'David Trimble and Seamus Mallon standing together to condemn the killing and pledging their commitment to finding a resolution to the parades issue.' The goal of peace was still worth striving for. Yet the sectarian attack on the family was conducted by those in a section of loyalism that, increasingly, would have no truck with such images, nor with the peace process itself.

The media debate on early releases of prisoners continued. By early August, such newspaper headlines as 'He Lost Five Loved Ones in the Troubles yet he is for the releases'[12] continued to pose the issue of prisoner releases alongside that of victims' feelings and experiences.

On 12 August, Adam Ingram announced the launch of a £250k Educational Bursary Scheme to provide educational assistance to those who had lost a parent in the Troubles, and a Memorial Fund with matching funding of £1m. Ingram also announced a formal review of the Compensation Scheme, which had been recommended in the Bloomfield Report.

In 20 August 1998, a massive explosion in Omagh town centre killed twenty-eight people, a twenty-ninth was to die later, and two unborn children. The bomb had been planted by the Real IRA. Shock and revulsion overcame the political process and Omagh was to become the focus of attention on the issue of victims for a considerable period. Ministerial visits to Omagh were followed by announcements of various public investments in the town and surrounding area over subsequent months. The Omagh Fund was established, and fund-raising for it was widespread. The Omagh bomb provided a clear focus for concern about victims; furthermore, there was political unity in condemnation of the bomb. It was reasonably clear what was needed in Omagh, and government and other public figures could do something positive about the victims issue. The scale and recency of the suffering of the people in the Omagh bomb served to temporarily sideline all other victims' concerns. This atmosphere prevailed, supported by events such as President Clinton's visit to the town and by continued fund-raising activities.

A growing number of new groups, FAIR (Families Acting for Innocent Relatives) and HURT (Homes United by Republican Terror, later changed to

Homes United by Recurring Terror), for example, had been formed over the previous months, many of them in the border regions. Many adopted 'exclusive' approaches to membership, claiming to represent 'innocent victims', 'victims of terrorism' or 'victims of Nationalist terror'. These groups began a round of meeting politicians and voicing opposition to prisoner releases. By November 1998, FAIR had been invited to join the Touchstone Group, a group established under Bloomfield's recommendations to advise the government on victims issues, although they did not take up their seats. From another quarter, the Victims Liaison Unit had already been under pressure to include prisoners in their remit, but with the increasing pressure from other quarters this became increasingly less likely to happen.

The Bloomfield Report had also drawn attention to the issue of the families of the 'disappeared' and recommended that 'every effort should be made to persuade and enable those with information about the disappeared to disclose it'.[13] Subsequently, legislation (Northern Ireland (Location of Victims' Remains) Act 1999) was introduced at Westminster on 26 May 1999. This legislation limited the use of the results of forensic testing of bodies and offered protection to those coming forward with information about the location of bodies. The Victims Commission in the Republic of Ireland played a key role in facilitating a number of excavations in the Republic of Ireland, in June 1999, and excavation work stretched over a number of months. In spite of all the efforts, only a total of three out of a total of twelve missing bodies were found. Either the information given by the IRA was inaccurate or environmental factors intervened to thwart the majority of the searches. The period of searches was one of increased tension and anticipation for the families of the disappeared and of growing embarrassment for republicans.

The political process, meanwhile, was stuck. On the one hand, the issue of decommissioning and on the other the failure to implement the Agreement and establish an Executive constituted a stalemate. After the resignation of the Deputy First Minister, Seamus Mallon, Ulster Unionist leader David Trimble presided alone, balking at any movement on further implementation. Complaints about the status of the IRA ceasefire, and about continuing paramilitary punishment attacks, offered evidence for his scepticism about Sinn Féin's intentions. FAIT, a group originally considered for funding under the provision for victims, monitored and regularly publicised such paramilitary punishment attacks, thereby providing evidence to support Trimble's scepticism. Added to this, recurrent media coverage of the expenditure on resettlement of prisoners[14]promoted an atmosphere of increasing cynicism about the peace process and the Agreement.

This was further crystallised by the announcement of the campaign for 'Protestant civil rights' in the form of a 'Long March'. This campaign incorporated many of the newly formed victims' groups. FAIR and HURT were among those who came together under the umbrella organisation Northern Ireland Terrorist Victims Together (NITVT). NITVT's campaign was for a range of demands including: a declaration by the IRA that the war is over; decommissioning including ballistic testing of weapons; destruction of paramilitary weapons; disbandment of terrorist groups; and an international tribunal to investigate the role of the Irish government in the development of the Provisional IRA. Anti-Agreement politicians, from the DUP and anti-Agreement UUP, marched alongside those from the victims groups, and other supporters, including Nell McCafferty from the 1960s Northern Ireland Civil Rights Association.

Finally, as the Ulster Unionist Party moved further away from the prospect of the establishment of an Executive, they, too, became more deeply involved with victims. Michelle Williamson, whose parents were killed in the Shankill Road bomb in 1993, was supported by the Ulster Unionist Party to take a court action seeking a judicial review of the secretary of state's ruling on the status of the IRA ceasefire. Should this ruling be overturned, Sinn Féin would be excluded from the political process. David Trimble accompanied her to court.

By the end of September 1999, Fraser Agnew, United Unionist Assembly Party member, resigned from the Long March campaign, saying, 'I believe innocent victims are being manipulated and exploited for political ends. It's almost like emotional blackmail.'

Definition of 'victim' and 'victim' status

Politically, it has been argued elsewhere[15] that, as a result of the particular history of Northern Ireland, the political cultures of contemporary loyalism and republicanism are cultures of victimhood. The status of victimhood brings with it certain dispensations and political advantages. The victim is deserving of sympathy, support, outside help, and intervention by others to vanquish the victimiser. The victim, by definition is vulnerable, and requires allies or outside rescuers for protection. Any attack conducted by the victim can be construed as self-defence and can therefore be justified, thereby legitimising violence carried out by victims. It is perhaps predictable that the armed factions in the conflict, particularly those who have killed and injured others, might wish to lay claim to victimhood. Without such a status, their violence becomes apparently politically inexplicable and morally indefensible.

Both loyalist and republican politics rely on their various senses of victimisation when justifying their recourse to armed conflict. Loyalists see themselves as victims of the IRA and of the incipient threat of Roman Catholic hegemony whereas republicans see themselves as the victims of British imperialism and of loyalist sectarianism. In the wider public political dynamic of conflict, neither protagonist can afford to portray themselves as the victimiser, since to do so would shift the moral argument to their disadvantage.

The implications for political culture where victimhood becomes an institutionalised way of escaping guilt, shame or responsibility are far-reaching. A political culture based on competing claims to victimhood is likely to support and legitimise violence, and unlikely to foster an atmosphere of political responsibility and maturity.

The conditions and atmosphere within which political violence takes place and its concomitant fears and divisions have pervasive effects, not merely on those who are injured or killed, but on a much wider section, if not all of the population. The social and political institutions within Northern Ireland have been shaped by the divisions within the society and have adjusted themselves in response to ongoing violent conflict. In that sense they can universally be regarded as 'victims'. Indeed, all residents of Northern Ireland – and beyond – have been variously adversely affected by the attritional effects of three decades of violence, its antecedents and consequences, and therefore could all be regarded in some sense as 'victims'. Official endorsement of this universalist definition was contained in the Bloomfield Report which found: 'some substance in the argument that no-one living in Northern Ireland through this most unhappy period will have escaped some degree of damage'.[16]

In practical terms, however, universal definitions of victims do not facilitate targeting of humanitarian resources, and mask the way in which damage and loss has been concentrated in certain geographical areas, communities, occupational groups, age groups and genders. Universal definitions are therefore impractical in social policy terms. Indeed, Bloomfield refers to the need of the Victims Commission 'to aim its effort at a coherent and manageable target group'.[17] However, the narrowing of the definition in the Bloomfield Report was not done in a way that excluded those who did not support the state, nor did it exclude victims of state violence. This was to occur in the local political arena.

The political nature and 'appropriation' of victims issues

L. M. Thomas[18] has described the prevalent view that those who have endured great suffering, Holocaust survivors for example, are potential or actual 'moral beacons' in the wider world. Thomas, in discussing the rivalry of suffering between Jews and blacks in the US, refers to what he calls the Principle of Job, namely that 'great suffering carries in its wake deep moral knowledge'[19] and that the victims of such suffering may become appointed or act as 'moral beacons' for the wider society.

Such figures are often held up to us, implicitly or explicitly, to point to some higher state that we should strive for, some feat of self-transformation that we should attempt to achieve. Their stories lead us to marvel at the resilience of the human spirit, and perhaps see something of ourselves in them. Gordon Wilson, whose daughter, Marie, was killed in the Enniskillen bomb was perhaps the best example of a moral beacon in the recent history of Northern Ireland. He was forgiving of his daughter's killers, and conciliatory in his political attitudes, although his acceptance of a seat in the Irish Senate compromised his acceptability in these terms to some unionists.

Thomas discusses who is eligible for such appointment, and it is clear that whilst Jews in the US have been appointed to such positions, blacks, although qualified by the suffering of slavery to fill the role, tend not to be so regarded. So suffering *per se* is not a sufficient qualification.

Neither is sustaining loss in the Troubles a sufficient qualification for such a role. The widow of the alleged informer, the victim of punishment beatings, or the wife of a prisoner are unlikely to qualify as moral beacons, in spite of their endurance of suffering. The suffering must be recognised as 'undeserved' according to dominant values. In deeply divided societies, attitudes to suffering are also divided; usually the suffering of one side is not easily recognised or acknowledged by the other. The production of a 'moral beacon' about which there is consensus is therefore problematic, since one side's suffering can be a source of the other side's triumph. Gordon Wilson's acceptance of a seat in the Irish Senate arguably disqualified him as a moral figure for sections of the loyalist community, for example. The moral beacon must be congruent with the dominant political values. The increasing political role of victims' groups which exclude sections of those bereaved or injured in the Troubles is the manifestation of this in Northern Ireland.

Moral qualifications of victims

It is often taken for granted that those who have suffered in this way are morally developed in some way by suffering, and are therefore suited to roles of moral leadership. However, Vicktor Frankl's[20] description of his experiences in the death camps of the Second World War would cast some doubt on this assumption. He describes how some prisoners jeopardised others' lives in order to save themselves, for example, and how suffering can destroy moral integrity. Furthermore, the experience of great suffering, in this case in Northern Ireland's Troubles, is also commonly used to explain subsequent violent behaviour. Colin Crawford,[21] for example, found that 30 per cent of the loyalist prisoners he interviewed had 'members of their family' killed by the IRA/republicans – although he does not give details of the closeness of relationship in his definition of 'family'. The implication that the experience of bereavement explains the motivation to violence and revenge is again taken for granted.

It seems that great suffering is perceived as having one of two main social, political and/or moral outcomes: as motivating revenge; or, if the sufferer manages to avoid being driven towards revenge, as morally educating and therefore qualifying the sufferer to act as a 'moral beacon'.

The media in Northern Ireland adopted a practice in interviews with the newly bereaved of asking immediate family members if they forgave the perpetrator – often within hours or days of the death. The bereaved person becomes a moral benchmark by which the public can 'read off' the degree of their own entitlement to anger, desire for revenge or impulses towards retaliation. Through the victim, a message is sent to the wider public about their own comparative state of forgiveness or blame, and how they measure up to those who are most entitled to blame and seek revenge – those closest to the loss. The victim functions as a potential or actual moral beacon. It is this function that politicians have striven to appropriate. By association with victims, they bring unassailable moral authority to their cause. The entry of the 'qualified' victim onto the political stage was, perhaps, always only a matter of time.

As the political profile of so-called 'victim issues' increases, attention is deflected from the humanitarian agenda. That the poorest people have suffered most in the Troubles, that they live in communities blighted with militarism and deprivation, and that the amount of humanitarian assistance to them is paltry is no longer a matter of public attention. Progress in the political arena on policy development on the victims issue, like many others in Northern Ireland, is a casualty of the remaining political chasm that yawns between unionists and nationalists. Such progress may well be made, but it is doubtful whether politicians will be those who achieve it.

Notes

1 See M-T. Fay, M. Morrissey and M. Smyth, *Northern Ireland's Troubles: The Human Costs* (London: Pluto, 1999) pp. 126–32.
2 *Ibid.*, p. 136.
3 See M. T. Fay, M. Morrissey, M. Smyth and T. Wong, *Report on the Northern Ireland Survey: The Experience and Impact of the Troubles*, 'The Cost of the Troubles' study (INCORE United Nations University/University of Ulster, 1999).
4 M. T. Fay, M. Morrissey and M. Smyth, *Northern Ireland's Troubles: The Human Costs* (London: Pluto, 1999).
5 *Ibid.*
6 Social Services Inspectorate, Department of Health and Social Services, *Living with the Trauma of the Troubles: A Report on a developmental project to examine and promote the further development of services to meet the social and psychological needs of individuals affected by civil unrest in Northern Ireland* (Belfast: The Stationery Office, 1998).
7 K. Bloomfield, *We Will Remember Them: Report of the Northern Ireland Victims Commissioner, Sir Kenneth Bloomfield* (Belfast: HMSO: The Stationery Office, 1998) p. 8.
8 See, for the Good Friday Agreement, Appendix 2.
9 Northern Ireland Office press release, 20 April 1998.
10 *Living with the Trauma of the Troubles*, p. 6.
11 *Ibid.*, para 5.26, p. 33.
12 *Sunday World*, 9 September 1998.
13 Northern Ireland (Location of Victims' Remains) Act 1999, para 5.38.
14 'Outrage Shock Costs of Giving Prisoners New Lease of Life', *Belfast Telegraph*, 4 June 1999.
15 M. Smyth, 'Remembering in Northern Ireland: Victims, Perpetrators and Hierarchies of Pain and Responsibility' in B. Hamber (ed.), *Past Imperfect: Dealing with the Past in Northern Ireland and Societies in Transition* (Derry/Londonderry: INCORE, 1998).
16 Bloomfield, *We Will Remember Them*, para 2.13; p. 14.
17 Bloomfield, *We Will Remember Them*.
18 L. M. Thomas, 'Suffering as a Moral Beacon: Blacks and Jews' in H. Flanzbaum (ed.), *The Americanization of the Holocaust* (Baltimore: Johns Hopkins, 1999).
19 *Ibid.*, p. 204.
20 V. Frankl, *Man's Search for Meaning* (Boston: Beacon Press, 1959).
21 C. Crawford, *Defenders of Criminals? Loyalist Prisoners and Criminalisation* (Belfast: Blackstaff, 1999) p. 132.

10

Northern Ireland: developing a post-conflict economy

MIKE MORRISSEY

Introduction

There has been long-term concern about the performance of the Northern Ireland economy, concentrated particularly on the region's disproportionately high unemployment. Isles and Cuthbert[1] demonstrate that as far back as 1939 male unemployment was nearly two and half times higher than in Britain while female unemployment was almost twice as high. Since then a plethora of reports have pointed to an economy with severe structural weakness:

- A worrying share of manufacturing concentrated in low-technology, low value-added industries.
- Since the Troubles, and compounded by the oil shocks, there have been difficulties in attracting and maintaining foreign direct investment.
- Reflecting the industrial structure, there are significant concentrations of low pay.
- The region has amongst the highest unemployment rates of UK regions and more of the unemployed are long-term. Indeed, over a quarter of unemployed men have been jobless for more than five years – twice the rate of the next worst British region, Mersyside.
- The region is characterised by a low rate of firm formation.
- Total factor productivity rates remain relatively low – about 80 per cent of comparable firms in Britain and 50 per cent in Germany.
- GDP per head remains stubbornly around 80 per cent of the UK level.

Nevertheless, unemployment and manufacturing growth did converge with UK rates during the 1990s (most rapidly during periods of ceasefire). The annual rate of growth exceeded that of the UK economy to the point where GDP per head, at 76.8 per cent of the UK's in 1988, rose to 83 per cent in 1995. Moreover, employment grew by 14 per cent between 1987 and 1996 compared to just 3 per cent in the UK.[2] Such positive developments, however, cannot conceal underlying problems –

Table 10.1   Gross weekly household income 1995–96

Income group	Northern Ireland (%)	UK (%)
Under £80	12.3	9.6
£80–£124	11.5	11.2
£125–£174	12.0	10.0
£175–£274	17.8	14.9
275–£374	11.5	13.8
£375–£474	12.4	12.3
£475–£649	11.8	12.9
£650 or over	10.6	15.4
Average gross weekly household income	£322.76	£380.89

Source: Family Expenditure Survey, NI Statistics & Research Agency, Office for National Statistics.

a region that competes primarily on price, where average wages are about 85 per cent of those in the UK and where productivity rates and GDP per employee are amongst the lowest of the UK regions.

Corresponding to the weaknesses of the economy, there are also concentrations of low income and poverty. Table 10.1 looks at the distribution of household incomes and compares it with the UK. Northern Ireland has higher proportions of its households in the lower income categories and fewer in the higher income groups. Average household income is almost £60 per week lower than for households in the UK.

These features of the local economy have been relatively constant over the past three decades despite substantial public expenditure of around £8 billion annually at current prices with £150 million in economic development. A weak region like Northern Ireland could not support this level of public expenditure from its own resources. Accordingly, the British Exchequer 'subsidises' public expenditure by about £3.5 billion annually. Part of this subsidy comes from Europe via investment in physical infrastructure, the Common Agricultural Policy (CAP) and training. Between 1994 and 1999 this amounted to a billion pounds. Thus, not only has the economy suffered from long-term structural weakness, but also the level of intervention designed to tackle these problems has been relatively higher than in other UK regions.

At the same time, since the inception of the state, there have been periodic challenges to its legitimacy by those who believe that the island of Ireland should be a single political entity. This cause has been pursued both politically by nationalists and militarily by republicans. In this respect, it should be clear that the contest in Northern Ireland is as much about its existence as it is about whether the state is fairly governed or adequately provides equal treatment for its citizens. Thus, the issues and problems are qualitatively different from, say, race relations in Britain. In the past three decades, this contest has resulted in 3,600 deaths, 40,000 injuries and substantial direct damage to buildings, infrastructure, jobs and tourism. The region is only slowly, painfully and with great difficulty emerging from this conflict. Moreover, the long conflict has generated a set of 'diseconomies of division' – barriers to development – that must be overcome.

In short, Northern Ireland faces a series of serious development challenges – it must shift its development trajectory upwards, an imperative that is strengthened by the rapid growth experienced by its near neighbour, the Irish republic; equally, it must address its high concentrations of deprivation and social exclusion; finally, in a region where the legitimacy of the state is in question, attention has to be paid to equal treatment for all.

The purpose of this chapter is to examine the impact of the Troubles on the regional economy as the context for assessing new development strategies. The annual size of the security budget (£770 million in 1998/89[3]) and the estimated costs of the conflict (on one calculation, £23.5 billion[4]) have led some to use the phrase 'a war economy'. For two kinds of reason, this is inappropriate:

- The term 'war economy' has been employed to describe those countries whose total productive assets have been devoted to the pursuit of war. Other than enormous investment in armaments manufacture and the incorporation of the large sections of the (mostly male) population into the armed forces, war economies are typically characterised by significant restrictions on personal consumption to fund the war effort. None of this describes Northern Ireland over the past thirty years, although the numbers in the local security forces (the RUC and UDR/RIR) have been considerably swollen because of the conflict.
- Second, the Northern Ireland conflict has been pursued ideologically, as well as politically and violently. Republicans wish to define their activities as a 'just war' against British imperialism with roots going back at least as far as the United Irishmen. The British state and unionists have instead described the situation as a terrorist conspiracy against the majority of the Northern Ireland population. The contest between those wishing to describe the conflict as a war and those who preferred the term terrorism was literally fought to the finish when ten IRA prisoners starved themselves to death in the pursuit of political status. Vocabulary is important here, since the use of the term 'war' implies the legitimacy of the republican cause. For those who are neither republican nor unionist, a vocabulary different to one that employs republican or unionist signifiers is required.

However, it is very difficult to separate out the impact of developments in the international economy, the effects of changes in the British economy, economic problems specific to Northern Ireland and the economic costs of the region's conflict. All were happening simultaneously and interacting with each other. As Bradley comments: 'The published direct analysis of the impact of the troubles on the whole economy, on sectors or on the public finances in isolation, is seriously flawed and cannot be reliably used to isolate the troubles from other factors.'[5] Nevertheless, the chapter looks at the performance of the local economy, particularly during the 1970s and 1980s, to assess the evidence that the economic performance of the region was deflected by violence. It also looks to the future by critically assessing development strategies that have emerged recently from the Northern Ireland departments and asks how the region is likely to fare within a rapidly globalising economy.

A good surrogate for the general level of conflict in Northern Ireland is the number of people who have died as a result of political violence. This correlates well with the numbers injured and with the number of reported violent incidents. The 'Costs of the Troubles' project has constructed a comprehensive database on all those who have died as a result of political violence. Table 9.1 (see preceding chapter) illustrates the distribution of deaths between 1969 and 1994, the year of the first IRA ceasefire. The period 1972–74 stands out, with more than 1,000 deaths over three years, followed by 1975–77. Almost a half of all deaths took place in this six-year period. Indeed after 1977, there was a relatively constant number of deaths in each period of between 200 and 300. Thus, in terms of intensity, the Troubles were primarily a phenomenon of the 1970s, but with significant blips, for example during the IRA hunger strike.

Even accepting that the economic impact of the Troubles was time-lagged, the major changes in the Northern Ireland economy over the period do not appear to be linked to the cycle of violence. The weaknesses of the local economy long preceded the current phase of the Troubles. Buckland, referring to Northern Ireland in the inter-war years, concludes:[6] 'It was not, however, a prosperous state. As the price for the security of a separate existence, it was condemned to years of economic and social stagnation as the most disadvantaged part of the United Kingdom.' Harris describes the post-war position as:[7]

> the average unemployment rate between 1949–59 was 7.4% compared to 3.0% for Scotland (which had the next highest regional rate) and 1.7% for the UK;
> net outward migration of the labour force was 7.2% between 1951–61, while in Scotland it was 5.7% (and –0.5% for the UK);
> earnings in industry were 83% of the UK for non-manual workers in 1951 and 80% for manual workers (the comparable figures for Scotland were 93% and 95%);
> the average growth in manufacturing net capital stock (plant and machinery) over the 1948–58 period was 0.3% per annum (which compares with 5.5% pa growth in the UK).

The problems of the Northern Ireland economy have been long-term and structural. Accordingly, economic decline cannot be attributed exclusively to the political violence of the past three decades. It might be argued, however, that the act of partitioning Ireland created the conditions under which the economy of the Northern state floundered. Cut off from the rest of Ireland and tied to macro-economic decision-making that favoured Britain rather than a peripheral region, the seeds of economic decline were already sown. Moreover, the existence of what was regarded as a 'disloyal minority' created economic problems through discrimination in housing and labour markets. Such factors are important. However, in the 1920s and 30s, the region's core industries suffered decline as a result of essentially international economic change. Local responsibility might be attributed to the failure to modernise in the face of a changing global economy although this charge tends to underestimate the substantial efforts to attract new industries, starting with aircraft manufacture and going on to artificial fibres. Other factors rather than just the local conflict have always been at work.

Bradley identifies three potential causes for poor economic performance during the 1970s:[8]

1 the Troubles, which became serious at just the time the decline in manufacturing employment started to get serious;
2 the weakening of regional and industrial policy in the UK, particularly after the election of a Conservative government in 1979;
3 the slower growth in the world economy that followed the OPEC I and OPEC II world recessions.

Northern Ireland is thus open to the cycles that affect the global economy, is sensitive to what is happening in the UK and has its own specific industrial characteristics. All three were changing during the period of the Troubles and many such changes would have occurred even in the absence of violence. Here, the impact of the Troubles is considered on three dimensions of the economy: changes in the level of unemployment; public expenditure trends; and patterns of inward investment.

Unemployment

Between the 1960s and the 1990s, unemployment in Northern Ireland steadily increased. In 1961, it was 31,980. In 1971, unemployment stood at 36,699. In 1981, it was 98,943, but in 1991, it stood at 100,400. (These are all unadjusted figures.) Because of the changes in the unemployment count after 1982, the final figure for 1991 is not comparable with the previous figures. Some estimates suggest that a comparable figure for 1991 should be around 140,000.[9] By 1991, unemployment was nearly three times higher than in 1961. Yet, despite the growing intensity of the Troubles, the decade of the 1970s saw some of the lowest numbers and rates of unemployment since the creation of the Northern Ireland state. Between 1970 and 1974, the numbers unemployed never rose above 40,000 and in the last year were below 30,000. Following the oil shock, however, unemployment increased by about 50 per cent to 59,700. This higher figure was still around half the average unemployment for the 1980s.[10] Moreover, while the proportion of the unemployed in the long-term category remained greater than in Britain (23.9 per cent in 1974 compared to 20.2 per cent), the relative size of this group was also dramatically lower than in the 1980s.

Reflecting the jobs' shakeout in the 1980s, unemployment in Northern Ireland substantially increased. Between 1979 and 1981 unemployment rose by over 60 per cent and continued to increase until 1986, when the official unemployment rate reached 18.1 per cent.[11] This represented a total of 127,800 unemployed people, with over 70 per cent men. Between 1978 and 1988 male unemployment as a share of the workforce more than doubled, from 9.4 per cent to 20 per cent. Female unemployment nearly doubled, from 6.1 per cent to 11 per cent in the same period. In 1989, official unemployment stood at 104,000, representing 15.1 per cent of the workforce, nearly two and a half times the UK rate of 6.3 per cent. As noted in an economic review at the time: 'The gap between Northern Ireland and the next worst region, the North of England, remains a wide one. If Northern Ireland had the same rate as the North of England (9.8 per cent) total unemployment would be 68,000 – 36,000 less than it is at present.'[12]

Despite changes in the unemployment count, and the expansion of government employment schemes (up by 30 per cent since 1979), the severity of Northern Ireland's jobless problem in the 1980s remained evident. Indeed, between 1979 and 1986 the percentage of the total unemployed in Northern Ireland in the long-term category doubled and for those out of work five years or more, it trebled – from 26 per cent to 55 per cent and 5 per cent to 15 per cent respectively. Between then and 1990, unemployment fell by over 30,000. However, this apparent reduction in unemployment has to be seen in the context of the labour market effects of motivation programmes such as Restart, availability-for-work tests on the number of unemployed claimants and rule changes that disqualified under-18-year-olds from benefit. There were over 33,000 people in government employment and training schemes in 1990, a substantial increase since 1979.[13]

It is thus difficult to trace a specifically Troubles-related effect on patterns of unemployment in Northern Ireland. Unemployment was actually low in the decade when the Troubles were at their most intense. The rise of unemployment can be better related to the impact of the oil shocks and the recession that afflicted the British economy post 1979. Nevertheless, a variety of commentators have made estimates of job loss because of the Troubles – Canning *et al.*[14] estimated job losses of 40,000 during the period 1971 to 1983, while Rowthorn and Wayne[15] estimated 46,000 jobs were lost during the period 1970 to 1985. Gudgin *et al.* estimate that between 1971 and 1977 job losses attributed to the Troubles amounted to 24,000.[16] Other analyses had similar findings – DKM suggested that the loss of 46,000 jobs in externally owned companies in the North could be linked to the troubles.[17] The Troubles were thus a factor in job loss and, consequently, unemployment. At the same time, other factors were equally, or, indeed, more, important. The Troubles were the extra pressure on an economy reeling from severe economic shocks. The employment picture was also confused by the fact that growing public expenditure absorbed an increasing proportion of local employment, thus offering a cushion to all of the processes leading to job loss. An additional factor was the widening of the spatial inequalities in the experience of unemployment. Areas where unemployment fell least were predominantly Catholic and nationalist, thus fuelling grievance.

Public expenditure

Westminster Rule in Northern Ireland responded to the problems of political crisis and an ailing economy by greater public expenditure. This was perhaps most noticeable in the allowances made by the Labour government (1974–79), which, while imposing greater fiscal restraint in Britain by 1976, treated Northern Ireland's expenditure with a greater latitude. This approach was characterised by some commentators as combining a tough military offensive against the IRA with a tender 'hearts and minds' campaign based on greater support for social and economic improvement. So, while up to 1970, public sector expansion in Northern Ireland was about proportionate to that in Britain, since 1970 about 50,000 jobs have been created in the public sector over and above what would have been expected given national trends.[18]

However, Northern Ireland was also adversely affected by the policy changes implemented in Britain after 1979. First, the Conservative government set about reconstructing key elements of the welfare state and tax system. Social security provisions are applied universally in the UK and so Northern Ireland residents suffered as a result of reforms in that area. The shift in emphasis from direct to indirect taxation disproportionately affects those on low incomes who were well represented in Northern Ireland's population.

Nevertheless, key policies in Northern Ireland were operated with greater autonomy. In certain respects, Northern Ireland was relatively protected compared to other regions of the UK. For example, public expenditure, excluding social security, grew in real terms annually by 1.3 per cent between 1982 and 1989 compared to −0.5 per cent in Britain. In 1980/81 public expenditure per head in Northern Ireland was about 33 per cent greater than in Britain. By 1986, this had increased to 42 per cent, a further confirmation of Northern Ireland's relative public expenditure advantage.[19]

However, the region's fiscal base could not sustain this level of expenditure and so the deficit was made up by a subsidy known as the 'British Subvention'. In 1972 at the beginning of Direct Rule, the Subvention was less than £100 million. By 1988/89, it had increased to £1.6 billion – £1.9 billion if the cost of sustaining the British Army and European Community receipts were included. Even the increased emphasis on Law & Order spending did not account for the differential. As a result of this 'protection', certain characteristics of Northern Ireland did improve, particularly in relation to poor British regions. The apparent paradox that the citizens of Northern Ireland did, in a sense, benefit from a government generally castigated for its approach to the poor, reflects but one of the ambiguities of the concept of Thatcherism.

Despite the public presentation of an ideology of non-intervention by the Conservative government, public sector employment in Northern Ireland steadily increased. Table 10.2 looks at public sector employment as a percentage of employees in employment for selected regions.

Table 10.2   Public sector employment as a percentage of employees in employment

	1971	1981	1991
North West	17.4	22.1	25.7
North	18.0	22.5	27.6
Wales	21.4	27.7	29.2
Scotland	19.1	24.9	28.4
Northern Ireland	23.1	36.5	38.9

Source: Northern Ireland Economic Council, June 1995, Table 2.1.

A simple statement of public employment probably understates the significance of the public sector in Northern Ireland since, on one hand, the very long-term unemployed have been almost permanently dependent on state benefits and, on the other, industry has been in receipt of long-term and substantial subsidy. The Northern Ireland Economic Council estimated that close to 7 per cent of the labour force had little prospect of finding work while Northern Ireland's share of UK Selective Financial Assistance to industry rose from 10 per cent in the early 1980s to 20 per cent in the early 1990s.[20] In 1996, industrial assistance amounted to 5 per cent of manufacturing GDP (compared to 0.3 per cent in Britain) and 9 per cent of average weekly earnings (compared to 0.5 per cent in Britain).[21]

By 1988, Northern Ireland was a service economy. As the private sector declined, public sector jobs partly compensated. Between 1979 and 1988 manufacturing employment fell by 40 per cent. At that time, nearly 90 per cent of the remaining manufacturing jobs were directly or indirectly subsidised by the state. Public support for manufacturing jobs averaged about £39 per employee per week. Yet, despite the degree of public support, manufacturing jobs continued to haemorrhage. The condition of the economy in the 1980s was summarised thus:

> Northern Ireland's manufacturing sector, together with agriculture, is probably capable of supporting a regional income at only half to two-thirds of the current level. As a result of the contraction of manufacturing, without replacement by other sectors producing externally tradable goods, the Province has become dependent on the public sector, much of it externally financed to support current levels of employment and income.[22]

There has been considerable comment that the relatively large scale of public sector operation in terms of employment, benefit transfers and industrial support has inhibited the capacity of the region's private sector to be competitive. As Bradley argues: 'a massive autonomous growth of the public sector may have exacerbated the cost competitiveness problems of Northern manufacturing by driving up wages in the North and absorbing too much of the talented workforce into the provision of high wage public services'.[23]

Moreover, generous support to industry can lead to a 'soft-budget culture'

Table 10.3   Employment in externally-owned manufacturing plants in Northern
Ireland 1973–90

Country of origin	1973	1986	1990
GB	64,445	22,331	25,259
US	17,344	11,654	9,282
Canada	606	808	951
Republic of Ireland	1,379	3,012	2,718
Rest of EC	2,579	2,875	3,155
Far East	0	13	1,496
Other	1,208	957	224
Total	87,561	41,650	41,085
Per cent of total manufacturing employment	52.8	39.5	38.6

Source: Northern Ireland Economic Council, November 1992 survey, Table 3.2.

where attention lies in the capacity to attract government assistance rather than
enhance competitiveness. Such problems were recognised in a series of strategy
documents from the Department of Economic Development – 'Building a Stronger
Economy' (1987), 'Competing in the 1990s' (1990) and 'Growing Competitively'
(1995). The 1987 document identified key weaknesses in the local economy including an over-dependence by industry on public subsidy, the lack of an enterprise
tradition and deficiencies in training, work and managerial competencies. The 1990
document emphasised the need for industrial competitiveness, suggesting that
public assistance should be targeted at potentially successful firms and concentrated
on training, R&D, quality and design rather than capital investment. This new
approach was reaffirmed in the mid-1990s, pointing to the necessity to target
assistance to remove obstacles to growth, to reduce of the share of public funding
(particularly for capital projects) and to generate an enterprise culture.

Inward investment

In the late 1950s, Northern Ireland embarked on an aggressive drive to attract
inward investment. By 1971, 34,000 jobs had been created in the manufacturing
sector. As noted by Canning, Moore and Rhodes: 'The dominant feature of the
period (1961–1971) is the large differential growth in Northern Ireland's
manufacturing employment after allowing for its industrial structure. We attribute
this primarily to the greatly strengthened regional policies.'[24] However, this process
halted and then went into reverse in the 1970s.

    The Troubles were not the only factor. The impact to two 'oil shocks' on the
artificial fibre industry, most of which used a crude oil base, was considerable.
Moreover, international mobile capital, upon which the drive to rejuvenate

depended, was both more scarce and subject to greater competition, given the whole process of the internationalisation of production and the related reorganisation of the global division of labour. In this changing world economy, Northern Ireland's comparative advantages were being eroded – a situation made worse by its steadily deepening political crisis.[25] Before the first oil shock, externally owned plants accounted for more than 50 per cent of all manufacturing employment. The biggest source of such plants was Britain, which accounted for almost three-quarters of all employment (83 per cent of all plants). Despite an overall decline in manufacturing employment over the next thirteen years, employment in externally owned plants fell faster, to around two-fifths of the total.

The most substantial study of the collapse of inward investment plants argued that the Troubles were not a significant factor.[26] Rather it was concluded that Northern Ireland plants were relatively vulnerable to general economic restructuring since they were small, lacked higher-order activities such as R&D and were making products close to the end of their production cycle. Other analysis suggests that peace and stability would bring significant gains for inward investment – around 1,500 jobs per year.[27]

How much of this poor performance in the 1970s and 1980s can be attributed to the Troubles? One way of looking at the issue is to compare Northern Ireland, not with the UK, a significantly larger economy, but with another of the weaker UK regions. This compares Northern Ireland with a region that suffered similar economic problems, but was free from political violence. Figure 10.1 presents Northern Ireland's GDP per head as a percentage of the North of England's between 1971 and 1994.

While there was some variation over the period, the range is just less than 10 percentage points. There does appear, however, to be some evidence that Northern Ireland's relative GDP per head fell during the first half of the 1970s, but improved by the end of the 1980s and the beginning of the 1990s.

The Troubles and the economy: a summary

The Troubles has been a significant feature of life in Northern Ireland over the past thirty years. The impact on the economy has undoubtedly been substantial. At the same time, it is difficult to estimate the precise effect because of the simultaneous operation of other processes, both economic and political. Equally, the preparedness of British governments to fund Northern Ireland, despite the fact that the region has been running on a growing deficit between income and expenditure, has acted as a significant cushion. If the region was independent and had to run at a loss of such magnitude through borrowing, it would also have had to face the interest payments on past debts, thus compounding the problem.

Nevertheless, it can be anticipated that thirty years of violence will have had severely negative consequences. These might be categorised as follows:

Figure 10.1   Northern Ireland compared with North of England (in terms of GDP)

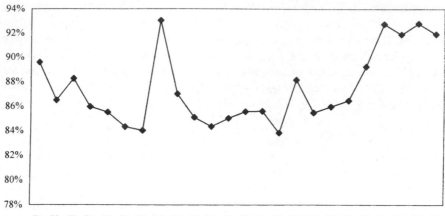

- The direct costs in terms of the dead, injured, damaged property/infrastructure and job loss within the economy.
- A swollen public sector (over the past twenty-five years the public sector has grown substantially, in no small measure due to the Troubles[28]) associated with higher need, additional costs (e.g. security) and a smaller private, wealth-generating sector.
- Political uncertainty inhibiting the ability of firms to plan for the longer term and set down long-lasting roots in any particular place: political risk can be expected to have a particular influence on the size of the tradable goods sector. This sector has an alternative to invest elsewhere, and, for a given rate of return, will seek out a lower risk environment.[29]
- Indirect costs in terms of the diseconomies of conflict – inefficient labour and housing markets generated by intimidation and community division – the lack of social capital, the complex matrix of trust, collaboration and shared responsibility that is a necessary precondition for successful development – community segregation that inhibits the scale on which local development can take place thus inhibiting opportunities for success.
- Other costs that are less easy to categorise – e.g. an increase in informal (and therefore non-taxed) economic activity.

Such factors suggest that peace and stability could have significant and bene-ficial effects on the local economy. At the same time, the region would be still subject to the competitive pressures facing any other weak region. The growing presence of international economic forces compels even small regions to achieve global standards of competitiveness. This is the environment for which Northern Ireland needs to prepare, but for which it is not yet ready.

Despite the good recent performance of the regional economy, there remain key structural weaknesses. In an article comparing the relative competitiveness of the standard UK regions, Gudgin described Northern Ireland thus:

> Its industrial base is small with little local competition in most sectors. Local suppliers or industrial services are limited in number and in the scope of products or services on offer. Like most of the northern regions of the UK, Northern Ireland's clusters (in linen and standard clothing) were established long ago and in most cases face intense competition from competitors with much lower labour costs. Local consumer and industrial markets in Northern Ireland are at the low income end of the UK spectrum and are not in general either sophisticated or fast changing. Although the upper third of the secondary education system is the best in the UK, the low level of local demand for highly educated manpower means that many well educated young people leave the region. This results in a labour force which is not particularly well educated even by the UK's low standard.[30]

Indeed ranked by underlying 'non-cost competitiveness factors', Northern Ireland came last in the UK. Nevertheless, growth in employment and GDP has historically matched that of the UK. The explanation lies in the fact that deficiencies in non-cost competitiveness have been compensated for by low labour costs. Low pay has thus been the crucial factor in sustaining regional development. A crucial issue for the future of the region is whether it will compete on the basis of low cost labour (with attendant social effects) or whether it seeks to enhance non-cost competitiveness factors.

Facing the future

A key challenge is to find a development model that will enable the region to compete economically on a global scale while retaining a commitment to social cohesion and social inclusion. This will be no easy task. Even large economic units, like the EU, are not immune to rapid changes occurring within the world economy.

A recent trend in this respect has been termed globalisation – the worldwide wave of liberalisation of trade, investment and capital flows and the consequent growing importance of these flows and of international competition in the world economy:[31]

- As world trade has become progressively liberalised, it has dramatically increased in volume. During the 1990s, the growth of exports exceeded the growth of world GDP, hence increasing the export-to-GDP ratios of most OECD countries. In order to be successful in this environment, enterprises have to produce at global prices – there is thus a permanent pressure to be price-competitive.

- Large corporations have internationalised their production centres and plan investment where long-term return is greatest. Foreign direct investment's annual average volume increased from $50 billion in 1981–84 to $212.5 billion in 1994.[32] This has meant the relocation of production from traditional sites and, indeed, the volatility of investment in new sites. Global production is changing faster than ever before, driven by a more deregulated world order, new systems of production and the pace of technological advance. International investment flows have grown in volume while the competition to attract foreign direct investment has become intense.

- Moreover, the world financial system has become substantially integrated so that large shocks in one part of the world affect all others.

The world has become more open, more complex and more interdependent. The end result is that international developments have had an increasingly significant impact on national economies and regions have become more open to competition from elsewhere. Accordingly, governments have come to regard competitiveness as the cornerstone of economic development policy. Garelli makes the point forcefully:

> Competitiveness has become to economics what gravity is to physics: one of the fundamental forces which underlie the major events that shape our world. Like gravity, it is a force that one cannot escape. It affects equally companies that need to grow, individuals that want to preserve their jobs and, of course, nations that wish to sustain and increase their standards of living.[33]

At the same time, however, there is no international consensus about how competitiveness can be achieved. The Asian model of export-led development sustained by a close alliance between enterprises, government and the banks has been tarnished by recent problems. The US approach of fiscal prudence coupled with deregulation has produced impressive growth and millions of jobs, but the bottom 40 per cent of US society has paid the price in terms of slow growth in real incomes and greater risk of job loss.

While Europe is committed to market integration, it also holds to the idea of a social compact as a means of moderating the extreme social costs of unrestricted competition. If this means no more than increasing tax burdens to pay for social compensation, it is unlikely to succeed. Governments are under pressure to contain the tax burden. Rather, there has to be a real synthesis between competitiveness and social cohesion whereby the latter contributes to the achievement of the former:

- Competitiveness is more dependent on 'created' rather than 'endowed' assets. This refers primarily to the quality of the labour force – investment in education and training and in improving the way people work contributes to economic development. Therefore, a need has emerged to upgrade skills, to enhance the diversification of employment selections, to benchmark training qualifications, to support the provision of complementary services and, finally, to exploit new and innovative economic sectors for the creation of new jobs.
- Simultaneously, social exclusion occurs primarily through marginalisation within the labour market. Enabling those at the fringes of the labour market to compete for jobs or to aspire to better jobs is an effective approach to inclusion.

- Enterprises have to 'raise their game' so that they are capable of competing in the global marketplace. This means being committed to quality, innovation, product development, marketing and systems of industrial relations that are constructively harmonious rather than conflict ridden.
- The need to find solutions to locally concentrated problems can be best served by the actors most immediately involved. They are motivated by the urgency to respond, they are the most able to assess the situation, to identify gaps in the provision of services, to propose upon, as well as to promote, methods protecting social cohesion.
- All these require new governance systems at local and national level. This implies partnerships amongst the main social actors and the participation of the proposed beneficiaries in all programmes.

Small, open regions have to be competitive – that means exploiting competitive advantage and finding the right competitive niche. Underdeveloped regions cannot rely on central subsidy to solve their problems. This does not deny the necessity for redistribution towards the most needy but suggests that social rights have to be balanced with social responsibility, obligation and entrepreneurship.

Although the situation is complicated by population movement, a key goal for most regions is to ensure that the quality of their human resources is better than the national average – i.e. looking critically at the form and content of existing education/training provision and finding the means to make it better and linked to the development process. If economies are driven by a combination of resources and knowledge, the latter has become dominant. The key to competitiveness lies in knowledge-intensive workers capable of constant innovation.

It is not the role of government to 'solve' regional problems – statutory agencies, the private sector, local politicians and the entire community have all to take on the responsibility for an area's development. Evidence from Europe suggests that regeneration is dependent on getting three things right – hardware (the appropriate physical infrastructure), software (education/training, business formation/attraction and social inclusion) and 'heartware' (a culture characterised by energy, enterprise, cooperation and the desire to get things done). All three have to come together at the right time to combine development with sustainability. In turn, this suggests that the role of the public sector should be redefined from provider to enabler, broker and entrepreneur.

The latest economic development strategy for Northern Ireland, Strategy 2010, embraces some elements of this emerging development agenda:

- Achieving international standards of competitiveness is the key to success in the global economy.
- This requires new forms of economic governance that are both more effective and more participative.
- Social cohesion, equality and social inclusion are central components of economic progress.

There is recognition that while the region's performance has more than matched that of Britain in the 1990s, there is still a long way to go before the region can compete in its own right in the global economy. Strategy 2010 sets ten targets to be achieved within a decade (for example, increasing regional GDP per head from 80 per cent to 90 per cent of the UK's GNP or reducing long-term unemployment from 4 to 2 per cent of the workforce) and makes sixty-two recommendations about how these targets could be achieved. In terms of scale and scope, it represents the most ambitious economic programme yet seen.

Nevertheless, Strategy 2010 has attracted severe criticism. The Northern Ireland Economic Council points to the failure to evaluate the implementation of previous development strategies (which it judges to be poor for the Department of Economic Development's biggest agency, the Industrial Development Board), the lack of coherence of the targets and the failure to cost proposals.[34] The trade union movement has suggested that it fails to take seriously a genuine social partnership approach to the economy. Bradley and Hamilton assert that Strategy 2010 has been poorly researched, that the social cohesion goals are to be achieved simply through the trickle-down effects of economic growth and that Strategy 2010 virtually ignores the all-Ireland dimension in the development agenda.[35]

At the same time, the opportunity exists, with a new administration at Stormont, to press for an innovative, integrative strategy for the local economy. Certainly, the Labour government has backed itself into a tight corner on taxation and spending. However, Labour is committed to the idea of investment-led development and to investing in quality training. In addition, each Labour budget has been redistributive in impact and targeted at economic growth. The overall policy environment is thus favourable to a new approach in Northern Ireland. As Quigley urged, we need to think ourselves into a higher destiny.[36] In that respect, he identified five goals as the components of a vision for regional regeneration: jobs growth, strong sub-regional economies, equitable economic activity and opportunity, a high standard of living and a good quality of life. While this remains no more than an outline agenda, it nevertheless provides a framework for development in Northern Ireland.

A new administration might thus commit itself to a policy framework which:

- fully implements the efforts to promote competitiveness that have been in place since the early 1990s;
- comprehensively operationalises Targeting Social Need;
- recognises that people are the fundamental resource of the Northern Ireland economy and therefore maximises efforts to improve the quality of its human resources;
- targets social inclusion together with economic development as the twin most important priorities of public policy; and
- Recognises that Northern Ireland has a rapidly growing near neighbour in the Irish republic and seeks to develop economic relationships across the island.

The new Northern Ireland governance arrangements that first came into force in December 1999 offer the possibility of a radical approach to economic development. Although the new ministers are counterbalanced by a committee system that some suggest will breed paralysis, parties new to government have much to prove and certain parties like Sinn Féin have adopted an explicitly radical posture. Despite the enormous policy agenda developed largely by civil servants prior to the formation of the new Executive, there remains scope for change, particularly in translating the rhetoric of Strategy 2010 (Competitiveness, Inclusion and Equality) into operational reality. Northern Ireland is small enough to permit experimental approaches to economic development that can incorporate the best from elsewhere.

Notes

1 K. Isles and N. Cuthbert, *An Economic Survey of Northern Ireland* (Belfast, HMSO, 1957).
2 P. Gorecki, *Industrial Policy in Northern Ireland: The Case for Radical Reform* (Manchester, Manchester Statistical Society, October 1997) p. 2.
3 Figures provided by the Northern Ireland Department of Finance and Personnel.
4 M. Tomlinson, *25 Years On: The Costs of War and the Dividends of Peace* (Belfast, West Belfast Economic Forum, 1994) p. 32.
5 J. Bradley, *An Island Economy: Exploring Long-Term Economic and Social Consequences of Peace and Reconciliation in the Island of Ireland* (Dublin, Forum for Peace and Reconciliation, 1996) pp. 63–4.
6 P. Buckland, *A History of Northern Ireland*, (Dublin, Gill and Macmillan, 1981) p. 55.
7 R. I. D. Harris, *Regional Economic Policy in Northern Ireland 1945–1988* (Aldershot, Avebury, 1991) p. 16.
8 Bradley, *An Island Economy*, p. 61
9 See *Unemployment Unit Bulletin*, various issues.
10 J. Trewsdale, *Unemployment in Northern Ireland, 1974–79* (Belfast, Northern Ireland Economic Council, September 1980) p. 17.
11 Northern Ireland Economic Council, *Autumn Economic Review*, Belfast, 1989.
12 Coopers & Lybrand, *The Northern Ireland Economy: Mid Year Review*, Belfast, 1989, p. 37.
13 Northern Ireland Economic Council, *Autumn Economic Review*, Belfast, 1991, Table 5.3.
14 D. Canning, B. Moore and J. Rhodes, 'Economic Growth in Northern Ireland: Problems and Prospects' in P. Teague (ed.), *Beyond the Rhetoric: Politics, the Economy and Social Policy in Northern Ireland* (London, Lawrence and Wishart, 1987).
15 Bob Rowthorne and Naomi Wayne, *Northern Ireland: the Political Economy of Conflict* (Cambridge: Polity Press, 1988).
16 Northern Ireland Economic Council, *The Economic Implications of Peace and Stability for Northern Ireland*, Occasional Paper 4, Belfast, June 1995, p. 17.
17 KPMG, Fitzpatrick Associates, Colin Stutt Consulting and the Northern Ireland Economic Research Centre, *The Social and Economic Consequences of Peace and Economic Reconstruction*, Forum for Peace and Reconciliation, Dublin, July 1995, p. 21.
18 Canning, Moore and Rhodes, 'Economic Growth in Northern Ireland', p. 223.
19 Northern Ireland Economic Council, *Economic Assessment*, Belfast, April 1989.
20 Northern Ireland Economic Council, p. 6.
21 Economic Development Strategy Review Steering Group, *The Economic Implications of Peace and Stability*, *Strategy 2010*, Belfast, Department of Economic Development, March 1999, Figure 7.7.
22 G. Gudgin, *et al.*, *Job Generation in Manufacturing Industry* (Belfast, Northern Ireland Economic Research Centre, 1989) p. 61.

23 Bradley, *An Island Economy*, p. 45.

24 Canning, Moore and Rhodes, 'Economic Growth in Northern Ireland', p. 221.

25 J. Freeman, F. Gaffikin and M. Morrissey, *Making the Economy Work* (Belfast, Transport and General Workers Union, 1987).

26 S. Fothergill and N. Guy, *Retreat from the Regions: Corporate Change and the Closure of Factories* (London, Regional Studies Association, 1990).

27 KPMG, *The Social and Economic Consequences of Peace*, p. 24.

28 Northern Ireland Economic Council, *The Economic Implications of Peace and Stability*, p. 4.

29 R. Barnett, 'Comment' in Northern Ireland Economic Council, *Through Peace to Prosperity*, Belfast, April 1995, p.49.

30 G. Gudgin, 'Prosperity and Growth in UK Regions', *Local Economy*, May 1996, p. 19.

31 International Labour Office, *World Employment 1996/97*, Geneva, 1996, p. 1.

32 *Ibid.*, Table 1.3.

33 Quoted in J. Dunning, E. Bannerman and S. Lundan, *Competitiveness and Industrial Policy in Northern Ireland*, Northern Ireland Economic Council, Research Monograph No. 5, Belfast, 1998, p. 68.

34 The Northern Ireland Economic Council, *A Step-Change in Economic Performance: a Response to Strategy 2010*, Occasional Paper 12, Belfast, September 1999.

35 J. Bradley and D. Hamilton, *Strategy 2010: a Critical Evaluation*, May 1999.

36 G. Quigley, 'Opening Remarks' in Northern Ireland Economic Council, *The Economic Implications of Peace and Stability*.

11

Whatever happened to the women? Gender and peace in Northern Ireland

KATE FEARON

Introduction

This chapter will begin by describing the role played by the Northern Ireland Women's Coalition (NIWC – for whom the author works as political adviser) in the talks process that led to the Good Friday Agreement of 1998. It will then identify those provisions that explicitly address women or gender equality issues in the Good Friday Agreement of 1998 as well as highlighting related issues that are of special interest in relation to women. It will then explore what happened when the provisions in the Good Friday Agreement were translated into legislation in the form of the Northern Ireland Act – what got 'left behind'; what remained new aspirations; and what became new actualities. The process of constructing the new institutions, in particular the Equality Commission, an amalgam of the existing equality agencies, is examined. The chapter will argue that the Good Friday Agreement presents great potential for change for ordinary women and men in Northern Ireland and reflects the views of women who live in anticipation of these potentials. It presents voices that volunteer an assessment of how much impact the Agreement has had on their lives in real terms in the period since it was signed and concludes by suggesting in what direction the long term benefits for women are likely to lie.

The NIWC and the talks process

The NIWC had been formed specifically to contest elections that determined delegates to the talks process chaired by George Mitchell. It had a deliberate cross-community base, and had organised around three core principles of human rights, equality and inclusion – which formed an 'ethical framework' by which the NIWC reached accommodation. From the outset, the NIWC declared that it was not going into talks in defence of a fixed constitutional position. It was concerned with the *interests*, not the *positions* of others, and how these interests might be accommodated within the NIWC's own ethical framework. For the NIWC it was better to have a different view of the possible in the given political norm, and to work towards it, rather than to declare the desirable and wait for others to share that view.

Parties to the Northern Irish negotiations had a tendency to spend most of their time and effort determining *if* any agreement was possible, rather than trying to devise a comprehensive and creative agreement. One of the roles that the NIWC engaged in very seriously was as advocates and protectors of the process. They placed an unequalled emphasis on getting the process right and believing in it. While patently process should never impede progress, the NIWC always raised the issue. For the NIWC there was never a question of *if there is* an agreement. It was always there will be an agreement, even in the face of much negativity from all political commentators, and, in late 1997/early 1998, a fearful and dangerous climate on the streets as a consequence of the UDA/LVF murder campaign.

The NIWC exercised its belief in the possibility of an outcome both inside and outside the talks process. By constantly engaging in an elliptic loop that involved the British and Irish governments, the talks chairs, the other participants and members of civic society, from grassroots community organisations to business and trade unionists, the NIWC was always well appraised of what was, or might be 'the acceptable' on any given question. This constant communication with the external community allowed the NIWC to provide resources for the talks on two planes. First, members of the NIWC became a trusted source of information and advice for the independent talks chairs and assisted them both to take judgement calls on specific issues and to present general options for the participants. Second, the NIWC submitted their own ideas for change and refinement to those persons outside the official process who were most likely to be affected by what was being decided inside the process. Many members of the NIWC had come from or were working in the vibrant community and voluntary sectors, and these contacts were optimally utilised. What the party lacked in size it made up for by forming and maintaining strategic alliances both inside and outside the formal process. It was able to evade or at least to elude the stunting effect of group-think precisely because of its heterogeneity, and the core-principles framework that guided its participation. This acknowledgement of difference proved liberating in another sense. Because they came from different political cultures, NIWC members were well placed to translate the different political argots used by other participants for each other. In turn, they were able to pass on this shared understanding to the other talks participants.

Gender issues in the Agreement

As the second draft of what eventually emerged as the Good Friday Agreement was being prepared, all of the participants were lobbying furiously, pushing for their priorities to be included in the text. This would entail discussions between various

parties and the government representative who was drafting the text, not necessarily between the parties themselves. Once included, however, they had to ensure
that the point, whatever it was, had to stay in, and thus the focus then shifted to
persuading others not to lobby to have it excluded. Traditional parties tended to
push for traditional demands. For instance, Sinn Féin advocated the release of all
politically motivated prisoners; the Ulster Unionist Party argued for the position of
Northern Ireland as an integral part of the UK to be secure. The NIWC, a relatively new party that adopted a counter-traditional approach to resolving the
conflict's fundamental questions, had an agenda that not only covered these questions, but went beyond them.

The NIWC as a party formed to highlight the dearth of women in politics
and, specifically, around the negotiating table, was keen to make the Good Friday
Agreement as inclusive and accessible a document as possible, to enable the public
to claim some ownership of the provisions it contained. One such provision was
that 'against the background of the recent history of communal conflict' the
participants affirmed a series of basic rights, including the right to free political
thought, and, *inter alia*, to freedom and expression of religion, to freedom from
sectarian harassment. Added to this list of fundamental freedoms was 'the right of
women to full and equal political participation'.[1] It was an uphill struggle to ensure
the drafters understood the rationale of having such a principle inserted in the
historic document. It only really became clear when an NIWC delegate suggested
to the drafters that it was because women had been living in an 'armed patriarchy'
that such a clause was necessary. None of the other parties lobbied to have it
excluded.

The Good Friday Agreement that eventually resulted from these myriad micro
and macro discussions was a complex, ambitious and ambiguous document. There
are over seventy separate 'action points' signalled in its various paragraphs and
clauses. Responsibility for implementing these lie with different sponsors, with
different degrees of authority. Some sponsors are explicitly named (like the British
and Irish governments in respect of establishing new international treaties). Other
action points are referred to more vaguely as being the general responsibility of all
the participants (like the affirmation to the principles of partnership, equality and
mutual respect). The British government is the premier body with responsibility for
implementing specific aspects of the Agreement, and these aspects may be codified
into three categories: (1) promoting principles, (2) giving practical effect to new
institutions and initiatives and (3) pursing policies. The following highlights the
principles, policies and practical aspects of the Agreement which have relevance for
women.

The government committed itself, in the period before devolution of powers to
the Northern Ireland Assembly, to pursuing 'broad policies for sustained economic
growth and stability in Northern Ireland and for promoting social inclusion,
including in particular community development and the advancement of women in
public life'.[2] The British government also neatly incorporated two pre-existing

public consultations dealing with equality issues into the Good Friday Agreement. One was the creation of a statutory obligation on public bodies to carry out all functions 'with due regard to the need to promote equality of opportunity in relation to religion and political opinion; gender; race; disability; age; marital status; dependants; and sexual orientation'.[3] The other was a statement of intent to merge the existing equality agencies: the Fair Employment Commission (FEC), the Equal Opportunities Commission (EOCNI), the Commission for Racial Equality (CRE)[4] and the Northern Ireland Disability Council.

Additionally, there were numerous pledges throughout the Agreement committing various parties to strengthen human rights. For example the European Convention on Human Rights was to be incorporated into domestic legislation. Without prejudice to this, there was provision for a supplementary Bill of Rights for Northern Ireland. The new Assembly (including any legislation it produces) should uphold the European Convention on Human Rights commitments, with the courts being given the power to overturn legislation that contravenes these human rights codes. A new Human Rights Commission was envisaged, with powers to monitor legislation and advise the government on rights issues; promote awareness of human rights issues; and bring court proceedings on human rights issues; or assist individuals to do so.

Further, the Irish government pledged to 'take steps to further strengthen the protection of human rights in its jurisdiction', including the implementation of enhanced equality legislation and the introduction of equal status legislation. When Ministers are eventually appointed to their posts, their Pledge of Office commits them to, *inter alia*, 'act in accordance with the general obligations on government to promote equality and prevent discrimination'.

Obviously the Good Friday Agreement provides for an elected body to administer the powers due to be transferred to Northern Ireland from the Westminster parliament. It also envisages a consultative Civic Forum, based again on the concept of broadening participation in politics; making democracy and decision-making more accessible to the people it directly affects. The Civic Forum planned to involve the social partners in issues of governance, in order to complement the work of the elected Assembly. Implicit in its composition was the fact of offering more opportunities for women to play a fuller role in public life than the Assembly might. Also implicitly recognising the work of women was the support the Agreement intended for victims of violence, and the groups that serve them.

Political aspiration to legislative fact

How well the Agreement actually serves women will depend on how it is implemented and the level of commitment to putting equality between women and men at the heart of the political agenda. Repeated commitments to 'inclusiveness' in the new institutions must take account of the inclusion of women, as well as inclusion of different political communities in Northern Ireland. Apart from the establishment of the institutions detailed above, and the impact of some of the more aspirational, policy-orientated principles, will the Review of the Criminal Justice System address the lack of female judges in the judiciary? Will the Commission on Policing address the procedures for handling domestic violence, and the role of women police officers in the service? While these major Reviews have not yet been published, and a cornerstone of the Agreement, the devolution of circumscribed powers to a power sharing local Assembly, has not yet been achieved, other components of the Agreement have been firmly embedded in the Northern Irish administrative establishment.

Lobbies to give legislative effect to the right of women to full and equal political participation proved unsuccessful, and thus it remains a principle that parties to the Agreement no longer affirm. In the event of any review, however, it may provide one measure of fairness in terms of how the Agreement overall has performed. Pledges by the government on pursuing policies that promote social inclusion are more difficult to assess. On the one hand, the government has provided 'listening' space, most notably in the 'Listening to Women' conference held in Belfast Castle in April 1998, hosted by Baroness Jay, the Minister for Women. Several legislative changes announced during the year, like the extension of maternity leave from fourteen to eighteen weeks, the introduction of the right to parental leave and the increase in child benefit were welcomed, and could be seen as fulfilling this commitment. But other areas of government policy mitigated against this commitment. Joan Smyth, chair of the EOCNI, writing in the *Belfast Newsletter*[5] shortly after the conference, highlighted other issues that fell into this category. The government's New Deal programme, for instance. The EOCNI believed this programme to be biased against women and signposted the potential gender bias in the working families tax credit, with the danger of money being transferred 'from purse to wallet'. In its Final Annual Report, the EOCNI highlighted how, in common with the rest of the UK, the New Deal is a benefit-based programme, access to which depends on receipt of the Jobseekers Allowance (JSA). Given that the very change from unemployment benefit to JSA resulted in a disproportionate number of women disappearing from the claimant register, women are less likely than men to receive JSA and have accordingly less access to the training and work opportunities provided for under the New Deal programme. Inadequacy of childcare in all of the New Deal options compounds these difficulties.[6]

Implementation of the policy and principle aspects of the Agreement are difficult to police. Those components that are principle-based have no named authority to champion them – they remain the responsibility of the participants, and require political leadership to embed. Those components that are policy-based are generally the responsibility of the British government, and in general social and economic terms have to fit within UK-wide policies. No particular effort appears to have been made to craft these policies in the general context of a society emerging from conflict, or in the specific wake of the commitments undertaken in the Agreement.

Both the human rights and equal opportunities initiatives signalled in the Agreement have, however, been put on a legislative footing in the Northern Ireland Act. The Human Rights Commission has been established, though it will be 2000 before any serious work is done on the separate Bill of Rights for Northern Ireland.

In introducing the final Annual Report of the EOCNI,[7] the chair, Joan Smyth, commented on the changed circumstances in which it was operating:

> The Northern Ireland Act was both an end and a beginning – an end, we all hope, to a long period of unhappiness for our society, and the start of a better future. In equality terms, for years we have called for public bodies to be legally obliged to equality proof their policies, and we welcomed the inclusion of this obligation in the Act. We look forward to seeing the practical outcomes of the statutory duty in balanced, fair and equal policy-making; not easy, we know, but what a fine goal to set.[8]

It remains a fine goal. The government, despite receiving a majority of correspondence against merging the equality agencies, pushed ahead with its plans, establishing an Equality Commission Working Group (ECWG), which published its Report in March 1999.[9] The general fear of respondents broadly against the merger was that 'their' particular agenda would be subsumed, and deprioritised, particularly as there would only be one pool of money to be divided amongst the different areas of discrimination. The ECWG did recommend that, in the first management phase of the new Equality Commission, four separate directorates reflecting the existing agencies should be maintained. Some argued that the intro-duction of the duty on public bodies[10] to promote equality of opportunity was such a massive new area of work that it required a separate directorate. This will not be the case and also, the government has confirmed that no additional resources will be made available to public bodies in the preparation of their individual 'equality schemes' which must be drafted and submitted to the Equality Commission[11] before possible approval by the secretary of state. Public bodies must pay for the prepara-tion of such schemes out of their existing, committed, budgets. Enforcement of the schemes will cost more again. It remains to be seen how meaningful, and how readily accepted the schemes will be, if they have these resource implications without any governmental assistance.

The general social and economic backdrop

So what impact does the establishment of these new institutions, principles and practices have on the lives of women in Northern Ireland? What does the Good Friday Agreement mean in real terms for women? In the past fifteen years, the general position for women in most areas of life – with the exception of the political arena – has been steadily improving, thanks in no small part to the vast amount of lobbying and campaigning undertaken by many women activists in the community and voluntary sectors.

The number of economically active women has increased by 23 per cent since 1984 (there are now 323,900 economically active women and 410,100 economically active men in Northern Ireland). The number of women in employment has increased by 34 per cent from 228,000 in 1984 to 305,900 in 1999. This compares with an increase of 16 per cent for men. The earnings gap is also narrowing, with women's weekly earnings now standing at 80.5 per cent of men's, though women are much more likely to be working in the service sector, particularly in clerical/secretarial and personal/protective occupations, and lower down the management ladder than their male counterparts.[12] Though the economic activity rate decreases as the number of dependent children increases, childcare provision has greatly increased. Daycare places in the past ten years have increased by 105 per cent, to 38,916 places, and there are many more registered childminders. But childcare costs money.

The outlook for young women before entering the labour force is decidedly bright, though this prospect does appear to become tarnished when the young women engage with the workplace, as detailed above. Young women tend to leave school better qualified than their male counterparts, and are more likely to progress to further or higher education: 60 per cent of students in further education colleges and 57 per cent of students at university were women in the academic year 1997/98. And there is some evidence that women are chipping away and making some indents in the glass walls marking off 'hard' and 'soft' subjects at third level, with almost 40 per cent of those enrolled for science courses at university now women.

Yet higher educational participation and attainment levels at second level do not necessarily mean all is plain sailing in the workplace. There continues to be a large number of legal complaints and enquiries regarding sexual harassment made to the EOCNI, as well as similar quantities (between 250 and 310) of complaints regarding maternity and pregnancy rights, and recruitment and selection procedures. Victimisation of employees at work on account of their gender constitutes a smaller category.[13]

The period coinciding with a lessening of violence on the streets has not resulted in reduced violence against women in the home, or outside it. RUC statistics show the number of domestic incidents attended by police has more than doubled in the past three years. Incidents of common assault in the home have risen dramatically. (See Table 11.1.)

Neither has the reduction in conflict-related deaths been reflected in a reduction of unlawful deaths of women. In the last three years the number of women killed in domestic violence incidents has risen sharply, from two in 1996, to eight in 1997, and ten in 1998. We have no 1999 figures yet, but the number to date at the time of writing in 1999 does not suggest a reverse in this trend. We do not know why the numbers have risen so dramatically, but we need to find out so that we can arrest and reverse the trend.

The one other area of life for women, which bucks the trend detectable in education and employment opportunities, is politics and public life. Statistics for

Table 11.1   Domestic violence (RUC figures) 1996–98

	1996	*1997*	*1998*
Domestic incidents attended by police	6,727	8,509	14,429
Physical violence involved	3,681	3,805	6,385
Female victims	89%	90%	89%
Common assault	1,758	1,899	3,223

Source: RUC Domestic violence statistics compiled by NI Women's Aid Federation.

public appointments find Northern Ireland marginally ahead of the rest of the UK at 33 per cent,[14] but the numbers of women in elected office are far behind Westminster. Northern Ireland has no women MPs or MEPs. Around 14 per cent of councillors in local government districts are women, and, of the twenty-six district councils, only five have a woman as a mayor/chair and a further 5 have a woman as deputy mayor/deputy chair. Of the 108 members of the new Assembly, only 14 are women. They are divided amongst the parties shown in Table 11.2.

The impact of political progress

It is against this rather patchy backdrop that one should examine whether or not the 'peace process' has had any impact on women, and, if so, what has been its nature. Women were marginally more likely than men to have voted for the Good Friday Agreement in May 1998, and, in a poll conducted in April 1999, though overall support was shown to have increased, the gap between women and men began to widen – women expressing a 75 per cent and men a 70 per cent affirmative to their voting inclination if another referendum were to be held. Women also professed to be marginally more supportive of compromise than men (72 per cent as opposed to 68 per cent).[15]

The women interviewed for this chapter (all 'Yes' voters) tended to be optimistic about the potential of the Agreement, in line with those interviewed for the above-mentioned poll, but they were worried about its non-implementation. Some were more cognisant than others of the new structures the Agreement established, and others were continuing to opt out. Caroline, aged 27, a student community relations adviser, feels that putting the equality agenda on a broader footing is one of the benefits. She sees potential in allowing parties who were uncomfortable with the notion of equality to the point of disparaging it to embrace it for themselves, to broaden ownership of the politics and practicalities of equal opportunities and human rights. But there are dangers in a beefed-up Equality Commission. Another of the women to be interviewed, Wilson, warns: 'The challenge for women is that gender issues are central, and equality is not just seen in terms of Catholic and Protestant.' Like other women, Wilson sees the very fact of devolution, of a localised power base as being empowering for women. As political

Table 11.2   Women in the NI Assembly 1999–2000

Party	Total number of seats	Women who hold seats
Ulster Unionist Party	28	2
SDLP	24	3
DUP	20	1
Sinn Féin	18	5
Alliance Party	6	1
NI Unionist Party	4	0
Ulster Unionist Assembly Party	3	0
PUP	2	0
NIWC	2	2
UK Unionist Party	1	0
Total	108	14

parties have begun to respond to the NIWC agenda of promoting women in public and political life, younger women students have begun to recognise women politicians speaking on a range of issues. Women students who stand for election in student unions are just as likely these days to stand for the positions of President or Deputy President as well as the more traditionally 'women's' posts of Education or Welfare officer, reports Wilson.

This impression of women becoming more overtly political is supported by Ann, 53, an administrator.

> Women's lives have changed – they've become more political. They're asking questions now about politics, starting to feel that they are more part of the political decision making. And its women now who are beginning to panic [about the Agreement not being implemented]. Women are working to protect the Agreement. Whatever is organised I guarantee it will be a majority of women involved – if there is some civic action women will not be behind the door in getting things done.

Like all of the other women asked for their opinion, Ann expresses the general feeling of hope that the Agreement generated, and the disappointment that has come in its wake. It is 'too early to tell' whether or not the Agreement will be capable of delivering on that hope, but what the peace process has delivered, and in particular the ceasefires, is a change in the nature of the natural worries a parent has about children growing up. Now when her children go out at night, it is the normal sort of worries 'speeding, drink driving' that occupy her, not like before, when it was the worry of them being caught up in political violence. This is echoed by Meta, 40, a mature student and Laura, 43, an administrator who feel 'more positive' after the Agreement, and they are grateful that they don't have to worry so much about their children as they grow up. Both tend to be optimistic, and although the Agreement has not resulted in any personal difference in their economic status, they recognise the potential investment opportunities it presents.

Sandra, 29, works with victims of those caught up in political violence. Through her work she is able to point to more concrete benefits that the Agreement has delivered in the past year. The inclusion of clauses recognising victims of the conflict, and acknowledging their pain was important, even though official policy on victims had been changing in the years prior to the Agreement. The majority of those involved in formal personal care delivery services are women – 70 per cent – as are the majority of those working in informal care delivery and support services.[16] For many years there were very few groups working with victims – support was offered in families, in communities, or by friends. Or people simply got on with life by themselves. Small self-help and support groups began to emerge, and these groups struggled on shoestring budgets or on a purely voluntary basis. The vast majority of those injured or killed in the troubles have been men, particularly young men, and women have had to pick up the pieces. The victim support groups were mainly run by women, 'Women', says Sandra 'have an understanding of the actual cost of the troubles.' In response to increasing lobbies, the government began to resource groups that were in effect carrying out an important area of work that should have been the responsibility of the health and social services departments. After the Agreement, the number of victims groups began to proliferate, and to reflect different political constituencies. The Agreement threw the focus on victims into sharp and stark relief. And it opened up space for people to tell their stories – people who have never spoken up before are coming forward now as adults who have sustained injuries or endured traumatic experiences in the 1970s when they were children. But Sandra, like many others, is witnessing a 'retreat' from the high hopes generated by the signing of the Agreement in 1998.

The current depression surrounding the political failure to give effect to the provisions in the Agreement is in stark contrast to the euphoria of 1998, and is reflected in the comments of all interviewees.[17] While the Agreement has not really resulted in much material change in their lives one way or the other, the introduction of new institutions has caused Kelly, 28, who works in skills-based training for women some concern. She is worried about that the move away from a conflict-ridden society to an extremely conservative one will further stymie the equal rights promised by the Agreement, and provided for in part by the institutions it establishes. It may take another thirty years before equality for women has real meaning, she believes. She understands that the clause referring to the right of women to full and equal political participation is virtually impossible to provide for legislatively, but believes it is not tokenistic. Political parties are the gatekeepers to women entering formal political life. Unless they change their structures, political life will not be truly reflective of the population it serves. Kelly believes the clause will be a useful lobby tool for women both within and outside party political structures to effect further positive change in this regard.

Supporting Ann's thesis, that 'women have become more political', Kelly has witnessed a prodigious increase in the number of women taking up the courses her centre provides for women and politics.

> Women have been active in community politics for years, and as far as we're concerned that is politics. But they've become much more interested – and less afraid – of formal politics now. You know, actual stuff about elections – council elections, they're really up for council elections! Women are really determined now – they're saying to politicians 'Go and get your finger out and get it sorted. We've managed to work together over the years, it's time you guys caught up.

What the Good Friday Agreement appears to have done, therefore, is to lift the veil on politics, to make it a less difficult enterprise to engage with. It has been revealed as an accessible, even an attractive entity. And this is how the Agreement will have perhaps the greatest import for women. Women within parties and women outside parties are demanding change in the way they are treated and represented. Another mechanism established by the Agreement which will aid this demystification process is the Civic Forum, a body designed to supplement, though not supplant, the work of the Assembly. The Civic Forum will be composed of representatives from the social partners – ten sectors in all – and is intended to be a more participative way of dispensing democracy in a deeply divided society. It will provide more opportunities for people to get involved in politics, and, unlike elected politics, the nominating bodies for each of the sectors must adhere to four guidelines when selecting representatives. One of these is that representatives should reflect a gender balance. A gender-balanced Civic Forum will create additional pressure on political parties to create a better gender balance in future Assemblies. When the current Assembly goes live, responsibility for 'Women's Issues' will lie within the remit of the First and Deputy First Ministers' Office. It will compete with twenty-five other areas of responsibility in the same Office. At the time of writing, no details were available on the number of staff planned for this specific remit.

Again, it is too early to tell whether or not these new institutional and administrative arrangements will have any meaningful impact on women's lives. That the peace process and specifically the Good Friday Agreement holds great promise and potential which people are poised to receive is in no doubt. It has recognised both politically and practically some of women's experiences throughout the conflict in terms of caring for victims and picking up the pieces in communities. The Agreement has accelerated the growing awareness of the true cost of the troubles, and provided a safer environment in which research exploring this could be publicly examined. And greater stability and economic growth, particularly in the service sector, should mean that women, particularly young women, will be well placed to benefit economically.

If it is implemented in full, women stand to make enormous gains in terms of political visibility and influence. The Agreement has been the catalyst for women asserting a 'claim of right' to full and equal political participation. It may take several generations before this claim is realised, and with it its full import: a truly inclusive polity that reflects and revels in the diversity of its population.

Notes

1 Belfast Agreement, Strand 3. (Belfast Agreement is another name for the Good Friday Agreement.)
2 Belfast Agreement, Rights, Safeguards and Equality of Opportunity, p. 19.
3 Belfast Strand 3, p. 16.
4 The CRE has only recently been established, 'opening for business' in August 1997. The Northern Ireland Disability Council did not enjoy any statutory footing.
5 'Government Lends Open Ear to Issues', *Belfast Newsletter*, Business Section, 4 May 1999, p. 23.
6 Annual Report, p. 9 (EOCNI, 1999).
7 In April 1999.
8 Annual Report (EOCNI, 1999), p. 2.
9 Report of the ECWG (Belfast, Department of Economic Development, March 1999).
10 Section 75 of the Northern Ireland Act 1998 deals with the duty to promote equality of opportunity, and Schedule 9 provides for its enforcement. Section 76 deals with the duty not to discriminate. There are some anomalies between the definitions of what constitutes a public body in each section. For instance, Section 75 does not include the Police Authority for Northern Ireland nor the RUC or RUC Reserve, while Section 76 does.
11 The ECWG Report recommends a possible eight-stage process before such schemes are approved. (Report of the ECWG, 1999, p. 84.)
12 DED, 1999, pp. 1–7.
13 Annual Report, EOCNI 1999, p. 14.
14 In the UK around 32 per cent of public appointments are women.
15 Ulster Marketing Surveys, 1999.
16 DED, 1999, pp. 6ff.
17 Eight women were interviewed for this chapter, four of whom were Protestant and three of whom were Catholic.

12

Promoting a culture of tolerance: education in Northern Ireland

FIONA STEPHEN

In late November 1999 following the Mitchell review[1] of the Belfast Agreement Northern Ireland was on tenterhooks, waiting to see whether David Trimble would gain sufficient support from the Unionist Council to proceed with the establishment of the new Northern Ireland Executive. This acute uncertainty followed by a delicate step-by-step sequence of events created a highly charged atmosphere – particularly around the sharing out of ministerial responsibilities between the various political parties and the key positions on the relevant supporting or overseeing committees. The Sinn Féin choice of the Education portfolio for Martin McGuinness was the *bombe surprise* in the carefully choreographed process. The surprise was quickly reinforced by his early statements in a flurry of interviews that he was keen to see more Irish language being taught, that he was utterly opposed to the 11 plus selection examinations and that he supported integration of schools. Education was suddenly guaranteed political and public attention.

Reactions to the McGuinness appointment – ranging from general surprise to absolute outrage – perhaps understandably focused on the personality and his political history rather than the significance of the choice of ministry. A seemingly orchestrated pattern of protests by school pupils – supported each time by a vociferous Democratic Unionist Party (DUP) representative – which, while reflecting the intensity of reaction to the political persona, also served to highlight how politically charged issues concerning school curriculum can be in Northern Ireland.[2] This chapter will look at the issues surrounding the expansion of integrated education, examine some of the assumptions underlying the Good Friday statement and consider what contribution education might realistically make towards the process of peace building and reconciliation.

Background

Housing and education – as the two primary areas where socio-political separation is most immediate in its impact on people's daily life – reflect the deep and persistent divisions within the Northern Ireland community. Currently, 95 per cent of the school-age population attend schools which are identified as belonging to one 'side' or the other.[3] While few would claim segregated schooling was responsible for social conflict, many have questioned how much educational separation has reinforced division and wondered to what extent shared or mixed education might help in overcoming it. The high response in repeated opinion polls supporting the principle of integrated or mixed education suggests that there is a widely held feeling that separate schools are not conducive to overcoming community division, but habit – perhaps masking feelings of insecurity or lack of trust – until now has mitigated in favour of continuing with what is familiar, tried and true within the immediate community.[4] Over the years there has accumulated an extensive body of research on the issue;[5] there have also been various policy initiatives ranging from reform of the curriculum to cross-community inter-school links. But by far the most radical, so far, has been the development of planned integrated schools.

From the founding of the Northern Ireland state, political tension along with the potential for conflict was present between the two sections of the community. The minority Catholic nationalist and majority Protestant unionist groups, each jealously guarding their political and religious distinctiveness, held clearly defined and conflicting agendas.[6] This fundamental separation of the population into two communities has been well documented and continued with little alteration, reflected at all levels, most notably in separate schools[7] and in segregated residential patterns.[8] The link between schools attended and an individual's 'religious' or community identity was such that asking which school an individual had attended was sufficient to identify a person without referring directly to their religion – 'Protestant' if a state ('controlled') school and Catholic if a Catholic church ('maintained') school. This practice of labelling was so widely used for discrimination by employers[9] that it was adopted as the basis for anti-discrimination monitoring. The Fair Employment Commission categorisation of individuals as 'Catholic' or 'Protestant' (for the purpose of monitoring employment ratios) is now based on which primary school was attended. From the beginning, Northern Ireland state schools – originally intended to be integrated (religiously mixed) – were viewed with deep suspicion by the nationalist community as an attempt to assimilate their young into the Unionist state. The parallel school system which developed became guarantor to each side of the community for their own distinctive identity.[10]

With the development of the civil rights movement and the subsequent political violence, the number and variety of analysts examining Northern Ireland and its 'troubles' proliferated. Mainstream academic explanations for the causes of the conflict have fallen broadly into three categories: socio-economic inequalities; differing cultural and political identities; and the deep historical religious division.

While putting a stop to violence and related security issues became the over-whelming political priority for the British government at Westminster, it was recognised that a whole range of economic and social issues needed to be addressed, particularly relating to discrimination in employment and housing. At the same time, ways of managing the division and attempting to bridge the gap between the two sides of the community needed to be found. James Callaghan, as early as 1969, made the suggestion that 'there should be a beginning to integration of education'.[11] He saw it as an incremental long term process, starting perhaps with various sixth forms coming together to discuss civic affairs, followed up by joint extra-mural activities, and gradually extending the programme to bring together younger age groups. His suggestion was rejected by Cardinal Conway, who dismissed integra-tion of education as merely ' a marginal factor'. In the intervening thirty years, the official position of the Catholic bishops has not changed significantly.

Integrated education

Planned integrated schools[12] in Northern Ireland are a relatively recent pheno-menon. The first twelve integrated schools, all established during the 1980s, were set up by parent groups and independently funded with substantial help from major charitable foundations and trusts, most notably the Joseph Rowntree Charitable Trust and the Nuffield Foundation. In 1989, Brian Mawhinney, then minister for education in Northern Ireland, included provision for integrated education in the education reform legislation. This was to be only where sufficient parent demand was shown to exist, but it allowed the newly formed voluntary organisation, the Northern Ireland Council for Integrated Education (NICIE), to actively encourage and support parent groups who wanted to establish integrated schools. The legis-lation also permitted existing schools to opt for integrated status. Ministerial approval for a change of status was subject to there being sufficient parental support as indicated by a ballot, backed up by credible potential enrolments from both sides of the community, substantial enough over a period of five years to make the trans-formation to integrated status meaningful. The legislative basis for an integrated school was loosely defined as one being likely to attract 'reasonable numbers' of both Catholics and Protestants which has subsequently been defined by the Department of Education, Northern Ireland (DENI) as a 30 per cent minimum enrolment from whichever side of the community forms the minority within a particular school. The integrated schools themselves adhere to a far more specific set of principles, including a commitment to all-ability schools at secondary level.[13]

Since 1990 and the enabling legislation, the number of integrated schools has rapidly increased, until at the time of writing there are forty-five recognised integrated schools, with more in the process of development. This rate of develop-ment, while impressive, represents provision for barely 4 per cent of the total school population. It also represents a substantial investment of resources during a period when stringent financial controls and cutbacks have been the perceived norm. This has given rise to claims from opponents that integrated schools have been treated more favourably than other schools, although the schools have been rigorously monitored by DENI and much of the capital development has been made possible by bank loans and charitable support through the Integrated Education Fund (IEF).[14] From the integrated schools' perspective, the situation has appeared very different, with the opening of each school representing a serious struggle to provide suitable accommodation,[15] in order to obtain both the necessary initial funding and the vital imprimata of ministerial and DENI approval. The integrated education movement as represented by NICIE and the IEF have the stated goal of making integrated school provision available for 10 per cent of the Northern Ireland school population by 2010. Both organisations believe this is the minimum level necessary to make integrated schools at both primary and secondary level available as a real option throughout Northern Ireland. Recently several new integrated schools have been forced to open without any government funding in the face of stringent DENI requirements. In 1994 the IEF in a review of the projected growth of integrated schools[16] identified three potential models for development:

1   *containment* – allowing for minimum growth and restricting the opening of integrated schools to one primary and one second-level school per year for five years;
2   *reactive* – in which NICIE simply responded to parental demand known at the time amounting to perhaps six primary and seven second-level schools over a five-year period;
3   *proactive* – where NICIE would actively stimulate demand for new schools amongst parent groups resulting in a potential twenty-two primary and thirteen second-level schools over a five-year period.

The capital costs attached to the three models ranged from £49.9 million for the containment model to £79.8 million for the proactive programme. The actual school developments for the five-year period 1994–98 amounted to five primary schools and ten second-level schools, matching the containment model at primary school level but exceeding the reactive model at secondary school level. As second-level schools are considerably more expensive to establish, the financial burden of development is far greater. DENI, nervous of the financial scale and slightly unpredictable element of integrated new school development, became keen to focus on the transformation of existing schools to integrated status.

Paradoxically, the rate of school development also assumes that the number of integrated school places, while continuing to increase, will still remain less than the level of demand. The resulting over-subscription then permits the continuance of a mixed enrolment, with enough pupils from both sides of the community to maintain cross-community confidence in the integrated nature of the school in question.[17] The integrated education supporters have always campaigned on the basis that integrated education was something which should be available by right as a real choice – alongside the traditional Catholic and state Protestant systems – not as a replacement. However, the reliance on over-subscription to maintain some form of religious balance in the enrolment carries an inbuilt exclusion factor with the implicit acceptance that not everyone can attend an integrated school who might wish to. This creates an uneasy tension alongside the aspiration that integrated education should be available to all as a basic right; a conundrum which has largely been created by the open enrolment legislation and exacerbated in some areas by Education Board refusals to permit the schools to increase their intakes.

The location of new integrated schools has in every case, been a sensitive issue. The sites chosen have been often a compromise between where suitable land was available and an array of other considerations such as the acceptability of a particular location to all sides of the community. In general, there has been an attempt to build on the edge of a town in an area where new housing was being developed rather than close to existing schools. There is, however, a finite number of children of school age and teachers, so an element of redistribution and change affecting controlled and maintained schools is unavoidable.

This issue is central to the opposition to planned integrated schools, particularly as voiced by the teachers' union UTU (Ulster Teachers' Union). Concern has also been expressed by representatives from both the maintained and the controlled sectors that the very act of developing integrated schools implied that both the Catholic maintained and the Protestant controlled schools were sectarian. A further criticism has been that the 'creaming off' of the more moderate or liberal parents and pupils by the integrated schools was likely to leave the Catholic and Protestant systems more polarised and divided than they were originally (an argument which might just as equally be levelled at the grammar school system for different reasons). More recently, DUP Assembly member Iris Robinson expressed yet another fear: that transformation of existing schools to integrated status was threatening to leave the Protestant community without any schools to call their own.[18] This echoes the dilemma faced by the Church of Ireland and Presbyterian Transferor[19] representatives, namely how to protect their interests without appearing sectarian. In the interests of parity, DENI has recognised the Transferor Representatives Council for representation along with the Council for Catholic Maintained Schools (CCMS) on consultative committees such as the working parties set up to consider the future development of integrated education and 'Education for Mutual Understanding' following the Good Friday Agreement.

The emergence of integrated schools, often in the face of fierce opposition has, it seems, stimulated the maintained and controlled school systems into participating in other initiatives within the cross-community contact scheme or the joint churches' organisation YouthLink – designed to bring the young people of both systems into contact out of school, but within a framework defined by both the Catholic and Protestant churches. Whatever the merits of the various arguments, the issue still remains as to what can be done more generally to encourage positive interaction not just between children and young people, but between people from all sections of the Northern Ireland community. This is a question which encompasses adult and further education and not simply the formal school system. Supporters of planned integrated schools would suggest that they go a long way towards offering this level of interaction, with the close involvement of parents within the schools, the parent councils and the cross-community composition of pupil enrolments, teaching and ancillary staff as well as governing bodies and all committee structures.

The basic premise of the planned integrated schools themselves – that integration should be available as a choice and not imposed – combined with the demography of Northern Ireland (the population is not equally or evenly distributed) – means integrating education in this formal sense cannot be the only educational strategy to overcome the religious and political division within the education system. The need for some educational programme to contribute towards improving community relations which could be delivered irrespective of which or what type of school an individual attended, has been the impetus for various curriculum initiatives and cross-community contact schemes. The 1989 education reform legislation included 'Education for Mutual Understanding'[20] and 'Cultural Heritage' themes within the prescribed Northern Ireland Core Curriculum (NICC). These were intended to open up the curriculum to include perspectives and content belonging to the 'other' tradition within the community and to encourage inter-school links. The striking limitation of this well-meaning approach was the potential for the creation and reinforcement of cultural and religious stereotypes,[21] along with the total lack of recognition for people within Northern Ireland society who did not fit into the 'Catholic/nationalist' and 'Protestant/unionist' cultural slots, most notably, for example, members of the substantial Chinese community. Furthermore, positive inter-group contact and collaboration could not be achieved by coercion: therefore, excellent and innovative though many school links were, involvement in inter-school links and cross-community contact schemes was entirely voluntary. The successful projects were completely reliant on the heroic efforts of a few individuals, usually operating on limited budgets and often dependent on support and assistance from outside community and voluntary workers. The programme was only as effective as the teachers and the individuals involved chose, or were able, to make it.[22] The lack of provision for a comprehensive teacher training programme in community relations was a serious flaw in the Education Reform Order, particularly as 'Education for Mutual Understanding' and 'Cultural Heritage' were compulsory cross-curricular themes which were supposed to filter through all subject areas. Often teachers who had volunteered for 'Education for Mutual Understanding' inset courses found themselves designated the 'Education for Mutual Understanding' 'person' on the staff, and were left with a responsibility for which many felt ill prepared and lacking in confidence, often in schools where the climate was at best indifferent and at worst hostile. While the level of contact projects has increased quite considerably particularly since 1994,[23] it has been recognised that 'Education for Mutual Understanding' as a curriculum area needed to be reviewed, particularly in the light of the Belfast Agreement.

The Belfast Agreement

'An essential aspect of the reconciliation process is the promotion of a culture of tolerance at every level of society and includes initiatives to facilitate and encourage integrated education and mixed housing.'[24]

In its emphasis on the need for an active approach to the process of reconciliation, the Agreement placed an implicit responsibility on all public and governmental bodies to ensure that their policies would support and contribute towards the creation of a culture of tolerance.

In response to the Belfast Agreement statement on the reconciliation process and the particular reference to encouraging integrated education, the Department of Education established a working party to 'consider ways of assisting the further development of the integrated school sector while taking account of the interests of other schools'. The working party numbering twelve members – only four of which represented the integrated education sector – started by rejecting the terms of reference as being 'too narrow'. The Progress Report, published in November 1998, revised the terms of reference and proposed the establishment of a separate working group to consider how a 'more coherent strategy for a pluralist society' could be developed.[25] In addition to discussion of suitable strategies for school development and the relative cost considerations of 'new' versus 'transformed'[26] integrated schools, the Report clearly highlighted the tension between 'parental choice' and 'prudent financial planning' and value for money considerations ('VFM concerns'). The Report also recognised that strategic planning for school provision had previously been carried out by the Education and Library Boards (local education authorities) and the CCMS which did not take into account any potential demand for an integrated, Irish medium form of education or any other forms of education. The suggestion was also made in the Report that the Boards 'should first examine the opportunity for establishing controlled integrated schools, before pursuing any other controlled option' in areas where major new housing was being developed. Interestingly, the CCMS recorded that they 'are content that the current methodologies for assessing school needs within the maintained sector are appropriate'.[27] The 'methodology' referred to is the use of baptismal certificates as a means of calculating future enrolment numbers. However, in areas where an integrated primary school is available, some of these children are being enrolled by their parents for the integrated school as well as being included by the parish in the numbers for the church school, creating an element of double counting which favours the CCMS in its projections. The Report, which many in the integrated education lobby had hoped would result in tangible improvements for the development of integrated schools in the spirit of the Belfast Agreement, was rather undermined by the fact that the proposal to DENI for Ulidia Integrated College at Whitehead in East Antrim had been turned down yet again. The College, already in its second year, was still entirely dependent on charitable funding.

In early 1999 a separate Working Group on the Strategic Promotion of Education for Mutual Understanding was established with a much wider membership. The resulting consultative report, 'Towards a Culture of Tolerance: Education for Diversity', published in September 1999 as a consultative document, focused exclusively on the education service, teachers and schools. The emphasis on 'pluralism' and segmented educational provision and interests as represented by the CCMS and the Transferor Representatives Council (representing the Church of Ireland and other Protestant churches as stakeholders in the state 'controlled' system) reflects the broader political reality of power blocks and checks and balances as seen in the Assembly. Parents are not mentioned at all and no suggestion emerges that the churches could perhaps look at the possibility of developing some form of shared integrated church school. Revd Professor Enda McDonough, speaking in Belfast,[28] suggested that perhaps the time had come for the churches to look at such a possibility. The fact that the Church of Ireland and Catholic, Presbyterian and Methodist Churches were able to agree a common Religious Education curriculum for Northern Ireland as part of the educational reforms in 1990, would indicate that shared church schools need not be out of the question on religious grounds. Furthermore, a successful model already exists in England where more than a decade ago, falling enrolments threatened the viability of church schools in some areas. Faced with the need to close down their respective schools, some of the Catholic and Church of England bishops there found it possible to join forces, successfully establishing shared schools in several places.[29]

In the longer term, particularly in Northern Ireland's rural areas, a shared school model might offer a solution to the trustees and transferor governors of Catholic and Protestant small schools struggling with falling enrolments and offer a felicitous step towards meeting the still growing parental demand for integrated education. At primary school level, establishing shared nursery or pre-school provision already offers a valuable opportunity for the first step – a suggestion which did receive a mention in the earlier 'Towards a Culture of Tolerance' Report. A proactive move such as this, accompanied by a joint demand for enabling legislation from the CCMS and the Transferor Representatives Council, would be a positive response to the lack of sufficient integrated school places. This would be particularly the case in the Western Education Board area where in 1999, the Board refused to allow the existing integrated schools to increase their enrolments because of the 'threat' they presented to other schools in the area. The NICIE newsletter in June 1999, reporting on the crisis of demand for integrated places far exceeding availability, estimated a shortfall of approximately 1,000 school places, ascribing the scale of the problem to a combination of ever-increasing parental demand combined with a slowing down of new integrated and transformation school developments. The situation was being further exacerbated by the opposition from some Education Boards and District Councils to proposals from the existing integrated schools to increase their enrolments. This was a less than encouraging situation. The recommendations from the 1998 'Towards a Culture of Tolerance'

Report had been firmly pushing the integrated education supporters to look to the Education Boards for the main thrust of future development through either new controlled integrated schools or the transformation of existing controlled schools. Combined with rejection of the Ulidia College proposal by the minister John McFaul some began to wonder whether the situation would become even more difficult for integrated schools under devolved government.

Education policy has been subject to the same over-arching policy guidelines as policy in all other Northern Ireland government departments and public bodies – Policy Appraisal and Fair Treatment (PAFT) and Targeting Social Need (TSN) being the two key initiatives which influence policy decisions and the distribution of resources. While PAFT considerations could be said to protect the interests of the integrated education sector against negative discrimination, TSN criteria dictate priorities for the direction of funding, particularly for capital development. In this context integrated schools are a tiny percentage and less likely to be considered eligible for priority consideration. The Irish medium schools while favoured by the new minister are also quite contentious and any attempt to treat them more advantageously will be rigorously scrutinised by the education committee. The principles behind PAFT and TSN are likely to provide policy continuity while the devolved government establishes its own agenda and reviews policy. The Queen's University research report on the impact of the 11 plus will be one of the first policy issues to be addressed, which will offer the minister and the education committee an opportunity to grapple with a contentious issue which crosses the constitutional and religious divide. The proposed 'Citizenship' curriculum will be another education issue which is likely to test the consensus process.

In spring 1999 the Curriculum, Examination and Assessment Council (CEAC) launched a pilot social, civic and political education programme involving twenty-five secondary schools. Currently the Citizenship Foundation in conjunction with the University of Ulster is drafting curriculum modules for 11 to 13-year-old pupils (Key Stage 3) and supporting teacher training programmes. In parallel, the BBC (Northern Ireland) has produced a series of programmes for schools titled 'Citizenship 2000'. This is in advance of the proposed UK 'Education for Citizenship' curriculum scheduled for 2002, and in keeping with recent curriculum development in the Republic of Ireland. Themes such as human rights, pluralism, democracy, social inclusion and justice form the core. The question though, is how effective can such programmes be if they are simply grafted on to the existing curriculum? Furthermore, how effectively can concepts such as 'parity of esteem', social inclusiveness and pluralism be transmitted within a segregated system? The 'Education for Mutual Understanding' and cross-community contact schemes have had some success but greater inter-school collaboration and use of focus groups will be necessary to give meaning and reality to curriculum developments. In isolation, teaching is vulnerable to 'interpretation' or simply the repetition of fine-sounding platitudes.

Martin McGuinness on taking up his ministerial post was quick to state his commitment to work for all sections of the community. In reality, the mechanisms of the new Assembly and its elaborate committee structures[30] with the various structural and procedural checks and balances have been created to make the introduction of sudden radical policy change in any area highly unlikely. Indeed the structure is designed to ensure that the new ministers in all departments will have to work hard within the committee structure, persuading and negotiating all the way, to arrive at any agreement on policy, be it consensual or by straightforward majority vote. McGuinness – who in his own words 'failed with flying colours' and left school at the age of 15 – knows at first hand the cost of being subjected to an education system which is still dominated by the 11 plus selection examination. Educational debates aside, the continuing selection of pupils for grammar school by means of the qualifying examination has ensured that the majority of secondary school pupils already segregated by religious background have been further subdivided. McGuinness, described by Edward Daly, the retired Catholic bishop from Derry, as ' a good father, a good husband and a strong churchgoer', was clear in the flurry of interviews following his appointment what his approach would be. Feeling in his own words well qualified for his new job after thirty years of 'the political education of a lifetime', he was keen to reassure his political opponents of his integrity and sense of responsibility.

> The reality is that the community I come from has been discriminated against for many years and the last thing we want to do … is turn round and treat other sections of our community in the way that we were treated. This is about children, not about unionism, nationalism, loyalism, republicanism. It's about children – our greatest resource, how we nurture them, care for them, protect them and primarily how we educate them.[31]

In another interview on the BBC 'Today' programme, he said he was 'totally and utterly opposed' to children of that age being put through the trauma of the 11 plus exam, that he favoured more integration of schools and was keen to see an increase in the teaching of the Irish language. The chairman of the Assembly education committee, Danny Kennedy (UUP), speaking on the BBC 'Talkback' programme, promised that the education committee would 'scrutinise all aspects of education policy. No minister is able to act independently or achieve their own particular political agenda.'

In this context the statement contained in the Belfast Agreement concerning the reconciliation process and the promotion of a culture of tolerance would appear to apply as much to the political process within the committee as to any policy as to what should happen in Northern Ireland's schools. The possibility that Sammy Wilson (DUP) and committee deputy chairman, might be faced with the choice of whether to support McGuinness on an issue such as abolishing the selection process (something Wilson has long advocated) or to oppose him as a matter of party principle is perhaps where the real potential for significant change lies.

Conclusion

After thirty years of civil strife, despite the emergence of a multitude of grassroot community groups and the development of government-sponsored initiatives designed to encourage cross-community contact and involvement from the late 1980s onwards,[32] residential segregation is greater than ever. Furthermore, the intimidation and violence which has been continuing since the signing of the Agreement, while condemned by the majority of people within Northern Ireland, does reflect the intensity and pervasive character of what has been labelled as the 'culture of violence' – a blanket term which covers sectarian intimidation and violence as well as the multitude of punishment attacks and threats. Since the official ceasefires the level of violence against school-boys from as young as 12 to 18 years old, has become much more apparent.[33] This highlights the critical distinction between an agreement to make peace and the much longer process of making peace. These young people are the very people who will ultimately be responsible for the success or failure of the process. The peace process will not immediately bring prosperity to all the families of children growing up in poverty (approximately one child in three according to Democratic Dialogue[34]), nor is it likely to rapidly and significantly reduce unemployment. With 40 per cent of the population under the age of 24[35] and 27 per cent of unemployed males being under 25 there is an urgent need for peace to be translated into meaningful terms. On the immediate level peace should mean personal security, but it will need to translate into a share in the economic development, a justice system based on a code of civil rights, and an effective cross-community police force which enjoys the support and confidence of all sections of the community.

It is in this context that education in Northern Ireland has to make its contribution to peace building. New curriculum content, conflict resolution workshops, more cross-community contact – all these can make a useful contribution. With a full-scale programme of professional development for teachers and supporting resources, much can be achieved over time. However, the most valuable initiative may be to use a consultative process with school, youth and community groups, asking them what they and others envisage 'peace' to be and how they see a culture of reconciliation and tolerance being developed. Further initiatives emerging from this process could involve the young people themselves both as part of the decision-making process and as participants. Young people need to believe that they can contribute to the peace development process and that it includes them in a brave new future.

The responsibility now rests with local politicians who will be held accountable. Martin McGuinness on his appointment as minister stressed that he was there to work for all communities. His ability to win the respect and confidence of people previously deeply suspicious or fearful of him, will be one of the key factors contributing to how successful the creation of any 'culture of tolerance' may be. The Minister began 2000 with an official visit to the offices of NICIE. While he was there he announced conditional approval for the proposals for both Ulidia College and the Millennium Integrated Primary School (Carryduff) which are due to open in September 2000. In his statement accompanying the announcement the Minister reiterated that his guiding principles would be equality, choice, accessibility and excellence. He went on to say:

> This is further evidence of the growing support for the development of the integrated sector. Such decisions are not taken lightly as new schools involve a very substantial investment of scarce capital resources. Although my Department will continue to support robust proposals for new integrated schools … the transformation of existing schools to integrated status must continue to be the most practical and affordable option for extending integrated education.[36]

He concluded:

> While I readily acknowledge that integrated education has an important contribution to make to the development of pluralism in our society, I must pay tribute to the valuable role played by schools in the mainstream sectors in promoting mutual understanding and tolerance. Over the next few months I will be considering how all schools can be supported and reinforced in their work in promoting a culture of tolerance and a respect for diversity.'

Pluralism and diversity are the key words which Northern Ireland politicians use freely. However, they are not necessarily concepts which sit easily with integration. In the short term 'reconciliation' would seem to waver between definitions. In the long term it may be possible to envisage Northern Ireland people united in harmony, in the medium term it is feasible that estranged members of the Northern Ireland community will win one another over to friendly terms, but for the immediate future the various antagonists are still – in the last analysis – antagonists. Reconciliation can mean many things, as the language development element of the Northern Ireland core curriculum may need to teach.

Notes

1 Senator George Mitchell returned to Northern Ireland in September 1999 to carry out a detailed review of the Belfast Agreement with all the parties involved to find a way forward towards the implementation of the Northern Ireland Executive alongside a solution to the decommissioning issue, thus breaking the stalemate into which the political process had become locked.

2 The protestors were preempting any suggestion that they should be compelled to learn the Irish language or play sports such as camogie (a game played in Catholic schools).

3 Catholic parents are encouraged to send their children to Catholic maintained schools (almost all of which are now fully state funded). The majority of Protestant parents usually send their children to state schools controlled by the area Education and Library Boards (the equivalent of local education authorities). The terms 'Catholic' and 'Protestant' continue to be widely used in Northern Ireland to describe people's community and cultural background, often being synonymous with political identity and not necessarily an indication of any specific religious affiliation.

4 Surveys have shown a high percentage in favour of integrated education being available, but

most notably in the survey for SACHR in 1990. A substantial percentage, while agreeable in principle, did not think they or their family would avail of an integrated option.

5 J. Darby, D. Murray, D. Batts, S. Dunn, S. Farren and J. Harris, *Education and Community in Northern Ireland: Schools Apart?* (Coleraine, University of Ulster, 1977); J. Darby and S. Dunn, 'Segregated Schools: The Research Evidence' in R. D. Osborne, R. J. Cormack and R. L. Miller (eds), *Education and Policy in Northern Ireland* (Belfast, Policy Research Institute, Queen's University of Belfast and The University of Ulster, 1987); S. Dunn, 'The Role of Education in the Northern Ireland Conflict', *Oxford Review of Education*, 12(3), pp. 233–42. For a comprehensive guide to the literature see S. Dunn, *Education and the Conflict in the Northern Ireland Conflict* (Coleraine, Centre for the Study of Conflict, 1986) and L. Abbott, S. Dunn and V. Morgan, *Integrated Education in Northern Ireland: an analytical literature review*, DENI Research Report Series No. 15, 1999.

6 See John Whyte, *Interpreting Northern Ireland* (Oxford, Clarendon, 1990); see also Denis P. Barritt and Charles F. Carter, *The Northern Ireland Problem: A study in group relations* (Oxford, Oxford University Press, 1962) pp. 77–92 which identifies education as a source of inter-group friction.

7 The state controlled and largely Protestant schools and the Catholic maintained system, running in parallel, is further segregated more or less on a social class basis as a result of the selection of pupils at the age of 11 for grammar school places.

8 See Richard Breen and Paula Devine, 'Segmentation and the Social Structure' in Paul Mitchell and Rick Wilford (eds) *Politics in Northern Ireland* (Oxford, Westview Press and PSAI, 1999) pp. 54–6. A. M. Gallagher, R. D. Osborne and R. J. Cormack, *Fair Shares! Employment, Unemployment and Economic Status* (Belfast, Fair Employment Commission, 1994) p. 61.

9 Martin McGuinness experienced this discrimination when he applied to a Protestant-owned garage to train as a mechanic. Instead he became a butcher's boy for a Catholic butcher. Profile, *The Sunday Times*, 5 December 1999.

10 See Sean Farren, *The Politics of Irish Education 1920–65* (Belfast, Institute of Irish Studies, Queen's University of Belfast, 1995), a seminal study of this process. The use of 'parallel' here should be taken to mean dual track, as the funding patterns were different and not equal.

11 James Callaghan, *A House Divided: The dilemma of Northern Ireland* (London, Collins, 1973) p. 79.

12 The first integrated school was Lagan College established in 1981, by All Children Together.

13 The NICIE Statement of Principles.

14 The IEF was established in 1992 (with money from the European Union Structural Funds, DENI, the Nuffield Foundation and the Joseph Rowntree Charitable Trust), to provide a financial foundation for the development and growth of integrated education.

15 The definition of what is 'suitable' as premises for a new integrated school has been one of the major issues for new school development, in that to obtain ministerial approval for a proposal, accommodation had to be adequate for the delivery of the common curriculum. They also have to meet DENI building branch requirements if the buildings are eventually to be considered eligible for capital grant. As most of the schools have buildings which have been bought with bank loans the payment of a grant is essential.

16 See *Towards a Culture of Tolerance: Integrating Education*, 1998 pp. 7–11 and *Ten Year Development Plan*, IEF, 1998 for a full discussion.

17 The issue of balance in enrolments has been one of the founding principles. See the Northern Ireland Council's *Statement of Principles* for the details and A. E. C. W. Spencer, 'Arguments for an Integrated School System' in Osborne, Cormack and Miller, *Education and Policy in Northern Ireland* for a complete outline of the thinking and research which provided the framework for the development of planned integrated schools.

18 Iris Robinson quoted in *The Star*, 18 June 1999, 'Parents Express Opposition to Suggestion of Status Change'.

19 The majority of Protestant church controlled schools transferred to the new Northern Ireland state school system immediately following the partition of Ireland. In return for

ceding control to the state the churches (mainly Church of Ireland and Presbyterian) were given transferor rights of representation on the management committees of the schools. Hence the transferor representatives are representative of the Protestant churches' interests in education.

20 For a detailed bibliography and other material on 'Education for Mutual Understanding' see the CAIN website http://cain.ulst.ac.uk/issues/education/education.htm.

21 A danger which was implicitly recognised by the authors of the project 'Create Not Learned Monsters'; see *Education for Mutual Understanding: A Guide* (Belfast, Northern Ireland Council for Educational Development, 1988) p. 11.

22 See A. Smith and A. Robinson, *Education for Mutual Undestanding: The Initial Statutory Years* (Coleraine, University of Ulster, 1996).

23 DENI estimate approximately 50 per cent of the school-age population are involved in either school or youth group originated cross-community contact schemes, although this figure may contain an element of double counting.

24 Strand Three, Section 13, Belfast Agreement (otherwise known as the Good Friday Agreement), see Appendix 2 of this book.

25 'Towards a Culture of Tolerance: Integrating Education. Working Party Progress Report', DENI, November 1998, p. 1.

26 The transformed integrated schools are existing schools with some element of mixed religious enrolment where the parents have voted to change the school to integrated status. The school then goes through a development process involving amongst other things increasing the religious 'mix' of the new intake in successive years.

27 'Towards a Culture of Tolerance', p. 10.

28 Enda McDonough speaking on BBC 'Good Morning Ulster', 23 April 1999.

29 St Bede's, Redhill was the first joint church school and founding member of the 'Educate Together' association.

30 Full details of the Northern Ireland Assembly and its committees can be found at http://www.ni-assembly.gov.uk.

31 *Irish News*, 1 December 1999.

32 The Cross-community Contact Scheme (DENI) and the founding of the Community Relations Council are two of the most notable examples.

33 'Men Save Schoolboy From Assault by Sectarian Thugs', *Irish News*, 2 September 1999, 'Paramilitary Beatings Put 189 Children in Hospital', *The Times*, 17 September 1999: 'It beggars belief … that the communities in which they live [victims of beatings] appear to accept such behaviour as part of life to the extent that some people have become blasé about it', Lawrence Rocke, senior consultant surgeon, Royal Victoria Hospital, Belfast.

34 *Politics: The Next Generation*, Report No. 6 (Belfast, Democratic Dialogue, 1997).

35 *Annual Abstract of Statistics, 16*, Belfast (Northern Ireland Statistics and Research Agency, 1998). Note: This percentage is based on 1996 figures.

36 DENI Press Release 7 January 2000

PART V
International and comparative dimensions

13

From Anglo-Irish to British–Irish relations

PAUL GILLESPIE

Four themes dominate relations between Britain and Ireland from 1969 to 1999. There was, first of all, a decisive shift from dependence to interdependence between the Republic of Ireland and the UK. Their relationship became more equal, despite the evident continuing asymmetries of size and power. This transformation is best understood as a process of internationalisation within the context of the EU and relations with the US – the second major theme. Without that there would not have been the confidence to tackle the transition from unity to stability based on inclusion and consent as the primary focus of the republic's policy towards Northern Ireland, the third theme. This culminated in the Belfast Agreement and is closely related to the normalisation of relations between Britain and Ireland, the fourth theme. It is occurring, crucially, at a time when the larger island is undergoing its own process of constitutional change, 'fundamental alterations in the arrangements of the UK, which amount to a reshaping of the British state'.[1] The Belfast Agreement directly involves Ireland in this historic process through the link-ups it proposes with devolved governments elsewhere in the UK.[2]

Taken together these changes may be described as a transition from Anglo-Irish to British–Irish relations.[3] Such is the argument of this chapter. First it looks critically at Anglo-Irish relations as conventionally described and written about; it goes on to examine each of these four themes in turn, with particular reference to the Northern Ireland peace process. This is not, therefore, a chronological narrative of Anglo-Irish diplomatic relations over these thirty years but a thematic commentary on them in the light of the peace process and the changing relations between Britain and Ireland.

Anglo-Irish relations

Anglo-Irish relations have been described as a 'label of convenience which confuses two distinctions, the first between nationalities and the second between geographical entities'.[4] The fact that both the nationalities involved in Anglo-Irish relations are themselves undergoing changes of identity also transforms the geographical relations between Britain and Ireland and should also change the terminology used to describe them. Scotland and Wales are brought into the foreground by devolution and European regionalism, as well as being promised a potentially fruitful new set of identities by developing their relations with Ireland through the British–Irish Council. The very reduction of the English domination of Britain after the end of empire and Cold War and the emergence of an Anglo-British question as it is constitutionally rearranged[5] can facilitate the resolution of traditional British–Irish quarrels – partly by offering dual or multiple identities as the Belfast Agreement does and as is central to Scottish and Welsh relations with England.[6] Historically and geographically Irish nationalism's quarrel was more with south-east England and its imperial governing class than with the British peoples over whom it ruled. Subliminally the term 'Anglo-Irish' recalls the Anglo-Irish ascendancy which was so integrated with that discredited socio-geographical system – 'it tends to imply a residual colonialism which most modern Irish writers would repudiate'.[7] It should perhaps be subjected to a critique similar to that applied to 'Anglo-Irish literature' in recent years.[8]

Traditionally Anglo-Irish relations have taken for granted that the two nationalities in question were the English and the Irish before and after the Treaty settlement. This presumption about nationalities made sense so long as the inherently ambiguous relationship between Englishness and Britishness was resolved practically by the unproblematic concentration of political power in London, Westminster and Whitehall. Such centralisation was a function of imperial rule and the development of the twentieth century big state through war, welfare, economic production and regulation. Inter-state relations between independent Ireland and the United Kingdom of Great Britain and Northern Ireland were automatically conceived as involving contact between the British and Irish governments in London and Dublin. That remains true despite the changing international context within which Britain now finds itself after the end of empire and Cold War, which froze many of its political structures in a centralist mode.[9]

Relations between Britain and Ireland in the years 1922–69 must, therefore, be put in the context of a British state whose structure and nature was for the most part taken for granted, even as argument about what it should do, and how the resources it could command should be distributed, dominated British politics. This coincided pretty well exactly with one of the principal motivations of British policy with regard to Ireland: the desire to ensure that the Treaty settlement removed the Irish Question from domestic British politics – 'disengagement was the objective and for the better part of a half century, from 1922 to 1969 ... was achieved to an extent that would have seemed inconceivable before the Great War';[10] Ireland 'was best managed with a barge pole'.[11] Hence the shocking realisation in 1969 that direct involvement would reintroduce Northern Irish affairs centrally to Westminster politics.[12] After Direct Rule was introduced in 1972 a great deal more parliamentary and political time has been taken up by Irish issues. One can plainly see in several of Mr Blair's comments a desire to see that reduced to more normal proportions in order to concentrate on other issues – including the development of closer relations with the republic in the context of the EU. As he put it in his speech to the Oireachtas: 'Northern Ireland is now helping to bring us together. But I do not believe Northern Ireland can or should any longer define the relationship between us. Our common interests, what we can achieve together, go much, much wider than that.'[13]

Anglo-Irish relations in the period 1922–69 have been studied extensively and there are a number of outstanding diplomatic and political histories, concentrating on inter-state relations conducted relatively secretively at the highest levels of government. The main themes include the development of Dominion status, the economic war, neutrality and the Second World War and the crisis leading to the declaration of the republic in 1949.[14] There are also fine studies of Anglo-Irish relations since 1969[15] and a flow of memoirs and autobiographies[16] – especially on the British side. But there are surprisingly few attempts to theorise or compare the relationship.[17] From the perspective of British–Irish relations – or, in the Hegelian phrase coined by Brian Lenihan and first inserted in the 8 December 1980 statement following the Thatcher–Haughey talks, the 'totality of relationships in these islands' – the narrow focus of this literature is unsatisfactory. It leaves too little room for the extensive social, economic and cultural interaction that continued and deepened after independence, creating one of the most intimate relationships between neighbouring states anywhere in the world. This is more apparent after the Belfast Agreement's definition of the British–Irish Council's task: 'to promote the harmonious and mutually beneficial development of the totality of relationships among the peoples of these islands'.

The extent to which the relationship continues to be dependent, post-colonial and politically contested obviously affects this literature and is a central concern of the debate on historical revisionism.[18] That debate has broadened studies of British–Irish relations insofar as they are intended to give a comprehensive account of how the peoples of the two islands relate to one another. But it also highlights their scattered disciplinary nature, subdivided between history,[19] economics,[20] sociology,[21] politics,[22] constitutional law,[23] international relations[24] and literary and critical studies.[25] With some notable exceptions, such as the volume edited by P. J. Drudy in 1986[26] there has been little attempt to bring them together. It was, extraordinarily, not until 1999 that an Institute for British–Irish Studies with a wide brief to examine the relationship was set up in an Irish university, University College, Dublin, despite the proliferation of Irish studies courses throughout the English-speaking world and beyond it. But this is probably symptomatic of a post-colonial dependence on Britain and its intellectual mindsets which took that relationship and those assumptions so much for granted.[27] Thus it has been precisely the relative escape from Anglocentricity roughly over the period 1969–99 that has enabled a more comprehensive approach to emerge in everyday life as well as in policy-making, the media and the academy – a point that Hegel would have appreciated.

From dependence to interdependence

When studying relations between Britain and Ireland it helps if one draws a distinction between independence and sovereignty. While British governments have traditionally been preoccupied with territorial sovereignty in the EEC/EU context, Irish governments have been readier to recognise that independence can be enhanced by pooling it.[28] Thus sovereignty is of little use if its exercise inhibits the pursuit of influence in a more interdependent world. That is above all the lesson to be drawn from Ireland's experience of European integration.[29]

For the first two generations after independence it had been taken for granted that political sovereignty would facilitate national economic development, even as arguments continued over whether it was best pursued by open or protectionist means. Neutrality in the Second World War was the ultimate assertion of independence and sovereignty in formal terms. 'When Ireland was dependent upon Britain, neutrality was the policy to which it aspired; when it became independent, neutrality was the policy it practised; and when Ireland and the UK became interdependent, military neutrality was a policy Ireland would still not relinquish.'[30]

Ireland's dependence on Britain in the period 1922–69 has been characterised as follows: 'The British influence on Ireland stemmed from the demographic fact of the unequal numbers of inhabitants, the geographical fact of nearness, the historical fact of political dominion and social and economic dominance, and the intellectual context of similarity of language and cultural blanketing.'[31] Paradoxically all this was reinforced by neutrality and its aftermath of international isolation in the 1950s, insulated from Europe by Britain – an island behind an island – and preoccupied politically by the border and partition. Nonetheless political independence, international boundaries and institution-building ensured that dependence did not amount to reabsorption. The republic and the North also grew apart; de Valera, no less, was to remark in 1963 that 'France was France without Alsace and Lorraine … Ireland is Ireland without the North.'[32]

From 1922 until EEC accession Ireland remained Anglocentric economically. The Irish economy was little more than a region within the wider British one in the 1920s, with 92 per cent of its exports and 78 per cent of its imports to or from there, making Ireland a part of Britain's informal empire; by 1937 these figures were still 91 per cent and 50 per cent respectively, despite the economic war between the Fianna Fáil government and Britain. It suited the British to bring the war to a close because Ireland was her second best and a highly profitable market, surpassing Australia, Germany and the US – and it remains by far the most important recipient of British exports on a per capita basis.[33] Agricultural goods in particular were bound up with the British market and its cheap food policy. Many Irish-owned businesses traded exclusively with the British market, while sterling parity meant that Ireland automatically devalued with the UK, most dramatically so in 1967. As a result Ireland had little option but to join Britain in applying again for accession to the EEC. Joint accession confirmed economic dependence, but was anticipated to reduce it; such has become the accepted interpretation of the Anglo-Irish Free Trade Agreement of 1965.

And this is indeed what happened in the economic sphere, so that by 1995 exports to the UK had reduced to 26 per cent and imports to 37 per cent.[34] Over the period 1970–93 the Ireland–UK trade ratio declined from 60 to 31.[35] Such overall figures admittedly conceal the continued existence of a dual economy, divided between largely domestically-owned firms for which Britain is the largest trading partner (although diversification is happening in that sector as well) and the extensive new multinational sectors which trade only marginally in that market.[36] Tension between their interests has been central in Ireland's strategy towards Economic and Monetary Union; within the euro–11 group Ireland has the greatest exposure to sterling volatility and the rate at which it would enter the single currency.

These changes represent a qualitative break from post-colonial economic dependence on the UK, confirmed by the decision in 1979 to join the European Monetary System without Britain and in 1999 similarly to join the euro. While argument understandably continues as to whether one set of dependencies have merely been substituted by others – on the larger EU powers for overall macroeconomic policy or the US for investment[37] – Irish capitalism has definitely diversified and developed away from what was a debilitating and exploitative relationship with the UK. The term interdependence best expresses the greater equality involved, in a framework of EU integration expressly geared to rebalance smaller and larger states by a system of international law and regulation that enmeshes nation-states together in a new system of governance.[38]

That such interdependence works its way through and transforms strong bilateral relationships as well as multilateral ones was recognised in 1994 by the then British Foreign Secretary, Douglas Hurd, in a speech to the Institute of European Affairs in Dublin: 'For the Irish membership in 1972 was about Ireland's place in history, confirming Ireland's position in Europe as a modern state ... and its decisive shift away from the embrace of Britain.'[39] That decisive shift was felt in the political and diplomatic spheres as well as in the social and psychological ones. Politically Ireland's perspectives were broadened by participation in a multilateral setting of the EU, as was its diplomacy. The same applied to its relations with the US over this period. Social change, too, fed in to a transformation of traditional social and cultural structures, as a new middle class asserted liberal and gender rights, consumer values and more secular attitudes.[40] All these interacted with the economic in a complex reorientation of Ireland's public policy and popular attitudes away from such a central preoccupation with and dependence on Britain over this period. Disparities of size and power often have their own psychological repercussions – and the British–Irish relationship has been marked historically by a superiority complex on the British side and an inferiority complex on the Irish one. There are similar asymmetries in the degree to which each is fixated by and knowledgeable of the other or informed about them in the media.[41]

Since a central aspect of unionist ideology concerned the supposed superiority of British political culture over Ireland's, as well as the superiority of British economic performance, of which the industrial North used to be such an integral part, it is not surprising that these changes profoundly influenced British–Irish relations. They inverted most of the presuppositions on which such judgements were based, including the supposed backwardness of the southern economy (it has in recent years caught up with the per capita income of the UK, including the North, and outproduced and outsold the North industrially); the supposed clericalist nature of southern society (after the undermining of the Catholic Church's legitimacy in a welter of scandals); and the exclusivist nationalist identities upon which it is perceived to be based (after the retrieval of its hybrid and genuinely republican as well as its cosmopolitan ambience – not to mention its Anglo-American popular culture which sits uneasily with its supposed European orientation).

Internationalisation

The Republic of Ireland now has one of the most open economies in the developed world; imports and exports come to over 150 per cent of GNP. This openness has developed rapidly over the period of the Troubles, although it is based on processes originating before they began, in the Lemass period. Coinciding with the economic opening there has been a political one: 'In order to understand the future evolution of Irish politics, it will be essential to see the state as a "small open polity"'[42] as well as a small open economy. That this affects Northern Ireland as well as the republic is increasingly recognised. The internationalisation process in fact includes the state's Northern policies, which have drawn on it systematically over the period 1969–99. Arthur suggests that this process should be examined under several headings, including the consequent reduction of dependency on Britain; the more dynamic influence of the Irish diaspora; the evolving debate on how to govern the North and contain its violence, which requires innovation in developing relations between Dublin and London; and the pervasive if usually indirect influence of the EU as a model and field for the transformation of contemporary political sovereignty.[43]

All this has transformed traditional Irish identities based on territorial sovereignty and added a certain post-national aspect to the new ones set out in the Belfast Agreement. Indeed the principles built into it, including consent, parity of esteem, recognition of diversity and power sharing amount to a lexicon of contemporary multiple identities and make it something of a model that other conflicts may follow.[44] Despite the evident hybridity that has characterised Irish identity over millennia, in the twentieth century we have experienced a classical set of exclusionary nationalisms and their associated essentialisms. That identity be defined as de-Anglicisation – Ireland as not-England – was inscribed canonically by Douglas Hyde as the task of Irish cultural nationalism in the following significant terms: 'But you ask, why should we wish to make Ireland more Celtic than it is – why should we de-anglicise at all? I answer because the Irish race is at present in a most anomalous position, imitating England and yet apparently hating it.'[45] This was perfectly understandable in the context of imperial power and cultural renaissance. But in Ireland as in Britain there has been a struggle between ethnic and civic nationalisms,[46] and effectively – as in many other European states – they become intermingled. The achievement of the civic modernisation project of the last generation has been rather through Europeanisation and Atlanticisation substantially to reduce Ireland's Anglocentricity. Diversification of economic, political and cultural life away from preoccupation with and over-dependence on Britain over the last generation of EC/EU membership has accomplished whatever independence is possible in a post-Westphalian world. Precisely because Ireland has been happier with this process than Britain, and *a fortiori* than unionists wedded to a zero-sum notion of sovereignty,[47] Dublin has had a certain advantage in pushing open the doors of political innovation involved in the Belfast Agreement by experimenting with a new liberal or cosmopolitan nationalism; thus integration and nationalism have reinforced each other, unlike in England.[48]

Europeanisation has awakened longstanding memories of previous engagement with the continent.[49] It has led to a greater realisation that Ireland's experience is more akin to central and eastern European nationalisms thrown up by the collapse of empires there after the First World War. The role of majorities and minorities is another similarity, which Frank Wright's pioneering study put in the context of ethnic frontiers.[50] Another is the triadic structure of political interaction between nationalising states, external homeland nationalisms and national minorities in central and eastern Europe, uncannily reflected in the structure of the Belfast Agreement.[51]

Ireland's engagement with Britain must be seen historically not only on a bilateral basis but in its wider European setting. As Fanning reminds us, 'crises in Anglo-Irish relations often either originated in or were subsumed by larger international crises in which British governments subordinated concern for harmony in Anglo-Irish relations to perceptions of what constituted their more vital national interests'.[52] That this applies as much to the end of the Cold War and the collapse of the Soviet Union as to previous major European convulsions is increasingly recognised by analysts. With the end of the Cold War the strategic issue that for hundreds of years determined Britain's presence in Ireland had fundamentally changed: 'When the Soviet Union ceased to exist as a legal and geopolitical entity in December 1991 it was to mark the beginning of the most dramatic change to Anglo-Irish strategic relations since the Act of Union in 1800.'[53]

Peter Brooke's important speech on 9 November 1990, in which he said 'the British government has no selfish strategic or economic interest in Northern Ireland', was specifically intended to influence Sinn Féin's thinking in its dialogue with John Hume at the time.[54] Similarly, suggestions were put forward that other regional conflicts, in South Africa or the Middle East, for example, would be more amenable to resolution after the end of the geopolitical conflict. The balance of forces in the special relationship between Britain and the US was also profoundly changed by the end of the Cold War.[55] Without that it is hard to see how President

Clinton would have been willing to offend the British so deeply by agreeing a visa for Gerry Adams to visit the US in February 1994[56] – despite the increasingly significant involvement of the US in Irish affairs during the Carter and Reagan presidencies, which abrogated the diplomatic fiction that Northern Ireland was an internal UK affair. The Irish diasporic involvement was central to that story and is a growing feature of contemporary internationalism. Clinton has regularly invoked the Belfast Agreement as a model for the resolution of other ethnic conflicts and regards it as one of his principal foreign policy achievements.

From unity to stability and consent

Over the time of the Troubles there has been a definite evolution of attitudes towards the conflict in Northern Ireland among the voting population of the republic. This has given political leaders the space to reach compromises on Northern Ireland and to cooperate closely with the British government. They had become more confident to do so after the internationalisation of Ireland's economics and politics during the 1970s and 1980s. Articles 2 and 3 of the Irish Constitution claiming jurisdiction over Northern Ireland, which were found to have a legal imperative by the Supreme Court, have been central features of the traditional political culture. But from 1986 to 1996 there was a fall from about 70 per cent to 30 per cent in the number of the republic's voters who identified a united Ireland as their preferred political settlement.[57] In that same poll only 7 per cent agreed that the Border is worth fighting over, 47 per cent that it mattered but is not worth fighting over and 42 per cent that it was not even worth arguing about.

These were dramatic findings given the long history of propaganda and conflict about partition and sovereignty in British–Irish relations in the twentieth century. It would be a mistake to interpret the figures as an abandonment of the aspiration towards Irish unification, however. This remained as a general but weak and shallow aspiration, based roughly on the assumption that 'partition was damaging and destructive to the whole of Ireland and reunification would bring certain benefits'.[58] A devolved, reformed, power sharing arrangement in the North with links to Britain and the republic is still seen as a stepping-stone to eventual unity of the island, at least as a Pascalian wager. An opinion poll for *The Irish Independent* published on 31 December 1999 found that 86 per cent support a united Ireland, with nearly half expecting it in ten years, and a further 21 per cent within twenty years. But 85 per cent reject the condition of higher taxation for unity; 59 per cent, Ireland returning to the Commonwealth; 42 per cent, joining NATO; and 25 per cent having unionists as part of a united Ireland government. The crisis certainly exposed the layers of unexamined attitudes in the republic towards sectarianism, partition and the British role in Ireland – and also the sheer ignorance and prejudice about the North built up during the years of partition.

Opinion shifted from unity to stability, based on consent of the Northern Ireland majority, inclusion of republicanism in negotiations and functioning North–

South institutions as the primary focus of the republic's policy towards Northern Ireland. There was often a failure to articulate this or a refusal to accept that the shift had occurred. As Fergus Finlay, special advisor to Dick Spring during the successive coalition governments from 1992–96, puts it in his political memoir: 'So far as I was concerned, this was never about unity. The process of 25 years, and the new process I was being invited into [in 1992], was about stability and peace.' Dick Spring added that 'both governments had to work together'.[59] Despite the unitary rhetoric – and whatever the inherent merits of a united Ireland – the logic of events and negotiations drove politicians of various tendencies to accept a formula based on consent, devolution, power sharing, North–South bodies and a growing realisation of the need to institutionalise relations between the Dublin and London governments.

That was the context within which the New Ireland Forum was convened in May 1983. Its deliberations facilitated a crucial rethinking of Irish nationalism after fifteen years of conflict in the North. Its three options, the unitary state, a federal/confederal Ireland and a joint authority solution, set the scene for negotiation of the Anglo-Irish Agreement in 1985. The Forum Report and the subsequent agreement with Britain took due account of two central features of the state's response to the Troubles: the need to protect it from paramilitary subversion;[60] and the need 'to strengthen constitutional nationalism in the North as an alternative to republicanism by offering it moral and political support and by pressing for reforms. Successive Irish governments hoped for a return to peace and stability.'[61] The possibility that the British might actually have contemplated withdrawal had created alarm in the coalition after the collapse of Sunningdale.[62] It was to prove an enduring motive for governmental caution in dealing with paramilitary violence and subversion or relaxing the media censorship directed against them. It also played to a potent mood of public disenchantment with things Northern Irish within significant sectors of Irish public opinion, anxious to protect itself from destabilising spillover and in any case increasingly disgusted by violent methods of pursuing Irish unity.

Inclusion of republicans was the other principle on which the emerging policy was predicated. Contacts between John Hume and the Fianna Fáil government with Sinn Féin were communicated to the British government and were taken up enthusiastically by Albert Reynolds, who had, as Mansergh says, 'a warm personal relationship' with Mr Major; this is confirmed in Major's autobiography, in which he says 'the great point about my relationship with Albert Reynolds was that we liked one another, and could have a row without giving up on each other'.[63] Three arguments made by John Hume in his dialogues with Gerry Adams were central: that the British are 'neutral' as between unionism and nationalism, which undermines the case for armed struggle; that European developments erode traditional notions of sovereignty; and that the Irish people could choose to accept the principle of consent within Northern Ireland as a valid exercise in self-determination.[64]

Normalisation of British–Irish relations

The notion of normality in inter-state relations craves definition – all the more so when the two states in question are as intimately linked as Britain and Ireland are. They have in common certain features of asymmetry comparable to other pairings of small and large neighbours – Austria and Germany, Canada and the US, Finland and Russia/Sweden, Norway and Sweden, or Estonia/Latvia/Lithuania and Russia. But most of these others did not have the precise combination of metropolitan and colonial interpenetration and domination, nor the same agonising setting of precedents on the theme of imperial decline that Ireland has had for Britain this century. The title of Erich Strauss's classic study, *Irish Nationalism and British Democracy*, captures another dimension of the relationship – the intimate connection between popular political mobilisations in the two countries over the whole period 1770–1922.[65]

Keatinge's study[66] is – surprisingly – the only systematic and detailed attempt to examine the modern relationship between Britain and Ireland in the light of comparative international relations theory and research. He looks at realist or power models of inter-state relations and contrasts them with the development of integration theory as applied to the EC. In between them is the study of complex interdependence proposed by Keohane and Nye and especially their application of the model to relations between Canada and the US.[67] Keatinge finds this more relevant than power models which emphasise conflict and the potential use of force (which is questionable in the light of Northern Ireland and the suggestion made above that dependency characterised the relationship until the last generation). He looks empirically at British–Irish relations in terms derived from the Canadian–US comparison under the headings of the patterns of interaction between the two states, the political processes employed, and the types of outcome that generally occur.

Examining the patterns of interaction he finds a case of very complicated interdependence indeed, using multiple channels of contact. Taking similar categories eighteen years on from his study one can readily see that this complex interdependence has both deepened and become less dependent and more normal – which is, indeed, 'healthy for both partners as it substitutes a greatly wider embrace for what had been an excessive intimacy'.[68] This applies in trade;[69] finance and investment;[70] migration, short-term mobility (business or personal visits, tourism[71]); churches, trade unions, sporting[72] or other networks that straddle the border; media and cultural penetration, especially television; the free travel area;[73] common citizenship provisions.[74]

These contacts show that the extent of direct human and family ties is probably unprecedented between two independent states, even if it is now more diversified than before.[75] Seven per cent of people born in Britain have at least one Irish parent, so that nearly 4 million people qualify automatically as Irish citizens; the 1991 UK census showed 830,500 Irish-born people living in Britain (174,000 from Northern Ireland and 656,500 from the republic); one quarter of Britons have an Irish relative; only 6 per cent consider those who come to Britain from Ireland to be foreigners; and the social class profile of the Irish in Britain is nearly identical to their British counterparts.[76] The volume of passenger traffic between Ireland and Britain is 70 per cent of the total travel from Ireland, although movement to the continent has been increasing in recent years. An estimated 9 million people travelled in 1997, a daily and vivid affirmation of normalisation, involving some 25,000 journeys daily across the Irish Sea.

Governmental goals and the intergovernmental agenda have been made much more explicit with the Anglo-Irish Agreement (1985), the Downing Street Declaration (1993), the Framework Document (1995) and the Belfast Agreement (1998). These were negotiated at the highest level at summits prepared by officials from cabinet offices, the Anglo-Irish division of the Department of Foreign Affairs and the Northern Ireland Office (less so, the Foreign and Commonwealth Office). The role of personal relationships between taoisigh and prime ministers – and between officials – has been crucial. Policy instruments used vary from the summit meetings; the institutionalised Anglo-Irish Inter-Governmental Conferences;[77] systematic use of meetings on the margins of European Councils since they were inaugurated in the mid-1970s – these deserve a separate study of their own – and complex networks between government departments looking after bilateral and EU business.[78] On the margins of the European Council at Luxembourg in December 1997 both governments issued a progress report on developing east/west relations, which covered almost every area of public policy, ranging from education to transport, crime, drugs, immigration, homelessness, defence, tourism, agriculture, health, trade, finance and arts and culture.[79] Cooperation is driven and coordinated by a joint steering group co-chaired by the Department of the taoiseach and the cabinet office. The secretariats of the British–Irish Council set up under the Belfast Agreement will carry on that work.

Alliances and concertation of policy within the EU are increasingly common, given the converging agenda between the two states and the British policy of pursuing selective bilateral alliances to amplify its European influence. In his Oireachtas address Blair suggested that 'increasingly we share a common agenda and common objectives', including completion of the single market and structural economic reform; better conditions for growth and jobs in Europe; successful enlargement; and cooperation on the Schengen agenda of crime, drugs and illegal immigration. He also included the need for flexible, open and accountable institutions. The Irish government shares many of these perspectives; there is general agreement among policy-makers that it is in Ireland's interest to have Britain participating fully in the EU, both to balance the other large states, especially France and Germany, and to ease the path of British–Irish relations. But there is also concern that Blair's preference for intergovernmental methods could herald a return to a *directoire* of the larger states rather than developing the supranational institutions which have so modified traditional balance of power politics in Europe. There are also different interests on agriculture and structural funds, both of which are expected to play out as closer relations are built up with Scotland, Wales and Northern Ireland.

There is, however, little evidence of explicit issue linkage.[80] Nonetheless security and defence policy became a relatively open issue in bargaining between Haughey and Thatcher in 1980–81[81] (and relations were undoubtedly soured by Ireland's refusal to accept EC sanctions against Argentina in the Falklands/Malvinas war). The issue has not been opened explicitly since then, although Bertie Ahern has raised relations with the UK and the US in a general sense in the light of his support for Ireland's membership of the Partnership for Peace.[82] Ireland has stated that it would be willing to sign up to a European defence arrangement if it is agreed, despite military neutrality; but in effect it has been content to base policy on the assumption that Britain's commitment to NATO would block the development of a more ambitious EU defence and security policy. That premise is changing following the St Malo agreement with France, the agreement at the June 1999 European Council at Cologne and the December 1999 agreement at Helsinki to develop such a policy more comprehensively following the Kosovo war. While there is little suggestion of a linkage with the Northern Ireland peace process, Ireland's security policy is converging towards the European norm. This is a considerable test of its residual commitment to sovereignty. That is also tested by reports that communications traffic between the two states is systematically monitored by British intelligence services and by differences over Sellafield.[83]

As for the types of outcomes that generally occur, a crucial consideration in the study of interdependence is the extent to which political cooperation has been institutionalised in a particular type of international regime, formally or informally. The Anglo-Irish Agreement of 1985 is a case in point. But many other aspects of British–Irish relations are worth examining from that point of view, including those organised under the Anglo-Irish Intergovernmental Council established by Thatcher and FitzGerald in November 1981,[84] informal contacts between policy elites in the annual British–Irish Association meetings, between civic and political leaders in Anglo-Irish Encounter (which is funded by the two governments since 1983) and in the British–Irish Inter-Parliamentary Body since 1990. They have endeavoured to overcome the inherently asymmetrical relationship and in many cases have been successful in doing so. This will be all the more important as relations are built up between the devolved assemblies and executives in Scotland, Wales and Northern Ireland, whether bilaterally or through the British–Irish Council. Comparative inter-state relations remain relevant. The Nordic Union is one possible analogue, with provision for concertation of policy across a wide span of issues; but it differs substantially in that a greater number of sovereign states are involved and the process is firmly rooted in inter-parliamentary contacts based on a wide popular consensus.[85] In time, however, such features could grow from the Belfast Agreement.

It will be important to understand these processes because if the Belfast Agreement fails or has to be parked for a prolonged period it will be up to the two governments to continue their close cooperation in administering Northern Ireland by implementing those substantial aspects of it that do not necessarily depend on the setting up of an Executive, including reform of the RUC, North–South bodies and equality agendas.[86] It must be remembered that British policy-makers and businesses look at Ireland as a whole. The balance of their interests, political stability, their international reputation and the need for EU cooperation all give priority to closer cooperation with Dublin. This confirms the argument that 'the two sovereign governments are primarily concerned with maintaining good relations with one another, rather than with working for the achievement of more fundamental objectives such as Irish unity or preservation of the Union'.[87] Symmetrical withdrawal of commitment to Northern Ireland on the part of the British and Irish governments has helped to create the conditions on which an autonomous political settlement can be based; but equally it can facilitate executive implementation of change if agreement is not reached to share power within Northern Ireland.

Conclusion: from Anglo-Irish to British–Irish relations

This chapter has traced the changing relations between Britain and Ireland over the last thirty years under four headings: the transition from dependence to interdependence; internationalisation; the shift from unity to stability as the major norm in Irish policy-making; and the normalisation of relations between the two sovereign governments. There is a great deal of interpenetration and overlap between these different categories. Interdependence implies normalisation and internationalisation reinforces the appeal of stability. But they do tap into various dimensions that have been left relatively unexamined in the British–Irish relationship because of the understandable concentration on Northern Ireland. Without these changes the Belfast Agreement would not have come about. The British government has a major interest in creating new institutional arrangements capable of reducing the crisis management aspect of the relationship and transferring them to political or bureaucratic routine in order to clear space for other business.

That is part and parcel of the ambiguity, perhaps the uniqueness, of the relationship between the two countries – as to whether they are genuinely 'foreign' to one another or not. The ambiguity of identity is reinforced by uncertainties created by two transformations which profoundly affect the British–Irish relationship: the constitutional changes introduced by the Labour government; and its efforts to bring Britain to the heart of Europe. Britain's crisis of state and political identity after the end of the Cold War operates in four dimensions: the international, transatlantic and global; the European; its internal constitutional arrangements; and its relations with Ireland.[88] They are interlinked and are being addressed by the Labour government. But there are tensions among them, notably between the desire to maintain the special relationship with the US and to integrate more with Europe; to devolve power within Britain while maintaining strong central control over the process; and whether and when to commit the UK to join the euro, given that this might affect the Labour government's ability to win the next election.

It is too early to say how the orchestration of such a complex agenda will affect British–Irish relations. This chapter has examined them largely from the Irish point of view, in what could be a methodological shortcoming given the asymmetries involved, since there is an inherent temptation to exaggerate the reciprocal response of the larger state to the necessarily persistent preoccupations of the smaller one. It is therefore important to understand the pressures bearing on the UK in this period of transition. Will they lead to the break-up of the UK or to its regeneration? What would the consequences of that be for relations between the two sovereign governments? The taoiseach disappointed members of the Scottish National Party by his failure to endorse independence when he spoke in Edinburgh in October 1998.[89] The question arises as to whether that would be in Ireland's interest. Arguably it would not be, given the close relationship built up through the peace process between Dublin and London.

Symbols are vitally important aspects of political reality in the relations between Ireland and Britain, none more so than the monarchy. The improvement of relations has been calibrated by state and private visits to Britain by Presidents Robinson and McAleese and that of Prince Charles to Ireland in June 1995. It would take a firm implementation and bedding down of the Belfast Agreement to enable a state visit to the republic by Queen Elizabeth II – that would be a real sign that abnormal business had been finished in the eyes of official Ireland. Other symbols also play a role. On the eve of Mr Blair's address to the Oireachtas, Mr Ahern suggested that a debate should open on whether Ireland should rejoin the Commonwealth, in order to avail of its networking and to indicate to unionists that reconciliation with British institutions is sincere and normalisation complete.[90] There was surprisingly little political reaction to the call; but a number of letter writers to *The Irish Times* argued in sharp terms that they felt such a move was premature, because it would be seen internationally as confirmation that Ireland is returning to the British fold (which seems to be daily confirmed in the retail and sporting spheres as a strong sterling and an undervaluation of Irish shares based on the persistent if mistaken belief in the City of London that the Celtic Tiger is a bubble economy make Irish firms vulnerable to takeovers).[91]

The letter writers have a point. If the case put forward in this chapter is sound, it can be seen that Ireland has finally attained independence from Britain by pooling sovereignty in the EU and participating effectively internationally, especially by creating its own special relationship with the US. Until Britain resolves its dual sovereignty and identity questions – by participating fully in Europe and constitutionally rearranging itself – such a normalisation would signify reabsorption rather than genuine interdependence. It is very much in Ireland's interest that this British participation and rearrangement happen. Until they do so Irish policy would best serve that normalisation by sticking to its path of achieving de Valera's objective of external association through European integration, in what has been aptly described as a policy of 'interdependent realism'.[92] That would also best serve the republic's new relationship with Northern Ireland.

Notes

1 Robert Hazell (ed), *Constitutional Futures, A History of the Next Ten Years* (Oxford: Oxford University Press, 1999), p. 4.
2 Elizabeth Meehan, 'The Belfast Agreement – Its Distinctiveness and Points of Cross-Fertilisation in the UK's Devolution Programme', *Parliamentary Affairs* 51(1), 1999, pp. 19–31. Vernon Bogdanor, 'The British–Irish Council and Devolution', *Government and Opposition* 33(2), 1999, pp. 287–98.
3 The External Affairs department was not renamed the Department of Foreign Affairs until 1972; and a specific Anglo-Irish section was not set up in it until the Troubles broke out in 1969, notwithstanding its responsibility along with the taoiseach's office for conducting relations with London from the beginning of the state (Patrick Keatinge, 'Unequal Sovereigns: the Diplomatic Dimension of Anglo-Irish Relations', chapter 8 in P. J. Drudy (ed.), *Ireland and Britain Since 1922* (Cambridge: Cambridge University Press, 1986)). Likewise in London, relations with Ireland were with first the Dominions Office until 1947 and then the Commonwealth Office, which was merged with the Foreign Office in 1968.
4 Keatinge, 'Unequal Sovereigns', p. 139.
5 See John Tomaney, 'New Labour and the English Question', *The Political Quarterly* 70(1), January–March 1999, pp. 75–82.
6 W. L. Miller, 'The Periphery and its Paradoxes', *West European Politics* 21(1), 1998, pp. 191–2.
7 Norman Vance, *Irish Literature, A Social History* (Oxford: Basil Blackwell, 1990) p. 12.
8 Declan Kiberd, *Inventing Ireland, The Literature of the Modern Nation* (London: Jonathan Cape, 1995) pp. 641–53.
9 David Marquand, *The New Reckoning, Capitalism, States and Citizens* (Cambridge: Polity Press, 1997) pp. 186–203. He makes the point at p. 200 that 'empire was not an optional extra for the British; it was their reason for being British as opposed to English or Scots or Welsh [or Irish, one might add]. Deprived of empire and plunged into Europe, "Britain" had no meaning.'
10 Garret FitzGerald, Paul Gillespie and Ronan Fanning, 'Britain's European Question: the Issues for Ireland', in Paul Gillespie (ed.), *Britain's European Question, the Issues for Ireland* (Dublin: Institute of European Affairs, 1996) p. 29.
11 Brendan O'Leary and John McGarry, *The Politics of Antagonism, Understanding Northern Ireland* (London: Athlone Press, 1993) p. 143.
12 Ronan Fanning, 'Anglo-Irish Relations – Partition and the British Dimension in Historical Perspective', *Irish Studies in International Affairs* 2(1), 1985, pp. 17–19. See also coverage of the 1969 State Papers, *The Irish Times*, 1 and 3 January 2000.
13 *The Irish Times*, 27 November 1998.
14 Among them Nicholas Mansergh, *The Irish Question 1840–1921* (London, 1965) and his *The Unresolved Question: The Anglo-Irish Settlement and its Undoing 1912–1972* (New Haven, CT: Yale University Press, 1991); David Harkness, *The Restless Dominion* (London, 1969); Deirdre MacMahon, *Republicans and Imperialists: Anglo-Irish Relations in the 1930s* (New Haven, CT: Yale University Press, 1984); Paul Canning, *British Policy towards Ireland 1921–1941* (Oxford, 1985); Robert Fisk, *In Time of War: Ireland, Ulster and the Price of Neutrality 1939–1945* (London, 1983); John Bowman, *De Valera and the Ulster Question 1917–1973* (Oxford: Oxford University Press, 1983); D. G. Boyce, *The Irish Question in British Politics, 1868–1996* (London, 1996).
15 Notably Paul Arthur's work – see 'Anglo-Irish Relations and Constitutional Policy' in Paul Mitchell and Rick Wilford (eds), *Politics in Northern Ireland* (Oxford: Oxford University Press, 1999) and references therein, and Paul Arthur, 'Anglo-Irish Relations in the New Dispensation: Towards a Post-Nationalist Framework?' in Malcolm Anderson and Eberhard Bort (eds), *The Irish Border, History, Politics, Culture* (Liverpool: Liverpool University Press, 1999), pp. 41–56; Patrick Keatinge, 'Unequal Sovereigns' and 'An Odd

Couple? Obstacles and Opportunities in Inter-State Political Co-operation between the Republic of Ireland and the United Kingdom', chapter 9 in Desmond Rea (ed.), *Political Coooperation in Divided Societies* (Dublin: Gill and Macmillan, 1982); Ronan Fanning, 'Anglo-Irish Relations', 'Small States, Large Neighbours: Ireland and the United Kingdom', *Irish Studies in International Affairs*, 9, 1998, pp. 21–30 and n.92 and James Downey, *Them and Us, Britain-Ireland and the Northern Question, 1969–1982* (Dublin: Ward River Press, 1983).

16 Garret FitzGerald, *All in a Life, An Autobiography* (Dublin: Gill and Macmillan, 1991); Edward Heath, *The Course of My Life* (London: Hodder and Stoughton, 1998); Margaret Thatcher, *The Downing Street Years* (London: HarperCollins, 1993); John Major, *The Autobiography* (London: HarperCollins, 1999).

17 But see Joseph Ruane and Jennifer Todd, *The Dynamics of Conflict in Northern Ireland: Power, Conflict and Emancipation* (Cambridge: Cambridge University Press, 1996); Frank Wright, *Northern Ireland, A Comparative Analysis* (Dublin: Gill and Macmillan, 1987); Adrian Guelke, *Northern Ireland: The International Perspective* (Dublin: Gill and Macmillan, 1988); Keatinge, 'Unequal Sovereigns' and 'An Odd Couple?'; Brendan O'Leary and John McGarry, *The Politics of Antagonism: Understanding Northern Ireland* (London: Athlone Press, 1993); John McGarry and Brendan O'Leary, *Explaining Northern Ireland, Broken Images* (Oxford: Blackwell, 1995); Fanning, 'Small States, Large Neighbours'.

18 D. George Boyce and Alan O'Day, *Modern Irish History, Revisionism and the Revisionist Controversy* (London: Routledge, 1996); Ciaran Brady (ed.), *Interpreting Irish History: The Debate on Historical Revisionism, 1938–1994* (Dublin: Irish Academic Press, 1994).

19 Roy Foster, 'Anglo-Irish Relations and Northern Ireland: Historical Perspectives', chapter 1 in Dermot Keogh and Michael H. Haltzel (eds), *Northern Ireland and the Politics of Reconciliation* (Cambridge: Cambridge University Press, 1993).

20 Dermot McAleese, 'Anglo-Irish Economic Interdependence: from Excessive Intimacy to a Wider Embrace', chapter 5 in Drudy, *Ireland and Britain*; M. Gallagher and D. McAleese, 'Ireland's Trade Dependence on the UK', *Irish Banking Review*, Spring 1994.

21 John Archer Jackson, *The Irish in Britain* (London: Routledge & Kegan Paul, 1963); Mary Hickman and Bronwen Walter, *Discrimination and the Irish Community in Britain* (London: Commission for Racial Equality, 1997).

22 Arthur, 'Anglo-Irish Relations' (both references).

23 Alan J. Ward, 'A Constitutional Background to the Northern Ireland Crisis', chapter 2 in Keogh and Haltzel, *Northern Ireland*.

24 Michael Cox, 'Bringing in the "International": the IRA Ceasefire and the End of the Cold War', *International Affairs* 73(4), October, pp. 671–94.

25 Terry Eagleton, 'Ascendancy and Hegemony', chapter 2 in his book *Heathcliff and the Great Hunger, Studies in Irish Culture* (London: Verso, 1995).

26 Drudy, *Ireland and Britain*.

27 J. J. Lee, *Ireland 1912–1985, Politics and Society* (Cambridge: Cambridge University Press, 1989), pp. 627–8. For reports on other British–Irish academic initiatives and networks see the Supplement on Scotland and Ireland, *The Irish Times*, 30 November 1999.

28 Arthur, 'Anglo-Irish Relations' (1999), pp. 245–6.

29 Brigid Laffan, 'The European Union and Ireland', chapter 6 in Neil Collins (ed.), *Political Issues in Ireland Today*, 2nd edn (Manchester: Manchester University Press, 1999).

30 Fanning, 'Small States, Large Neighbours', p. 25.

31 Basil Chubb, *The Government and Politics of Ireland*, 2nd edn (London: Longman, 1982), p. 329.

32 Bowman, *De Valera*, p. 312.

33 Mike Cronin, 'An Anatomy of Dominion Status and After: the Case of Ireland Since 1922', BISA/PSA Political Science Group, workshop conference on The Dominion Concept: Inter-state and Domestic Politics in the British Empire, University of Warwick, July 1998; Gillespie, *Britain's European Question*, p. 9.

34 Gillespie, *Britain's European Question*, p. 23.

35 Gallagher and McAleese, 'Ireland's Trade Dependence'.

36 Seamus Bannon, 'EMU and Ireland's Sterling Trade', paper to Statistical and Social Inquiry Society of Ireland, 28 March 1996.

37 See Denis O'Hearn, *Inside the Celtic Tiger: The Irish Economy and the Asian Model* (London: Pluto Press, 1998); Peadar Kirby, *Poverty Amid Plenty, World and Irish Development Reconsidered* (Dublin: Trocaire and Gill and Macmillan, 1997); John Kurt Jacobsen, *Chasing Progress in the Irish Republic, Ideology, Democracy and Dependent Development* (Cambridge: Cambridge University Press, 1994); Brendan Keenan, 'Can the IDA Make it Two in a Row?', *The Irish Independent*, 13 January 2000.

38 Brigid Laffan, Michael Smith and Rory O'Donnell, *Europe's Experimental Union: Rethinking Integration* (London: Routledge, 2000).

39 Quoted in Gillespie, *Britain's European Question*, p. 7.

40 Patrick Clancy, Sheelagh Drudy, Kathleen Lynch and Liam O'Dowd (eds), *Irish Society: Sociological Perspectives* (Dublin: Institute of Public Administration, 1995); J. E. Goldthorpe and C. T. Whelan (eds), *The Development of Industrial Society in Ireland* (Oxford: Oxford University Press, 1992); Dermot Keogh, *Twentieth Century Ireland, Nation and State* (Dublin: Gill and Macmillan, 1994), pp. 243–388.

41 Garret FitzGerald and Paul Gillespie, 'Ireland's British Question', *Prospect*, 12, October 1996, pp. 22–6.

42 Patrick Keatinge and Brigid Laffan, 'Ireland in International Affairs', chapter 12 in John Coakley and Michael Gallagher (eds), *Politics in the Republic of Ireland* (Galway: PSAI Press, 1992), p. 220.

43 Arthur, 'Anglo-Irish Relations', pp. 244–6.

44 Paul Gillespie, 'Multiple Identities in Ireland and Europe', in Ronit Lentin (ed.), *The Expanding Nation: Towards a Multi-Ethnic Ireland* (Department of Sociology, Trinity College Dublin, 1999), pp. 8–16; Cathal McCall, *Identity in Northern Ireland, Communities, Politics and Change* (Basingstoke: Macmillan, 1999).

45 Douglas Hyde, 'The Necessity for De-Anglicising Ireland', in Charles Gavan Duffy, George Sigerson and Douglas Hyde (eds), *The Revival of Irish Literature* (London: T. Fisher-Brown, 1894).

46 Hugh Kearney, 'Contested Ideas of Nationhood', *The Irish Review*, 20 Winter/Spring, pp. 1–22.

47 See Elizabeth Meehan's chapter in this volume.

48 See James Goodman, 'The Republic of Ireland: Towards a Cosmopolitan Nationalism?', chapter 5 in James Anderson and James Goodman (eds), *Dis/Agreeing Ireland, Contexts Obstacles Hopes* (London: Pluto, 1998); James Goodman, *Single Europe, Single Ireland? Uneven Development in Process* (Dublin: Irish Academic Press, 2000); James Anderson, 'Rethinking National Problems in a Transnational Context', chapter 6 in David Miller (ed), *Rethinking Northern Ireland, Culture, Ideology and Colonialism* (London: Longman, 1998).

49 Brigid Laffan and Rory O'Donnell, 'Ireland and the Growth of International Governance', in W. Crotty and D. Schmitt (eds), *Ireland and the Politics of Change* (London: Longman, 1998).

50 Wright, *Northern Ireland*; Paul Gillespie, 'Optimism of the Intellect, Pessimism of the Will', *Transit*, 18, Winter, 2000.

51 Rogers Brubaker, *Nationalism Reframed: Nationhood and the National Question in the New Europe* (Cambridge: Cambridge University Press, 1996).

52 Fanning, 'Anglo-Irish Relations', p. 2.

53 Geoffrey Sloan, 'Geopolitics and British Strategic Policy in Ireland: Issues and Interests', *Irish Studies in International Affairs*, 8, 1997, p. 134. See also G. R. Sloan, *Geopolitics of Anglo-Irish Relations in the Twentieth Century* (Leicester: Leicester University Press, 1997).

54 Michael Cox, 'Northern Ireland: the War that Came in From the Cold', *Irish Studies in International Affairs*, 9, 1998. p. 78. Mrs Thatcher refused to allow Brooke to make the speech before the end of the Cold War because of her concern to protect British nuclear submarines passing near Northern Ireland, according to Nicholas Watt, 'Thatcher Gave Approval to Talks with IRA', *Guardian*, 16 October 1999.

55 Paul Gillespie, 'Britain and Europe: the Politics of Identification', in Gillespie, *Britain's European Question*, p. 86.
56 See Michael Cox, John Dumbrell and Adrian Guelke in this volume. For a vivid account of the story see Conor O'Clery, *The Greening of the White House* (Dublin, Gill and Macmillan, 1996).
57 *The Irish Times*/MRBI poll, 2 February 1996.
58 Ruane and Todd, *The Dynamics of Conflict*, p. 250.
59 Fergus Finlay, *Snakes and Ladders* (Dublin: New Island Books, 1998), pp. 182–3. The 1969 State Papers reveal that in autumn of that year the Department of External Affairs formulated a policy based on cooperation, agreement, consent, the rejection of violence and maximal if discreet contact with Whitehall – 'a turning point in Dublin's policy towards the Northern question' – according to John Bowman, 'Dublin Opts for "Hard Realities" as Belfast Burns', *The Irish Times*, 1 and 3 January 2000.
60 Eunan O'Halpin, *Defending Ireland, The Irish Free State and its Enemies since 1922* (Oxford: Oxford University Press), pp. 342ff.
61 Ruane and Todd, *The Dynamics of Conflict*, p. 262.
62 FitzGerald, *All in a Life*, pp. 244ff.
63 Martin Mansergh, 'The Background to the Peace Process', *Irish Studies in International Affairs*, 6, 1995, p. 153; Major, *The Autobiography*, p. 452.
64 Finlay, *Snakes and Ladders*, p. 184.
65 London: Longman, 1951; new edition, London: Greenwood Press, 1994.
66 Keatinge, 'An Odd Couple?'.
67 Robert O. Keohane and Joseph Nye, *Power and Interdependence: World Politics in Transition* (Boston: Little Brown, 1977). Keohane and Nye have revisited their study of complex interdependence recently in the light of the information revolution, in 'Power and Interdependence in the Information Age', *Foreign Affairs* 77(5), September/October 1998, pp. 81–94. They agree that realist assumptions about the dominance of military force and security issues remain valid – 'information does not flow in a vacuum but in political space that remains occupied'. And power is distributed through communications facilities in such a way that relations between large and small states are not fundamentally affected. Keohane pays tribute to the contribution made by the literature on international regimes, neo-institutionalism, transnational actors, networks, game theory and bargaining and globalisa tion to the study of interdependence (Robert O. Keohane, 'International Institutions: Can Interdependence Work?', *Foreign Policy*, 110, Spring 1998, pp. 82–96). But there has been little attempt to apply them to Britain and Ireland, which remains a very special relationship in comparative terms.
68 The phrase comes from Eamonn Gallagher, 'Anglo-Irish Relations in the European Community', *Irish Studies in International Affairs* 2(1), 1985, p. 35.
69 Bannon, 'EMU and Ireland's Sterling Trade'.
70 T. Baker, J. FitzGerald and P. Honahan (eds), *Economic Implications for Ireland of EMU* (Dublin: Economic and Social Research Institute, 1996).
71 Elizabeth Meehan, *Free Movement between Ireland and the U.K.: from the 'common travel area' to the Common Travel Area* (Dublin: The Policy Institute, 2000).
72 Michael Holmes, 'Symbols of National Identity and Sport: the Case of the Irish Football Team', *Irish Political Studies*, 9, 1994, pp. 81–98; Mike Cronin, *Sport and Nationalism in Ireland*, (Dublin: Gill and Macmillan, 1999).
73 Meehan, *Free Movement*.
74 *Ibid.*
75 FitzGerald and Gillespie, 'Ireland's British Question'.
76 James O'Connell, 'British Attitudes to Ireland and the Irish: A Special Relationship', *Irish Post* survey reported in ten parts, 19 November 1994–4 February 1995, cited in Simon Partridge, *The British Union State, Imperial Hangover or Flexible Citizens' Home?* (London: Catalyst, January 1999), pp. 12–13. This is not to say the Irish in Britain do not have their problems. They do, as recent studies demonstrate, see Hickman and Walter, *Discrimination*.

And 50 per cent of the 20,000 ill-educated and marginalised people who emigrate from Ireland go to Britain, where 'they experience high rates of unemployment and illness, a low rate of upward social mobility, live in poor housing, enter unrewarding occupations, suffer a distinct level of discrimination and present high rate of social problems, including alcoholism and suicide', Irish Episcopal Commission, reported in *The Irish Times*, 19 May 1999.

77 Their communiqués are recorded in successive issues of the journal *Irish Studies in International Affairs*, 1986–.

78 The former British Ambassador in Dublin, Veronica Sutherland, referred to the complications of diplomacy when prime ministers and taoisigh are in direct touch by telephone on Anglo-Irish and EU business, as are governmental departments, sometimes without contacting the embassy, see Maol Muire Tynan 'Departing Envoy Admits Concern about NI Peace', *The Irish Times*, 16 January 1999.

79 *Progress Report on Co-operation between Ireland and the United Kingdom, Developing East/ West Relations*, 12/13 December 1997; Mark Brennock, 'Report Shows Wide-ranging East–West Links Being Forged', *The Irish Times*, 13 December 1997.

80 An exception is the abortive attempt by Anthony Crosland to link fishery issues with broader cooperation, recorded in FitzGerald, *All in a Life*, pp. 172–5; see also John Horgan, 'Irish Foreign Policy, Northern Ireland, Neutrality and the Commonwealth: the Historical Roots of a Current Controversy', *Irish Studies in International Affairs*, 10, 1999, pp. 135–48.

81 Patrick Keatinge, *A Singular Stance, Irish Neutrality in the 1980s* (Dublin: Institute of Public Administration, 1984), pp. 77–83.

82 Bertie Ahern, speech to European Movement seminar on Partnership for Peace, 29 March 1999.

83 Miriam Donohue, 'Report on Phone-Tapping Claims "Inconclusive"', *The Irish Times*, 5 August 1999; reports in *The Irish Times* and *The Irish Independent*, 13 January 2000 on Dail committee hearings on the matter.

84 Anglo-Irish Joint Studies Report (HMSO, Cmnd 8414), 1983.

85 *The Nordic Council: Lessons for Council of the Isles*, November 1998 (London: The Constitution Unit, University College, London).

86 See Gerry Moriarty, 'Trimble, Adams Still Need Each Other', *The Irish Times*, 27 September 1999.

87 Feargal Cochrane, 'Any Takers? The Isolation of Northern Ireland', *Political Studies*, XLII, 1994, pp. 378–95 and the exchange between him and Paul Dixon in the following volume, XLIII, 1995, pp. 497–508.

88 Paul Gillespie, 'Britain in Europe: the Politics of Identification', chapter 6 in Gillespie, *Britain's European Question.*

89 Bertie Ahern, 'The Western Isles of Europe at the Millennium', The Lothian European Lecture, Edinburgh, 29 October 1998.

90 Interview with Bertie Ahern, *The Times*, 26 November 1998. See also Bertie Ahern, address to Kevin Barry Fianna Fáil cumann, University College, Dublin, 13 January 1999, text in *European Document Series*, 22, Summer 1999 (Dublin: Institute of European Affairs), pp. 6–9.

91 Letters page, 10, 18, 21, 23 and 24 December 1998; 7, 9, 20 and 25 January 1999 and 5 February 1999.

92 Ronan Fanning, 'Irish Neutrality – the Diplomatic Perspective', in Michael Kennedy and Joseph Morrison Skelly (eds), *Irish Foreign Policy, 1916–66, From Independence to Internationalism* (Dublin: Four Courts Press, 2000).

14

Europe and the Europeanisation of the Irish Question

ELIZABETH MEEHAN

> One of the striking things about the Belfast Agreement is that, to any one who knows the European Union, one immediately recognises that it was written by people who also know the EU and have worked its systems quite extensively.[1]

Introduction

The links between Europe and the Europeanisation of the Irish Question are complex and disputed. First, 'Europe' as the European Convention on Human Rights (ECHR) coexists with 'Europe' as the EU – and together both have some part in the Europeanisation of the Irish Question. Secondly, the significance of the EU on the Irish Question was complicated by the coincidence of timing in the imposition of Direct Rule on the one hand, and negotiations by the UK and the Republic of Ireland on the other to join the then European Community (EC) back in 1972. This caused the Europeanisation of the Irish Question to be both 'domesticated' into the Northern Ireland conflict and promoted as a new factor in its potential resolution. Thirdly, insofar as the literature on Northern Ireland attends to the EU's effects, it comes to contradictory conclusions.[2] Most commentators agree that common EU membership has helped Irish and British governments to cooperate effectively in the quest for a solution. But there is sharp disagreement about the EU's impact on North–South cooperation or sectarianism.

Assessing the impact of Irish and British membership of the EU upon Northern Ireland is complicated by the interaction of four factors. These are:

- that, unlike Ireland, the UK has been ambivalent towards European integration;
- that, in Northern Ireland, Direct Rule overshadowed UK and Irish accession to the EC;
- that, however, unionists saw Direct Rule and UK accession as a twin blow;
- that constitutional nationalists, not only reversed their previous indifference to the EC, but, from the early days of Direct Rule, looked positively upon it as a means of transcending conflict over territory and sovereignty.

In impinging upon one another, these factors led the question of EU influence to become, not a matter of disinterested intellectual enquiry, but politicised. That is, prior outlooks on Northern Ireland affected the extent to which people were able or willing to 'see' actual or potential EU influences upon conflict resolution.

The thesis of this chapter is that there *has* been some Europeanisation of the Irish Question, the results of which can be seen in the three Strands of the Belfast Agreement and outside them. The chapter thus begins with the sphere where most commentators agree that this is so; that is, in the transformation of British–Irish relations in the EU context which enabled the two states to cooperate over Northern Ireland and to accept the more complicated set of East–West relations adumbrated in the Belfast Agreement.

It might be expected that attitudes towards European integration on the part of the two states might be expected to find parallels in the 'two communities' in Northern Ireland. The chapter thus explores the extent to which the centrality of the EU to Ireland's interests and the UK's ambivalence about it are reflected in nationalist and unionist outlooks in Northern Ireland. Here, it is suggested that, before Direct Rule, attitudes in Northern Ireland did not simply parallel those of the two states with which the 'two communities' identified. The imposition of Direct Rule changed this, dividing unionist opinion on Europe more fundamentally than before on its import for Northern Ireland and providing the circumstances for nationalists to promote the EU as a factor in bringing about what is now called 'an agreed Ireland'.

The chapter then moves to areas in which there is less agreement in the literature about EU influence – disagreement partly stemming from differences over Europe between the Social and Democratic Labour Party (SDLP) and the Ulster Unionist Party (UUP). In dealing first with North–South cooperation, the chapter suggests that the very existence of the EC, even when Ireland and UK were not yet members, prompted consideration of the necessity of closer links between the two parts of the island. However, the main impact came as the EC, itself, began to develop a more systematic regional policy in the form of support for integrated development programmes for internal and cross-border regions (and, more recently, in the context of special funding for Northern Ireland after the ceasefires). Here, it is argued that unionists have moved considerably but that a heightened awareness on their part of the 'spillover' effects in neo-functionalist explanations of European integration makes them wary of a similar logic in North–South cooperation resulting in 'rolling reunification'. All the same, pro-Agreement unionists accept that such cooperation is a corollary of nationalist acceptance that Northern Ireland remains, for the time being, British – and that there is a legitimate EU dimension to this. Moreover, it is acknowledged amongst those who are practically engaged in cooperative projects that the EU may be more acceptable than the two states, because more neutral, as an umbrella for such activity.

Next, the chapter discusses the impact of the EU on relations within a still British Northern Ireland, suggesting that, though the EU's impact may be disputed in terms of the budgetary significance of structural funding, the conditions of eligibility for support have contributed to new forums for inter- and cross-community participation. It is also suggested that this was reflected in the talks leading up to the Belfast Agreement and in some of its provisions.

The chapter, having – by and large – followed the three Strands of the Belfast Agreement, closes by touching upon matters outside them. It is here that ECHR influences are most apparent. It is concluded that while the influence of the EU (and ECHR) should not be overstated, it is equally a mistake to minimise the impact of external developments.

The Europeanisation of British–Irish relations and the East–West dimension of the Belfast Agreement

In the early 1960s, both states sought to accede to the then European Economic Community (EEC). Though one opinion in Ireland favoured entry regardless of any British decision,[3] the general view was that simultaneous accession would suit Ireland's interests, given the pattern of trade between the two states. Both states had different political perspectives. The UK's decision to try to enter was reluctant, part of coming to terms with the decline of empire and its loss of status as a world power. Ireland pursued accession wholeheartedly because membership was expected to raise its international status. As in the case of the Benelux countries before it, 'pooling sovereignty' would be the means of escape from the shadow of a single, dominant neighbour. In the course of actual membership from 1 January 1973, Ireland's political expectations were vindicated and the EU is now a core Irish interest. From the British–Irish point of view, the greater equality of status between the two states contributed to their ability to act jointly to 'pacify' Ireland by 'pooling sovereignty'[4] over the North. This process was helped by the familiarity between each state's civil servants induced by their interaction in the EU and by the opportunities at the interstices of intergovernmental meetings for discreet high-level exchanges of political views.

Early Irish speculations about a possible EEC impact on the status of the whole island took place before Direct Rule and, hence, were more North–South than East–West in focus (thus, discussed below). Conversely, the British prime minister's overriding determination during 1970–72 finally to succeed in joining the EC made the Northern Ireland crisis at best a distraction and at worst a threat to his European policy.[5] The main EU impact on a seriously joint British–Irish focus on Northern Ireland began in 1980 in which there was a 'dawning of a new era in Anglo-Irish relations'.[6]

Anglo-Irish intergovernmentalism, starting with Charles Haughey and Margaret Thatcher, survived tensions over the hunger strikes in 1981, the lack of an Irish dimension in a proposal for a new Northern Ireland Assembly in 1982, Ireland's attitude to the Falklands war, and the preference in the New Ireland Forum Report of 1983 for reunification. It was given an explicit European gloss by

Garret FitzGerald in his hope for 'a new and dynamic relationship with both communities in Northern Ireland, with the British Government and with our European friends' and in his determination to use the 1984 Irish Presidency of the EU 'to smooth the path of Anglo-Irish rapprochement'.[7]

The 1985 Anglo-Irish Agreement has been described as a 'compromise between Irish demands for joint authority and British reluctance to cede sovereignty'.[8] Even so, 'spillovers' from 'pooled sovereignty' in functional matters at the European level can be seen in the Agreement's institutionalisation of cross-border relations and the subsequent expansion after 1989 of areas for cooperation. The Intergovernmental Conference Report of 1993 explicitly refers to the relevance of the Single European Market and, in general, shows that membership of the EU 'increasingly encroached upon the work of the IGC'.[9] More specifically, the INTERREG, a programme of the EU (see below), and related programmes have been exploited to develop the functional agenda of the Anglo-Irish Agreement, particularly in connection with transport and the movement of goods. On the political front, British antipathy to joint authority, as symptomatic of ceding sovereignty, became less obvious as negotiations proceeded through the 1991 talks, the Joint Declaration of 1994 and the New Framework for Agreement Document of 1995.

The institutions and responsibilities outlined in the 1995 Document refer in some detail to the EU. It was suggested that it become a specific responsibility for a proposed North–South body and that the two governments might try to reach an agreed approach for the whole island in respect of EU issues.[10] This is somewhat reflected in the Belfast Agreement (see section on North–South cooperation). (See Appendix 2.)

The Agreement, however, widens intergovernmental relations beyond the joint authorisation of North–South cooperation. If implemented, the machinery of the Anglo-Irish Agreement will be replaced by two innovative institutions. There will be a new British–Irish Intergovernmental Council whose decisions will be informed by consultation with the Assembly and a British–Irish Council. The latter will consist of representatives of the two governments, the devolved institutions in Northern Ireland, Scotland and Wales, the Isle of Man, the Channel Islands and, if they are established, devolved assemblies in England. Though the analogy is imperfect since only two of the members are independent states, the proposed institutional relationships and functional responsibilities (including European matters) bear the hallmarks of that sense of interdependence lying behind the 'pooled sovereignty' arrangements of the EU. Though these innovations arose first from proposals by unionists to offset the North–South body, it is difficult to see how they could have come about without changes outside the confines of Northern Ireland; e.g., a more relaxed British understanding of sovereignty in the EU context and of the distribution of power within the UK.

It has been suggested[11] that a 'Council of the Isles' would ameliorate unionist disquiet over nationalist insistence on a North–South body by enmeshing it in a network of channels of cooperation towards the east. But this innovation may have a potential to transform relations amongst the component parts of the islands more radically than was intended by its proposers; that is, given its scope for bilateral agreements amongst the members in the context of a Scottish nationalist aspiration for 'independence in Europe' and inspiration from the success of a 'Europeanised Ireland'.

Northern Ireland; the Europeanisation of the Irish Question or the 'domestication' of the European Question?

It might be thought that Irish enthusiasm for and British ambivalence about accession to the EU would be reflected in a similar contrast between nationalists and unionists in Northern Ireland. There is a certain truth in this but patterns of support and opposition to European integration, in itself and in respect of its potential for ameliorating domestic conflict, have varied.

Superficially, unionists look like the last defenders of the imperialist values that led Winston Churchill and Ernest Bevin to be for European integration but against being in Europe. There is an overlap of personnel amongst Tory Euro-sceptics and Friends of the Union. This is explicable by their common concern to highlight the significance of borders for the preservation of national sovereignty and identity and, hence, the danger, especially for a disputed territory, of membership of a body whose *raison d'être* is to eliminate frontiers or to make them more permeable. Such disquiet is fuelled by the mirror-image approach of modern nationalists. In 1973, the SDLP adopted a policy of 'a United Ireland in an EC context'.[12] Since 1979, John Hume has used the resolution, through the EU, of the Franco-German territorial conflict as a metaphor for Northern Ireland and has promoted the idea of a 'Europe of the Regions' as the means of resolving conflict over territorial sovereignty. In the 1990s, his party took the further step of proposing that the EU play a part in the governance of Northern Ireland – to the disquiet of unionists and the Conservative government because of the implications for sovereignty.[13]

However, at the time of the first UK efforts to join the EEC – before Direct Rule – unionists, though divided over prospective membership, were more enthusiastic than the Nationalist Party (predecessor to the SDLP) and republicans. Unionists simply sought certain safeguards, especially the preservation of the Stormont legislation on the Safeguarding of Employment[14] (which prohibited the recruitment of Irish nationals from the South). Conversely, nationalists and republicans maintained the then conventional nationalist aspiration of autarky.[15] Direct Rule altered that pattern and, to some extent, 'domesticated' Europe as an additional angle to the conflict – in distinction to the Europeanising the Irish Question.

On the one hand, the coincidence of accession to the EC and Direct Rule divided unionism more fundamentally than before.[16] 'Moderate' unionists remained pro-European, especially the new Alliance Party. But 'hardline' unionists took the view that unionist values and interests had been doubly betrayed by the two events. On the other hand, the SDLP began to espouse European integration. Although it was intended to be temporary, Direct Rule was followed by the Sunningdale Agreement and a short-lived new Assembly. Its Executive, including its SDLP members, was pro-European. Since then, support for the EU in the SDLP at large has grown to a level comparable with that of the Alliance Party. And, as indicated above, its leaders have increasingly seen the Europeanisation of the Irish Question as the way forward. Reflecting a postnational or postmodern nationalist outlook which takes account of interdependence (also found in nationalist parties elsewhere which call for 'independence in Europe'), John Hume has declared that the days of the (autarkic) nation-state are gone.[17] Republicans, however, were more opportunistic converts to the EU, their strategists being forced by the 'Europeanisation of Ireland' to reformulate their ideas of Irish nationalism and their planning for Northern Ireland.[18] The reluctance of the shift is illustrated by Bernadette McAliskey's retort to John Hume – that she had not yet had her nation-state – and in the fact that Sinn Féin supporters still tend to be more similar to the Democratic Unionist Party (DUP) over Europe than to other nationalists.[19]

In what John Taylor, deputy leader of the UUP, called the 'New Unionism' to be seen in the Belfast Agreement, there is some renewal of the idea that European integration could be good for Northern Ireland. Thus, once again, 'Europe' is less 'domesticated' into the local conflict, attitudes to the Europeanisation of the Irish Question no longer coinciding so starkly with constitutional positions or schisms between the largest parties of the 'two communities'. However, as explained in connection with North–South cooperation, acceptance of a European dimension is accompanied by an awareness of competing theories of integration – functionalism and neo-functionalism. These different understandings of integration do coincide with unionism and nationalism.

The Europeanisation of North–South cooperation

The impact of the EU on North–South relations has economic and political dimensions. As noted, Irish opinion in the early 1960s favoured simultaneous accession to the EEC by Ireland and the UK. Though this did not stem from Ireland's northern interests, a European Commission report on regional economies occasioned a passing reference in 1962 to the possibility of 'the 32 counties being designated as one region'.[20] While unionist policy did not oppose UK efforts to join the EEC, the prime minister of Northern Ireland, Lord Brookeborough, raised the stakes by alleging during an election campaign that the taoiseach, Sean Lemass, had told his party that Irish entry into the EEC would effectively end partition.[21] The taoiseach claimed to have been more modest, suggesting that 'the gradual disappearance ... of the Border as a barrier in the economic and many other fields ... would, in time, tend to promote a common desire to remove the political barrier also'. In explaining his remarks, he drew upon the late Lord Craigavon's words: 'In this island, we cannot live always separated from one another. We are too small to be apart or for the border to be there for all time.'[22]

The first two applications by both states to join the EEC were unsuccessful but, it was observed that, in or out of it, the 'establishment of the European Community had affected both Irish and Northern Irish States'.[23] This was the background to a number of proposals which prefigured the areas of cooperation that are now accepted in the 1990s agenda. They were initiated by the secretary of the Department of Finance, T. K. Whitaker, familiar with the thinking of northern politicians, and pursued in 1965 by the taoiseach and the new prime minister of Northern Ireland, Terence O'Neill.[24] But the 'dynamism' of the mid–1960s disappeared during the Lynch premiership in the wake of renewed suspicions about the possibility of a hidden political agenda behind functional cooperation, the arms smuggling scandal implicating the Irish government, escalating violence in Northern Ireland and the imposition of Direct Rule.[25]

As noted, the coincidence of Direct Rule and EC accession divided unionists. Terence O'Neill and Brian Faulkner were excoriated for their 'un-Ulster values' of 'compromise, cross-border dialogue with the annexationist Irish Republic and power sharing with Republicans'.[26] This was compounded during British re-negotiation of the terms of membership and the 1975 referendum. Prospects for North–South cooperation remained stymied by the domestication of the European Question, especially as the European Parliament sought in the mid–1980s to intervene in political as well as economic affairs relating to internal and North and South matters.[27]

But change began with the development of European regional policy in the late 1980s and 1990s which provided a more comprehensive basis for the potential seen by the SDLP in a 'Europe of the Regions'. A new programme, INTERREG, started in 1989, was intended to foster 'bottom-up' initiatives reflecting the common interests of contiguous territories in different member states throughout the EU. There is also a cross-border dimension to what is now called the Special Support Programme for Peace and Reconciliation (SSPPR), initiated for Northern Ireland in the wake of the 1994 ceasefires.

This is not the place to assess the intrinsic details and merits of either pro-gramme or projects funded by them.[28] The point is to consider the extent to which they have Europeanised the Irish Question. Commentators are agreed that, because of centralisation and weak local government in Ireland and the UK, INTERREG I and II have not been a 'radical catalyst in the redefinition of relationships for the governance of the border region'[29] (i.e., 'bottom-up', joint administration). But the INTERREG initiative activated local interest among business people, councillors, and the voluntary sector in cross-border networking, administration and policy delivery and the 'bottom-up' approach has become more successful in the SSPPR.[30] This interest in cooperation may be, and sometimes is, fostered by the perception that the EU is a more neutral framework for it than intergovernmental initiatives.

Indeed, the existence of INTERREG initiatives coincided with a shift in some post-Direct Rule unionist ideas about sub-state cross-border cooperation: opposi-tion to it at all; that it should be spontaneous, market-led or otherwise voluntary;[31]

and, now, that it can be tolerated even with administration in joint, local hands. In the early 1990s, 'a remarkable upsurge in business enthusiasm for North–South economic integration' was noted.[32] 'Hardline' unionists berated a leading local banker and others for pursuing the idea of a 'North–South economic corridor'[33] – even without a superstructure. But, about the same time, the UUP was prepared in the 1992 Talks to concede the sense of some cross-border bodies, provided the remit of their joint management was functionally specific and limited to those functional objectives.

Strand Two of the Belfast Agreement reflects emergent recognition among unionists of the legitimacy of the nationalist interest in cooperation (in the absence of a majority for reunification); and that for unionists, too, there are some common North–South interests. The pursuit of these are now institutionalised in a North–South Ministerial Council which, in plenary form, will comprise representation from the Assembly led by the First Minister and Deputy First Minister and from the Irish government led by the taoiseach – reminiscent of the European Council. Reminiscent of the Council of Ministers, it will also meet in sectoral format under the leadership of ministers from both sides according to the topics under discussion. Its work will be directed at economic and social matters (including common EU interests), such as agriculture, fisheries, transport, waterways, tourism, urban and rural development, education, health, certain aspects of social security and the environment.

This was a difficult part of the Agreement upon which to reach consensus. Both sides had to come a long way; nationalists from immediate reunification and unionists from opposition to a political-administrative superstructure which they believed would be a Trojan horse for a reunited Ireland. While EU initiatives helped to foster such convergence, as mentioned above, greater awareness of theories of integration also induced reservations and, hence, complicated the reaching of agreement on just what shape, powers and responsibilities the new body should have.[34]

For the same reason that theorists of functionalism prefer the allocation of collaborative functions to a variety of bodies rather than to a single body, unionists would have preferred North–South cooperation to have been carried out by several bodies set up for narrowly-defined, specific purposes. Having lost that argument, they would have preferred an overarching institution to be advisory rather than to be required, in EU style, to develop common policies for implementation in the two jurisdictions.

Nationalists have a more neo-functionalist way of thinking – that as people are accustomed to cooperation in one area the habit will 'spillover' into others – as implied earlier in Sean Lemass's speculations and John Hume's references to the EU's origins and development. Even so, they are puzzled by what they see as a lack of unionist confidence in being able to say 'no' to some future proposal or another. But unionists observe neo-functionalist 'spillovers' leading, in theory and actuality, into 'ever closer union' in the EU. This means that they expect their potential 'no's' to be seen as irrational and dysfunctional to the full benefits of cooperation. Hence, the rashness of the comment during the negotiating period by David Andrews, the Irish foreign minister, that the proposed North–South Ministerial Council would be 'a kind of government'.[35]

One account of the North–South dimension[36] is sceptical of both 'irredentist nationalist hopes' and corresponding unionist fears that the EU will bring about 'rolling integration' by neo-functionalist means. But its authors do suggest that North–South economic cooperation could 'square the circle between Nationalism and Unionism' within a 'British Northern Ireland'.

The impact of Europe on relations within a British Northern Ireland

As noted, commentators disagree about whether the EU has made any difference to 'the warring factions' within Northern Ireland.[37] It is suggested here that, while direct effects may not be obvious, EU initiatives have contributed to the conditions under which it has become possible for people from different communities to negotiate with one another. There is evidence of new ways of thinking, facilitated by the EU, in the institutional provisions of Strand One of the Belfast Agreement.

Despite the domestication, in the 1970s, of the European Question, from 1979 – the year of the first direct elections to the European Parliament (EP) – the EU 'provide[d] an unsuspected opportunity for common cause'[38] and Northern Ireland's MEPs worked together in Europe. For example, action by John Hume (SDLP), supported by Ian Paisley (DUP) and John Taylor (UUP), led to the Martin Report by the European Parliament which called for special assistance for Northern Ireland.[39] Throughout the 1980s, various individual initiatives or problems (agriculture, lobbying for Objective 1 status, additionality) attracted the combined attention of the three MEPs[40] (John Taylor replaced by Jim Nicholson). More recently, the MEPs cooperated in helping to secure (and renew and enlarge), the 1994 SSPPR. The EU also provides 'common cause' opportunities for politicians in local government, albeit that, following Direct Rule, their powers to act and scope of action are limited. Most notable, perhaps, is the partnership of the twenty-six district councils in an initiative started by the Law Society and the private sector to set up and fund a Northern Ireland Centre in Europe (Northern IrelandCE). And there is their role in the SSPPR (see below).

Political cooperation arises in part from perceived defects in constitutional conventions which, despite the high profile of Northern Ireland secretaries of state,[41] unionists, as well as nationalists, see as causing Northern Irish interests to be poorly defended in the Council of Ministers.[42] According to Ian Paisley, the three MEPs work together so closely that, on seeing this, their colleagues in the EP 'thought they had worked a miracle'.[43] But, they have been slower to show themselves as being able to transcend their differences at home. In 1983, Ian Paisley boycotted a banquet in Belfast to celebrate ten years of membership because of the presence of the Irish taoiseach and John Taylor boycotted it because of the presence of Edward Heath.[44] Manifestos for European elections, especially those of the DUP, still tend to convey the electoral contest as a plebiscite on the constitutional status of Northern Ireland. Notably, the European election of 1999 was presented and interpreted as a competition between pro- and anti-Agreement forces.

While elected political leaders may behave outside Northern Ireland as though there is a positive symbiosis between the Irish and European Questions but not at home, in the domestic politics of civil society there is some ameliorative link between Europe and inter-community relations. This has stemmed from the operation of structural funds programmes, available hitherto to Northern Ireland as an Objective 1 region (as the whole of the Republic of Ireland), and under the SSPPR. Eligibility for the former is based on the inclusion of social and local partners (as well as regional, national and European) at all stages of the life of a project. While, as in the case of INTERREG programmes, structural funding planning within Northern Ireland has been criticised as too state-driven, it is also argued that, over time, the special problems of Northern Ireland encouraged Conservative governments to permit a degree of popular participation in European policy issues that was not regarded as suitable in Great Britain.[45] The SSPPR institutionalises cross-community partnership. Twenty-six district partnerships are comprised of equal proportions of people drawn from business and trade unions, from elected councillors from a variety of parties, and from the community and voluntary sectors. Funding decisions by the partnerships are intended to secure the participation of all sections of the community and, where appropriate, to promote cross community cooperation. In 1997, it was suggested that they would not bring about 'the big solution' but had 'the potential for making a solution more possible'.[46] This seems to be borne out by the fact that community workers involved in such partnerships and projects include ex-prisoners from both sides, now working together and some of whom were on the teams supporting Sinn Féin and the new loyalist parties at the Talks.

Another European dimension to community politics and the peace process comes about through women. Women are particularly visible in community action and negotiation with the statutory sector over the politics of everyday life and, at the same time, alert to the potential of EU initiatives to improve their situations – in employment conditions and social policy at home, and through the greater acknowledgement outside Northern Ireland of their skills in partnership and rights to effective political participation.[47] The EU, through the Northern Ireland Women's European Platform, provides a network, operating internally and at the interstices of the EU and the United Nations' international human rights policy community. Combined with community networks, this was the basis upon which the Northern Ireland Women's Coalition (NIWC) was able to be brought into being.[48] It was the NIWC which proposed the Civic Forum that is in the Agreement as a symbol and a means of a more pluralist and inclusionary political system. (There is also the possibility of a north–south civic forum.) The NIWC Talks Team deliberately examined the workings of the EU Economic and Social

Committee and institutions in other European countries in deciding the details of what to propose and what to avoid.

The Civic Forum may be construed as a kind of power sharing in that it grafts the politics of inter-community interaction or cross-community participation on to the 'pillared' political representation of the 'two communities'. But power sharing in its formal sense belongs to the chamber of elected representatives. This, too, has a European dimension. It could be argued that power sharing is a domestic form of 'pooling sovereignty'. More directly, the practice of consensual decision-making or coalition politics elsewhere in Europe informed the thinking of the Executive of the short-lived Assembly of 1973.[49] The Alliance leader, Oliver Napier, pointed out that power sharing was 'the rule rather than the exception throughout Europe'[50] and, when the Assembly was on the brink of being brought down, Brian Faulkner warned that 'Europe's eyes will be upon us to see if we can pull together'.[51] In contrast, the Assembly's opponents equated 'softness on Europe' with 'softness on power sharing'. Power sharing was not wanted at any level, 'within Northern Ireland, between Northern Ireland and the Republic of Ireland ... or within Europe'.[52] Twenty-six years later, however, conflating the EU and power sharing negatively has not figured prominently in opposition to the Belfast Agreement.

Power sharing in the Agreement involves the allocation of committee and ministerial offices in proportion to party strengths. In addition, there are two forms of qualified majority voting, which are controversial because they protect nationalists and unionists but not those who define themselves as 'other': for the selection of the First and Deputy First Ministers, dismissal from office, standing orders, budgetary allocations and policy issues defined in advance as 'key'. The present impasse over the implementation of the Agreement does not involve opposition to those institutional features which Napier saw as the norm in Europe – only the conditions under which the institutions might begin to work.

Conclusion

There are other aspects of the politics of Northern Ireland and British–Irish relations to which Europe is relevant. Three issues – Economic and Monetary Union, formalised police cooperation, and freedom of movement between Ireland and the UK and within the EU – are important; the first for North–South transactions in the current constitutional set-up, the second legitimating what has been happening for a long time,[53] and the third because of arrangements allowing there to be an open North–South border.[54] But these are not directly connected to the Belfast Agreement. Several issues, not mentioned so far, in Strands One to Three and outside them show signs of the Europeanisation of the Irish Question, or, at least, the interaction of indigenous ideas and developments elsewhere. For example, Assembly legislation will have to be 'equality proofed' and comply with ECHR standards. The two governments will strengthen human rights standards to meet those of the ECHR and to match one another; for example, in provisions for minorities and their languages, the status of women, and socioeconomic equality regardless of class, religion, disability or ethnicity. A charter of human rights for the whole island is mooted.

Acceptance of some harmonisation owes something to both the ECHR and the EU. That discrimination against homosexuals is unlawful in both North and South (affirmed in the Agreement explicitly by the UK and implicitly by Ireland) stems from actions in the respective courts which led, eventually, to rulings in the European Court of Human Rights. The EU has long been argued to have contributed to the emergence of commitment in the South to sex equality and its reinforcement in the UK. Legislation to incorporate the ECHR in the UK and proposals for human rights legislation in Ireland were completed and introduced, respectively, at the same time as the ratification of the Amsterdam Treaty. The first text of the Treaty, drafted by the Irish Presidency in 1996, declared that ECHR principles are also the EU's fundamental principles – and this remained in the final version.

It has not been the intention of this chapter to overstate the European dimension to the reformulation of the Irish Question and answers to it. Obviously the roots of the Irish Question long pre-date European integration. But if Europe was irrelevant to the causes, it can be relevant to the solution. Indeed, it has been shown that moves similar to provisions now in the Belfast Agreement were on the agenda in the 1960s, before either state belonged to the EU. Europe, however, is a new factor in the context in which a solution is being sought. Even in the 1960s, the existence of the EEC, although the UK and Ireland were not in it, was considered relevant to the well-being of both parts of the island.

This proposition became less persuasive in mainstream Northern Irish unionism as a result of Direct Rule, of nationalist hopes that the EU could 'blur' the status of Northern Ireland, and of an overlap between unionists and 'Euro-sceptics' at Westminster, especially in the Conservative Party. But such forces did not eliminate a Northern Ireland unionist sense that the EU could have benevolent effects. The Belfast Agreement, as indicated in the opening quotation to this chapter, shows that an EU impact has been accepted, albeit on a less ambitious scale than speculated upon in the South in the 1960s and envisaged in subsequent SDLP aspirations. In everyday life, the EU has become palpable to people in community politics and it is implausible that it should have no meaning. My only claim about the meaning is that the language, conventions and institutions of EU policy-making have helped, after a shaky start, to create spaces for contending parties in formal and informal politics to discuss solutions to old problems in new ways, to act upon that opportunity, and to do so in a context in which the states with which they identify themselves have become more equal partners than they ever were before.

Notes

1   Rory O'Donnell, 'Fixing the Institutions' in Robin Wilson (ed.), *No Frontiers; North–South Integration in Ireland* (Belfast: Democratic Dialogue, 1999), pp. 70–3. Quotation taken from p. 70.

2   In addition to works cited here, other brief (mostly) or extensive references to the EU and Northern Ireland are reviewed by Elizabeth Meehan in her E. H. Carr Memorial Lecture, University of Wales, Aberystwyth – published in the *Review of International Studies,* January 2000.

3   Letter from Garret FitzGerald to T. K. Whitaker, secretary, Department of Finance, 29 April 1961, D/T S16023C/61.

4   John McGarry and Brendan O'Leary, *Explaining Northern Ireland* (Oxford: Blackwell, 1996), esp. pp. 279–82, 302–6.

5   Paul Hainsworth, 'Northern Ireland in the European Community' in Michael Keating and Barry Jones (eds), *Regions in the European Community* (Oxford: Clarendon Press, 1985), p. 130.

6   Etain Tannam, *Cross-Border Cooperation in the Republic of Ireland and Northern Ireland* (Basingstoke: Macmillan, 1999), pp. 75–6.

7   Quoted by Hainsworth, 'Northern Ireland', pp. 128, 130.

8   Tannam, *Cross-Border Cooperation*, pp. 77, 83, 85. The Agreement was hated by unionists who had been excluded from the intergovernmental negotiations (unlike the SDLP which had an informal channel of communication with the Irish government).

9   *Ibid.*, p. 81.

10 *Ibid.*, pp. 90–4.

11 Richard Kearney and Simon Partridge (and with them elsewhere, Robin Wilson), 'Nordic-Style Institutions Recommended for Irish-British Islands', *Eagle Street,* Newsletter of the Finnish Institute in London, Issue 7 (January 1998), no page number.

12 Hainsworth, 'Northern Ireland', p. 123. See also Cathal McCall, 'Postmodern Europe and the resources of communal identities in Northern Ireland' in *European Journal of Political Research*, 33, (1998), pp. 398–411, esp. 397–8.

13 Paul Bew and Elizabeth Meehan, 'Regions and Borders: Controversies in Northern Ireland about the European Union', *Journal of European Public Policy* 1(1), (1994), pp. 95–113; Tannam, *Cross-Border Cooperation*, p. 95.

14 Letter from Irish Ambassador in London to the secretary, Department of External Affairs, 24 November 1961, D/T S15273B.

15 Michael Cox, 'Bringing in the "International": the IRA Ceasefire and the End of the Cold War', *International Affairs* 73(4), (1996), pp. 671–93.

16 Hainsworth, 'Northern Ireland', pp. 121–3.

17 James Anderson, 'The Shifting Stage of Politics: New Medieval and Postmodern Territorialities?', *Environment and Planning D: Society and Space*, 14, (1996), pp. 133–53, esp. pp. 137–8, from where the John Hume quotation is taken. He also reviews commentaries by, for example, Richard Kearney and Robin Wilson, in this area. Also see McCall, 'Postmodern Europe', on both Kearney and the impact of postmodernity and developments in the European state system upon Irish identity.

18 Cox, 'Bringing in the "International"'.

19 Anderson, 'The Shifting Stage', pp. 689–92 on McAliskey and, on Sinn Féin (as well as the other parties), Gavin Adams, 'The Impact of European Integration on Northern Irish Politics set in a Comparative Perspective with Confessional Parties in the Netherlands', PhD thesis to be submitted at The Queen's University of Belfast.

20 File note to taoiseach, 4 January 1962, D/T S16877X/62.

21 *Irish Press*, 31 February 1962.

22 Dail Debates, Vol. 194, No. 0, Cols 1427–8, 5 April 1962, D/T S17246E/62. He attracted public correspondence about whether or not Lord Craigavon had actually said such a thing; *The Irish Times,* 11 April 1962 and 13 April 1962, D/T S17246F/62.

23 Tannam, *Cross-Border Cooperation*, p. 51.

24 *Ibid.*, pp. 50–7.

25 *Ibid.*, pp. 58–60, 83–4.

26 Hainsworth, 'Northern Ireland', p. 122.

27 E.g., the 1983 Haagerup Report which recommended joint British–Irish responsibilities, as well as cross-border cooperation and also attempted in Strasbourg to debate the Anglo-Irish Agreement in 1985; Tannam, *Cross-Border Cooperation*, pp. 174–5 and Hainsworth, 'Northern Ireland', pp. 111, 129.

28 Accounts are available in: Tannam, *Cross-Border Cooperation*, chs 4–7; Cathal McCall, 'Fledging European Union Social Partnership and the Irish Border Region', unpublished paper (1998), given to this author; James Corrigan, 'Cross-border Programmes' in Mary Browne and Dennis Kennedy (eds), *Northern Ireland and the European Union: Discussion Papers on the Intergovernmental Conference and other European Issues* (Belfast: Institute of European Studies, The Queen's University of Belfast, 1996), pp. 35–6.

29 Tannam, *Cross-Border Cooperation*, chs 4–7; McCall, 'Fledging European Union Social Partnership'.

30 *Ibid.*

31 Anderson, 'The Shifting Stage'.

32 Respondent to Opsahl Commission; A. Pollak (ed.), *A Citizens' Enquiry: The Opsahl Report on Northern Ireland* (Dublin: The Lilliput Press and Initiative 1992, 1993), p. 75.

33 Dr George Quigley, chairman of the Ulster Bank and former senior civil servant, introduced the idea of a corridor. An economic and political critique of it is provided by Paul Bew, Henry Patterson and Paul Teague, *Between War and Peace: The Political Future of Northern Ireland* (London: Lawrence and Wishart, 1997), ch. 7.

34 Tannam, *Cross-Border Cooperation* deals with this from the standpoint of an observer. But politicians, themselves, also use these categories and theories. See Anderson, 'The Shifting Stage', pp. 136–7 on how they have done so in the past and Bew, Patterson and Teague, *Between War and Peace*, pp. 192–5 on the present. See also McCall, 'Postmodern Europe', pp. 393–4.

35 Rory O'Donnell alludes to postmodern political theories that state power now seeps outwards, downward and upwards to a variety of non-governmental, semi-public bodies and supranational regimes by saying that 'one smiled' at this 'unfortunate phrase' – 'because nobody knows what a government is like nowadays', 'Fixing the Institutions', p. 73. This fits in with postnationalist ideas but unionism is, perhaps, still 'modern'; see references at n.17.

36 Bew, Patterson and Teague, *Between War and Peace*, p. 199.

37 McGarry and O'Leary, *Explaining Northern Ireland*, pp. 198–9.

38 Hainsworth, 'Northern Ireland', p. 128.

39 *Ibid.*, p. 110.

40 *Ibid.*, p. 128.

41 *Ibid.*, pp. 113–4.

42 Bew and Meehan, 'Regions and Borders', pp. 105–6.

43 In an interview with Bew and Meehan, 'Regions and Borders', p. 103.

44 Hainsworth, 'Northern Ireland', p. 122.

45 Susan Hodgett, *Community Infrastructure: The Northern Ireland Voluntary Sector and European Union Regional Policy* (Belfast: Northern Ireland Council for Voluntary Action, 1998).

46 Paul Sweeney, then Director of the Northern Ireland Partnership Board, the 'umbrella' for the twenty-six boards; quoted by McCall in 'Fledging European Union Social Partnerships'.

47 *Women and Citizenship in Northern Ireland; Power, Participation and Choice.* No named author; written by a research group (Belfast: Women's Education and Resources Centre and Equal Opportunities Commission, 1995).

48 Bronagh Hinds, 'Women Working for Peace in Northern Ireland' in Yvonne Galligan, Eilis Ward and Rick Wilford (eds), *Contesting Politics: Women in Ireland, North and South* (Boulder, Colorado: Westview Press/Political Studies Association of Ireland, 1999).

49 Hainsworth, 'Northern Ireland', p. 122.

50 *Ibid.*

51 *Ibid.*
52 *Ibid.*, p. 123.
53 Jason Lane, 'The Development of Irish Cross-Border Police Cooperation: Influences and Effects of the European Union', PhD thesis submitted at The Queen's University of Belfast, 1999.
54 Elizabeth Meehan, *Ireland's Choice to Prioritize Free Movement with the United Kingdom over Free Movement in the European Union* (Dublin: The Policy Institute, 1999), ch. 5.

15

'Hope and history': the US and peace in Northern Ireland

JOHN DUMBRELL

In late December 1993, following a White House review of policy, President Clinton decided to take a proactive stance on Northern Ireland. For an Administration frequently accused of directionless 'channel surfing' on foreign policy, this was a key decision and one which produced a coherent and resolute commitment to the province's affairs. As a turning point in the history of the peace process, Clinton's decision has many rivals. Yet few would deny Clinton's activism a central place. When the IRA leadership attempted to explain its August 1994 ceasefire decision to IRA supporters, it specifically invoked the opportunities stemming from Washington's new attitude.[1] Washington intervened at key stages to revive the process. George Mitchell's contribution – as US special envoy to Northern Ireland and chairman of the peace negotiations – was praised publicly in 1998 by representatives both of Sinn Féin and the Ulster Unionist Party (UUP). A year later of course he was critical in ensuring the setting-up of the new Northern Ireland executive. His role in the peace negotiations developed, from one of even-handed absorption of different viewpoints, to dynamic and proactive reconciliation in the days and hours leading up to the 1998 Good Friday Agreement.[2]

Clinton's active involvement in the North has been derided – by various unionist politicians, by British politicians and journalists, by political opponents in the US, and, most famously by Raymond Seitz (US Ambassador to London, 1991–94). Journalist Simon Jenkins described Clinton's conduct at the 1999 St Patrick's Day reception at the White House as follows: 'He flashed his sequins and put some more bourbon on ice. Resolving Northern Ireland has always seemed that simple to the expatriate Irish of America.'[3]

For Seitz, 'the Clinton White House took little account of … simple constitutional and democratic facts' such as that Northern Ireland is part of the UK and that London has 'responsibility for bridging the historic mistrust between majority and minority'. Jean Kennedy Smith, sister to Senator Edward Kennedy and Clinton's first Ambassador to Dublin, 'was', he continued, 'an ardent IRA apologist'.[4] In awarding Sinn Féin leader Gerry Adams a US entry visa in early 1994, Clinton stood accused of rewarding terrorism. Yet, as Vice President Al Gore put it (in characteristically unClintonesque rhetoric), threads were 'being woven, one stitch at a time, into the shimmering cloak of peace'.⁵ Clinton's activism was an integral feature of the peace dynamic, not an optional add-on or *deus ex machina*. Despite Seitz's accusations about Kennedy Smith, Washington did manage to achieve a degree of credibility with loyalists. Progress would scarcely have been possible otherwise. At times it actually appeared that Washington *was* the peace dynamic. Reflecting such (excessively heightened) expectations, *The Times* announced in a March 1999 headline: 'Hope for peace rests on Clinton's clout'.⁶

This chapter will review the Clinton administration's role in the peace process and consider various explanations for the new American activism. It will set the Northern Irish initiatives in the context of the Administration's developing post-Cold War foreign policy priorities.

Ripeness and the American dimension

Before 1993, executive branch leaders in Washington tended to favour an 'ancient enmities' understanding of the Troubles, combining this with (on this issue at least) an 'empathetically interdependent'⁷ interpretation of US–UK relations. What went on in the North of Ireland was London's business. Washington would try to avoid embarrassing its Cold War ally. Washington's interests and sympathy were identified with London. The State Department made its position clear in 1969: 'The United Kingdom is a friendly country which, unlike certain other countries with civil rights problems, has a basic structure of democratic institutions and political freedom.'⁸ Despite public and Congressional pressure to do otherwise, official Washington shunned involvement in a conflict which was generally viewed as obscure, ancient and probably intractable. In the terminology used by the Bush Administration (1989–93), the conflict was not 'ripe' for American mediation.⁹

From the late 1960s to the early 1990s, the American dimension to the conflict primarily involved the various Catholic Irish-American lobbies and Congressmen who were sympathetic to the republican cause. The IRA gained funds, especially during the hunger strikes of the early 1980s, as well as access to weapons.¹⁰ Yet, even before Clinton, the White House did show signs of breaking with the cautious, pro-London 'ancient enmities' understanding of the Troubles. Key indications of a more proactive approach were President Jimmy Carter's 1977 statement on the province – linking American investment to a power sharing solution – and the Reagan Administration's pressure on London prior to the 1985 Anglo-Irish Agreement. This US counter-policy laid the foundations for Clinton's activism and for the abandonment of the more conservative, 'ancient enmities' approach. It was associated with various lobbying networks, all of which sought to promote both US governmental involvement and the cause of constitutional nationalism. Key players included Senator

Kennedy, SDLP leader John Hume and various Dublin politicians and diplomats (notably Sean Donlon).[11]

Clinton did not immediately jettison the non-interventionist policy. Gerry Adams was twice refused a visa in 1993. Clinton's call, made ten days before the 1992 Presidential election, to appoint a 'peace envoy' was not followed up until Mitchell's appointment (initially as special adviser on economic initiatives) in January 1995. Yet, even early on, there were important changes of emphasis. In February 1993, Raymond Seitz lectured business leaders to the effect that Northern Ireland should be distinguished from ethnic conflicts which are 'so primordial that they lie beyond the reach of rational resolution'.[12] Various forces – most particularly the end of the Cold War and Presidential efforts to articulate a new internationalism – were leading the new Administration towards intervention. Central to this momentum was a reconfiguration of the elite Irish-American lobby; Clinton's 1992 call for a 'peace envoy' came in a letter to a group of 'Irish Americans for Clinton and Gore'. Coordinated for campaign purposes by Clinton aide Chris Hyland, 'Irish Americans for Clinton and Gore' represented a body founded by ex-Congressman (and former law school classmate of Bill Clinton), Bruce Morrison: Americans for a New Irish Agenda (ANIA). ANIA was a potent configuration of well-funded, business-oriented Irish-American opinion: geared towards constitutional nationalism, concerned that Washington should abandon the traditional non-involvement, and also prepared to woo moderate loyalists. Leaders included Niall O'Dowd, editor of the Irish-American journal *The Irish Voice*, and businessmen William Flynn and Charles Feeney. The group was not merely an outgrowth of the Hume-Kennedy network. (Both John Hume and Senator Kennedy were, for example, far less enthusiastic about the MacBride principles than the ANIA (these set 'fair employment' quotas for US-owned firms in Northern Ireland)). Yet the period 1992–3 did see an important alliance between these representatives of corporate Irish America, the Kennedy forces and Dublin. Nancy Soderberg, long-serving Kennedy aide, drafted the 1992 statement and was appointed to the National Security Council staff. The White House drew closer to taoiseach Albert Reynolds, who succeeded Charles Haughey in February 1992. A formidable alliance was now promoting White House proactivity.[13]

Clinton's involvement

The December 1993 White House policy review was a direct response to the Downing Street Declaration. Clinton kept in touch with Albert Reynolds during the Declaration's genesis and development. At one time the US President appears to have been persuaded by Reynolds to shelve the 'peace envoy' idea as a way of easing London into the agreement.[14]

The decision to admit Adams reflected the ANIA view that – in Niall O'Dowd's words – 'Sinn Féin were looking for another, wider outreach in America'.[15] Reynolds presented this view directly to Clinton: 'No fundraising, short-term visa, send him home with a message, that you want him to join the peace train and leave violence behind and that if he doesn't he'll never get another one.'[16] Soderberg later described how the White House made its decision. The President 'decided that it was worth the risk of reaching out to Adams a little bit in the hope he would then deliver on the ceasefire'. If ceasefire hopes were disappointed 'we could go back and say this person is not serious about peace ... we thought we would win either way'.[17] Bruce Morrison saw it as Sinn Féin's 'opportunity to come in from the cold'.[18]

It was Morrison's group which had invited Adams, and some unionist politicians, to the US. A visit by the group to Belfast in August 1993 had been accorded a week-long IRA ceasefire. When the ceasefire of 1994 came, the strategy seemed to have been vindicated. The Morrison group, acting as a kind of deniable White House surrogate, visited Belfast immediately before the August 1994 announcement. The White House concentrated on dangling the 'peace dividend', as well as pressuring both London and Sinn Féin into establishing a peace dynamic.[19]

Central to the strategy was the conscious desire to avoid a replay of more or less solid loyalist opposition to the 1985 Anglo-Irish Agreement. Official Unionist leader James Molyneaux entered into dialogue with Vice President Gore. He was promised that Northern Ireland's Protestant majority would not find the US seeking to impose an unwanted settlement. The period 1993–94 saw a distinct wedge being driven by Washington between the different brands of unionism; such a strategy had long been advocated by Senator Kennedy. Upon emerging from the Senate Office Building in April 1994, Molyneaux remarked: 'I never thought I would see the day that Senator Edward Kennedy would sit across a table from me and ask, "Mr Molyneaux, what can we do for you"'.[20] Despite the application of the intra-unionist wedge, ritual overtures were made to Ian Paisley. It was also constantly emphasised that the 'peace dividend' which the US was prepared to inject would benefit all. In May 1995, Gary McMichael reported on a major Washington investment conference on Northern Ireland for *The Irish Voice*. (McMichael, leader of the UDP, was invited by O'Dowd to write for the *Voice* as part of the inclusionist strategy):

> I watched as Ulster Unionist MPs sat at one end of the bar, while Adams was a few feet away, each engaging in their own particular activities. This is something we would not have seen six months ago. Even though the DUP (Democratic Unionist Party) was fleeing from room to room in strict formation and scanning the area with hands firmly in pockets least they be compromised by some opportunist Republican, they were there and that is important.[21]

(As if to underline the fragility of the process, not only Paisley but also Molyneaux boycotted the conference since Northern Ireland secretary Patrick Mayhew was to meet Adams informally.)

Adams met National Security Adviser Anthony Lake, now leading Clinton's Irish strategy, at the White House in November 1994. On St Patrick's Day 1995, he received an unphotographed handshake from the Chief Executive himself. In early

1995, Washington lifted the ban on Sinn Féin fundraising in the US, citing Adams' promise to move on arms decommissioning. Pressure was applied on Sinn Féin to respond to the new American strategy by giving ground. (The need for the IRA to make some actual, tangible start to decommissioning later became known as 'Washington Three'. In March 1999, Clinton was still reportedly telling Adams: 'You are going to have to move. It's not viable for you to say it can't happen.')[22]

The White House organised visits to Washington by loyalist paramilitary representatives, following their 1994 ceasefires. Various high-level trips to Belfast culminated in Clinton's own November 1995 visit – 'hope and history'.[23]

The breaking, in February 1996, of the IRA ceasefire exposed burnt fingers at the White House and stimulated cries of 'I told you so' from London. Between February 1996 and May 1997 – the date of the British general election – the Clinton initiative in Ireland seemed to be discredited. An international commission, chaired by Mitchell, backed Clinton's view that decommissioning should occur in parallel with talks. Yet when talks began, in June 1996, Sinn Féin was excluded. Rifts appeared, even within the O'Dowd-Morrison group, over the withdrawal of Sinn Féin fundraising rights. A leading Irish-American Democrat, Senator Christopher Dodd of Connecticut, actually condemned the whole Clinton strategy.

Following Tony Blair's victory, Clinton's involvement was reactivated. In stark contrast to the John Major years, it was now actually welcomed by London. In March 1998, journalist John Carlin noted: 'Every public declaration made by Mr Clinton, [taoiseach] Mr Ahern and [Northern Irish secretary] Mo Mowlam appeared almost as if it had been carefully orchestrated and jointly rehearsed.'[24] Adams, John Hume, McMichael, David Trimble and Lord Alderdice of the Alliance Party were all seen personally by Clinton during their 1998 St Patrick's Day visit to Washington. Clinton's direct telephonic interventions during the subsequent Stormont talks were a predictable, yet arguably indispensable, feature of the Agreement's emergence. In his memoir, *Making Peace*, George Mitchell referred to calls to Trimble, Hume, Adams and others: 'The delegates know the President well from their prior meetings … They were impressed that he would stay up all night, to follow the negotiations, to talk with them.'[25] Following the Agreement, Clinton urged a 'vote for peace' in the ensuing referendum and assembly elections. He was dissuaded from campaigning in person, but visited Ireland again in September 1998.

Clinton's activism: explanations and context

Various explanations for Clinton's activism spring to mind. The President had a personal interest in the affairs of the province, stemming from student days at Oxford. The abandonment of non-interventionism also had a strong 'bureaucratic politics' dimension. Clinton's Irish strategy involved a bureaucratic victory for the White House European foreign policy staff over the State Department. (Aside from State and the London Embassy, the Justice Department and the Central

Intelligence Agency were also opposed to the granting of a visa to Adams in 1993–94.) At one level, Clinton was responding to Congressional and Democratic party pressure. Edward Kennedy was an important influence. Clinton was also responsive to the new alignment in elite Irish America represented by the Morrison–O'Dowd group. The policy evolved alongside a reinterpretation of the 'special relationship' with London. Two clusters of explanatory context stand out: one involving the Presidential relationship with Irish America; the other relating to the development of American internationalism after the Cold War.

For *The Nation* columnist Eric Alterman, Clinton's Irish policy was 'a stunning success' for ethnic lobbying.[26] Michael Mates, who had been sent by prime minister John Major to Washington to protest Clinton's early interventions, wrote in 1996 of 'Clinton's cynical playing to the green Irish vote'.[27]

Presidents, especially first term ones, are interested in votes and popularity. Although criticised by Republicans for damaging US–UK relations, Clinton was hardly likely to suffer much domestic damage in advancing his new activism. Irish America – a vast constituency of around 40 million people, represented by some powerful Congressional figures – would probably like it. At worst, a highly assimilated Irish America would be indifferent, though surely willing to applaud any settlement. Irish-Americans were also widely thought to be prominent in the ranks of 'Reagan Democrats', who had defected to the Republicans in the 1980s, and needed to be reclaimed. The new policy was not entirely risk-free, even if we discount the impact on Anglo-American relations. Nancy Soderberg later recalled the problems of heightening expectations, about 'the President pulling a rabbit out of the hat'.[28] The policy clearly offended specialists at the State Department. However, it is possible to concoct an argument to the effect that Clinton was primarily concerned to please various sections of Irish America.

The problem with this type of analysis is that it is frequently pushed much too far. Commentators understate the complexity and overstate the intensity of political Irish America. David Trimble acknowledged, as the peace process developed, that Irish America was 'complex, politically'.[29] For one thing, though arguably more assimilated than their Catholic counterparts, Protestant Irish Americans represent a significant component in the ethnic mix. Congressman Joseph Kennedy estimated in 1994 that around one-quarter of Irish-Americans in his Massachusetts constituency were Protestant in origin.[30] Prominent Irish-Americans also often disagree about what is best for Northern Ireland. In 1993–94, House of Representatives Speaker Tom Foley, a highly influential Irish-American politician whom the Clinton Administration had every reason to cultivate, *opposed* the granting of Adams' visa. There is no cohesive 'shamrock vote' in the US. In 1992, Clinton actually won reasonably clearly in states with large Irish-American populations.[31] Indulging in high-profile and time-consuming policy departures in Northern Ireland was hardly a rational way of electioneering. It is also worth recalling that Clinton (like Senator Kennedy) has clashed with Irish Catholic lobbies over issues such as abortion and the waning Administration enthusiasm for the McBride principles.[32]

Strong arguments can be mustered to link both the entire post–1992 peace initiative, and Clinton's own part in it, to the global context – particularly to the end of the Cold War. As Michael Cox has argued, 'it was inevitable that, as the tide of global radicalism began to retreat after 1989, this would feed into republican thinking'.[33] With the Soviet threat removed, it indeed did appear that London had neither selfish strategic nor economic interest in Ulster. The Clinton–ANIA strategy was a coherent and successful attempt to reinforce republican doubts about the rationale for the armed struggle and to talk up the benefits of peace.

The new strategy was also rooted in a reinterpretation of Britain's relationship to the US. In Keohane's terminology, an 'instrumentally interdependent' under-standing of US–UK relations (in the Irish context) supplanted the traditional 'empathetically interdependent' line. Clinton's annoyance at the Major govern-ment's clumsy efforts to advance the Bush cause in the 1992 Presidential election may have played a part in the shift. Much more central, however, was the sense of release felt by the White House following the Cold War's end. The (asymmetric) strategic symbiosis, which characterised US–UK relations in the era of the Soviet threat, was now unravelling. Washington was now far less bothered with the prospect of anti-Americanism crossing from Calais to Dover. Prime minister John Major's anger[34] was simply not a matter of great concern to the White House. Some Clinton aides actually relished what they saw as a long-overdue puncturing of British stuffiness and hypocrisy on Ireland. Conor O'Clery attributes the following comment on the Adams visa issuance to senior adviser George Stephanopoulos: 'It obviously ticks off the Brits but equally obviously that is acceptable to a lot of us.'[35]

By late 1993, the White House had accepted not only that the 'special relation-ship' was no longer a major obstacle to intervention, but also that intervention was actually desirable. Contacts with the developing situation in Northern Ireland were available through the Kennedy–Hume–ANIA network. Judgements were made to the effect that conditions were now 'ripe' for intervention. A combination of war weariness and Dublin–London cooperation appeared to have created conditions where US involvement might achieve results. Moreover, the US leadership actually *wanted* to become involved.

My last task in this chapter is to set his wish for involvement in the context of Clinton's developing foreign policy. Upon assuming power in 1993, the Administration sought to reconcile various foreign policy objectives. From the Bush Administration, it inherited a commitment to free trade, multilateralism and internationalism. The Clinton team sought to devise a foreign policy of selective engagement – a policy linked both to military spending cuts and to the achievement of a new balance between ideals and interests. Prioritisation of the domestic reform agenda was, however, not to be bought by sacrificing internationalism. For all its pragmatism, the Administration stressed its commitment to human rights, to the legacy of Woodrow Wilson. It even (though less publicly) looked to the legacy of President Carter, for whom Secretary of State Warren Christopher had worked with a special human rights brief. As the years passed, the Administration developed a stronger commitment to an activist, moralistic foreign policy: what has been called, in the context of Kosovo, 'liberal hawkism' or 'Carterism (with bullets)',[36] but without ground invasions. (US activism in the Balkans after 1994 involved an abandonment of 'ancient enmities' interpretations of conflict, parallel to that which had already taken place in respect of Northern Ireland.)

Against the developing foreign policy background,[37] intervention over Ulster had some obvious attractions. Risks, as we have seen, did exist; but they did not include any possibility of troop engagement. Internationalist and peace-promotion precedents could be set;[38] and Republican neo-isolationists in Congress confounded. The commitment to Europe could be underlined, and with no great expenses. (The US, as secretary of state Ron Brown emphasised, might benefit from the economic opportunities – not least a bridgehead into the European Union – of involvement.) The policy could plausibly be described as one of principle. It might even help to balance those arenas, such as China, where public advertisement of a foreign policy of ideals was less convincing. It would demonstrate that the foreign policy of a lonely, internationalist superpower need not be one of 'mindless muscle'.[39]

Of course, in Northern Ireland as elsewhere, interests and ideals are intertwined. The US has an interest in internationalism as well as an idealistic commitment to it. Robert Fisk has argued that America's Irish interventions were 'calculated to produce a winner, a side with whom Washington feels comfortable, an ally upon which it can depend'.[40] Whatever their origins, the forces set in play by the December 1993 policy review were bound to transform the search for peace. No party to the conflict could sensibly ignore pressure from the global hegemon. The final outcome could not, and still cannot, be predicted. A short-to-medium judgement, however, is that a reasoned, measured and appropriate intervention brought Clinton his greatest diplomatic success.

Notes

1 H. Patterson, *The Politics of Illusion: A Political History of the IRA* (London, Serif, 1997), p. 253.
2 See D. de Breadun, 'George Mitchell: Irish American of the Year', *Irish America*, April/May 1999, pp. 36–41. Also, G. J. Mitchell, *Making Peace* (London, William Heinemann, 1999), pp. 143–83.
3 S. Jenkins, 'A Song for Ireland', *The Times*, 19 March 1999.
4 R. Seitz, *Over Here* (London, Weidenfeld & Nicolson, 1998), pp. 285, 299.
5 Quoted in C. O'Clery, *The Greening of the White House* (Dublin, Gill and Macmillan, 1996), p. 206.
6 M. Fletcher, 'Hope for Peace Rests on Clinton's Clout', *The Times*, 13 March 1999.
7 The phrase is from R. O. Keohane, *After Hegemony: Cooperation and Discord in the World Political Economy* (Princeton, Princeton University Press, 1984), p. 122.
8 Quoted in S. Cronin, *Washington's Irish Policy 1916–1986: Independence Partition Neutrality* (Dublin, Anvil Books, 1987), p. 291.
9 R. N. Haass, *Conflicts Unending: The United States and Regional Disputes* (New Haven, Yale University Press, 1990), pp. 27–8, 122–37.

10 See J. Holland, *The American Connection: US Guns, Money and Influence in Northern Ireland* (Dublin, Poolbeg, 1989) (also revised edition, Boulder, Roberts Reinhart, 1999); A. J. Wilson, *Irish America and the Ulster Conflict: 1968–1995* (Belfast, Blackstaff Press, 1995).

11 See J. Dumbrell, 'The United States and the Northern Irish Conflict 1969–94: from Indifference to Intervention', *Irish Studies in International Affairs*, 6 (1995), 107–25.

12 *The Independent*, 25 February 1993.

13 See T. P. Coogan, *The Troubles* (London, Hutchinson, 1995), pp. 348–9.

14 O'Clery, *The Greening of the White House*, p. 40.

15 Quoted in E. Mallie and D. McKittrick, *The Fight for Peace: The Secret Story Behind the Irish Peace Process* (London, William Heinemann, 1996), p. 280.

16 O'Clery, *The Greening of the White House*, p. 90.

17 BBC Northern Ireland interview, September 1994, quoted in A. J. Wilson, 'From the Beltway to Belfast: the Clinton Administration, Sinn Féin, and the Northern Ireland Peace Process', *New Hibernia Review*, 1:3 (1997) 23–39, at 31. See also K. Cullen, interview with Soderberg, *Fortnight*, 345, (December 1995), pp. 23–4.

18 *Newsweek*, 12 September 1994, p. 10.

19 See *Public Papers of the Presidents of the United States: William J. Clinton*, 1994, Vol. 2 (Washington DC, US Government Printing Office, 1995), pp. 2–7.

20 O'Clery, *The Greening of the White House*, p. 138.

21 G. McMichael, *An Ulster Voice: In Search of Common Ground in Northern Ireland* (Boulder, Roberts Reinhart, 1999), p. 80.

22 M. Fletcher, 'Clinton Orders Adams to Give Up Arms', *The Times*, 13 March 1999.

23 The phrase comes from Seamus Heaney's 'The Cure at Troy'. It was taken up by the President from Hope, Arkansas as a policy slogan. See B. Clinton, *Between Hope and History* (New York, Random House, 1996).

24 *The Independent on Sunday*, 22 March 1998.

25 Mitchell, *Making Peace*, p. 178.

26 E. Alterman, *Who Speaks for America? Why Democracy Matters in Foreign Policy* (Ithaca, Cornell University Press, 1998), p. 146. See also J. O'Grady, 'An Irish Policy Born in the USA', *Foreign Affairs*, 75:3 (1996), 2–7.

27 *Mail on Sunday*, 25 August 1996.

28 K. Cullen, interview with Soderberg (n.17 above), p. 24.

29 O'Clery, *The Greening of the White House*, p. 138.

30 Interview on the BBC *Today* programme, 22 September 1994.

31 See M. J. Brady, 'Democratic Audit', *Fortnight*, 345 (December 1995), p. 8.

32 See K. Cullen, 'The Fraying of the Green', *Fortnight*, 351 (June 1996), p. 8.

33 M. Cox, 'Cinderella at the Ball: Explaining the End of the War in Northern Ireland', *Millennium: Journal of International Studies*, 27:2 (1998), 325–42, at 330. See also M. Cox, 'The War that Came in From the Cold: Clinton and the Irish Question', *World Policy Journal*, 16:1 (1999), 59–67.

34 See A. Seldon, *Major: A Political Life* (London, Weidenfeld & Nicholson, 1997), pp. 363–4, 443–6, 538–40, 621–2.

35 O'Clery, *The Greening of the White House*, p. 98.

36 See P. Starobin, 'The Liberal Hawk Soars', *National Journal*, 15 May 1999, 1310–16.

37 See W. G. Hyland, *Clinton's World: Remaking American Foreign Policy* (Westport, Praeger, 1999).

38 See A. Guelke, 'The United States, Irish Americans and the Northern Ireland Peace Process', *International Affairs*, 72:3 (1996), 521–36, at 536.

39 For a critical (Irish) perspective, see 'American Foreign Policy: Mindless Muscle?', *Times Change*, 16 (1988–89), 4–5.

40 R. Fisk, 'No Use Relying on Uncle Bill', *Fortnight*, 346 (January 1996), p. 19.

16

'Comparatively peaceful': South Africa, the Middle East and Northern Ireland

ADRIAN GUELKE

Comparison in politics is far from simply being an academic exercise that is the preserve of those who study the subject. On the contrary, it is a vital part of political discourse itself, frequently having an impact on the course of events in different societies. The 1990s have been notable for peace processes and/or transitions in places that have been characterised as deeply divided societies, most prominently, South Africa, Israel/Palestine and Northern Ireland. In the process, polities associated with long-running conflict have been transformed to cases that have been seen to a greater or lesser extent as models for the resolution of conflict in other political systems beset by conflict. These include Angola, Mozambique, Kashmir, Sri Lanka, Cyprus, Corsica and the Basque Country, to name examples where the South African transition and/or the Good Friday Agreement has been seen as having provided inspiration for political settlements or attempts to achieve them. The problems that the Middle East peace process has encountered make it less commonly presented as a positive model, though that does not diminish its relevance to other cases in which difficulties have been encountered in the implementation of agreements.

Because comparison of the three cases of South Africa, Israel/Palestine and Northern Ireland attracted considerable academic and even political interest before the 1990s, it did not prove difficult to gain acceptance in each of the three societies of the proposition that the experience of the other two cases has potential relevance to political developments in the society in question. The result has been a disposition to regard the peace processes/transitions in the three cases as analogous so that to some degree their experience of the transformation of the conflicts has come to be seen as shared. For example, when the Shell Oil Company placed an advertisement in the South African press that proclaimed 'Enough tears. Enough blood. It is time for peace'[1] as part of its campaign to demonstrate the company's support for the South African transition, it could take it for granted that readers would pick up without prompting the allusion to Yitzhak Rabin's words on the White House lawn in September 1993.

The quest for a unionist de Klerk

The most common metaphor that the South African transition inspired in Northern Ireland was the notion that what the province needed was a unionist de Klerk. However, it was not a role that any unionist wished to volunteer to fill. In an interview a few days before the 1997 British general election with the Northern editor of *The Irish Times*, Deaglan de Breadun, the leader of the Ulster Unionist Party (UUP), David Trimble, responded to a question about the desire of many nationalists to see a de Klerk figure emerging from the ranks of unionism by declaring that the analogy was 'quite obviously incorrect'[2] as de Klerk came from the minority population. He went on to argue that what the peace process needed was the emergence of a de Klerk figure from republican ranks. Trimble has not been alone in responding to the notion of a unionist de Klerk by suggesting that what is needed is a nationalist leader ready to acknowledge the rights of the majority within Northern Ireland. More usually, however, it was linked to criticism of the leader of the Social Democratic and Labour Party (SDLP), John Hume, particularly in the context of his oft-expressed opposition to an internal settlement.

The focus on Hume partly arose because of the frequency with which Hume himself referred to the 'unionist de Klerk' analogy. For example in *Personal Views: Politics, Peace and Reconciliation in Ireland*, Hume put the case as follows:

> In many ways what we need is a unionist de Klerk. There are parallels between the South African situation and our own. If the solution to the problem in South Africa had been to draw a line on the map, create a small white state, with two whites to every black person, and to make the rest of South Africa independent, would there ever have been a possibility of peace? Would not the whites have been forced to discriminate totally against the black minority in order to ensure that it never became a majority? This is precisely what happened in Ireland, and we are still living with the consequences.[3]

The use of the South African comparison to de-legitimise unionism explains why unionists have tended to react strongly against the analogy with South Africa, even though during the early years of the troubles, it was commoner for unionists to make reference to the situation in southern Africa and the Middle East as similar to their own in being under siege than it was for Irish nationalists to compare their cause to that of the Palestinians or of black South Africans. In particular, there was widespread sympathy among unionists for the view that Ian Smith of Rhodesia had been let down by Britain. After Zimbabwe's independence in 1980, this sympathy tended to be transferred to whites in South Africa.

Hume's comment echoed a strained comparison of the two societies put forward by Kevin Kelley during the early 1980s, which was widely quoted among republicans in justification of the armed struggle. Kelley set out the comparison in an epilogue to his book, *The Longest War: Northern Ireland and the IRA*, published in 1982.

> Suppose for a moment that apartheid South Africa was still an English or Dutch colony and that the black majority population has now risen up in arms to demand

independence and freedom. After a five-year struggle against the colonizer and a civil war between factions of the liberation forces, England or Holland will then grant a Free State, neo-colonial designation to four-fifths of the country which is now called Azania. The area around Johannesburg will remain a directly-ruled colony, however, with its own local parliament and with a two-thirds majority of its population being Afrikaners. Fifty years pass, during which the Afrikaners consolidate their rule and exclude the blacks from any meaningful political representation. The minority inside this white-supremacist statelet then revolts and demands unity with the rest of Azania. The colonial power dispatches its army to aid the Afrikaner police and militia in putting down a rebellion described as terrorist. Where does the fair-minded onlooker stand? Does she or he condemn the uprising as 'an outbreak of criminal violence'? Does one point to a handful of modest reforms that may have been introduced as a sop to the rebel minority, or does one conclude that the fighting will never be stopped until this land is made whole again and until Afrikaners come to terms with their own identity and make peace with the Azanians? An imprecise analogy, granted. But one that is still worth contemplating.[4]

The importance attached by republicans to the comparison was underlined by Gerry Adams's 1986 book, *The Politics of Irish Freedom*, which was packed with references to similarities between Northern Ireland and South Africa.[5] The obvious reason for the popularity of the comparison among republicans was the apartheid regime's lack of international legitimacy – in Jack Spence's redolent phrase, it was 'the most popular corpse in history'.[6] The hope of republicans clearly was that the comparison might make British rule in Ireland appear as illegitimate.

Comparison of the conflict in Northern Ireland with other struggles was an important theme of republican propaganda and rhetoric in the wake of the campaign by republican prisoners for the restoration of special category status for politically motivated offenders. The crisis in the prisons saw a flourishing of wall murals in Catholic areas. During the duration of the crisis these focused on the plight of the prisoners. However, this gave way to the depiction of wider themes after the hunger strike ended. A number highlighted similarities between other lands and Northern Ireland. For example, a 1983 wall mural pictured women militants from the Palestine Liberation Organisation (PLO), the South West African People's Organisation (SWAPO) and *Cumman n mBan* (the women's section of the IRA). A 1982 mural showed a member of the PLO and a member of the IRA holding a rocket launcher aloft, with the slogan 'one struggle' underneath.[7] A prominent mural of the mid–1980s quoted the words of an African National Congress (ANC) martyr, Benjamin Moloise, alongside those of Bobby Sands, the first of the republican hunger strikers to die in 1981.[8]

Intractable conflicts

South African interest in Northern Ireland had a somewhat different motivation. It was based on the search for models for the resolution of conflict in deeply divided societies, particularly outside of Africa. In this context, the work of Arend Lijphart on consociationalism was seen as especially pertinent. In particular, power sharing, as had occurred under the 1973 Sunningdale Agreement in Northern Ireland, was regarded as having relevance to a political settlement in South Africa both by the government and by liberal opinion, though it was opposed by African nationalists whose goal was majority rule in a unitary state. However, prior to 1994 that goal seemed almost as out of reach as a united Ireland. South African comparison of the three cases focused on the intractability of conflict in the three societies.

That was the main theme of a conference, principally of academics, on the three cases in Bonn in September 1989. The conference was hosted by the Institute for a Democratic Alternative in South Africa, which has been renamed the Institute for Democracy in South Africa, and the Friedrich Naumann Foundation, which provided the funding for the conference and is a body associated with the Free Democratic Party in Germany. A book edited by two well-known South African political scientists, Hermann Giliomee and Jannie Gagiano, based on revised versions of the papers delivered at the conference was published in 1990. In his introduction, Hermann Giliomee described the problem the book posed as follows: 'Why are the conflicts in Northern Ireland, South Africa and Israel so intractable and why is the search for peace so elusive?'[9]

In a key chapter in the book, Bernard Crick pronounced the three cases 'insoluble'. He gave two formal reasons for this characterisation of the three situations. The first was 'that no internal solution likely to guarantee peace can possibly satisfy the announced principles of the main disputants'; the second, 'that any external imposed solution or enforced adjudication is likely to strengthen the desperation and self-righteousness of the threatened group'. He added a third contingent reason: 'the virtual impossibility of successful armed rebellion against each of the governments concerned'. Crick expressed the hope that a meeting of leaders on both sides might arise out of the very existence of a 'stalemate of subversive terror versus state terror' and concluded: 'concerned persons should be less concerned to predict and support most favoured outcomes and more willing to imagine and to accept many possible and often quite unexpected outcomes'.[10]

Ironically, the popularisation of this comparison started to occur just as all was about to change in the three societies. The first to change was South Africa. In February 1990 President de Klerk announced the unbanning of the ANC and the release of Nelson Mandela as the prelude to negotiations on the country's future. Next came Israel/Palestine. The Oslo agreement and the handshake between the Israeli prime minister and the PLO chairman on the White House lawn in September 1993 marked the start of its peace process. Of course, in both cases these dramatic steps could be placed in the context of earlier developments that had presaged these possibilities, but such judgements were made with the benefit of hindsight. At the time, these breakthroughs exceeded most commentators' expectations of what was possible in the circumstances. An important factor in each case was the impact of the end of the Cold War.[11]

The *zeitgeist* of peace processes

The end of the Cold War was of much less obvious *direct* relevance to the conflict in Northern Ireland. The Soviet Union had supported the Official republican movement, a marginal force in both paramilitary and political terms. The weapon of the Provisional IRA's campaign of violence was associated with the American Armalite not the Russian Kalashnikov. It therefore seemed possible that alone of the three societies, Northern Ireland might not undergo a similar process of significant change. However, the *indirect* influence of the end of the Cold War proved very considerable through the *zeitgeist* of peace processes, which the parties in Northern Ireland were unable to disregard. Whether one takes as the start of the Irish peace process the Joint Declaration by the British and Irish governments in December 1993 or the actual announcement of a cessation of military operations by the Provisional IRA at the end of August 1994, the influence of the analogy between Northern Ireland and the other two cases was omnipresent at its birth. In the period leading up to the Joint Declaration, both John Hume and the Irish government vigorously pressed the analogy. A week before the Joint Declaration, *The Christian Science Monitor* linked the three cases in an article headed 'PLO, ANC and IRA Embark upon a New Pragmatic Path'.[12] After the Joint Declaration, *Le Monde* carried a cartoon showing John Major arm in arm with a member of the IRA entering a café of peace where Rabin and Arafat and de Klerk and Mandela were already celebrating.[13] In response to the Joint Declaration, a number of Irish-American business leaders placed a full-page advertisement in *The New York Times* appealing for peace, referring to 'the backdrop of the unprecedented peace initiatives in the Middle East and South Africa'.[14]

Similarly at the time of the IRA's announcement of its ceasefire, much of the commentary dwelt on the comparison with South Africa and, to a lesser extent, the Middle East. Significantly, this focus was not confined to enthusiasts for the peace process. For example, in a column entitled 'The Irritated Person's Guide to the Peace Process' in *The Independent*, James Fenton referred to the ceasefire scathingly as 'the Mandela manoeuvre'.[15] A concern of a number of British commentators was that Adams was using the ceasefire to pass himself off as a Mandela-like figure. Andrew Neil complained that in the US, the British and Irish governments had done little to counter Sinn Féin propaganda. He concluded: 'Only the republican message has been coming across in America since the ceasefire was announced ... [and that] had left Gerry Adams looking like another Gandhi, Yassir Arafat or Nelson Mandela.'[16] Such concerns did little to prevent the tidal wave of comparison. Thus, the normally parochial evening newspaper in Johannesburg, *The Star*, reported the ceasefire under the banner headline, 'IRA Takes "SA Option"'.[17] Another South African newspaper reported the President of the European Commission, Jacques Delors, as describing the ceasefire as 'a ray of light, on a par with events in South Africa and the Middle East'.[18] Archbishop Tutu's reaction that 'his excitement was similar to the day that Nelson Mandela was released from jail' figured prominently in coverage of international reaction to the ceasefire in the Sinn Féin paper, *An Phoblacht/Republican News*.[19]

During the seventeen months of the first IRA ceasefire, Sinn Féin continued to press the analogy with South Africa. In June 1995 Gerry Adams visited South Africa at the invitation of the ANC. He met Mandela but in his capacity as ANC President rather than as South Africa's head of state. His visit was extensively and most sympathetically covered in the South African media.[20] Republicans were not alone in continuing to draw inspiration from South Africa's experience. Northern Ireland's small band of liberals also drew inspiration from the South African experience.[21] Deputy President de Klerk was invited to address the Forum on Peace and Reconciliation in Dublin in November 1995 on the implications for Ireland of the South African transition. Even after the IRA ended its ceasefire in February 1996, *The Irish Times* continued to argue that there was 'much to be learned from the comparison',[22] while during her visit to South Africa in March 1996, President Mary Robinson stressed the inspiration that events in South Africa had provided to those seeking peace in Ireland.[23]

In May 1997 well before the resumption of the IRA ceasefire in the second half of July, the South African government invited representatives of Sinn Féin and of all the parties taking part in the multi-party negotiations in Northern Ireland to South Africa for a weekend seminar on the lessons of the South African transition.[24] All of the parties accepted the invitation, with the exception of the United Kingdom Unionist Party, though the other unionist parties insisted on arrangements for the conference that kept them separated from the representatives of Sinn Féin, a stance widely satirised as an echo of the policy of apartheid. It was evident from the emphasis that the South African government placed on Sinn Féin's participation that part of the motive for the event was to assist Sinn Féin back into the negotiating process in Northern Ireland.

Sinn Féin and the ANC

The ideological sympathy between the ANC and Sinn Féin was further underlined following the Good Friday Agreement. Thus, one of the most extraordinary aspects of the Sinn Féin leadership's efforts to convince rank and file members of the value of the Agreement was its enlistment of aid from leading figures in the ANC. The first opportunity for the Sinn Féin negotiators to explain the deal to a representative group of the party's members occurred at the party's annual conference a week after the Good Friday Agreement. The only decision on the Agreement made at the conference was that it would reconvene in a month's time to debate the deal. However, the party leadership used the occasion to explain the deal in an effort to promote a positive view of the Agreement among the rank and file. They were assisted in this by an array of foreign speakers, including the Deputy Secretary-General of the ANC, Thenjiwe Mtintso. She spoke of when she was an MK cadre and negotiations on the South African transition began, and she feared that the ANC leadership had sold out, and how she had been gradually persuaded that this was not the case. That was followed by the visit of an ANC delegation to

Northern Ireland at the end of April, including such senior figures as Cyril Rama-phosa and Mac Maharaj. They spoke at a number of Sinn Féin meetings, as well as visiting IRA prisoners in the Maze.

South African interest in the Good Friday Agreement has continued. After a further round of abortive talks on the issues deadlocking implementation of the Agreement at the end of June and the beginning of July 1999, the President of Sinn Féin, Gerry Adams, when asked for his message for republican activists in an interview, underscored South Africa's role:

> There is huge goodwill for the peace process and particularly for Sinn Féin stewardship of it. That must be consolidated. An indication of the strength of the republican position outside of Ireland is that both South African President Thabo Mbeki and President Clinton contacted us by telephone. These two world leaders from two different political cultures have shown consistent support for the quest for peace in our country. The South African involvement may have been over-shadowed on the world stage by the US endeavours but those who have attended Sinn Féin Ard Fheiseanna and listened to the ANC contribution will know how much they want this to work. Both Nelson Mandela and President Mbeki have made wonderful contributions to this process. So as well as the outreach work that is required in Ireland, the international dimension needs also to be built upon, particularly in Britain.[25]

The South African connection was also played up by Sinn Féin leaders in their recounting of the success of the Mitchell review. Thus, according to Niall O'Dowd,

> At times even the leadership began to despair of progress as the talks dragged on. This is where ANC thinking was influential. The South African negotiators had long advised Sinn Féin to follow 'a bush strategy' where the participants are re-moved from the normal surroundings, and in the case of the South African peace talks, when the two sides got away to the bush for fishing trips and discussions. Sinn Féin's version of the bush turned out to be the palatial surroundings of the American embassy in London, where on two successive nights the breakthroughs occurred with the inspired help of Senator George Mitchell.[26]

It is reasonably easy to demonstrate that the comparison with South Africa has exercised a powerful influence on political discourse on Northern Ireland and that to a lesser extent the comparison with the Middle East has also had an impact on the rhetoric about Northern Ireland. It is somewhat more difficult to establish that these comparisons have influenced political behaviour to any significant degree. During the 1980s there were a number of stories in the press in Northern Ireland of links between loyalist paramilitary organisations and South Africa. At the close of the 1980s the involvement of the South African arms corporation, Armscor, in the supply of weapons to loyalists came to light. In return the South Africans hoped to secure surface-to-air missile technology to assist them in battles in southern Angola. In 1992 a project of South African Military Intelligence to link the ANC and the IRA (drawing in part it seemed from research being carried out by a British Conser-vative MP) was exposed during the course of an inquest into a lawyer murdered by the agents of the state. Ironically, while Project Echoes seems to have yielded relatively meagre results, ANC leaders in their own pronouncements on the Irish Question frequently alienated allies in both Britain and Ireland by expressions of sympathy for the republican movement as being engaged in an anti-colonial struggle.[27]

The influence of the South African transition

In the case of Sinn Féin, the intensity of the commitment of its leaders to the analogy with South Africa and their claims that the transition in South Africa has influenced their own strategy does provide some basis for concluding that they have internalised the comparison to the point where it has had an impact on their decision-making. The huge attraction of the relationship with the ANC to Sinn Féin is that the ANC is a political organisation with immense international prestige which at the same time shares what the Sinn Féin leadership calls the republican analysis of the conflict in Northern Ireland. That is to say, the ANC agrees with Sinn Féin's anti-colonial model of the conflict and rejects the more common ethnic model. When the ANC embarked on negotiations with the South African government and suspended the armed struggle, pressure was indirectly put on the republican movement because of the extent to which it relied on the analogy with South Africa to sustain the legitimacy of its own armed struggle. Of course, it would be silly to suggest that the South African transition was the only reason why the IRA declared a ceasefire in August 1994. At most, it was one of a number of factors that brought about that decision, including fatigue at the sheer duration of the long war and a combination of other internal and external factors.

It is also important to stress that the South African transition has exerted an influence on many people in Northern Ireland outside the republican movement who do not accept the republican view of the nature of the Northern Ireland problem. In particular, President Mandela is widely revered in Northern Ireland as someone who stands for reconciliation following conflict. For this reason the non-party 'yes' campaign sought to invite Mandela to Northern Ireland to support the Belfast Agreement. Mandela was willing to come. The suggestion ultimately foundered on opposition from pro-Agreement unionists who feared that damage would be done by opponents of the Agreement portraying Mandela as a paramilitary leader who had achieved power without decommissioning.[28] Interest in the South African transition has led to borrowings from it both in terms of expert opinion and of ideas, most notably the use of 'the principle of sufficient consensus' as the basis for decision-making in the multi-party negotiations. This has been interpreted in the context of Northern Ireland as the requirement that substantive decisions should have the support of majorities of both unionists and nationalists. With qualifications, the principle has been made part of the working of the Agreement itself. It might be objected that what has been borrowed from South Africa is simply the label rather than the concept, which has long figured in schemes for political accommodation between the communities in Northern

Ireland. However, that understates its significance. Its use in South Africa's multi-party negotiations was important in helping to legitimise its employment in Northern Ireland. There has also been much interest in the South African Truth and Reconciliation Commission as a possible model for Northern Ireland.

The much greater emphasis on the South African than on the Israel/Palestine comparison is largely a reflection of the much greater success of the South African process. However, the difficulties that the Northern Irish process has encountered even after the achievement of the Good Friday Agreement suggest a closer correspondence between the process in Northern Ireland and that in the Middle East. While optimists in Northern Ireland were comparing Trimble to de Klerk, Trimble's decision in July 1999 to put the unity of his party before implementation of the Good Friday Agreement suggested that a comparison with Netanyahu might have been more apposite. The obvious preference of republicans for the South African comparison also underpins their view of the Good Friday Agreement as transitional (or at any rate that it can be made to be so through the republican movement's pursuit of its peace strategy). Indeed, the way the comparison was presented at the Sinn Féin *ard fheis* in the week after the Good Friday Agreement was as if Northern Ireland was at the same point in the process as South Africa was in 1990. It may be that some republicans harbour illusions that the nature of the Northern Ireland settlement can be transformed in a manner analogous to the way the ANC managed to secure South Africa's democratisation on its terms in 1994 out of the liberalisation of the political system in 1990. The report in the Dublin *Sunday Tribune*, though not confirmed by other sources, that a meeting of the Provisional IRA's Army Convention in December 1998 had decided on an extension of the ceasefire to 2002, might suggest the influence of the chronology of the South African transition on republican thinking.[29]

However, an important lesson of the way different parts of the political spectrum have used the analogies of South Africa and Israel/Palestine to make political points in relation to Northern Ireland is that the comparisons do not remain static, but undergo substantial changes as the situation in the societies concerned, as well as in the wider world, changes. Indeed, from a historical perspective, the current identification of Irish nationalism with African nationalism in South Africa and sections of unionism with Zionism represents a reversal of lines of sympathy that existed in previous generations, when Irish nationalism identified with Afrikaner nationalism and unionism regarded Zionism with hostility as an anti-colonial movement. The ANC's dominant position in the South African political system makes the South African analogy attractive to Sinn Féin since it suggests a much larger role in the future of Irish politics than the republican movement is likely to achieve.

Conclusion

While the off–on again success of the Mitchell review has lifted Northern Ireland out of the debilitating impasse that the Middle East peace process had succumbed to during Netanyahu's premiership, the analogy with Israel/Palestine arguably remains more relevant to Northern Ireland than the South African transition. Thus, in both cases, the process tends to be viewed, even by some of its supporters, less as a way of resolving their differences through the medium of new institutional arrangements than as a continuation of their political struggle by other means. In both cases, too, winning the support of the external parties is seen as a significant element in influencing political developments in a positive direction from one particular point of view. In 1990 Meron Benvenisti expressed scepticism that the steps being taken to promote negotiations in the Middle East would achieve the objective of political accommodation as long as 'the protagonists consider conflict resolution devices only through the prism of their respective gains and losses, not as a means to resolve their differences amicably'.[30] As a characterisation of the attitudes of some of the key parties towards implementation of agreements, his words have considerable resonance both for the Middle East and Northern Ireland. This, in part, reflects the fact that only in South Africa do the changes of the 1990s appear utterly irreversible by reason of the shift in political power that accompanied the settlement.

It also reflects the fact that the settlements achieved in Israel/Palestine and Northern Ireland, unlike those in South Africa, were more frameworks than final outcomes. Admittedly, that was much truer of the Israeli/Palestinian Declaration of Principles than it is of the Good Friday Agreement, which created a much more complete blueprint for implementation. But, in practice, the ambiguities and loose ends of the Good Friday Agreement have provided ample scope for argument and even after the resurrection of the Executive in May 2000 seem likely to provide the possibility of fresh crises in the future. Thus, in both Northern Ireland and Israel/Palestine, the full shape of the settlement is only likely to be unfold in a matter of several years, and it remains conceivable that the difficulties encountered in the implementation of the settlement might ultimately prompt the collapse of the peace process. However, the pressures that led the parties to sign up to agreements in the first place seem bound to remain, so a return to the situation that prevailed prior to the peace process is unlikely in either case. Just as Israeli public opinion swung back to support for the peace process after Netanyahu's premiership, so a majority of Unionists can be expected to support the continuation of the Northern Irish peace process and the settlement it gave rise to, even if there are crises along the way.

Notes

1 *The Weekly Mail and Guardian* (Johannesburg), 25–30 March 1994.
2 *The Irish Times*, 29 April 1997.
3 John Hume, *Personal Views: Politics, Peace and Reconciliation in Ireland*, Dublin: Town House, 1996, pp. 95–6.

4   Kevin Kelley, *The Longest War: Northern Ireland and the IRA*, Dingle: Brandon, 1982, p. 354.
5   Gerry Adams, *The Politics of Irish Freedom*, Dingle: Brandon, 1986, pp. 5, 27, 28, 113, 118.
6   J. E. Spence, 'The Most Popular Corpse in History', *Optima*, Vol. 34, No. 1, March 1986.
7   See Bill Rolston, *Drawing Support: Murals in Northern Ireland*, Belfast: Beyond the Pale Publications, 1992, pp. 49–50.
8   The mural adorns the cover of Kevin Boyle and Tom Hadden's *Northern Ireland: The Choice*, Harmondsworth: Penguin, 1994.
9   Hermann Giliomee and Jannie Gagiano (eds), *The Elusive Search for Peace: South Africa, Israel and Northern Ireland*, Cape Town: Oxford University Press, 1990, p. 3.
10 In *ibid.*, pp. 265, 270, 271 and 274.
11 See Adrian Guelke, 'The Impact of the End of the Cold War on the South African Transition', *Journal of Contemporary African Studies*, January 1996, pp. 87–100.
12 *Christian Science Monitor*, 9 December 1993.
13 Reproduced in *The Irish Times*, 6 January 1994.
14 *The New York Times*, 27 December 1993.
15 *The Independent*, 5 September 1994.
16 Interview on 'Breakfast with Frost' (BBC TV), 4 September 1994.
17 *The Star*, 1 September 1994.
18 Quoted in *Business Day* (Johannesburg), 6 September 1994.
19 *An Phoblacht/Republican News*, 8 September 1994.
20 See, for example, the profile of Adams under the heading of 'To Heal a Nation' in *The Sunday Times* (Johannesburg), 13 August 1995.
21 See *The South African Experience – Lessons for Northern Ireland?*, Belfast: *Ad Hoc* Group on South Africa, 1995.
22 *The Irish Times*, 9 July 1996.
23 *The Irish Times*, 27 March 1996.
24 Joe Carroll, 'Senior NI Politicians to Visit South Africa to Study its Peaceful Transition from One-party Rule: Reports that Mandela Would Act as Mediator Dismissed', *The Irish Times*, 13 May 1997.
25 'Time for Republicans to Hold their Nerve' – Gerry Adams interviewed, *Irish Republican News and Information*, Galway, Ireland (http://irlnet.com/rmlist/), 7 July 1999.
26 Nial O'Dowd, 'Obsession with decommissioning misses historical breakthrough', *The Irish Times*, 18 November 1999.
27 On South African Military Intelligence involvement in Northern Ireland, see, for example, the reports in *The Independent*, 15 July 1992. On ANC attitudes towards the Irish Question, see, for example, 'Mandela's IRA Remarks Criticised', *The Irish Times*, 21 October 1992.
28 On the invitation to Mandela from the non-party 'yes' campaign, see Quintin Oliver, *Working for "YES": The story of the May 1998 referendum in Northern Ireland*, Belfast: The "Yes" Campaign, (December) 1998, pp. 77–8. See also Martina Purdy, 'Mandela "Was Set to Boost Yes Vote"', *Belfast Telegraph*, 15 December 1998.
29 17 January 1999.
30 Meron Benvenisti, 'The Peace Process and Intercommunal Strife' in Giliomee and Gagiano, *The Elusive Search for Peace*, p. 130.

17

Peace in the Basque Country and Corsica?

FRANCESCO LETAMENDIA

AND JOHN LOUGHLIN

Of all the cases of violent conflict that have arisen in Western Europe over the past four decades, three regions stand out by reason of the longevity, degree of political organisation of the armed groups involved, and their challenge to the traditional nation-state: Northern Ireland, the Basque Country and Corsica. Today, each of these regions is lurching toward some kind of peace settlement although in all three the obstacles to obtaining this are formidable. The Northern Ireland case is the most advanced; Corsica is still on the way; while the Basque Country seems to have taken several steps backwards with the collapse of the ETA ceasefire at the end of 1999.

The three cases are very different in many respects: there is considerable variation between the historical origins of the conflict, the issues at stake, the composition and political orientations of the regional populations, and even the degree of organisation (or disorganisation) of the armed groups. Nevertheless, all three illustrate the problems associated with a notion of the nation-state whereby this is supposed to integrate minority groups into the national system and to exercise absolute sovereignty over every piece of its territory. The existence and activities of the IRA, ETA (Euskadi ta Askatasuna which is Basque for 'Freedom') and the FLNC (Front de Libération nationale de la Corse), in their various manifestations and guises, demonstrate the limitations of these supposed attributes of nation-states. Each of these movements challenges the legitimacy of the state to exercise a complete monopoly over the means of violence. In all three cases, the groups went through a historical development, more or less at the same periods, through which they passed from regionalism or federalism to one of adopting the unitary state as their final goal. Thus, all three movements have, in the past, defined their objectives in terms reminiscent of the stato-nationalism of the state which they oppose: each sought a nation-state independent of the state within which they are included (or felt excluded). This development involved in the three regions a use of Marxist ideology sometimes consciously borrowed from Third World liberation movements in the 1960s and 1970s, sometimes drawing on internal colonialism analyses. Each of the movements has managed to garner sufficient support from the local population, although varying considerably from case to case, to continue in existence over a very long period of time and to ensure that, at least in these territories, the writ of the state did not run completely smoothly. Furthermore, each of the three movements exercised a kind of negative veto over attempts to pacify the region and, in this way, swayed the public and political agendas in each area. Finally, in all three cases, the armed movements in each region have, over the past several years, declared a willingness to seek a non-violent approach to achieving their political objectives, through a process of dialogue and alliance with other political forces.[1]

It is clear that these recent developments coincide with changes at the level of the nation-state itself.[2] Globalisation, Europeanisation, the application of 'New Public Management' approaches to public administration systems and the emergence of subnational authorities as policy actors in their own right have all considerably altered the nature and significance of nation-states, at least in Western industrialised countries. It is outside the scope of this chapter to go into these changes in detail but one of the most important consequences has been the decoupling of the concepts of 'nation' and 'state' that was developed at the time of the French Revolution and has been the basis of modern liberal democratic systems ever since. This concept postulated that nations ought to have states and states ought to be coterminous with nations and has underlain nationalist mobilisation right up to the present day. Irish, Basque and Corsican nationalisms, at least in their more extreme separatist manifestations as represented by the IRA, ETA and the FLNC, have also been driven by this logic of seeking to gain (or recover) a state that would be appropriate to their 'nations'. However, if, today, the concept of nation-state itself is being called into question, then this quest is increasingly meaningless. Nationalist movements are being forced therefore to reformulate their basic ideological concepts – nation, sovereignty, self-determination, etc. – as well as their strategy and tactics in new ways. This is most strikingly illustrated in the Northern Ireland case where a strategy of dialogue among nationalists (SDLP, Sinn Féin and Fianna Fáil) coincided with a process of devolution in the UK that made a real breakthrough possible. UK devolution itself was made possible both by new ways of thinking about the state and by the new context of European integration which the reformers have embraced with much more enthusiasm than any previous British government. These developments have rippled across Europe and have influenced both the Basque Country and Corsica. There is not a direct causal link between the Irish peace process and these two regions. However, Ireland has provided a boost and an example for already existing political forces seeking a new way of resolving their conflicts. This chapter will outline the main features of these situations of conflict and the recent moves towards peace, while emphasising that the peace processes in all of these countries are far from solidified and there is still plenty of scope for the continuation of violence.

The Basque problem

The Basques are an ancient people with a unique language, occupying a territory at the western end of the Pyrénées straddling the French and Spanish borders, so that there are, in fact, two parts to the Basque Country.[3] Most of the violence has taken place in the South although there have also been some violent groups in the North[4] and militants from the South have used it as a refuge and a base for conducting military operations in the Spanish state. The southern Basque Country is, however, divided politically and administratively between the Autonomous Community of the Basque Country and the Autonomous Community of Navarre, which nationalists claim as part of their territory. The Basques in Spain, as a border people occupying the border with France, have had, since the Middle Ages, privileges known as the forals or the right to a certain fiscal independence, which lasted into the modern period but were abolished by the Franco regime.

The Basques thus developed a strong sense of identity based on their linguistic uniqueness, the mystery surrounding their origins, and their special position within the mediaeval Spanish monarchies.[5] At the end of the nineteenth century, they differentiated themselves from the rest of Spain because of the high degree of industrialisation. This attracted Spanish immigrants who settled in the cities, joining socialist and trade union movements, while traditional Basque society was faithful to the Catholic Church.[6] This dichotomy worried early Basque nationalists such as Sabino Arana, the founder of the Basque Nationalist Party (Partido Nacionalista Vasco – PNV) in 1896, who formulated the early doctrine of Basque nationalism in terms more racist than linguistic or cultural and was quite opposed to this intermingling. Fortunately, this aspect of Arana's doctrine was quietly abandoned by later nationalists.[7] Nevertheless, Basque nationalism offers an interesting contrast to Catalonia where the emphasis is much more on culture and language as identity markers.[8]

During the Spanish Civil War, the majority of Basques of all political tendencies opposed Franco.[9] In the 1960s, the PNV re-emerged but some members of its youth wing founded ETA in 1959. ETA was a coalition of different groups some of which emphasised political actions, while others were more inclined to military action. We can thus distinguish three political 'blocs' in the Basque Country at the time of the transition to democracy (1976–1978): a moderate nationalist bloc represented by the PNV; a radical nationalist bloc represented by the various groups emanating from ETA such as Herri Batasuna (HB, meaning Popular Unity in Basque), created in early 1978; and a pro-Spanish bloc, represented by the Spanish political parties such as the Spanish Socialist Workers' Party (Partido Socialista Obrero Espanol, PSOE, or Socialists) or the right-wing parties such as the UCD (now defunct) and the Popular Alliance (Alianza Popular – AP) which would later become the Popular Party (Partido Popular – PP), and attracting supporters either from the working-class constituencies of non-Basque origin[10] or from some sections of the industrial and financial bourgeoisie.

Although the moderate nationalists of the PNV have ruled the Basque Autonomous Community (AC) since its inception in 1980, sometimes alone, sometimes
in coalition with the Basque Socialist Party (Partido Socialista de Euskadi – PSE-
PSOE), most Basque nationalists are unenthusiastic about the 1978 constitutional
settlement which, in their eyes, divided the southern Basque Country by creating
two separate communities and did not go far enough in recognising its national
character. Another source of dissatisfaction has been the failure to implement fully
the foral laws which would allow the Basques to gain control over their fiscal and
tax regimes.[11] Basques feel they pay too much to the central government to
subsidise the southern Spanish ACs.[12] Even more intense has been the conflict
between the PNV and the various radical nationalist groups clustering around
ETA and HB. But radical nationalists have also been bitterly divided into different
factions.[13]

The radical nationalists succeeded throughout the 1980s in shaping the political
agenda of the Basque Country and, to some extent, of Spain itself.[14] This provoked
a repressive response from the Spanish state which sometimes used its own anti-
terrorist organisations of dubious legality, such as the Anti-terrorist Liberation
Groups (Grupos Antiterroristas de Liberación – GAL), responsible for more than
twenty-five deaths.[15] By the mid-1990s, however, ETA was in a position similar to
that reached by the Provisional IRA in the mid–1980s – they could only disrupt the
system but could not achieve a positive outcome of any of their declared aims. In
other words, it could not go forward politically but neither could it abandon the
armed struggle. This was especially important as there were a considerable number
of prisoners in different parts of Spain outside the Basque Country. To give up the
armed struggle would have seemed like abandoning them. Nevertheless, by the
1990s, it was clear to many Basques that nationalists needed to go beyond the
armed struggle.

Richard Gillespie lists six factors which led to the 1998 ceasefire: political
setbacks experienced by ETA and HB; decline in ETA's military capacity with
more members in prison than active outside; isolation of the militarists from the
mainstream of Basque society; generational change in which younger militants
were less convinced by the old Marxist discourse; the changing international
context, especially Europe and the Irish peace process; and, finally, developments
within Basque nationalism as a whole. This author also points to the influence of
the Irish peace process and the close links between Sinn Féin and HB which
encouraged the latter to follow a similar path.[16]

The Basque peace process

The peace process began with a series of developments originating from within the
moderate nationalist movement. In 1988, the parties represented in the Basque
parliament, the PNV, the PP and the PSOE, but excluding HB, signed the Pacto
de Ajuria-Enea (henceforth – the Pact) which had two aims: to oppose ETA

violence and the radical nationalism of HB and to create the conditions that would permit the full implementation of the Basque Country's Statute with the transfer of more competences from the centre.

To achieve the first aim, the Pact signatories sought the coordination of already existing peace movements opposed to ETA violence, such as Gesto por la Paz (Association for Peace – close to the PNV), and the creation of new ones. The traditional pacifist groups rejected ETA as a valid partner in political negotiations since renouncing violence was a prerequisite to finding a solution. In 1992, however, the Elkarri movement, made up of environmentalist movements close to radical nationalism and describing itself as a 'Social Movement for Dialogue and Agreement in the Basque Country' (Movimento Social por el Diálogo y el Acuerdo en Euskal Herria), came into existence. It sought to overcome the multiple cleavages within the Basque Country through dialogue involving all the protagonists.[17]

After an initial hostile reception from the pacifist organisations involved in the Pact, contacts between the two movements developed in the 1990s. From 1993, the PNV, like its coalition partner the EA (Eusko Alkartasuna, meaning Basque Solidarity), was embarrassed by the fact that the Pact was being used by the PP and the PSOE simply to pressure radical nationalists and not for completing the transfer of competences promised by the Basque Statute of 1979. Gesto por la Paz, close to the PNV, shared the latter's disappointment and moved closer to the Elkarri. Then, in 1994, the revelation of the activities of the GAL brought Elkarri and Gesto por la Paz closer together and they began to collaborate on concrete initiatives.

The PNV initiated its own distinct peace process, involving a rapprochement with HB through a 'dialogue without limits' to find a solution to the Basque conflict. The PNV's position was made known at a Peace Conference in 1995: the Basque problem was a political one; the PNV was ready to engage in a dialogue with ETA; it would support a reform of the Spanish Constitution recognising the right of self-determination; and, finally, this should lead to sovereignty and thence to peace. Constitutional Basque nationalists modelled this approach explicitly on both the Downing Street Declaration and the dialogue between SDLP and Sinn Féin. Alongside this *rapprochement* between moderate and radical nationalists was a series of actions by two Basque trade unions – the ELA (ELA-STV Solidaridad de Trabajadores Vascos, or Basque Workers' Solidarity) and the LAB (Laugile Abertzalean Batzordeak, or Nationalist Workers Union) – close to radical nationalism.[18] In early 1995 ETA published *Alternativa Democrática*, which took account of these developments and advocated a change of approach from one of dialogue between ETA and the Spanish state to one that would give a voice to ordinary citizens and other social and political forces within the Basque Country, while insisting that the state recognise the right of self-determination and the entire territory of the Basque people.

Despite these burgeoning peace movements even within the heart of radical nationalism, the latter remained deeply divided for a further three years. While HB attended Elkarri's Peace Conference in 1995, increasingly indiscriminate military actions on the part of ETA led to increased tension between HB and Basque society. ETA, hounded by the Spanish and French police after the arrest of its leadership in Bidart, in the French Basque Country, intensified the armed struggle, attacking both Basque and Spanish politicians. PP representatives in the Basque Country were assassinated in retaliation for the prisons policy of the PP government in Madrid after its election in 1996. These actions set off alarm bells among constitutional nationalists who feared they would lessen their capacity to influence the further implementation of the Basque Statute. At this point, the Lehendakari (President of the Basque Government) José Antonio denounced 'the political bartering' through which the parties in power in Madrid exchanged support in the Spanish parliament for the transfer of a few powers, and the 'political prejudices' of those parties in favour of a symmetrical and homogenous state.[19] In October 1997, ELA organised a meeting in Guernica attended by the leading figures of all the Basque nationalist parties, during which its secretary general Elorrieta, while criticising the on-going campaign of ETA, announced that 'the Statute [of the Basque Country] was now dead'.

In 1998, discussions continued among the nationalist parties and, in September of that year, the Declaration of Lizarra was signed by the PNV, EA, HB and Ezker Batua (Basque branch of the Spanish coalition Izquierda Unida (United Left) led by the Communist Party), by the ELA and LAB trade union movements, and by social movements such as Elkarri and Bakea Orain (Paz Ahora, or Peace Now – a pacifist organisation).[20] The Declaration was signed partly under the influence of the Belfast Good Friday Agreement and, indeed, the meeting was known as the 'Irish Forum'.[21] Even if the central state and the centralist political parties become stuck in immobilism, it was felt that Basque political and social actors should build their own national consensus. An indefinite ceasefire should be the beginning and not the end of the peace process. The Declaration invited all the interested parties, including the Madrid government, to participate in the agreement. However, their presence was not an essential precondition to begin the process. The Declaration of Lizarra recognised the existence of a political conflict between the Basque Country and the Spanish state involving unresolved questions of territory, decision-making and sovereignty. It laid out a negotiation process open to all actors in conjunction with Basque society. Following an initial phase of multilateral discussions without any preconditions, there would be a final phase of negotiation which would tackle the causes of the conflict. However, these negotiations could happen only following a complete and permanent cessation of violence. This should lead to a resolution of the conflict without any imposition or coercion which would respect the 'pluralism' of Basque society and treat all political positions on the basis of equality. The Spanish and French governments were asked to respect the Declaration, which did not envisage definitive and closed scenarios but an open and innovative approach.

In the AC elections in October 1998 and the municipal (local) elections in the Spring of 1999, the parties which had signed the Declaration triumphed.[22] In the Basque AC elections, they won 65 per cent of the vote. If Navarra is included, the entire southern Basque Country (that is, in Spain), this comes to 55 per cent. Herri

Batasuna, which had stood under the name Euskal Herritarrok (Basque Citizens), saw a spectacular increase of one-third in the numbers voting for them.

At the end of 1998, the Spanish parliament unanimously approved a resolution which requested the PP government to modify its policies towards Basque prisoners. With the formation of a Basque government consisting solely of a coalition between the PNV and EA, Basque radical nationalists had, for the first time, to take on responsibilities within the political system and to subscribe to a programme of government with the governing parties. Doubtless, the peace process in the Basque Country was unlike what had happened in Northern Ireland. The Spanish right-wing government, fearful of the questioning of national sovereignty which the Declaration of Lizarra implied, adopted an immobilist position, and were supported in this by the opposition Spanish Socialist Party, which shared the same fears. It ignored the massive street demonstrations in the Basque Country at the beginning of the year in favour of the Declaration. It dragged its heels on the moving of prisoners closer to the Basque Country. The PP government declared that it would not pay any price for peace. This really meant it refused to discuss any change in a political model clearly opposed by a majority of Basques. The French Socialist government, which regarded with suspicion the demand for a unified Basque *département* in the French part of the Basque Country, shared Spain's obstructionist attitude. The French minister of the interior, Jean-Pierre Chevènement, continued to collaborate with the Spanish police in arresting ETA militants as if the latter had not declared a ceasefire. Those arrested included a woman who had taken part in the only meeting between ETA and the Spanish government in Switzerland in May 1999.

The intransigent centralism of the Spanish authorities is reminiscent of the attitude of the John Major government during the first IRA ceasefire of 1994 and, like this, has contributed directly to breakdown of ETA's ceasefire in December 1999. It has also irritated the Basque government and certainly slowed down the peace process. This casts a shadow over the future and whether there can be a negotiated solution to the Basque problem. Groups of young radicals who are sympathisers but not members of ETA have carried on a low-level campaign of violence against public buildings and property belonging to Socialist and PP activists. Euskal Herritarrok took a decision, in contrast to the other signatories of the Pact, not to stand for the Spanish general elections which will take place in 2000. These groups are beginning to think that the Good Friday model of multilateral negotiations is not viable. They are now swinging around toward the Quebecois model of an agreement on sovereignty among nationalists.

The Corsican problem

Corsica's position in the French state differs radically from either Northern Ireland or the Basque Country. It is an island in the western Mediterranean and was a colony of the city-state of Genoa for several centuries. It came under French control in 1769 following a forty-year revolt by Corsicans. During the second half of this revolt (1749–69), Corsicans, led by Pascal Paoli, set up an embryonic democratic republic whose constitution was inspired by Jean-Jacques Rousseau. The French monarchy intervened at the request of the Genoese and quelled the revolt. The Genoese then 'leased' the island to France but Corsica only became fully French when most Corsicans expressed a desire to be fully incorporated into the French state rather than return to Genoese rule. However, Corsican culture, language and society owed more to Italy than to France. Even as late as the nineteenth century, many mayors of villages conducted their official business through Italian while the spoken language of the people was Corsican, closely related to Tuscan Italian. There were in fact two Corsicas: the Corsica of the towns built, mostly by the Genoese,[23] around the coastline and the village Corsica of the interior. These reflected two kinds of society and ways of life. Bastia was originally the capital and oriented toward Italy. Ajaccio became the capital during the Second Empire when Bonapartism was at its height. It developed a way of life typical of a French provincial town. In the mountainous interior, society resembled that found in southern Italy, Sardinia and Sicily, with their traditions of family honour, banditry and the vendetta. This dichotomy is a pointer to the ambiguities of Corsican identity which is both French and Italianate.

Throughout the nineteenth and twentieth centuries, most Corsicans identified with the French state which they perceived to be the source of their continued survival as an island community. Corsicans joined the army, the police, customs and other branches of the French civil service and identified strongly with France's imperialist expansion as administrators or soldiers. Identification with France reached its apex during the First and Second World Wars when thousands of islanders gave their lives for *la patrie*. They rejected identification with the surrounding Italian regions and islands which they regarded as inferior.[24] Furthermore, Corsica had exactly the same political and administrative institutions as the rest of France, with only some minor fiscal advantages granted as a result of its geographical situation. On the other hand, the island, despite its rejection of Italianateness, bore a strong resemblance in its culture and society to its Italian neighbours in southern Italy, Sardinia and Sicily. French political institutions were recast into a mould of clientelism and patronage and were operated by the political clans of the island.[25] These were basically powerful political families who divided the island among themselves. They adopted the official labels of the French political parties, usually of the left and the right, although their political practices were fundamentally similar to each other and far removed from those of mainland France. The clans acted as mediators between the local society and the state, ensuring the loyalty of the local population in return for resources of various kinds channelled in a clientelistic manner from the state to the locality. It was an exaggerated form of the *système notabiliaire* which operated in other parts of the French periphery.

While the system worked well it went largely unchallenged either by Corsicans or by state officials such as the *prefect*. During periods of economic crisis, however, as at the end of the nineteenth century, in the 1930s, and after the Second World War, regionalist groups emerged to criticise and challenge the clan system. They blamed the economic crisis on the clans and the French state. Until the most recent period, regionalist groups tended to be right-wing or even extreme-right. During the Second World War, some of their number collaborated with the Italian and Fascist occupants of Corsica.[26] However, the economic crisis of the 1950s, when Corsica was in a state of ruin and collapse, led to a much more broadly-based regionalist mobilisation, this time led by the Communist and Socialist Parties but containing under its umbrella more radical autonomist and nationalist tendencies.

The traditional French response to Corsican problems was benign neglect. However, following the success of Breton regionalists in obtaining a Regional Action Plan[27] in the 1950s, Corsica was also granted such a Plan in 1957. This emphasised tourism and agricultural development related to the tourism industry. It failed, however, to satisfy the more radical Corsican regionalists. When de Gaulle came to power in 1958, the plan was shelved at first but resurrected following Algerian independence in 1962. In effect, around 17,000 *pieds noirs* returned to Corsica where many had family contacts and where the climate and landscape resembled North Africa. Most integrated without difficulty or moved on to mainland France. However, about 500 *pied noir* families were granted farm land under the Regional Action Plan which had been cleared for use by Corsican farmers. Not surprisingly, Corsicans reacted vigorously to this and this was the immediate cause of the emergence of the first violent clandestine groups in the mid-1960s with bombings of *pied noir* property and crops.[28]

It is unlikely that these early groups had clear political aims such as more autonomy or independence. On the contrary, the evidence suggests that they were actually close to the *Algérie française* movement which fought against Algerian independence. However, the *pied noir* question and a number of other affairs led to the emergence of more radical regionalist movements in the 1960s and early 1970s.[29] Some of these, such as the autonomist UPC (Unione di u Populu Corsu), sought greater autonomy within the French republic and recognition of the existence of a distinct Corsican *ethnie*.[30] Others, such as the FRC (Front Régionaliste Corse), created in 1973, mainly by students on mainland France, adopted a more Marxist analysis and espoused the then fashionable internal colonialism model to explain Corsica's backwardness. Violence continued in the background to these more overt political movements. The autonomists of the UPC, led by Edmond and Max Simeoni, engaged in more symbolic violence, that is one-off spectacular events, such as the occupation in 1974 of the wine cellars of a *pied noir* wine grower. The UPC soon afterwards renounced the use of violence because of deaths caused by this incident. This was not the case of the more radical nationalists.[31] Several groups, such as the FPCL (Fronte Paisanu Corsu di Liberazione, of the period 1973–76) and GP (Ghjustia Paolina, of 1974), existed until the FLNC was created in 1976. The FLNC was the main clandestine group until 1990 when it split into several competing factions.

These movements never attracted the support of the majority of the Corsican population who continued to support the main French parties. Nevertheless, they did succeed in dominating the political agenda on the island and, to a lesser extent, in France and provoked several responses from the French government. Until the election of François Mitterrand to the French Presidency in 1981, the response was a mixture of repression and concessions which were usually too little and too late. The Socialists, however, launched their decentralisation programme in 1982, part of which involved setting up elected regional governments. Corsica received special treatment through a *Statut Particulier* which recognised its specificity through a Regional Assembly (rather than a Regional Council) and some extra committees related to culture and economic development because of its island status.

Decentralisation deeply divided the nationalist and autonomist movements, some of whom participated in the new institutions, while others continued to boycott them. In fact, the violence increased in both quantity and intensity.[32] There followed several years of splits and then feuds between rival groups. However, all nationalists and autonomists were in agreement that the *Statut* did not go far enough in recognising the existence of a Corsican *'peuple'*, let alone a Corsican 'nation'. The Corsican Assembly also failed to function well, with continual crises due to the fissiparous nature of the political groups elected to it. There were problems of electoral fraud and financial corruption. Meanwhile, the economic situation deteriorated further, adding to the sense of foreboding and crisis on the island. Social movements and trade unions launched strikes which left the island isolated from France and the outside world. We should not exaggerate the extent of this crisis or the effect of the violence which never reached Northern Ireland proportions. Nevertheless, it was sufficient to prevent the economic development of the island and contributed to the failure of the political institutions to function in a democratic manner.

A first step towards resolving the problem came in 1991 when the then Socialist minister of the interior, Pierre Joxe, promulgated a revised version of the *Statut Particulier* which raised its legal status to the same level as the *Territoires d'Outre-Mer*.[33] The bill setting up the new Assembly also recognised the existence of 'the Corsican people, part of the French people'.[34] The bill passed through the National Assembly with a small majority but was struck down as unconstitutional by the Constitutional Court (*conseil constitutionnel*) on the grounds that the Constitution only recognises the 'French people' and not the 'Corsican people'. Nevertheless, the new institutions were set up and began to function but the refusal to recognise a Corsican people further radicalised the nationalist movement.

But radicalisation was accompanied by more dramatic splits and an increase in internal feuding.[35] This was related, at least partly, to control of different kinds of criminal activities engaged in by some of the clandestine movements. French governments of both right and left tried at various points to enter into negotiations with different factions to meet some of their demands but these usually ended in failure and infuriated the groups left out of the dialogue. The final straw for the government came with the assassination of the *prefect*, Claude Erignac, in 1998, as he left the *prefecture* in Ajaccio.[36] This caused a wave of revulsion on the part of most French people, similar to that caused in Britain by IRA activities. A Parliamentary Commission published a report on the use of public funds in Corsica which was highly critical of mainstream Corsican politicians on the island whom it accused of corruption. The Jospin government dispatched a hardline *prefect*, M. Bonnet, who favoured a hard law-and-order crackdown. However, this backfired when it emerged that the prefect had sent some senior policemen to burn down a restaurant which had been erected illegally! He in turn was arrested along with the policemen and detained in custody. Relations between the island and the mainland reached their lowest point ever with criticisms coming from mainstream Corsican politicians as well as nationalists and autonomists, most of whom were beginning to realise that Corsica's institutional and political relationship to the French state needed to be reappraised.

A Corsican peace process?

Despite these problems, there developed, in the 1990s, a willingness to come to grips with the Corsican problem and a dialogue opened up between nationalists, autonomists and some mainstream political groups on the island. The IRA ceasefire and peace process also exercised an important influence on the radical nationalists of the various armed groups emanating from the FLNC. John Hume's role was particularly admired by the autonomists of the UPC (roughly the equivalent of the SDLP).

At this point, a project was launched by the European Centre of Minority Issues (ECMI)[37] which invited a group of Corsican politicians and activists to a conference on 'Island Regions in the New Europe', held on the Åland Islands in Finland.[38] This conference seems to have been a turning point in internal Corsican relations, for two reasons. First, Corsicans as bitterly opposed as nationalists and unionists in Northern Ireland came together for the first time and found themselves largely in agreement on a whole range of issues. Thus a dialogue among Corsicans was begun that would not have been possible on the island itself. Second, by couching the Corsican problem in terms of European regions and in the context of European integration, the vocabulary of Corsican politics began to change.[39] The word 'autonomy', hitherto taboo in the political lexicon of certain traditional French parties, now began to be used more freely. Mr Paul Giacobbi, President of the Conseil Général of upper Corsica and heir of the Radicaux de Gauche political clan,[40] caused a sensation at the conference by declaring that he was in favour of many positions hitherto espoused by the regionalists. In fact, he demanded a statute of 'regional citizenship'[41] for Corsica and a radical reduction of the island's political and administrative institutions.[42] The conference participants, including Pierre Joxe, referred on several occasions to the Northern Irish peace process during the Åland Islands conference. On the island itself, some time after the conference, following the success of nationalist lists in the March 1999 elections to the Corsican

Assembly,[43] fifteen nationalist groups came together and declared a common programme and renounced violent acts against each other – the Declaration of the Fiumorbu. There was a great willingness to engage in a constructive and open dialogue with the French government and other political forces on the island.

On a visit to the island in September 1999, the prime minister, Lionel Jospin, failed to respond very positively to most of these demands. However, this is probably to be expected given the strong Jacobin factions within his own party such as the Mouvement des Citoyens, led by the Minister of the Interior, Jean-Pierre Chevènement, bitterly opposed to anything which seems to threaten the unitary state. The instransigence on the part of the French government and parliamentary reports which criticised the functioning of the island's legal system soured relations between the islanders and the mainland. Some nationalists stepped up the violence with car-bombs exploding during the day in the centre of Ajaccio. The entire political class in Corsica, including the Gaullist chair of the Regional Executive, Jean Baggioni, and the centre-right chair of the Assembly, José Rossi, felt alienated from the hardline position of the government. Rossi, in particular, was engaged in dialogue with the nationalists and both politicians called for further modifications of the island's institutions. At first, the Jospin government, under pressure from its own hardline Jacobins, refused to enter into dialogue with elected representatives unless these first condemned the use of violence. However, in December 1999, Jospin appeared to adopt a less intransigent line by dropping this demand and inviting representatives of the main groups elected to the Corsican Assembly to an open-ended dialogue on the island's future, to take place in Paris. Eight of the nationalist groups which had signed the Fiumorbu Declaration came together under the umbrella of a group called Unita in order to participate in this dialogue. Thus, despite the difficulties, it may be remarked that the peace process in Corsica has begun and the potential is there for peace to break out on the island.

Conclusions

The three cases of Northern Ireland, the Basque Country and Corsica have many features that differentiate one from the other. What is remarkable, however, is that the phasing of the different conflicts seems to correspond quite closely, moving from early regionalism to separatist nationalism. In all three cases, however, while the armed struggle did influence the political agenda, it could not achieve the nationalists' political goals of setting up independent states.

In the late 1980s and 1990s there was a completely different context. Political activity was no longer confined to the nation-state but occurred in a system of European governance marked by a complex variety of public actors. Regions and local authorities, despite their great diversity within European states, have found a new role as political actors with this new European system, for example in the Committee of the Regions.[44] Small nations such as Catalonia and, more recently, Scotland and Wales recognise that this new situation offers windows of opportunity to them that had not existed before. Moderate nationalists have been quick to exploit these opportunities, often as a way of putting pressure on central governments such as Madrid. Furthermore, the new context radically changed traditional conceptions dear to nationalism such as sovereignty which, confronted by both globalisation and a more integrated EU is increasingly meaningless. It is this broader context which, combined with the realisation by republicans that the armed struggle had reached its limits, made it possible for the nature of the Northern Irish problem to be redefined in such a way that the IRA could get off the hook of violence while saving face in front of their own followers. The same processes have been at work in the Basque Country with the *rapprochement* between the PNV and HB and in Corsica between radical nationalists and traditional parties of the left and right. The path trodden by the Irish and British has been an important stimulus to the Corsicans and Basques in finding an alternative to political violence. It is difficult to say at this point where the direct influences have been. Certainly, there have been some, such as a visit by Gerry Adams to the Basque Country or of John Hume to Corsica. However, it is probably truer to say that the influence of the Irish peace process has been more indirect, encouraging especially radical nationalists to rethink their political project and to study the method which led to the Good Friday Agreement. One key difference, however, is in the attitude of the national governments involved. Neither the French nor the Spanish feel much desire to emulate the initiatives taken by the Blair government, fearing that this might encourage further separatist trends. Another difference lies in the nature of the nationalist movements. The Provisional Republican movement is, by and large, a unified movement with a solid base in almost half of the Northern Irish Catholic community. They have shown a remarkable discipline in holding to the ceasefire. In the Basque Country and especially in Corsica, the nationalist movements are deeply divided and find it difficult to present a unified front to enter into dialogue with both the government and other political forces within their regions.

Nevertheless, despite the breakdown of the ceasefire in the Basque Country, we can end this chapter on a note of optimism, although this needs to be tempered by caution. The positive point is that in Northern Ireland, the Basque Country and Corsica violence has been considerably scaled down and there is a new spirit of dialogue at least among nationalists and sometimes with non-nationalists. On the other hand, the difficulties of achieving a final settlement should, perhaps, not be underestimated. Peace may not be impossible, but as the Northern Irish case illustrates, an agreed 'solution' is far more difficult to achieve.

Notes

1 In Northern Ireland and the Basque Country, the radical nationalists have done so with the moderate nationalists in the SDLP and PNV, while in Corsica, the radicals are dialoguing with non- and even anti-nationalist groups such as elements within the French centre-right or sections of the Socialist Party.

2 See John Loughlin, 'The "Europe of the Regions" and the Federalization of Europe',

Publius: the Journal of Federalism, Autumn 1996.

3 These are usually referred to as the Spanish Basque Country and the French Basque Country. Basques, however, especially those in Spain, tend to use the terms the North Basque Country (in France) and the South Basque Country (in Spain).

4 See John Loughlin, *Regionalism and Ethnic Nationalism in France: a Case-study of Corsica* (Florence: European University Institute, 1989).

5 See J. Cara Baroja, *Los Vascos* (Minotauro: Madrid, 1958).

6 See Daniel-Louis Seiler, *L'exemplarité du nationalisme basque: une perspective comparée* (Iruña: Fundación Sabino Arana, 1996).

7 See Francesco Letamendia, 'Basque Nationalism and the Struggle for Self-determination in the Basque Country', in B. Berberoglu (ed.), *The National Question* (Philadelphia: Temple University Press, 1995).

8 This is understandable given the high percentage of Catalans who speak Catalan and the ease with which a Castilian immigrant can understand and learn the language, while Basque is much less accessible. An excellent comparison of the two nations may be found in Daniele Conversi, *The Basques, The Catalans and Spain: Alternative Routes to Nationalist Mobilisation* (London: Hurst & Co., 1997).

9 The upper bourgeoisie and the Spanish military stationed in the Basque Country supported Franco.

10 This needs to be qualified by stating that many Basque nationalists and even members of ETA and HB are also from this group of immigrants.

11 The foral laws give the Basque Country and Navarre a great deal of financial autonomy. The Foral Deputation, not the Spanish state, first collects taxes of various kinds. These are then divided according to a complex formula between those which remain in the AC and those which go to the central state.

12 The sentiment on the part of richer regions that they are subsidising the poorer is not confined to the Basque Country and may also be found in Italy's northern regions such as Lombardy.

13 See Joseba Zulaika, *Basque Violence. Metaphor and Sacrament* (Reno: Nevada University Press, 1988).

14 They have been responsible for over 800 deaths and many bombings in different parts of Spain.

15 See Francesco Letamendia, *Juego de espejos, Conflictos nacionales centro-periferia* (Madrid: Ed. Trotta, 1997).

16 Richard Gillespie, 'Peace Moves in the Basque Country', *Journal of Southern Europe and the Balkans*, Vol. 1, No. 2, 1999, pp. 119–36.

17 See M. Uranga Gomez, I. Lasagabaster, F. Letamendia, R. Zallo (eds), *Un nuevo escrenario: democracia, cultura y cohesión social en Euskal Herria* (Aranguiz: Instituto Manu Robles, 1999).

18 See Letamendia, *Juego de espejos.*

19 Whereas Basque, Catalan and Galician nationalists argued in favour of an 'asymmetrical state'.

20 Twenty-three groups and parties signed the Declaration, see Gillespie, *Peace Moves,* p. 125.

21 *Ibid.*

22 *Ibid.,* p. 127 and Gomez *et al., Un nuevo escrenario.*

23 Ajaccio, Bastia, Calvi, Bonifacio etc. were built mostly by the Genoese. Ile-Rousse was built by Pascal Paoli during the revolt against the Genoese as a way of having access to the sea.

24 Italians came from different Italian regions to work on Corsica and were referred to pejoratively as 'I Lucchesi' even if few actually came from Lucca in Tuscany.

25 See Jean-Louis Briquet, *La Tradition en mouvement. Clientélisme et politique en Corse* (Paris: Belin, 1997) and Loughlin, *Regionalism and Ethnic Nationalism.*

26 *Ibid.*

27 This was basically the introduction of a regional dimension to the National (Economic) Plans, invented by Jean Monnet, which covered France as a whole.

28 See John Loughlin, 'Les Pieds Noirs en Corse', *La Guerre d'Algérie et les Français* (Paris: Fayard, 1989).

29 See Loughlin, *Regionalism and Ethnic Nationalism*; E. Bernabéu-Casanova, *Le Nationalisme corse. Genèse, succès et échec* (Paris: L'Harmattan, 1997).

30 Some members of this movement were, in fact, old-style regionalists and nationalists who did not wish to use this terminology given the discredit it had earned because of the collaborationist activities referred to above.

31 There was a shift from regionalism to nationalism on the part of these groups as their way of defining the nature of Corsican society. See Loughlin, *Regionalism and Ethnic Nationalism*.

32 Much of the early FLNC violence had taken the form of *propagande armée* (symbolic actions) rather than *lutte armée* (armed struggle). The latter involved more serious destruction of property and led inevitably to the taking of human life. There was also an intense campaign against non-Corsican French people (*les continentaux*) who had settled on the island as teachers, civil servants, etc.

33 See Helen Hintjens, John Loughlin and Claude Olivesi, 'The Status of Maritime and Insular France: the DOM-TOM and Corsica', in J. Loughlin and S. Mazey (eds), *The End of the French Unitary State: Ten Years of Regionalization in France (1982–1992)* (London: Frank Cass, 1995). The TOMs are in fact, ex-colonies, and have the right to independence if they so wish. Although the French state refuses to place Corsica in this category of being a colony, the Joxe Statute goes some way to recognising its special circumstances.

34 Article 1 of the Law of 13 May 1991 (*loi* no. 91–428 *Statut de la Collectivité territoriale de Corse, Journal officiel de la République française*, 14 May 1993, p. 6318–29) on the Special Statute of the Corsican Region reads: 'The French Republic guarantees to the historic and cultural community constituted by the Corsican people, component of the French people, the right to preserve its cultural identity and to defend its specific economic and social interests. These rights related to insularity are to be exercised with respect for national unity, in the framework of the Constitution, of the laws of the Republic, and of this present statute.'

35 An organigramme of the different nationalist and autonomist groups may be found in John Loughlin and Farimah Daftary, *Insular Regions and European Integration: Corsica and the Åland Islands Compared*, ECMI Report No. 5, November 1999 (Flensburg: European Centre for Minority Issues), p. 62.

36 This was the only time, at least since the Second World War, that a French *prefect* was assassinated.

37 ECMI, based in Flensburg, Germany and financed by the Danish, German and Schleswig-Holstein governments, is an institute devoted to the study but also to contributing to peaceful solutions to minority conflicts. John Loughlin, co-author of this chapter, and Claude Olivesi, a Corsican academic and politician, acted as academic and political advisors to ECMI on this project.

38 Also present were Pierre Joxe (in a private capacity), several French and Corsican journalists, and politicians and administrators from Finland and the Åland Islands. A full report of the conference may be found in John Loughlin, Claude Olivesi and Farimah Daftary (eds), *Autonomies Insulaires. Vers une Politique de Différence pour la Corse?* (Ajaccio: Albiana, 1999).

39 It is true that many Corsicans such as Claude Olivesi had begun to speak in these terms but this was the first time that the language was used by such a diverse gathering of political tendencies.

40 His late father, François, had been the chief of this political clan and was bitterly opposed to nationalism.

41 'Regional citizenship' was the basis of the Åland Islands' autonomy state and could be obtained only if one possessed Finnish nationality, was resident on the islands for at least five years, and had a competent mastery of the Swedish language, spoken by 95 per cent of the islanders. See Loughlin *et al.* (eds), *Autonomies Insulaires*.

42 Besides the regional assembly, there are two departments with all their cantons and about 350 communes for a population of around 220,000.

43 In the second round, the list Corsica Nazione, led by Jean-Guy Talamoni, won 16.77 per cent of the vote and 8 seats, third behind the centre-right list Rassemblement pour la République (RPR)-Démocratie Libérale (DL), who won 27.9 per cent of the vote and 17 seats and the left-wing list Gauche 'plurielle', who obtained 22.7 per cent and 11 seats.

44 See John Loughlin, 'Representing Regions in Europe: the Committee of the Regions', *Regional and Federal Studies: an International Journal*, Vol. 6, No. 2, Summer 1996, pp. 147–65.

18

Northern Ireland after the Cold War

MICHAEL COX

Introduction

If students of international relations can readily be accused of failing to take the Northern Ireland seriously enough, then analysts of the conflict in the North can be criticised with equal force for ignoring the complex ways in which the outside world has impacted upon the province since the struggle for civil rights rapidly and tragically evolved into a military campaign in the late 1960s. This is not only historically indefensible insofar as the tangled web of relations between Britain and Ireland make no sense unless they are situated within a wider international context; it is also analytically parochial. Indeed, far too many historians of the Troubles have discussed them as if they stood in some splendid isolation from the rest of the world. The approach adopted here is quite different, and while in no way seeking to deny either the local causes or the specific character of the conflict, insists that the conflict in its various phases can only be fully explained if we 'bring in the international'. Northern Ireland does not stand and has never stood outside international history. It was certainly not true when the Troubles began and – as we shall see below – has not been the case in the 1990s when the 'long war' finally began to show very clear signs that it was coming to an end.

But how should we set about explaining the deeper causes of the end of the war and the quite extraordinary events that began with the Good Friday agreement in April 1998 and concluded with the creation of a new Northern Ireland executive in December 1999? While in no way ignoring the role of key individuals like Hume or Trimble, the negotiating patience of US Senator George Mitchell, or the critical part played by republican persuaders like Gerry Adams and Martin McGuinness, theorists of the peace process have tried to explain the new politics of Northern Ireland in one of three ways.

First, there are those who see the winding down of the conflict in terms of what some like to call public opinion and others 'people power'. According to this thesis, the voiceless and the powerless in Northern Ireland had simply had enough after twenty-five years of civil disorder, and conveyed this directly and indirectly to the main paramilitary organisations.[1] Not surprisingly, this populist explanation is rejected by the 'realists'. Not for them romantic stories about popular pressure for peace, but the hard logic of power and the successful long-term containment of the IRA by the Army and the intelligence services. Some would even insist that loyalist terror also played its part in persuading the IRA to give up the gun. Taken together, these pressures, it is suggested, forced republicans to rethink their militant tactics and in the end (and somewhat reluctantly) accept a ceasefire followed by serious negotiations.[2] Lastly, there is a very powerful school of thought that would explain the ending of the war not in terms of a changing balance of power between conflicting parties, but as the result of organised cooperation between the two states which had most to lose if the war continued. The combined efforts of both Ireland and the UK, it has been argued, first helped isolate the republican threat though the instrument of the Anglo-Irish Agreement of 1985; and then drew republican leaders in from the cold through a series of carefully designed accords whose ultimate purpose was to undermine the case for violence by implying that there might be another, non-violent way of them achieving their goal. The basic reason for the war coming to an end in Northern Ireland, therefore, had less to do with the exercise of military power, and more to do with policy-makers from legitimate states working together to resolve a conflict that most people had hitherto thought to be insoluble.[3]

The thesis advanced here does not reject what might be termed 'internalist' explanations of the end of the IRA war but rather suggests that we cannot isolate the 'peace process' in the North from changes taking place in the wider international system.[4] Nor should we try to do so, and while in no way seeking to downplay the importance of other factors such as war weariness, military containment and inter-state cooperation, it is argued here that the winding down of the 'armed struggle' was also the result of transnational pressures upon the most immediate reason for the conflict: the Provisional IRA. The IRA may well have been a quintessentially Irish phenomenon. However, it could not escape the world or ignore what was happening outside Ireland. In particular, it could not escape the impact of the several tidal waves thrown up by the collapse of the Cold War system in the late 1980s. This is not to imply a simple reductionist relationship between the end of the Cold War and the conclusion of its campaign of violence. Nor is it to argue that the end of the war in Northern Ireland is reducible to a single 'essential' cause. What is being suggested, however, is that the conclusion of the Cold War made it far more difficult for the IRA to continue with its military campaign – not because the organisation did not have the capacity to do so, but rather because in the post-Cold War era, its campaign of violence could no longer be so readily justified.[5] Furthermore, the ending of the Cold War precipitated a number of critical changes in the wider structure of the international system. These not only weakened the republican movement's rationale for fighting the British presence in Ireland, but even more importantly perhaps, made it possible for a 'Third Party', the US, to play a far more decisive role in Northern Irish affairs. Finally, as a self-proclaimed revolutionary organisation with a project of changing Ireland, it was inevitable that as the tide of global radicalism began to retreat after 1989, this would feed into republican thinking. Indeed, there is strong evidence to suggest, that as radicalism around the world began to ebb in the 1990s, this had a marked influence on a number of key figures in the republican movement; enough it seems to force some of them at least to rethink what they had been doing since the heady days of the 1970s.

The complex narrative of how the IRA was finally persuaded against all known expectation to try the unarmed road has been told in a number of compelling accounts of the peace process. The purpose here, therefore, is not to retell a story which others have already told, but to explain how and why the end of a larger competition which apparently had very little to do with the local conflict in Northern Ireland, had such a big impact upon the theory and practice of the Irish republican movement.[6]

Farewell to national liberation

The Provisional IRA did not begin life in 1970 as a fully formed guerilla organisation, but as a poorly equipped group whose first task, as they saw it, was to defend the besieged Catholics of the North against the perceived threat posed by the Protestant majority.[7] Those who created the Provisionals also saw their job as rebuilding a movement along traditional and authentically Irish lines. Thus, according to the early 'Provos', there was no need for republicans to look outside Ireland for inspiration or guidance. Indeed, at a time when national liberation movements around the world were exciting the sympathy and the support of student radicals in western Europe and the US, the Provisional leadership almost seemed to go out of its way to distance itself and the new IRA from these other struggles – especially if they were led by revolutionary Marxists. Yet in spite of this apparent narrowness of outlook, the IRA was impelled by both military necessity and a genuine sense of political solidarity to forge links with other movements of national liberation. This move was also hastened by the collapse of the IRA's original scenario of quick victory over the British.[8] This not only caused a shift in its tactics, but also led to the emergence of those in the organisation more sympathetic to socialist ideas and more inclined to build serious bridges to other revolutionary groups and regimes. Even Cuba began to get a more sympathetic hearing, which Castro later appeared to reciprocate during the hunger strikes when he praised the bravery of the freedom fighters of the IRA. Of course, this hardly made the republican movement agents of the Soviet Union, as some on the conservative right argued at the time.[9] On the other hand, its continuing campaign against America's most special ally – the British – certainly made the USSR sympathetic towards their cause. It would be something of an exaggeration to talk, as one writer has done, of the IRA now becoming 'Pravda's Provos'.[10] Nevertheless, Soviet coverage of the situation in Northern Ireland remained broadly sympathetic to the republican cause and only changed significantly following the collapse of the USSR itself in 1991.

There was and remains no simple or direct connection between the settlement of other regional conflicts after the Cold War and the change of strategy by the IRA. Some have even argued that because the relationship between the conflict in Northern Ireland and the larger Cold War was somewhat tenuous, that it would be wrong to believe that an end to the larger struggle had very much impact on Ireland.[11] As a leading figure in the republican movement noted at the time, 'only a fool would argue that there are direct parallels' between the situation in the North of Ireland and other Third World conflicts.[12] However, as Mitchel McLaughlin also conceded, those who had already gone through the difficult transitional process leading from war to peace elsewhere, might have something to teach the Irish. He even admitted that those who had made peace in other countries had given 'tremendous support' to those in Ireland trying to do the same.[13] The Sinn Féin president, Gerry Adams, made much the same general point. Ireland, he accepted, was different and it would be a 'mistake' to think otherwise. Nonetheless, if conflicts as apparently intractable as those in the Middle East and South Africa could be resolved, then this obviously held out hope for the people of Ireland. Furthermore, because these other conflicts had been brought to an end, according to Adams, it created 'an international climate' which made the resolution of all conflicts, including the one in the North, far more likely. Northern Ireland might have been different. But it was neither unique nor immune to change taking place in the wider international system.[14]

In effect, having become part of a wider revolutionary project, Irish republicanism could hardly avoid being affected by its collapse in the latter half of the 1980s. Logistically of course they could fight on, as they did most effectively with weapons supplied by Libyan leader President Qadaffi. But having the capacity to bomb and shoot was one thing: this was hardly the same as being part of a broader movement whose larger aim was nothing less than the destruction of imperialism as a system. And inevitably, as this movement began to retreat, republicans in Ireland started to lose their various points of ideological and political reference around the world. Even more critically perhaps, those who earlier had made solidarity with their 'Irish brothers and sisters', now began to advise them to follow the path of peace. It was one thing when your enemies suggested you abandon the armed struggle. It was something else entirely when those with enormous moral standing in the republican movement – figures like Mandela and Arafat – told you to do the same.[15]

The Soviet threat and after

If events in the Third World after the Cold War increased the IRA's sense of isolation, developments in the larger strategic landscape helped undermine its analysis of why it was necessary to fight the British. To explain why this should have been so, we have to understand the republican movement's theory of why it believed the British were in Ireland in the first place.[16]

According to republicans, Britain remained in Northern Ireland because this provided them with a vital (albeit costly) platform from which to exercise economic control over Ireland as a whole. As a Sinn Féin document of 1988 argued, though the annual British subvention to the North was high, it would be quite 'wrong to conclude that this level of spending negates any British economic interest in Ireland'. But economics was only one part of a complex set of ties linking the two countries. Of even greater importance was an abiding British fear of what might happen if Ireland were ever to be united. For locked as it was into what seemed like a permanent Cold War conflict with Russia, Britain – according to republicans – stayed on in the North to secure one part of Ireland for NATO and to prevent the creation of a united and neutral Ireland outside the NATO alliance. Economics might have been important in maintaining the Union. There was even something to the argument that the 'British establishment' had a historic attachment to the Union, if not necessarily to unionists themselves. But these were second-level explanations of why Britain went to such 'lengths' to 'remain'. As one republican source put it before the Berlin Wall came tumbling down, though Britain's 'continuing involvement in Ireland' was based upon a number of calculations, including an exaggerated fear of Ireland becoming a 'European Cuba', by far and away the 'most important' consideration 'now' was its concerns about Irish neutrality and the serious threat which that posed to NATO and Britain's 'strategic interests'.[17]

The collapse of communism in Eastern Europe in 1989 followed two years later by the implosion of the USSR itself, clearly posed enormous problems for the republican movement's analysis of why Britain hung on to Ireland. After all, with no Soviet Union, there could be no Soviet threat; and this inevitably left Sinn Féin in desperate need of a new argument to explain both the British presence and why force was needed to remove it. It also created an intellectual opening for John Hume, leader of the Social Democratic and Labour Party. Hume was already involved in detailed negotiations with Gerry Adams about the best way of resolving the situation in the North. Significantly, part of these negotiations had revolved around the critical issue of British intentions. Adams, not surprisingly, insisted that the British had powerful reasons for staying in Ireland, and the only way to get them to go therefore was by physical means. Hume, on the other hand, believed that the British were either agnostic about or indifferent to Irish unity. In fact, as he pointed out to Adams, they had already indicated as much in Article 1 of the Anglo-Irish Agreement of November 1985 where it was clearly stated that if a majority in Northern Ireland wanted a united Ireland, the government of the UK would not stand in the way. Now, four years later, with Soviet power in retreat across Europe and the Warsaw Pact in free fall, it seemed to Hume that the republican argument (and the strategy which flowed from it) was now more than ever quite fatally flawed.[18]

In a quite deliberate move designed to support Hume in his discussions with Adams, the secretary of state for Northern Ireland, Peter Brooke, made a significant intervention. In a remarkable speech in London in November 1990 he outlined British policy towards Ireland, in the course of which he not only displayed a genuine sensitivity to nationalist history, but insisted that the government itself had no 'selfish strategic or economic interest in Northern Ireland'.[19] The response of Sinn Féin to this very real challenge was to cast doubts on both Brooke's motives and his analysis. Nonetheless, its display of bombast could not hide its very real uncertainty about what to do next. Indeed, in private, some of its leaders at least were beginning to accept the possibility that Britain's declared neutrality 'might be real and that the IRA might, therefore, be open to persuasion on the merits of armed struggle'.[20]

Of itself, the collapse of the Soviet threat would not have induced an IRA ceasefire. That said, it would be wrong to underestimate the impact which the change in the wider East–West relationship had upon the republican movement; and in particular upon the leadership of the movement and its ability to persuade the sceptics that because of new global realities, there was not much point fighting an enemy which might want to go anyway now that it had no reason for staying. Martin McGuinness in particular played a crucial role in convincing the hardliners about the need for a deal; and one of the ways he was able to do this was by stressing that he too was now certain that 'in the new European and post-Cold War situation, Britain no longer had any strategic interests in Ireland'.[21] Furthermore, once it became apparent to the two governments in London and Dublin that the question of British interests was critical, they did everything in their power to address the issue in an attempt to convince republicans that violence was no longer necessary. It was no coincidence of course that the crucial Downing Street Declaration of December 1993 reiterated the now familiar post-Cold War line that 'the British government' had 'no selfish strategic and economic interests in Northern Ireland'.[22] It would be plainly absurd to suggest that the inclusion of this phrase led directly to the first IRA ceasefire. However, without it, a cessation of violence would have been unthinkable.

No longer 'special'?

Taken together the collapse of the Warsaw Pact and the disintegration of the wider revolutionary project, created a set of international conditions which made an IRA ceasefire feasible. There was always a possibility however that in spite of this critical convergence of circumstances, one of the key actors would fail to act decisively. The Conservative government in particular had good reason to be cautious. After all, on two occasions the IRA had tried to kill its key leaders and had murdered two of Mrs Thatcher's closest friends. Many in the government also doubted whether Adams and McGuinness could deliver a ceasefire; and even if they could, whether such a ceasefire would last. Moreover, they feared that if they were now to include

Sinn Féin in the political process, it would create enormous political problems in terms of their relations with the main Unionist parties at Westminster. Finally, as formal guardians of the Union and keepers of the faith on law and order, the Conservative Party could hardly be expected to be enthused about negotiating with those whose method was murder and primary aim the destruction of the link between one part of the UK and the rest.

The likelihood therefore of a Conservative government seizing the opportunity and pushing ahead with some sort of agreement was never likely to be high. This is why the US role in the early stages of the peace process especially, was to be crucial.[23] The details of what happened are now fairly well known. As an aspiring presidential candidate, Bill Clinton had forged a close alliance with the Irish-American lobby, a fact which did not go unnoticed by Sinn Féin. Naturally enough this lobby expected him to play a more active role over Northern Ireland than his predecessor. He did not disappoint them. First, in the autumn of 1993 he backed an important, and fairly high-level fact-finding delegation to Ireland. Significantly, while it was in Ireland, the IRA announced a temporary ceasefire. In December 1993, the US then played what many regard as a crucial backstage role supporting Dublin against London in the difficult negotiations that in the end led to the signing of the Downing Street Declaration. Finally, and critically, in January 1994, President Clinton reversed an earlier decision, and against the advice of the State Department, the CIA and the FBI, personally sanctioned a visa for Gerry Adams to visit the US. Though a crushing defeat for the British government, this decision and the extraordinary visit which followed in February was of enormous importance in the peace process. Certainly, without it, the IRA would not have declared a ceasefire six months later.[24]

It might well be argued that Clinton's decisive intervention on Northern Ireland had very little to do with the end of the Cold War as such, and was simply another example of an American President playing the Irish card for reasons of domestic politics. Clinton's activism might also be read (and indeed has been) as reflecting the growing influence in the US of a new type of Irish-American: powerful instead of poor, organised in the boardrooms and not just in the Democratic precincts of Chicago and New York, and desperately keen to help Ireland in a constructive way rather than sending money to Ireland to help the 'boys'. It could also be seen as the measure of the power of the Kennedy family – including that of the new ambassador to Ireland, Jean Kennedy Smith. Some have even argued that Clinton's intervention was a pure act of revenge against his political enemies in the British conservative establishment who had done everything in their power to get one George Bush and not William J. Clinton elected to the White House back in 1992.

Though there is clearly some truth in all these various explanations of Clinton's Irish policy, they do not add up to the whole story. They can hardly explain, for instance, why Clinton was prepared to ignore the advice of key foreign policy officials over the decision to admit Adams into the US. Nor do they really help us understand why he tilted as far as he did towards Dublin. And most importantly of all, they cannot account for a series of decisions which almost seemed designed to alienate the one country which many still regarded – even in the post-Cold War era – as America's special ally. And alienated the British undoubtedly felt. Hence, when John Major was informed of the White House decision to allow Adams into the US he is reliably reported to have been 'furious', and for a short time thereafter refused to talk to Clinton. This in turn was followed by a campaign of vilification against Clinton in the British press that rumbled on for months. In fact, well over two years later, Clinton's policy on Ireland was cited on the front page of *The Times*, no less, as an important indication of his general foreign policy ineptitude.[25] Even in Ireland itself many were genuinely astonished by how far Clinton had been prepared to go. As one highly astute and well-placed analyst later put it, there is little doubt that the 'US input' on the North was 'tough for [the] British to swallow'.[26]

Of course Clinton's intervention, though critical in bringing about the first IRA ceasefire, could not in the end prevent it breaking down: and it was to take a good deal of effort by a new and energetic Labour government in Britain to persuade Irish republicans to restore the peace in July 1997. But with or without 'New' Labour and Clinton's close personal ties to Tony Blair, the US was still going to pursue its own agenda in Northern Ireland. No longer would it defer to London or treat the question of Northern Ireland (as it had done until 1989) as an internal British affair. Moreover, even with a new UK administration in control of Northern Ireland, the peace process continued to require the support of the US. Indeed, one of the key players in brokering the deals in April 1998 and then again in late 1999 was none other than the former Senate majority leader, George Mitchell.[27] But it was not just Senator Mitchell who made Good Friday possible.[28] It was Clinton too. In fact, it was only a 'last-minute appeal by Clinton' to the Irish prime minister, Bertie Ahern, to Unionist leader, David Trimble, and finally to Gerry Adams, that broke the deadlock on 10 April 1998 and made the Good Friday Agreement possible. It was this same support through the figure of Mitchell that made the executive a reality eighteen months later. Little wonder that Blair later praised his political ally and friend across the Atlantic for his 'unswerving support and commitment to the peace' in Northern Ireland.[29]

New Europe: new Ireland

Finally, any analysis of the republican decision to halt its campaign of violence, has to take account of the changing position of Ireland in Europe and changes in the very structure of Europe itself.[30] In fact, it might well be argued that it was these changes – as much as anything else – that made the peace process possible. To understand why, we have to return beyond 1989 to 1972 and the Irish republic's original decision to become a member of the EC.

Initially motivated by a recognition of the failure of economic nationalism to bring genuine prosperity to Ireland, Ireland's decision to 'join' Europe transformed the country in a myriad of ways. In straightforward material terms of course it made Ireland altogether more prosperous and far less dependent on the British market. But more subtly, it brought about an important alteration in what has been termed the Irish national project.[31] Hitherto, Irish politics and culture had been dominated by the idea of Irish unity and opposition to British rule in the North. Now, as a result of deeper integration into Europe, this project seemed to make a good deal less sense. Indeed, as Ireland became more part of Europe, the old nationalist dream of making the country whole once again looked increasingly irrelevant. Certainly, in the minds of most Irish people, it seemed far less critical than the Common Agricultural Policy, getting large amounts of aid from Brussels, or proving to its European neighbours that it had at last become a 'normal' country.[32] Moreover, as the dreary military campaign in the North continued unabated, many in the South began to think about the costs of running the other part of Ireland: and wondered too whether or not their new-found prosperity in Europe would be threatened by unification. And having concluded that it might be, began to revise their views about Ireland's traditional claims to the 'six (heavily subsidised) counties' of Antrim, Down, Tyrone, Fermanagh, Armagh and Derry.[33]

Joining Europe thus transformed Ireland, and in the process created a wider and wider gap between traditional nationalist or republican aspirations and new Irish realities. Hence, whereas old-style nationalists may have dreamed of fighting for Ireland (as they were still doing in the North), more and more citizens in the Irish republic itself saw their future in acquiring an education and either working in Europe or possibly at home. Equally, whereas it had once been normal to call for the protection of Irish industries, in the new Ireland the state itself now made every effort to encourage foreign investment. Naturally, this was anathema to classical republicans who argued that this would both undermine a particular way of life and mean the loss of economic independence. The new political class in Dublin and the overwhelming mass of the Irish people brushed aside such objections. The more cynical amongst the Irish intelligentsia even suggested that there was only one thing worse than being 'exploited' by large multinational corporations which introduced new skills and new jobs into Ireland, and that was not being exploited at all! This may have been a poor joke, but in the Irish context was not an insignificant one and reflected an important shift in the wider debate about the nature of 'imperialism' and its impact upon Ireland.[34]

If Ireland's insertion into the wider European space undercut old republican truths, it also changed the nature of the Anglo-Irish relationship. Until joining Europe and becoming a partner of Britain's, Ireland had had few real incentives in cooperating with the UK in the management of the North. However, the experience of partnership in Europe literally forced Dublin and London together. This did not change their different perspectives on Ulster. Nevertheless, by uniting the countries in the same organisation it did help break down the distrust which had previously poisoned relations between the two. It also led them to the fairly obvious conclusion that their division had not only contributed to the conflict in Northern Ireland, but that the disturbances in the North posed a serious threat to Ireland as a whole. Thus the two – it was now clear – had to work in tandem to ensure that instability in Northern Ireland did not spill over and render Ireland ungovernable. This of course was the true meaning of the Anglo-Irish Agreement of 1985 and the Downing Street Declaration of 1993. Whilst both were designed to deal in the short term with the political and military threat posed by Sinn Féin and the IRA, neither could have happened without the longer term revolution that had transformed Anglo-Irish relations after Ireland and the UK joined the EC back in 1972.[35]

Finally, if dynamic change in Europe and in Ireland's relationship to Britain did much to weaken the appeal of traditional republicanism, developments after 1989 seemed to undermine the republican case altogether. They did so firstly by showing that deep, and apparently permanent divisions could be overcome by peaceful means. Moreover, as many were quick to point out at the time, if it was possible to heal the scars that had once disfigured Europe, was it not feasible to do the same in Northern Ireland itself? Indeed, according to those engaged in trying to persuade the IRA to give up the armed road (notably the influential John Hume), unless and until the chasm between the two communities in the North had been overcome, there was little point fighting for Irish unity. It was also left to Hume to draw another lesson from the events in Europe. In the new post-Cold War Europe, borders, he argued, were becoming increasingly irrelevant. Hence, what exactly was the purpose of a military campaign aimed at eliminating something that was, in effect, just an imaginary line across the Irish countryside? Hume was quite blunt in his assessment. In an increasingly integrated Europe he argued – where the very notion of sovereignty itself was being brought into question – the IRA campaign and the pre-modern assumptions which underpinned it, were basically irrelevant.[36] Furthermore, what exactly were republicans fighting for anyway? Before 1989 at least the movement could claim (and key figures like Adams and Morrison regularly did) that its objective was to build an Irish form of socialism on the island of Ireland. But with the left now in headlong retreat across Europe, this project seemed like a utopian pipe-dream; a product of old thinking rendered irrelevant by the disintegration of the old European system.

Again, the extent to which these various changes played a part in transforming republican theory and practice is difficult to calculate with any mathematical precision. However, there is strong evidence to suggest that key figures in the leadership were not insensitive to the fact that irreversible alterations in the European landscape posed a series of difficult questions which traditional republicanism could not easily answer. A key figure in Sinn Féin indeed conceded that one of the important factors that made the peace process possible, was (to use his own words), 'the Single European Act and the dominance of the EU on the island of Ireland'.[37] Certainly, the highly revisionist Sinn Féin programme of 1992 bore witness to the influence which changes in Europe were having upon republican thinking. One can also detect the same processes at work in the less radical language that key figures in the movement began to employ. Though a few clearly remained committed to their vision of a socialist Ireland standing outside the capitalist club of Europe, most began to sound decidedly less enthusiastic about constructing what amounted to a siege economy in opposition to the EU. Many also started to wonder about the wisdom of struggling for something in Ireland that had apparently failed elsewhere. As one of their number pointed out, though republicanism had traditionally been a movement of economic resistance, by the mid–1990s its attitude towards the market and private enterprise had undergone a good deal of change. As he put it rather pithily (at a time when Adams himself was trying to convince American multinationals to invest in Catholic West Belfast) republicans no longer had a serious 'problem with capitalism'.[38] Before the ideological earthquake of 1989 such thoughts would have been considered pure heresy in an organisation devoted to liberating the 'men of no property'. With the passing of the old Europe and the collapse of planning across the continent, this was no longer the case. Neither Ireland it seemed, nor those who had fought to unite it for over twenty-five years by violent means, could escape the irresistible logic of globalisation.

Conclusion

I have been concerned in this chapter to show how and why a particularly brutal and lengthy military campaign, conducted by one of the more effective guerilla organisations of the twentieth century – against one of the most effective democratic states – finally came to an end. Whether the 'war' would have come to an end of its own accord – the result of war weariness and military stalemate between the British state and Irish republicanism – is of course an open question.[39] Nor should we forget the role of contingency in translating the possibility of peace into a reality. The election of a Labour government in 1997, the carnage caused by the Omagh bombing, and the respective roles performed by Mo Mowlam and Peter Mandelson at crucial moments in the discussions, all played their part in making some form of settlement more likely. No doubt, what key actors did and said, and said to each other, also mattered a great deal. However, this does not mean we should not look for deeper causes nor, in the case of Northern Ireland, treat the conflict as if it stood apart; and as I have tried to show here, the winding down of the 'Troubles' was strongly influenced by shifts and changes in the larger international system. Born of the turbulent 1960s, sustained indirectly by the Cold War in the 1970s and 1980s, it finally came to a conclusion in the settling 1990s – along with a number of other conflicts which had drawn more direct inspiration from the larger struggle between East and West.

Yet even though the 'war' in the North has come to an end like most other wars,[40] this does not in itself mean that the underlying causes of the conflict have completely disappeared.[41] It is one thing to make peace; it is quite another to construct a stable society where all can unite around the same institutions. It has not happened in the Middle East, it has not happened in Bosnia and there is still a chance it will not happen in the North of Ireland. Any number of issues from decommissioning, police reform and the establishment of serious North–South bodies can easily upset any negotiated political settlement. Then there is the even deeper issue of identity which neither the Good Friday Agreement nor the formation of a Northern Ireland executive are ever likely to resolve.[42] Many questions remain unresolved and possibly insoluble. That said, Northern Ireland has managed to travel an enormous distance from there to here, and where we now find ourselves as we enter the new millennium would have been inconceivable a few years ago when the Cold War – along with many other factors – continued to breathe life into what was once regarded as being one of Europe's most intractable conflicts.

Notes

1 Thus writes one commentator of the peace process: 'As so often happens, in real life, the power of the people in Ireland is triumphing over defective political theories and flawed political structures which they spawned.' See David Bleakley, *Peace In Ireland: Two States, One People* (London, Mowbray, 1995), p. viii.

2 This idea that the armed struggle was brought to an end by the successful containment of the IRA is articulated in Peter Taylor's study (later made into a four-part TV series), *Behind the Mask: the IRA and Sinn Féin* (New York, TV Books, 1998).

3 See Arwell Ellis Owen, *The Anglo-Irish Agreement: the First Three Years* (Cardiff, University of Wales Press, 1994).

4 See also Garrett FitzGerald and Paul Gillespie, 'Ireland's British Question', *Prospect* (Vol. 12, October 1996), pp. 25–6.

5 A leading figure in Irish republicanism later conceded that 'the end of the Cold War and its effects on the strategic and the regional interests of the West made it possible for a number of peace processes' [including the one in Ireland] to emerge'. See interview conducted with Mitchel McLaughlin, 23 July 1996.

6 The two most detailed narratives are by Brendan O'Brien, *The Long War. The IRA & Sinn Féin: from Armed Struggle to Peace Talks* (Dublin, O'Brien Press, 1993), and Eamonn Mallie and David McKittrick, *The Fight for Peace: the Secret Story Behind the Irish Peace Process* (London, Heinemann, 1996).

7 There is now an extensive academic literature on the history of the modern IRA. This includes a range of work from the critical anti-republican left – see for example Henry Patterson, *The Politics of Illusion: Republicanism and Socialism in Modern Ireland* (London, Hutchinson Radius, 1989) – through to the more strategically oriented study by M. L. R. Smith, *Fighting for Ireland? The Military Strategy of the Irish Republican Movement* (London, Routledge, 1995). There are also a number of more 'journalistic' studies on the organisation. See, for example, Patrick Bishop and Eamonn Mallie, *The Provisional IRA* (London, Heinemann, 1987), Tim Pat Coogan, *The IRA* (London, Fontana, 1987) and Martin Dillon, *25 Years Of Terror: The IRA's War Against the British* (1994; London, Bantam edition reprinted, 1997).

8 Thus, according to a leading Irish republican in the early 1970s: 'if we could continue to inflict high British casualties and step up the sabotage campaign, it would be difficult for them to bear the strain and drain on their economy and no government could be prepared to continue indefinitely in such a situation'. Sean MacStiofain, *Memoirs of a Revolutionary* (Edinburgh, Gordon Cremonesi, 1975), p. 261.

9 Claire Sterling, *The Terror Network: the Secret War of International Terrorism* (New York, Holt, Rinehart and Winston, 1981).

10 See Chris Skillen, "'Pravda's Provos": Russian and Soviet manipulation of News from Ireland', *Irish Political Studies* (Vol. 8, 1993), pp. 73–88.

11 See Adrian Guelke, 'The Peace Process in South Africa, Israel and Northern Ireland: A Farewell to Arms?', *Irish Studies in International Affairs* (Vol. 5, 1994), pp. 93–106.

12 Interview conducted with Mitchel McLaughlin, 23 July 1996.

13 *Ibid.*

14 See Gerry Adams, *Selected Writings* (Dingle, Brandon, 1997), pp. 274–5.

15 Both Arafat and Mandela visited Dublin in the early 1990s and had extensive discussions with the leadership of Sinn Féin. A delegation from Sinn Féin also visited South Africa in 1995. See *An Phobacht/Republican News* (No. 363, July–August 1995). For a fine discussion of the impact of the peace process in South Africa on Sinn Féin see Adrian Guelke, 'Comparatively Peaceful: The Role of Analogy in Northern Ireland's Peace Process', *Cambridge Review of International Affairs* (Vol. XI, No. 1, Summer/Fall 1997), pp. 28–45

16 On the strategic dimension in Anglo-Irish relations see G. R. Sloan, *The Geopolitics of Anglo-Irish Relations in the Twentieth Century* (London, Leicester University Press, 1997).

17 The information in this paragraph is drawn from the discussion in Mallie and McKittrick, *The Fight for Peace*, p. 83.

18 See John Hume, 'A New Ireland in a New Europe' in Dermot Keogh and Michael H. Haltzel (eds), *Northern Ireland and the Politics of Reconciliation* (Washington, Cambridge University Press, 1993), pp. 228–9.

19 Speech by Peter Brooke, secretary of state for Northern Ireland (London, 9 November 1990).

20 O'Brien, *The Long War*, p. 212.

21 *Ibid.*, p. 305.

22 Joint Declaration, Downing Street (15 December 1993).

23 For important background see the excellent study by *Irish Times* journalist, Conor O'Clery, *The Greening of the White House* (Dublin, Gill and Macmillan, 1997).

24 For an assessment see Paul Arthur, 'American Intervention in the Anglo-Irish Peace Process: Incrementalism or Interference', *Cambridge Review of International Studies* (Vol. XI, No. 1, Fall 1997), pp. 46–62.

25 'US Links with Britain "Worst Since 1773"', *The Times* (16 August 1996).

26 See Garret FitzGerald, *The Irish Times* (9 December 1995).

27 For details on the role of George Mitchell between 1993 and 1996 see the numerous entries in Paul Bew and Gordon Gillespie (eds), *The Northern Ireland Peace Process, 1993–1996* (London, Serif, 1996).

28 After the Agreement, David Trimble, the leader of the Ulster Unionists, praised George Mitchell 'whose patience and fairness won universal praise'. See David Trimble, 'Ulster Should Say 'Yes', *Daily Telegraph*, 13 April 1998. The American senator also became something of a star figure amongst the British media. See the profile on him by Nicola Jennings, 'George Mitchell: Man in the Middle', *Guardian*, 6 April 1998.

29 See *The Financial Times*, 11 April/12 April 1998, p. 1.

30 This section on Europe draws heavily upon the excellent work by Professor Elizabeth Meehan. See in particular her 'British–Irish Relations in the Context of the European Union', *Review of International Studies*, Vol. 26, No. 2 (2000).

31 See Richard Kearney, *Postnationalist Ireland – Politics, Culture, Philosophy* (London, Routledge, 1997).

32 By the end of 1995, total net transfers to Ireland from Europe amounted IR£18.45 billion. The bulk of these came from the Common Agricultural Policy and the Structural Funds. See *Challenges and Opportunities Abroad: White Paper on Foreign Policy* (Dublin, Department of Foreign Affairs, 1996), p. 59.

33 On the rise of historical revisionism in Ireland see John Whyte, *Interpreting Northern Ireland* (Oxford, Clarendon Press, 1996), pp. 119–33.

34 For a guide to Ireland in Europe see Patrick Keatinge (ed.), *European Security: Ireland's Choices* (Dublin, Institute of European Affairs, 1996) and Paul Gillespie (ed.), *Britain's European Question – the Issues for Ireland* (Dublin, Institute of European Affairs, 1996).

35 See the essays on Ireland's place in the new Europe, collected in *Irish Studies in International Affairs* (Vol. 8, 1997).

36 See *Derry Journal* (18 February 1994), p. 10.

37 Interview with Mitchel McLaughlin, 23 July 1996.

38 Quoted in Suzanne Breen, 'Sword in the Stone', *Fortnight* (No. 340, June 1995) p. 7.

39 See Anthony McIntyre, 'Modern Irish Republicanism: The Product of British State Strategies', *Irish Political Studies* (No. 10, 1995), pp. 97–121.

40 Fred Ikle, *Every War Must End* (New York, Columbia University Press, 1977).

41 Karin Aggestam and Christer Jonsson, '(Un)Ending Conflict: Challenges in Post-War Bargaining', *Millennium*, p. 792.

42 On the relationship between identity and interest in Northern Ireland see Bill McSweeny, 'Identity, Interest and the Good Friday Agreement', *Irish Studies in International Affairs*, Volume 9.

19

The effect of violence on the Irish peace process

JOHN DARBY

Ceasefires never bring an end to violence. The word itself acknowledges that there has been a truce rather than a treaty. By implication neither side has abandoned the option of returning to the use of force. At best a ceasefire may trigger a peace process which, if completed successfully, will allow violence to diminish and return to forms which can be handled by normal policing and legal procedures. The greatest obstacle to this conclusion is violence itself, and the effect it may have on the process. This chapter examines the relationship between violence and the peace process in Northern Ireland. It presents a chronicle of the violence, followed by an analysis. The argument advanced is that, even when political violence has been ended by a ceasefire, it has reappeared in other forms to threaten the evolving peace process. Eight main forms of violence are identified. Each has a different effect and requires different policy approaches.

A habit of violence

The conflict in the North of Ireland has been exceptionally persistent. No generation since the Plantation of Ulster has escaped its heritage of violence. In Belfast alone there were nine periods of serious rioting between 1835 and 1969, and many other years where some disturbances have been recorded.[1] The recent violence was the longest and most sustained of all. It was uninterrupted, except for variations in form and intensity, from 1969 to 1994. During the early 1970s many observers believed that the upsurge of violence in Northern Ireland could lead to only two outcomes: either the belligerents would be shocked into an internal accommodation, or they would be propelled into genocidal massacre. Neither occurred. The initial rioting in 1969 between Catholics and Protestants, during which eight people were killed, was soon replaced by more structured violence after the arrival of the British Army and its confrontations with the Catholic community. The emergence of the Provisional IRA, strengthened by the introduction of internment in 1971, converted the violence to a more organised confrontation between the IRA and the British Army. During the 1990s the pattern shifted again, with loyalist paramilitaries causing more deaths than any other group in the years immediately preceding the ceasefires. All three main actors were both perpetrators and victims of violence.

The violence of the Troubles reached a peak in 1972, when 468 people died. In subsequent years, a succession of particularly dramatic events periodically raised the casualty rate: the killing of fourteen Catholics by paratroopers on Bloody Sunday, 30 January 1972;[2] the loyalist UWC strike in May 1974; the activities of the 'Shankill butchers' in the mid–1970s, the IRA hunger strikes in 1981. By the 1990s the violence had gradually declined to an annual average of below 100 deaths. Between 1969 and the declaration of the ceasefires by republican and loyalist paramilitary organisations in 1994, the Troubles had claimed 3,173 deaths in Northern Ireland, and a total of 235 in Britain, the Irish republic and the rest of Europe. Thousands of people were intimidated from their homes, and thousands more injured.[3]

Inevitably the prevalence of violence affected legal and policing procedures. There was practically a standing army on the streets after 1969. Public opinion on the state's handling of these problems was divided, and fluctuated during the years of violence. There was concern that the barrage of special powers infringed individual rights, that emergency powers were not exercised impartially, and that the surveillance apparatus installed by the British Army collected information not directly related to security concerns.[4] Unionists often complained that security policies never amounted to more than *ad hoc* responses to IRA violence. With the exception of a short period in the late 1970s, the role of security policy had largely been one of containment, maintaining what the British home secretary Reginald Maudling called 'an acceptable level of violence'. The result was stalemate. Each set of combatants, the security forces and the paramilitaries, was able to frustrate the other, but unable to secure victory.

Violence and the peace process: a chronicle

Most people in Northern Ireland only became aware that a peace process had started when the IRA announced a ceasefire on 31 August 1994. The main loyalist paramilitary organisations followed suit in October. Since then every stage in this process was obstructed by violence, in its various forms. The transition from war to peace had started during the late 1980s, when elements within Sinn Féin shifted to the view that resilience was not enough to deliver a united Ireland. IRA violence was not only driving greater divisions between Catholics and Protestants in Northern Ireland, but also alienating the population of the Irish republic. The Dublin *Sunday Tribune* voiced a growing condemnation of IRA intransigence by the Dublin media shortly before the ceasefire. 'The IRA campaign, although not the only obstacle to this [peace] process, is now beyond all reasonable doubt the most substantial one. That is why the killing must stop.'[5] The British government's entry into secret negotiation with Sinn Féin reflected a growing view that the IRA could not be defeated within the political constraints of a liberal democracy. Secret talks enabled them to test the seriousness of the Sinn Féin leadership. The nervous courtship carried an equilibrium of risk for both sides – for republicanism the historical tendency to split at the first suggestion of compromise and for John Major's precarious Conservative government the risk of alienating Unionist support in parliament.

The ceasefires produced immediate and tangible benefits. Fifty-one people had been killed during the six months before the 1994 IRA ceasefire. Although the ceasefires did not end paramilitary violence in Northern Ireland, only two people were killed as a direct result of political violence in the six months following July 1994. The euphoria did not last long. By the end of 1995 the stalemate over decommissioning – the demand that the IRA hand over its weapons – forced the British government to agree to the establishment of the International Body on Arms Decommissioning chaired by Senator George Mitchell. The resulting Mitchell Report, published in January 1996, laid down conditions for admission to all-party negotiations, requiring participants to replace violence with political negotiation, to disarm and to accept any resulting agreement.[6] The British government response on the same day downplayed these major proposals in favour of a marginal suggestion that elections should be held for a Northern Ireland Forum. Two weeks later, on 9 February 1996, the IRA ended its ceasefire by planting a bomb in Canary Wharf in London.

The IRA's justification was that the British government had deliberately constructed a succession of obstacles to Sinn Féin's entering political talks. For unionists the bomb simply confirmed their warning that the IRA would resort to force to resist any developments they opposed. A senior London police source alleged that what 'some people call a ceasefire' had never been more than 'a period of terrorist preparation'; others pointed to evidence that the IRA had been preparing for a resumption even during the ceasefire period.[7] Whatever the balance of blame, the ending of the ceasefire did not lead to an immediate resumption of the IRA campaign as it had operated before the August 1994 ceasefire. The bombings were largely confined to Britain, the worst explosions in London in February and Manchester in June 1996. The loyalist paramilitary organisations decided to preserve their ceasefires, and paramilitaries from both sides kept out of the confrontations which accompanied the Orange celebrations in July 1996.

The traditional Orange parade from Drumcree church down the mainly nationalist Garvaghy Road in July, which had led to serious confrontations a year earlier, was banned by the RUC. The Orange Order responded with a serious of pre-planned demonstrations, blocking roads, bridges and airports and converging in increasing numbers at Drumcree in the days immediately preceding the parade. Catholic families were intimidated from their homes. On 10 July the RUC reversed its decision and escorted the parade down Garvaghy Road, physically removing local protesters from the road. That evening nationalist parts of Belfast were curfewed to prevent their anticipated protests. The sectarian confrontations of the early 1970s had returned.

The IRA declared a second ceasefire in July 1997. The orchestra unpacked its instruments and the pre-negotiation dance started for the second time. This time it was greeted by wariness rather than euphoria. Not only had the first ceasefire collapsed, but the high level of communal and sectarian violence within the loyalist and republican communities continued and, in some respects, increased. 'Concerned Residents' Groups', fomented by Sinn Féin according to some unionists, were formed in nationalist communities to resist Orange marches. A Parades Commission was formed in 1997 to determine which marches should be permitted to proceed and which banned. The renewed talks were directly balked by violence. Loyalist prisoners in the Maze Prison voted to oppose any agreement, following the British government's refusal to release political prisoners. The crisis was relieved following a visit by Mo Mowlam, the secretary of state for Northern Ireland, to hold direct talks with the loyalists in the Maze Prison, declaring her willingness to 'take risks for peace';[8] within hours the loyalists agreed to continue their support for the process.

The Mitchell principles, which had been signed by all participants in the talks, were soon tested when the all-party negotiations started in January 1998. There was increasing evidence that both loyalist and republican paramilitaries were still engaging in violence. In January 1998, after the Ulster Freedom Fighters confessed to three murders, the UDP was expelled from the talks. The expulsion of Sinn Féin followed in February, when the secretary of state attributed at least two murders to the IRA.[9] Both expulsions were for a limited period – four weeks for the UDP and two weeks for Sinn Féin. This was contemptuously dismissed by Peter Robinson of the DUP as 'a spell in the sin bin',[10] but the expulsions were the minimum action required to justify claims that the Mitchell Principles would be enforced. The Good Friday Agreement was eventually reached in April 1998. The Agreement, and the referenda and elections which endorsed it, had a constitutional as well as a moral impact on Irish republicanism. Its ratification by substantial majorities on both sides of the Irish border provided an up-to-date all-Ireland mandate. This legitimisation, bolstered by the fact the Sinn Féin was participating in the negotiations and campaigning for its acceptance, effectively undercut the traditional justification for violence for many mainstream republicans.

After two summers of violence associated with Orange parades and the protests against them, the summer of 1998 brought the Good Friday Agreement to the edge of collapse. The decision by the Parades Commission to ban the march down the Garvaghy Road led to protests in many parts of the province. Supporters of the Orange Order gathered at Drumcree, apparently determined to force through the march. Public roads were blocked. Sectarian killings increased. The number of families intimidated from their homes rose from 112 in 1997 to 278 in 1998.[11] Arson attacks reached alarming levels. The Good Friday Agreement, signed four months earlier, was seriously threatened, until circumstances were changed dramatically by two violent events during the summer. On 12 July three Catholic children from Ballymoney, Richard, Mark and Jason Quinn, aged 10, 9 and 7, were burned to death in one of the arson attacks which accompanied the Drumcree disturbances. The reaction was unprecedented. Support among Orangemen for the increasingly violent protest at Drumcree was severely eroded. Many withdrew and some openly opposed it. The atrocity allowed those unionists who opposed the Orange activities to harness the general feelings of outrage. The Drumcree protest continued, but Ballymoney had knocked the heart out of it.

A month later, on 15 August, a splinter republican group, the 'Real' IRA, planted a bomb in the country town of Omagh, killing twenty-nine afternoon shoppers. This was the last in a series of spoiler bombs planted by the 'Real' IRA in market towns in order to undermine the peace process. The bomb struck indiscriminately against both communities. It appeared to spurn the popular feeling expressed in the recent referenda in both parts of Ireland. Consequently, it allowed Gerry Adams to underline his party's rejection of violence by condemning a republican bomb 'without any equivocation whatsoever'. Martin McGuinness of Sinn Féin even went further: 'We see our job to be one of stopping the activities of these people.'[12] The Omagh bomb also provided the opportunity for both governments to harmonise and toughen their anti-terrorist powers with virtually no opposition. This in turn allowed the Unionist leader David Trimble to compliment the Irish republic's swift decision to introduce more legislation, and even to contrast this favourably with UK provision. The British government reacted immediately to deny the charge in a spiral of over-trumping security condemnations. In other words, Omagh licensed a number of actors who had intellectually accepted the need to make concessions actually to do so.

The Omagh bomb caused consternation among the splinter republican groups. Within four days of the bomb those responsible for planting it, the 'Real' IRA, had declared a ceasefire. Three days later the Irish National Liberation Army, one of the most violent of the republican groups, followed suit with 'a complete ceasefire'. The political wings of dissident groups also came under pressure. Much anger was directed at the 32-County Sovereignty Committee, which was associated with the 'Real' IRA. One of the Committee's leading figures, a dissident IRA quarter-master, felt compelled to claim that he 'had neither hand, act nor part in this thing [Omagh]'.[13] The Provisional IRA seized the opportunity to discipline other republican spoilers. They visited the houses of sixty dissidents during one September night with threats from the IRA Army Council that 'action would be taken' against the 'Real' IRA if it did not disband within a fortnight.[14] Violence, or rather spoiler violence, had become temporarily unfashionable.

By 1999, however, the failure to resolve the decommissioning issue, and the arrest of republican gunrunners in the US in August, demonstrated again the fragility of the peace process. It was also a reminder that the control of violence was the central condition for its success.

Violence and the peace process: an analysis

In 1988 Bertie Ahern, the Irish taoiseach (prime minister), suggested that 'it is an observable phenomenon in Northern Ireland, and elsewhere, that tension and violence tend to rise when compromise is in the air'.[15] The greatest political violence in South Africa, for example, occurred during the transition to agreement between 1990 and 1994, when almost three times as many people were killed as in the previous four years. The use of terror also rose dramatically during the Middle East peace process, and more than two-thirds of victims were killed while the Rabin–Peres negotiations were under way.[16] In Northern Ireland too the Downing Street Declaration, which cleared the ground for the peace process, in December 1993, led to an increase in violence; fifty people were killed during the six months after the Declaration, up from thirty-two during the equivalent period in the previous year.

Nevertheless, in the months following the 1994 ceasefires political violence declined significantly. It was replaced by other forms of violence, each in its own way a threat to the peace process. The eight forms identified here (dealt with under eight subheadings) fall into three main categories:

1   The violent activities of the paramilitaries fragmented into their component elements; these included the possible return of political violence, 'strategic violence', internal feuding and violence from splinter groups. (See the heading 'The paramilitary fall-out' below.)
2   Violence spread into the community at large, through a return to sectarian confrontations and a rise in conventional crime. (See under 'Violence in the community' below.)
3   New substantive issues emerged – the release of prisoners, decommissioning of paramilitary weapons, the reform of policing, as well as the dismantling of the security apparatus. (See under 'New substantive issues' below.)

Let us deal with each in turn.

The paramilitary fall-out

Disaffection within paramilitary organisations is perhaps the most obvious threat to peace progresses. These are rarely the monoliths presented by their opponents. They are complex organisms performing a variety of functions and providing umbrellas for different interests. The diversity allows paramilitary leaders to assume the high moral ground by emphasising their political and civil roles, while turning a blind eye to punishment beatings and murders. It also helps to explain strategic shifts between war and negotiation, as different elements within the organisations win temporary dominance. During ceasefire periods the varied interests sheltering under the paramilitary parasol become diffused and fragmented. At least four posed separate threats to the peace process:

A return of political violence

Ceasefires may bring an official end to political violence, but they are never unanimous. The more disaffected members of the militants may desert to splinter groups or perform individual acts of violence. The less disaffected may go along with the majority view, but their agreement is conditional. Their continuing allegiance depends on measurable rewards from negotiation, most notably prisoner releases and the dismantling of the security apparatus. These rewards are rarely immediate. Consequently the pendulum may swing back towards the militants, as when the London bombs ended the IRA ceasefire in 1996.

The journalist Mary Holland pointed to discontent within a number of IRA units as the most plausible explanation for Canary Wharf: 'On previous occasions since Ireland became independent, every move by the IRA away from violence and into constitutional politics has involved a split between the men of violence and the politicos. Provisional IRA was itself born from such a development.'[17] The insistence that all participants in multi-party talks sign up to the Mitchell Principles was a useful device for regulating political violence. The suspension of Sinn Féin and the UDP for breach of the principles, however temporarily, was necessary to sustain credibility. Their acceptance of the suspension, however truculently, indicated their determination to remain within the peace process.

Tactical violence

The willingness of some negotiators to exploit violence is a common feature during peace negotiations. When the Irish parliamentary leader Charles Stuart Parnell was jailed during the Home Rule campaign in the 1880s he forecast correctly that 'Captain Moonlight will take my place', thus positioning himself as the only alternative to revolutionary violence.[18] The paramilitaries' minimum price for ceasefire was their inclusion in negotiations. The main apprehension for some constitutional parties was that their political surrogates would use the threat of violence for strategic advantage, and that the pace of negotiation would be determined by the gunmen outside the negotiating rooms. To paraphrase Clausewitz, they feared that paramilitary negotiators would approach politics as the continuation of war by other means.

Any acts of violence during the process were taken as confirmation of this fear. During the early stages of the peace process, unionists constantly warned that Sinn Féin would use IRA violence to remind other negotiators of their power. Indeed, there were occasions during the ceasefire period when the Sinn Féin leaders appeared to feed unionist fears, as when Gerry Adams drew the attention of a republican rally to the fact that 'they [the IRA] haven't gone away, you know', an implied threat that the IRA would resume the war if Sinn Féin did not profit during the negotiations. The triumphalist appearance of newly-released republican prisoners at the Sinn Féin *ard-fheis* before the May 1988 referendum was cited as further evidence of conspiracy. Despite these apprehensions, however, the unwillingness of

Sinn Féin or the loyalist parties to resort to tactical violence was one of the more remarkable aspects of the multi-party negotiations leading to the Good Friday Agreement.

Internal paramilitary violence

Punishment beatings continued throughout the peace process as both loyalists and republicans carried on what they regarded as their policing role in a number of communities. People were expelled from the community and severely beaten for 'anti-social behaviour'. Alleged drug dealers were attacked in both communities, and at least seven were killed by the IRA during the period of the first ceasefire.[19] These and other crimes were often disowned by paramilitary sources as unauthorised or the actions of mavericks. Mitchel McLaughlin, one of Sinn Féin's main spokesmen, protested in January 1996 that Sinn Féin was '"powerless" to stop the IRA engaging in drug-related beatings and killings',[20] a claim regarded with scepticism by unionists. The desire for peace encouraged, at least initially, a public tolerance for paramilitary violence. The need to maintain clear water between officially condoned violence and the general lawlessness inherited from thirty years of paramilitary violence was a crucial test of the ceasefires.

Spoilers: zealots versus dealers

The very entry of paramilitary interests into negotiations implies that the purity of their cause has been compromised. It imposes strains on organisations which are essentially military, and it is difficult to find any instances when such a move was not accompanied by a split between two main groups – the zealots and the dealers. The zealots often comprise radical groups who picked up the torch (sometimes literally) they believed had been surrendered by the dealers. Their aim is not to influence the content of a peace agreement. It is to ensure that agreement is not reached or, if reached, is derailed.

The emergence of spoiler groups[21] was not unprecedented in Irish politics. The Irish writer and IRA member Brendan Behan once said that the first item on the agenda for any republican meeting is 'the split'. The Provisional IRA itself was formed in 1969 after a split from the Official IRA. The Irish National Liberation Army had also broken away from the Official IRA in 1972, and thirteen INLA members were killed during its own internal split in 1987. In 1986 the newly formed Republican IRA and Sinn Féin broke away from the Provisionals in opposition to its allegedly softer line. A new epidemic of splits followed Sinn Féin's signing up for the Mitchell Principles in October 1997. More than twenty Provisionals resigned in protest at Sinn Féin's entry to the peace process, and the INLA stepped up its violence.

Two new republican paramilitary groups, the Continuity IRA (CIRA) and the 'Real' IRA, emerged, committed to continuing the armed struggle. These challenges to the Provisionals' authority had some bizarre manifestations. The Continuity IRA accused the Provisionals of destroying one of their bombs south of the border before it could be transported to Northern Ireland. In another incident in Derry a member of the Provisional IRA punched and kicked a CIRA man in an attempt to stop him planting a bomb in a bank. Later the CIRA, without apparent irony, criticised his action as placing innocent people in danger. Spoilers were not restricted to the republican family. The growing involvement of the PUP and UDP in the peace process also brought charges of betrayal and defections by loyalist splinter groups. The Loyalist Volunteer Force, which had been formed in 1996 by dissidents from the more established groups, was further reinforced during the period of negotiations.

Violence in the community

The fragmentation of paramilitary organisations was not the only violent accompaniment to the peace process. Two other forms of violence also threatened it – the revival of direct confrontations on the streets, and a rise in the conventional crime rate.

Return to the streets

The declaration of the ceasefires was marked by a return to more direct violence between Catholics and Protestants, especially during the marching seasons from 1996 to 1998. The switch is not surprising. During the period of organised violence, paramilitaries must be dominant and disciplined to be effective. When a ceasefire is declared the discipline of the military campaign diminishes, but the underlying sectarian hatred remains, taking the form of riots and undisciplined confrontations with ethnic rivals or the police. The paramilitary representatives who entered negotiations were not divorced from the instincts and antagonisms of their communities, and some felt the need to support them. The danger is that such confrontational violence may swing the balance from negotiation back towards a military campaign.

'Ordinary decent crime'

Was there any relationship between this confusing mixture of paramilitary violence and the 'normal' non-security crime rate? When the Troubles started in 1969 Northern Ireland had the lowest per capita prison population in Western Europe. The conventional, as opposed to politically-motivated, crime rate continued to be low during the years of the Troubles. Rates of victimisation for burglary, assaults and thefts were substantially lower than in England and Wales.[22] Initially this pattern continued after the ceasefires, in contrast to the dramatic increase in normal crime during the comparable period in South Africa. In 1997 the prison population in Northern Ireland showed a decrease for the fourth consecutive year and the crime rate was the lowest for nine years. The major exception to the low crime rate was a 22.2 per cent increase in offences against the state, mainly public order offences, reflecting the increase in sectarian violence.[23]

South Africa presents a sombre warning. By the mid–1990s the high level of conventional crime had far outpaced political violence as a destabilising factor. By 1998 the average daily homicide rate was sixty-eight, and still rising. More ominously, the barrier between ordinary crime and South Africa's underlying racial tensions, never sharp, became increasingly blurred. Fifteen hundred white farmers were attacked between 1994 and 1998, resulting in more than 200 murders, and threatening to create a loop back from post-settlement civil violence to the pre-agreement struggle.

New substantive issues

Violence as an issue during negotiations

When talks began, a number of new substantive issues emerged, most of them security related. The three most notable among them were the decommissioning of illegal weapons, policing and early prisoner releases. The stubbornness of Ulster unionists in demanding decommissioning and of Sinn Féin in rejecting it, however irritating, arose from the need of each side to keep its primary constituency on board, and on the symbolic association between decommissioning and surrender. Police reform is an equally emotional issue in negotiations. It is axiomatic that divided societies require a police force which reflects the divisions. Section 195 of the 1996 South African Constitution, for example, insisted that the police and defence forces 'be broadly representative of the South African people' and by 1996 16,000 former guerrillas had been absorbed into the army; it seems likely that a similar principle will apply in Northern Ireland.

The agreed release of prisoners after the 1998 Agreement led to an increased demand that the victims of violence should be accorded a greater priority. The establishment of a Victims' Commission failed to stem concerns than those who had suffered most had been sidelined in the desire for a political settlement. In June 1999 the IRA revealed where their 'disappeared' victims had been disposed, but was embarrassed when police were unable to find the missing bodies. The depth of Northern Ireland's sectarianism was confirmed in July of the same year by the 'long march' on behalf of innocent victims; the protest was confined to Protestant victims of violence, and the march culminated at Drumcree during the height of the annual Orange demonstration.

The security apparatus

Thirty years of violence had absorbed a security apparatus into Northern Irish society. It had penetrated deeply into its social structures: heavy recruitment of military, police and prison personnel, emergency legislation and procedures, information gathering and sometimes abuses of power. Within six months of the 1994 ceasefire security ramps were removed and border roads with the Irish republic, many of which had been closed by the Army, were gradually re-opened. The pace quickened after the Good Friday Agreement. Militants are released instead of imprisoned. The security forces augmented during the violence were reduced in number. Demands were made to reform the police force which regarded itself as the bastion against terrorism. The occasional arrest of members of the security apparatus for terrorist offences underlines the threat left after all internal wars; unless steps are taken to ease their return to civilian life, dissatisfied and well-armed professionals are as serious a threat to stability as their paramilitary counterparts.

Violence as a catalyst for peace

Occasionally, in Northern Ireland and elsewhere, certain atrocities provoke universal condemnation and galvanise popular reaction against the perpetrators. After decades of kidnappings and murders, hundreds of thousands of Basque protesters took to the streets to protest against the murder of a Basque town councillor by ETA. During the South African peace process the murder of twenty-eight ANC supporters in Bisho in 1992 was not followed by the same violent internal reaction which had followed the massacre of forty-eight people at Boipatong three months earlier; instead it persuaded the ANC to advance the negotiations rather than to withdraw from them.[24]

What is the nature of these atrocities that converts them into catalysts for peace? Why did Ballymoney and Omagh have a greater effect in Northern Ireland than so many awful actions in the past? War-weariness is part of the explanation, but this had been evident for years before Omagh. The reason why certain violent events, at certain times, can become catalysts for peace lies not in the nature or severity of the violence, but in its timing. Support for the Good Friday Agreement by both communities enabled public outrage after Omagh to be harnessed, as opposed to simply vented. Outrage without a mechanism to enforce it fades away, as the Peace People had discovered in the 1970s. What can convert outrage to action is condemnation within the context, or at least realistic hope, that agreement is possible, and that further violence could threaten it. Such violence is almost inevitable, as this chapter demonstrates. The opportunities provided by public abhorrence of violence are constantly placed under siege by renewed acts of violence.

So catalytic episodes are transitory. The often-mentioned 'window of opportunity' is barely ajar and soon slams shut. The most important effect of the Ballymoney and Omagh atrocities was not that they ended spoiler violence; it was that they enabled the middle grounds of unionism and nationalism to find their voice at a time when the voice of moderation could make a difference. Important progress in the peace process followed, including agreement on the number of departments that would be established under devolved government and the remit and functions of cross-border bodies. However, even after the creation of a Northern Ireland Executive in late 1999, the central issue dividing the parties remained – and the apparent incapacity of the Ulster unionists and Sinn Féin to resolve their differences over decommissioning only served to draw attention to the narrow ground upon which the peace process had been built.

Notes

1 See Andrew Boyd, *Holy War in Belfast*, Tralee, Anvil, 1969.
2 Thirteen people died on the day; a fourteenth died later.
3 Marie-Therese Fay, Mike Morrissey and Marie Smyth, *Northern Ireland's Troubles: The Human Costs*, London, Pluto Press, 1999, pp.136–41.
4 Paddy Hillyard, 'Law and Order" in John Darby (ed.), *Northern Ireland: The Background to the Conflict*, New York, Appletree, Belfast and Syracuse University Press, 1983, pp. 46–8.
5 24 August 1994.
6 For text of the report, see Appendix 10.
7 *Belfast Telegraph*, 5 January 1996.
8 *Belfast Telegraph*, 13 January 1998.
9 *The Irish Times*, 25 March 1998.
10 *The Irish Times*, 16 February 1998.
11 *Magill* (Dublin), November 1998.
12 *Observer*, 16 August 1998.
13 *The Times*, 19 August 1998.
14 *The Irish Times*, 4 September 1998.
15 *Observer*, 22 September 1997.
16 See Tamar Hermann and David Newman, 'The Peace Process in Israel-Palestine' in John Darby and Roger MacGinty (eds), *The Management of Peace*, London, Macmillan, 1999.
17 *Observer*, 22 June 1996.
18 Parnell's Imprisonment in Kilmainham Jail in 1881 was accompanied by increased agrarian and political violence. He was released the following year after the 'Kilmainham Treaty' was signed with the British prime minister Gladstone.
19 *Belfast Telegraph*, 5 January 1996.
20 *The Irish Times*, 8 January 1996.
21 See S. J. Stedman, 'Spoiler Problems in Peace Processes', *International Security*, Vol. 22, No. 2, Fall 1997.
22 Ray Geary and John Morison, 'The Perception of Crime' in Peter Stringer and Gillian Robinson (eds), *Social Attitudes in Northern Ireland*, Belfast, Blackstaff, 1992, p. 68.
23 Royal Ulster Constabulary, *Recorded Crime*, Belfast, Central Statistical Unit, 1998.
24 Pierre du Toit, 'The Peace Process in South Africa' in Darby and MacGinty (eds), *Management of Peace*.

20

Peace processes in the late twentieth century: a mixed record

FRED HALLIDAY

The charms of singularity

The purpose of this chapter is to examine the peace negotiations in Ireland of the 1990s in a broader, comparative, context – that of the worldwide set of peace agreements and settlements, partial and plenary, which marked the decade following the end of the Cold War. The most obvious points of comparison are those which, on self-evident grounds, appear most like Ireland – the Basque Country, Corsica and, at a stretch, Palestine. It is comparison of this kind which has, in the first instance, attracted the attention of those who have sought to cast light on the Irish conflict by a comparative analysis of fragmented societies.[1] Such international contextualisation of the Irish case can also examine the ways in which the broader changes of the 1990s have affected it. There may, of course, be some resistance in Ireland to the drawing of such analogies. Nationalism, with its investment in particularism, would have it no other way. The first step may, however, lie in reducing that appearance of singularity, and uniqueness, to which all inter-ethnic, and nationalist, conflicts are so easily prone, even while avoiding any facile reduction of any individual case to a broader international pattern.[2]

Comparison is often more easily made from outside. Certainly there are those in such contexts who, for one reason or another, look to Ireland for their own inspiration: in Palestine, both Arabs and Jews have in the past sought succour from the Irish case, the Jews taking, at various times, the Catholics and Protestants as their model.[3] In the Basque Country and Corsica, but not Sardinia, the matter is simpler – a generic sympathy for the 'Irish' cause, meaning Sinn Féin, is evident in both contexts.[4] Those seeking peace have also looked to the Irish peace agreements for support: 'Stormont en Euzkadi?' was the title of one such, hopeful, article published after Good Friday.[5]

The Cold War, however, and hence its termination, presents a particular problem, since, in comparison with many other international processes that did influence Ireland – Reformation, industrial revolution, romantic Mazzinian nationalism of the 1840s, the First World War, the European Union, to name but some – the Cold War seems not to have affected Ireland in an overt manner. Ireland was, along with Cyprus and the Iranian revolution, one of those post–1945 conflicts that had only a tangential relation to the Cold War. Communism was weak in both North and South, and the republic did not even have diplomatic relations with Moscow till 1973. The North's role in NATO's Atlantic strategy was without direct political impact on the island. The republic, for its part, did play its role as a neutral state, be it through the promotion of a cooperative European neutrality, or participation in peacekeeping. But the extent of this should not be exaggerated – NATO membership did not prevent the Danes or the Norwegians from playing their role in peacekeeping, and neutrality was, in Cold War as in World War, as much a ticket to free-riding as to an effective, alternative international role.[6] When violence returned to the North in 1969 it was striking that this had little or no Cold War component to it, some adoption of Third-Worldist rhetoric by sections of the republican movement aside.

This apparent insulation is, however, open to some challenge. The argument as to the relevance of the end of the Cold War itself to the Irish process has been made elsewhere, and to great effect.[7] If not the end of the military and ideological Cold War, then the broader international context of economic interdependence, and demilitarisation and deideologisation of politics, had a, partial, role in promoting negotiation in the 1990s. Here I shall discuss another kind of relation, showing how, in a comparative perspective, this general record of peace negotiation and enduring conflict in the 1990s may throw light on the progress, and certain limits of progress, in the Irish case.

Peace processes and the Cold War

The record of peace negotiations in the Cold War was, in large measure, a reflection of the relative degree of incorporation of the local conflicts into strategic rivalry. Where the conflicts had a clear Cold War character, or where the local states were closely allied to, or dependent on, the Cold War rivals, agreement was sometimes possible: ceasefires in Korea and Vietnam, and in the successive Arab-Israeli wars, reflected the ability of Washington and Moscow to impose peace on their local allies. The agreements on the neutrality of Austria and Laos, in 1955 and 1962 respectively, reflected similar understandings. It was significant, however, that in the main these agreements, like agreements on arms control, were reached through direct, bilateral, negotiations between the major states, not through the United Nations (UN) or other multilateral fora. Independent third party mediation had almost no role. The UN had, however, a role, in various forms of peace processes, provided this was an area in which the Cold War antagonists were willing to allow the involvement of other parties.

For its part, the UN often found its activities undermined by the collapse of local agreements – as was the case in the Congo in 1961 – or marginalised as local forces decided to prosecute their wars irrespective of the UN presence – as in the Lebanon. Elsewhere, a UN presence may have kept, or helped to keep, the peace, as in Kashmir and Cyprus, even as the overall conflict was very much frozen, not resolved. In the context of the 1990s there was a temptation to look back at the classic peacekeeping of the Cold War, as some kind of 'golden age', where mandates were clear, peacekeeping was independent of great power involvement, and the peacekeepers represented benign, smaller, states. There was no golden age, in a world beset with regional and local conflicts, and overshadowed by the threat of nuclear annihilation, a threat itself increased by the adventurist initiatives of local states and political forces.

Peace processes after the Cold War

The period following the end of the Cold War saw an apparent transformation in the character of peace processes, at first in an optimistic sense, then in more doom-laden vein. In the first place, the proclamation of a new collaborative spirit between the USSR and the US, and then of a new collaboration between the West and post-Soviet Russia, led to a set of substantial, and interrelated, peace initiatives. Gorbachev in his 'New Thinking' proclaimed a set of principles for dealing with what he termed 'regional' issues: deideologisation, reduction in arms supplies, 'national reconciliation', an end to the zero-sum approach by international and local forces. Bush, in 1991, proclaimed a 'New World Order'. This was a term much misused and abused: yet it had, at the time, a limited, and relevant, meaning, namely active collaboration between the two major powers to resolve, and if possible prevent, conflicts.

The elements of this new positive approach were evident in several respects. At the UN itself the US and the USSR, and more broadly the Permanent Five members of the Security Council, began to collaborate more actively and to shed Cold War antagonism. The result was a set of peace agreements that were brokered, in whole or in part, through the UN: in Angola an international agreement in 1988 led to the withdrawal of Cuban and South African forces; Namibia, long ruled in the face of international condemnation by South Africa, attained independence in 1991; in Mozambique, years of war between FRELIMO and RENAMO were ended by a compromise peace in 1992; in Cambodia, where war had been raging since the 1960s, the UN negotiated a compromise agreement in 1992, which in time brought the Khmers Rouges to a political settlement; in Central America – in El Salvador, Guatemala and Nicaragua – peace agreements, followed by elections and by internationally backed 'peace-building' (a term that came into fashion in the 1990s), ended decades of civil war;[8] in South Africa, international pressure, and cross-party participation in negotiations, produced the democratic settlement of 1994.

In three of the most dramatic international conflicts of the 1980s there were also negotiated settlements. In 1988 Iran and Iraq reached a ceasefire agreement, after eight years of war – an event preceded by a letter from Khomeini to Gorbachev urging him to embrace Islam. In Afghanistan, the Soviet Union agreed in April 1988 to withdraw its forces, a process completed, on schedule, in February 1989. In the Arab-Israeli dispute, a Palestinian recognition of Israel in November 1988, as much under US and Swedish as under Soviet pressure, and the discrediting of Arab militarism in Kuwait in the Gulf War led to the Madrid conference of October 1991 and, in time, to the Oslo Accords of August 1993. Elsewhere, and with all sorts of local variations, and prevarications, agreements, and/or ceasefires, occurred: in Western Sahara, POLISARIO and the Moroccan government agreed on a ceasefire in 1991, to be followed by a referendum to determine the territory's status; in the two major armed conflicts of Western Europe – Ireland and the Basque Country – ceasefires were proclaimed in 1994 and 1998 respectively. In Corsica most of the fragments of the armed cause took the hint as well, notably FLNC-Canal Habituel in 1992, even if to a degree greater than in either Ireland or the Basque country, political fragmentation, internecine fighting and racketeering led to a continuation of bombing and killing.

The optimistic perspective on peace was confirmed by other developments in the aftermath of the end of the Cold War. One was the Kuwait conflict of 1990–91: here a clear act of aggression by one state against another led to an unprecedented action to expel the aggressor. All political entities act in the light of past failures, and international organisations are no exception: the UN response to the Iraqi attack on Kuwait owed much to a realisation, drilled into UN officials during the long Iran-Iraq war, that the Security Council's failure to act in September 1980, when Iraq attacked Iran in clear breach of the Charter, had antagonised Iran and so greatly prolonged the war.[9] Now, with broad US-Soviet agreement, the UN could, and did, act: it appeared that this form of action under Chapter VII of the Charter, of which there had been rather few instances in modern times, would prevent conflict.[10] The subsequent Allied action to protect the Kurds of northern Iraq, in effect occupying part of Iraq in defence of the human rights of the inhabitants, appeared to confirm this trend, as did the unprecedented, intrusive, arms control regime subsequently imposed on Iraq. Resolute, and cooperative, enforcement was now, it seemed, possible.[11]

This optimism was reflected in the statements of the UN secretary-general Boutros Ghali himself, and above all in his statement *Agenda for Peace* of 1992. This outlined the possibility of a more secure world. It stressed several measures to maintain the peace which were, in the secretary-general's view, now possible: a greater emphasis on pre-emptive diplomacy, to prevent conflicts breaking out; a more secure financial base for peacekeeping operations; a permanent standing force, to act as a rapidly deployable peacekeeping forces; a greater investment in post-conflict action, what was now termed 'peace-building' in countries where precarious agreements had been reached.

All of this optimism from above was accompanied by a wave of what one may term 'optimism from below'. In a convergence of neo-liberalism from the right and promotion of social movements and civil society from the left, greater roles were being allocated for private, non-governmental and social forces in societies. Much of this remained confined to national societies, but an increasing interest was shown in transnational or global civil society – in the work of human rights and development groups, in activities of ecological and feminist organisations. At the same time, and across several continents, there was a wave of democratisation, a process that not only removed authoritarian, and often violent, regimes at the top, but also encouraged a mellowing, and pacification, of opposition below: armed struggle had lost much of the romantic appeal of the 1960s, but it was only in the late 1980s that many of those who had taken up the gun, in Latin America, Africa, the Middle East, were able credibly to contemplate entering the political arena.[12]

Before we enter into a cascade of pessimism, it is worth noting that much of this optimistic scenario held true. The record of agreements, bringing peace in whole or in part to a dozen countries, was substantial enough in itself. The threat of strategic nuclear war did recede. Military expenditure in major states declined between 1985 and 1995 by, in real terms, around 20 per cent.[13] The process of democratisation, and of promotion of civil society in a broad sense, sustained itself, in Eastern Europe, though not the former USSR, outside the Baltic states, and in Latin America, with even holdouts like China changing substantially. In the field of international humanitarian law, there was significant progress – from the establishment of an International Criminal Court, to the Tribunals for war criminals, to the arrest of Pinochet in October 1998.

The unravelling of peace

In retrospect, however, the turn to peace was far from being the whole picture. In the first place, the record of peace agreements was a very partial one. Some agreements were, in the context of the ensuing decade at least, broadly successful: Namibia, Mozambique, Lebanon, Central America, South Africa. The UN (in effect US) intervention in Haiti did promote, if not conclusively stabilise, a democratic transition. Other processes were shaky, perhaps imperilled, but by no means returning to war, or the *status quo ante*: in Palestine, matters did not proceed as planned, or expected, but nor did the whole process break down – the phrases 'on a knife edge', and 'in serious danger of collapse' were too easily used. Elsewhere, however, serious regression occurred. In Afghanistan, the Soviet withdrawal and the collapse of the PDPA regime in 1992 led to new, and unprecedented, levels of killing and savagery, culminating in the seizure of Kabul by the *taliban* in 1996. In Sri Lanka, despite many mediation attempts, war between the state and both its Tamil and Sinhalese foes continued. In the Horn of Africa the apparent resolution of Africa's longest war, that between Eritrea and Ethiopia in 1993, with the Ethiopian assent to the restoration of Eritrean independence, was followed five years later by the outbreak of a new, murderous border war between these two former guerrilla allies. In Angola a UN-brokered peace process did not prevent

UNITA from relaunching its war. In Cyprus and Sahara there was a cold peace, but no diplomatic movement. In Sudan, Somalia and Colombia, wars that had begun in the 1980s or before intensified in scope and fatalities. In Turkey the PKK insurrection begun in 1984 continued through the decade, until 1999.

The balance-sheet of the old, Cold War, agenda itself was, therefore mixed. But the overall balance-sheet of world peace and conflict was placed more in deficit by the new conflicts that emerged after, and in considerable measure as a result of, the end of the Cold War itself. These were located, above all in two areas. One was in what had been multinational communist countries – the former USSR, and the former Yugoslavia. In the first, there were wars in independent Transcaucasia (Ossetia, Nagorno-Karabagh, Abkhazia) and in the northern Caucasus, still part of the Russian Federation (Chechnya, Dagestan), in Tajikistan, and in Moldova. In the Balkans the secession of Slovenia in 1992 was followed by, some would argue led to, the wars of Croatia and Bosnia (1992–95) and Kosovo (1998–99). The second arena of conflict of the 1990s was Africa: in the Horn every significant state was affected; in the Maghreb, Algeria was riven by civil war, along indeterminate battle lines; in West Africa, civil conflict ravaged Liberia and Sierra Leone; in Central Africa, the massacres of Rwanda in 1994, in which an estimated 700,000 people died, were followed by an internationalisation of conflict in the Congo, drawing on a range of regional states: from Sudan in the north-east, to Angola in the south-west, Africa was, it seemed, in flames.

Nor was the sense of regression confined to such a proliferation of small and local wars: as was the case after the end of other great, strategic, conflicts an initial period of great power cooperation and trust appeared to be yielding, as the 1990s wore on, to a new and more antagonistic pattern of inter-state competition. The consolidation and expansion of the NATO–EU bloc in the Atlantic occasioned growing anxiety in Russia, at both state and popular levels. In the Far East, the triangle of China, Korea and Japan, the locus of the inter-state strategic military rivalry that had, a century before, presaged the wars of the twentieth century, was once again witnessing growing tension, as China and Taiwan failed to resolve their differences and internal political and social tension in China prompted a resort to greater nationalism. In the Gulf, there was no resolution of the unstable, triangular, inter-state conflict involving Iraq, Iran and Saudi Arabia. Most immediately, and with the greatest possible potential for promoting a return to worldwide military competition, the decision by India to explode a nuclear device, in May 1998, following by a similar action by Pakistan, marked the start of a new defiance of the international non-proliferation regime that stimulated states throughout Asia, from the Middle East to the Far East, to consider following suit. As far as inter-state military competition was concerned, the first post-Cold War decade ended on a note of more ominous uncertainty.[14]

A crisis of international peacekeeping

This proliferation of war and uncertainty led some to argue that the world had, in some significant way, entered a new period of conflict, one that perhaps posed greater threats than did the conflicts of the Cold War period itself. For some writers, the post-Cold War period was indeed marked by a greater degree of global disorder, anarchy, chaos, in which nationalism and the growing independence of economic and financial activity from state control, contributed to producing a dangerous instability, a 'new middle ages'.[15] The American writer Robert Kaplan wrote of a new period of savagery and anarchy that threatened to consume the west.[16] Michael Ignatieff, in books covering the rise of ethnic nationalism and the disregard by contemporary military forces of the traditional restraints of war, stressed the dangers of these new conflicts.[17] Mary Kaldor and others analysed the nature of the 'new' wars: these were ones in which the traditional aim of controlling territory was replaced by the dissemination of fear, in which political goals were linked to narco-trafficking and other forms of transnational financial activity, aided and often encouraged by powerful diasporas, in which the majority of casualties were civilians, in which traditional codes, and boundaries, seemed not to operate. Beyond the hatred which these generated, such wars acquired their own dynamic and were, therefore, all the more difficult to control and conclude.[18]

This sense of growing chaos was fuelled by an apparent weakening of precisely that new intergovernmental cooperation that had marked the early post-1989 period. The critique of international institutions, starting with the UN itself, had begun well before the end of the Cold War, and encompassed a range of concerns – lax managerial standards, corruption, a tendency to rhetoric. In British diplomatic circles it was common to talk of two kinds of international institutions, the 'talking' and the 'doing'. The hope expressed by many was that, with the end of the Cold War, and a general bracing air of institutional reform, these difficulties could be overcome.

There was also, in the new managerial spirit, much talk of decentralisation and reorganisation in the field of security – of encouraging regional organisations and influential states to play a leading peacekeeping role, or a range of institutions, not just the UN, being responsible for security. The initial post-1989 years seemed to bear this out: the UN involvement in the range of peaceful settlements, and the operations over Kuwait and the Kurds, seemed to confirm optimism. There was even talk of reviving the Military Staff Committee, mentioned in the Charter but never implemented. In the run up to the fiftieth anniversary of the UN, in 1995, there were many proposals, building on *Agenda for Peace*, for a strengthened peace-keeping capability.

All of this was, however, overtaken by events. In the first place, the traditional resistances to reform of the UN continued to prevail. The Permanent 5 did not want to see their prerogatives diluted, by Security Council reform, or by the creation of a standing military force. The regional organisations encouraged by the

Charter and the secretary-general did, to some measure, operate, but they did so in a way that appeared to highlight the dangers of allowing regional hegemons to act: one person's devolved peacekeeping became another's bully on the bloc – be it Nigerian troops in West Africa, Japanese in Cambodia, Russians in Georgia and Moldova, let alone NATO in former Yugoslavia. Throughout the developed world, i.e. in those countries from which the troops and/or funds for peacekeeping would disproportionately be drawn, there was widespread resistance to the despatch of such forces, and to the casualties peacekeeping might entail. The 'debellicisation' of developed societies came to act as a major constraint on the international operations of these countries.

More significantly, the optimism about UN peacekeeping itself that had culminated in *Agenda for Peace* was to crumble in the face of a series of cases where the UN proved ineffective. Two of these were relics of the Cold War itself: Afghanistan and Angola. Despite long-term UN involvement in peace-making, and the deployment of observers and advisers, the local parties in each case pursued their conflicts, and were encouraged to do so by regional states, at great cost to their own countries and to the neighbouring region. In two African cases the UN proved ineffective: in Somalia an initial deployment for 'humanitarian' purposes in 1992, in the sense of providing food and basic services, degenerated into a military and political conflict with local forces, and an abject retreat; in Rwanda, the outbreak of violence in 1993, between Tutsi and Hutu, one long foreseen by diplomats and UN officials, prompted no effective international response. In the bland and irresponsible neo-liberal language that had become fashionable in the 1990s, 'there were no takers for Rwanda'.

Most sustained, and visible, and most evocative of the weaknesses of the whole UN machinery, were the wars in south-east Europe. It was one of the unexpected ironies of the post–1989 period that UN peacekeeping, which had hitherto been confined to the third world or the remoter European periphery, was now concentrated on the mainland of Europe itself. Whereas in 1987 there were 5 UN peacekeeping operations, with 10,000 personnel, there were in early 1994 17 such operations, with 72,00 personnel, military and police. The majority of these personnel were now deployed in Europe, which also became the theatre for the proliferation of institutions called for in the new neo-liberal institutional doctrine: in contrast to a monopoly of one institution, the UN, on the classical model, there were now at least seven such international security organisations involved in European security.[19] The changed character of peacekeeping was, also, evident in a shift in the composition of the forces involved: in the Cold War the major powers had kept out of peacekeeping, even if they provided logistical, financial and diplomatic support. Now they participated, in a leading role, obstructive or constructive.

The nemesis of the new peacekeeping optimism was to be Bosnia and then Kosovo. In the end, of course, action was taken – in support of Bosnia in 1995, in support of Kosovo in 1999. But the story of these operations underlined the limits of the UN and other diplomatic actors. First, the inability of the UN to prevent the outbreak of war demonstrated the limits of what had become one of the leitmotifs of the early 1990s optimism, pre-emptive diplomacy: put simply, foresight and preemptive diplomacy had little impact where one, or all, of the local actors wished to proceed with war. This was the case with Serbia, as it was with India and Pakistan and their nuclear tests, and with Ethiopia and Eritrea. It is doubtful what difference it would have made in, say, June 1990 if Western and Arab capitals had realised, as they did not, that Saddam Hussein was going to occupy Kuwait.

Secondly, the delays in action over Bosnia and Kosovo highlighted the gap between rhetoric and action in UN, and more general diplomatic, policy. It is easy to suggest, with hindsight, what should or could have been done, but even the best-intentioned of critics would notice how confused, mixed and ineffective the response of the international community to these crises was. All too often resolutions passed with solemn authority in New York were ignored, or proved ineffective, on the ground. Many times the Serbs were solemnly warned to cease their activities, to no avail. In 1995 sanctuary was offered by the UN to thousands of Serbs at Srebrenica: nothing was done to prevent the massacre in which thousands of Bosnian males were killed.

The problems highlighted by Bosnia and Kosovo were not, however, only ones of determination and coordination: there were also very real dilemmas, of policy and principle, involved here. These were dilemmas which no amount of coherence at the policy level could automatically have resolved. When, for example, does an ethnic group have the right to secession? What of the rights of minorities? How far should the pursuit of justice, including the arrest of suspected war criminals, be carried if this undermines agreements to keep the peace? What levels of corruption are tolerable, amongst local political elites, and peacekeepers themselves? These are problems which arose in the Bosnia and Kosovar cases, but were by no means specific to them. The problems associated with UN activities in Bosnia were on occasion blamed on imprecise mandates and 'mission creep': but others saw this as inevitable or even desirable – reference was made to 'robust' peacekeeping, or to 'Chapter Six and a Half', a constitutional position somewhere between peace-keeping and peace enforcement.

The cost of these accumulated problems was, however, substantial and widespread: the optimism of the early 1990s was dispersed, the institutional fragmentation and paralysis intensified. At the end of the 1990s, and without accepting the more dramatic claims about historical regression or the prevalence of new forms of anarchy, the crisis of international peacekeeping, and of global governance with regard to peace and security, was arguably greater than it had been a decade before.

The limits of peace agreements

It may well be asked what relevance all this has to the Irish case. For all the temptations of comparison, instrumental or even well-intentioned, it is evident that in many key respects the Irish case is distinct from, and largely insulated from, this history of expectations, rising and falling, in the 1990s. The Irish conflict, most importantly, was not caused by the Cold War, nor did it to any significant extent acquire a Cold War character. Its course after 1969 was not, in any significant way, the subject of attempts at international third party mediation, nor was any international organisation, the UN or any other, directly involved in seeking a solution. Even in those cases most conventionally associated with Ireland there were significant differences: in contrast to the two other main western European cases, Corsica and even more so the Basque Country, there was no rise of social movements to oppose the armed struggle and unite different communities – the history of civil society in the Northern Irish conflict is recurrent, but intermittent, strangely silent, when not silenced. The women's movement of the 1970s petered out: there was, for example, no counterpart to demonstrations for peace organised by trades unions and other groups, or the mass rallies in the Basque Country, in July 1997, after the murder of the Popular Party municipal councillor, Miguel Angel Blanco.[20] Ireland is divided in a way neither Corsica nor the Basque Country are: here the space for democratic and social forces is far less.

Yet, as Michael Cox has argued, there were in three respects international changes that did affect Ireland: the decline of national liberation as a legitimate goal, the changed nature of the Anglo-US relationship, and the enticements, economic and civil, of Europe. Such a survey of peace, and war, in the post–1989 world therefore prompts a revised version of Winston Churchill's famous question.[21] If, in this case, after the Cuba missile crisis, the Korean and Vietnam wars, and the rise and fall of the Berlin wall, the twin steeples of Fermanagh and Tyrone, the dismal streets of the Falls and the Shankill, will indeed rise again. We cannot be sure, and for a conflict that has gone over eight hundred years, going back, as I once remarked to an Arab audience, to the time of Saladin and the Abbasid Empire, the Cold War may appear as just a blip.

On the side of caution, if not pessimism, there are five lessons which this comparative panorama of the 1990s may suggest as far as Ireland is concerned. First, if Ireland is to be set in the international context of the 1990s this is not a context in which peace, and the resolution of problems, have overwhelmingly prevailed. The record is, as we have seen, a mixed one, and the implications for Ireland are also, therefore, mixed. Ireland is, to be sure, located in the region of the world where military conflict, between and within states, has been overcome more than anywhere else in the world: but the mixed character of the global pattern, including in certain parts of Europe, suggests a degree of caution as far as invocation of world trends is concerned. We do not have to buy into the more exaggerated talk of a 'new' world anarchy, or of 'new' nationalisms or wars, to see that there are several international patterns which Ireland could, arguably, fit.

Secondly, the conditions for lasting peace are neither wholly internal nor external. Both are necessary. A change in the international environment, and active international involvement, is not, on its own, sufficient to guarantee peace: there are, simply, limits to what outsiders, be they states, facilitating individuals, or non-governmental organisations, can do. Neither threat, nor money, are on their own sufficient. To criticise the failure of the international community anywhere, in Ireland, Afghanistan, Sri Lanka or Rwanda, is to imply that *on their own* such changes or mediations can resolve the conflict. They cannot. In the Irish case the range of external circumstances, and not least an active US involvement, were propitious: but as in Palestine, or Angola, or Cambodia, such an external involvement is not on its own enough. A changing European context also helped, in offering a more decentralised, and subsidy-providing, context: this was most evident in the Basque Country, less so in Ireland and Corsica.

Thirdly, when it comes to the internal conditions, the central issue remains the intentions of the main military and political players. Peace does not come, as many in the rush of 'civil society' expectations of the early 1990s may have hoped, through the replacement of the nasty people by nice people: would that it did. Protest, denunciation, scorn may play a role, but this not enough to sway 'hard' men and women, *duros* and *duras*. It comes through a decision by the nasty people that it is, at a particular moment, more advantageous to pursue peace than to pursue war. The term 'hurting stalemate', pioneered by William Zartman to refer to a situation in which a party decides it cannot attain its maximum goals, identifies such a decision.[22] It was obvious that this is what occurred in, say, Afghanistan, Palestine, Bosnia. In the Irish case it applied, to some degree, to all three parties. By the late 1980s the British state and the unionists realised the IRA could not be destroyed. On their side it would seem evident that, at some point the republican leadership realised it could not achieve a purely military victory: there was no 'last push'. For the IRA, there *was* a stalemate on the military front.

What else was rethought is less clear: in this sense a military stalemate may lead to a ceasefire, but not necessarily to a complete settlement. As far as armed nationalists are concerned, we do not have an authoritative analysis as to why the IRA called the ceasefire of 1994 nor why Sinn Féin signed the Good Friday Agreement. It cannot be asserted, with confidence, that the hurting stalemate in the full sense of an acceptance of politics had been reached: it would appear, however, that it had, and indeed that the IRA leadership, or the more far-sighted elements within it, had come to this conclusion ten or more years previously.[23] The element of doubt about this, and the continuing uncertainty about IRA intentions associated with the 'decommissioning' issue, in effect a mechanism for stalling, of political rather than military utility, leaves this question open.[24] Those in the unionist camp who were opposed to any political compromise used this issue to advantage. Perhaps IRA goals were more limited – a cessation of violence. Perhaps political optimism ebbed in the face of new difficulties, within the nationalist camp or in dealing with the UK government and the unionists.

Fourthly, in Ireland, as elsewhere, it is important not to lose sight of the interests which a conflict of this kind creates. The majority of the people in Ireland may well be tired of the war, but there is a minority for whom, emotionally and economically, the war is a way of life – through employment in military and security forces, through the funds available from grants and racketeering. The social and security-related expenditures of the UK government in the North may have reinforced this, by insulating 80 per cent of the population from conflict. One of the central problems in building peace in former war-torn societies – Lebanon, Guatemala, El Salvador – has been that of providing employment for former paramilitaries. In societies where the drugs trade is linked to guerrilla opposition the financial obstacles to peace-building may be even greater.

More broadly, and fifthly, there is a special problem about bringing peace in societies that are ethnically fragmented, as Ireland is, as distinct from riven by predominantly social divisions, as was the case in, for example, Central America, or where the conflict appears at least to be one between locals and outsiders, as in Corsica and the Basque Country. In fragmented societies, the war creates or reinforces, more the latter in the Irish case, a deep suspicion and cleavage in the society which no rush of optimism or agreement, let alone international involvement, can overcome. Here we find that displacement of conflict and demand from the fundamental issues – land, discrimination, violence – means a move to secondary but now no less acute issues – prisoners, investigative commissions, nomenclature and symbolism. What the French call *l'évolution des esprits*, a broad change of mind, is much slower to come than initial enthusiasm might suggest. The voting patterns after Good Friday and the wary respect which politicians of all stripes have shown to the concerns of their communities indicate that the past, for all that people are tired of its negative side, weighs heavily on the present, stoked up, of course, by those with an interest in preserving it.

This suggests, by way of conclusion, that a comparative study of peace processes and agreements must include the possibility of failure, as political paralysis or as regression to violence, as well as success. Indeed, based on the record of the 1990s, one can suggest a set of four kinds of peace process: (1) those that are broadly successful within a five- to ten-year period; (2) processes where political discussion continues, but with protracted and initially unanticipated delays and disappointments; (3) processes where a suspension of military hostilities is accompanied by a complete political stalemate, usually policed by external forces; (4) those that break down and return to the previous levels of conflict. Category one would include Namibia and El Salvador. Category two, Palestine, Cambodia, Haiti and Ireland. Category three, Bosnia, Cyprus, Nagorno-Karabagh and Western Sahara. Category four, Afghanistan, Sri Lanka, Sudan, Angola, Colombia.

It may be important to maintain the division between Categories two and three: the failure to reach full implementation of an agreement does not equal a return to the anterior situation, prior to the signing of such an agreement. This is why the most relevant parallels for Ireland may, in addition to the post–1998 Basque Country, be Palestine: the Oslo Accords of 1993 were meant to have led, by May 1999, to a final status settlement and an independent Palestinian state. Given these goals, the longer-term outcome is still in balance: but to say that the broad goals of the initial Palestinian-Israeli Agreement of 1993 were not met does not mean that the situation has, or is likely to, return to the *status quo ante*. A slippage from Category two to three does not equal return to the wars of earlier years. If there is no deterministic timetable for peace, some kind of historical ratchet may nonetheless operate.

This is all the more evident if cases of stalled peace processes, of which Ireland is also one, are contrasted with the real regressions of Category four or with cases where a ceasefire holds, but without *any* significant political or economic progress. In this perspective, and even allowing for some, controlled, return to paramilitary action, Ireland remains, with Palestine, in the second of four categories of peace process – stalled, but not paralysed, or collapsed. As ever, Ireland is not alone, or unique, whatever its communities, as well as those who despair of it overcoming its nationalisms, may sometimes assert.

Notes

1 See, *inter alia*, Brendan O'Leary and John McGarry, *The Politics of Antagonism: Understanding Northern Ireland* (London: The Athlone Press, 1993); Ian Lustick, *Unsettled States, Disputed Lands* (Ithaca: Cornell University Press, 1993; Adrian Guelke, *Northern Ireland: the International Perspective* (Dublin: Avebury, 1988); Frank Wright, *Northern Ireland: a Comparative Analysis* (Dublin: Gill and McMillan, 1987).

2 I have gone into this in greater detail in 'Irish Problems in International Perspective: a Personal View', *Irish Studies in International Affairs*, Vol. 7, 1996 and 'Irish Nationalism in Comparative Perspective', Torkel Opsahl Lecture, 1997, Democratic Dialogue, Belfast.

3 I have written on this in 'Letter from Dublin', *MERIP Reports* (Washington) 1991.

4 The analogies between the three Western European cases of nationalist paramilitary activity are several: all three broke out in the late 1960s, as a younger generation of nationalists rejected authoritarian political systems and their own 'bourgeois' nationalist political leaderships alike; all three operate on the basis, pellucid to everyone, of a supposed political-military division – Sinn Féin/IRA, Herri Batasuna/ETA, Cuncolta Naziunalista/FLNC; all three enjoyed a minority but enduring support from their own constituencies; all three indulged in romantic, sentimental, cultural nationalism that manipulated local language. The differences were, however, several: casualty rates in Corsica and the Basque Country were around 800, as opposed to 4,000 in Ireland; the two continental causes lacked the triangular Catholic/Protestant/UK character of Ireland. In ideological terms, the Corsicans and Basques, for all their invocation of a struggling past, lacked the historic dimension of 'physical force' republicanism that marked the SF/IRA – this being one of the factors that made them relatively more open to third-worldist rhetoric and solidarity. Organisationally, SF/IRA was distinguished by a much tighter, centralised, command structure: the ETA leadership had, from the early 1970s, been dispersed across prisons and places of exile, while the Corsicans had since 1992 divided into two main factions – FLNC-Canal Historique and FLNC-Canal Habituel, the former continuing armed activity, the latter not. I am grateful to Keda Sodupe, Bernardo Atxaga, Jose Maria Montero and Bob Sutliffe for providing background on the Basque conflict, interviews San Sebastian/Donostia July 1991, Bilbao/Bilbo, July 1996. For critiques of ETA see *Cuadernos de CIP*, Madrid, including Mariano Aguirre, 'Sobre las Pequeñas Patrias', June 1997. The absence of a 'physical force' tradition in Sardinia, despite grievances aplenty, may owe much to the strength of the socialist movement there and to the influence of the most famous Sardinian, the Marxist Antonio Gramsci.

5 Cesareo R. Aguiler de Prat, 'Stormont en Euskadi?', *Mundo*, November 1998. De Prat, one of the leading Spanish students of the Irish conflict, warns, in particular, of the dangers of

imposing numerical majorities in fragmented societies, but stresses that the big difference between the Basque Country and Northern Ireland is the division between communities in the latter. Relations between Sinn Féin and Herri Batasuna were close; one Sinn Féin official Pat Rice was fluent in Spanish and could also, so I was told in Bilbao, talk in *eukera*.

6   I have gone into this in greater detail in 'Irish Neutralism in Cold War Politics: A Harder Look', Sheffield Papers in International Studies, Department of Politics, University of Sheffield, 1990.

7   Michael Cox, 'Bringing in the "International": the IRA Cease-fire and the End of the Cold War', *International Affairs*, vol. 73, no. 4, October 1997; Roger MacGinty, 'American Influences on the Northern Ireland Peace Process', *The Journal of Conflict Studies*, vol. XVII, no. 2, Fall 1997.

8   I have drawn here on the informative analysis by a former UN participant in the Guatemala process, Peter Barwick, 'Multi-Dimensional Peacekeeping in Guatemala: Mixed Success', MSc dissertation, Department of International Relations, London School of Economics, p. 199.

9   In response to Iraqi pressure, the Security Council delayed for several days before passing a resolution at all, and then failed either to name the aggressor or to call for a return to the pre-conflict boundaries. The latter was only stipulated in Security Council Resolution 514 of July 1982.

10 Much was made by critics of the action to support Kuwait of 'double standards', and cases were cited where the UN had failed to act: Palestine, Cyprus, Kashmir, Tibet, Sahara, Timor. These were, however, cases where territories that had not yet attained independence and international recognition were occupied prior to their establishment of a substantive independence.

11 For discussion see James Mayall (ed.), *The New Interventionism 1991–1994: United Nations Experience in Cambodia, Former Yugoslavia and Somalia* (Cambridge: CUP, 1996); Adam Roberts, *Humanitarian Action in War. Aid, Protection and Impartiality in a Policy Vacuum*, London, International Institute for Strategic Studies, 1996.

12 For a comprehensive and perceptive account of the shift from *lucha armada* to democratic politics in Latin America, see Jorge Castañeda, *Utopia Unarmed*, New York: Knopf, 1993.

13 International Institute for Strategic Studies, London, *The Military Balance 1998/9*, Table 46, pp. 295–300.

14 For documentation of recent and current wars see amidst a large literature Dan Smith, *The State of War and Peace Atlas*, London: Penguin, 1997; Thomas Rabehl, *Das Kriegsgeschehen 1998*, Opladen, Leske and Budrich, 1999; and Mariano Aguirre (ed.), *Anuario CIP*, Madrid.

15 Alain Minc, *Le nouveau moyen age*, Paris: Gallimard, 1993; Robert Harvey, *The Return of the Strong. The Drift to Global Disorder*, London: Macmillan, 1995.

16 Robert Kaplan, 'The Coming Anarchy', *Atlantic Monthly*, February 1994.

17 Michael Ignatieff, *Blood and Belonging. Journeys into the New Nationalism*, London: Chatto & Windus, 1993 esp. pp. 1–2, where he argues: 'The key narrative of the new world order is the disintegration of nation states into ethnic civil war; the key architects of that order are warlords; and the key language of our age is ethnic nationalism.' Amongst the nationalists he cites as 'new' are Germans, Québecois, Kurds and Northern Irish. See also *The Warrior's Honour*, London: Chatto & Windus, 1998.

18 Mary Kaldor, *New and Old Wars: Organized Violence in a Global Era*, Cambridge: Polity, 1999; Mary Kaldor and Basker Vashee (eds), *New Wars*, London: Pinter 1999.

19 UN, NATO, OSCE, WEU, Council of Europe, EU, Partnership for Peace.

20 'An Atrocity Too Far for Spain', *The European*, 17–23 July 1997.

21. 'The whole map of Europe has been changed … but as the deluge subsides and the waters fall short we see the dreary steeples of Fermanagh and Tyrone emerging once again'. *Hansard*, 16 February 1922, Col. 1270.

22 'A hurting stalemate begins when one side is unable to achieve its aims, resolve the problem, or win the conflict by itself; it peaks when the other side arrives at a similar perception. Each

party must begin to feel uncomfortable in the costly dead end that it has reached. This plateau must be perceived by both sides not as a momentary resting ground but as a flat, unpleasant terrain stretching into the future, providing no later possibilities for decisive escalation or graceful escape.' I. William Zartman and Saadia Touval, 'Mediation: The Role of Third-Party Diplomacy and Informal Peacemaking' in Sheryl Brown and Kimber Schwaub (eds), *Resolving Third World Conflicts: Challenges for a New Era,* Washington: US Institute of Peace, 1992. See also William Zartman, *Elusive Peace. Negotiating an End to Civil Wars*, Washington: Brookings Institution, 1995.

23 Kevin Bean, 'The New Departure. Recent Developments in Irish Republic Ideology & Strategy', *Occasional Papers in Irish Studies, No. 6*, Institute of Irish Studies, University of Liverpool, 1994.

24 Michael Cox makes this point well in 'Bringing in the "International"'.

Conclusion: closure for the Irish Question?

MICHAEL COX, ADRIAN GUELKE
AND FIONA STEPHEN

On 22 May 1998 voters in both Northern Ireland and the Republic of Ireland went to the polls to give their verdict on the political settlement that had been reached on 10 April. In Northern Ireland over 71 per cent of those voting endorsed the Good Friday Agreement, as it was commonly and popularly known. (The document of the text distributed to every household in Northern Ireland referred to it simply as the Agreement. Its eventual official designation was the Belfast Agreement.) There was a very high turnout of 81 per cent of the electorate. Voters in the Republic of Ireland, required under the terms of the Good Friday Agreement to approve alterations to the wording of Articles 2 and 3 of the Irish Constitution, were even more overwhelmingly in favour, with over 94 per cent of those casting a ballot voting 'yes' to the Agreement, though the turnout was lower, with just 56 per cent of those entitled to vote doing so. In Ireland as a whole that day the deal had been endorsed by over 85 per cent of those who had voted. Those who disputed that this constituted an authentic act of self-determination by the people of the island as a whole had to take refuge in the rather lame argument that the difference in wording between the two referenda nullified the exercise as a test of opinion of the whole island of Ireland. The nub of the issue was that both electorates had consciously endorsed the principle of consent, i.e. that unity could only come about with the consent of majorities in both jurisdictions.

No previous Irish settlement has attracted such overwhelming support from the population. That might seem reason enough for regarding the Good Friday Agreement as qualitatively different from its predecessors, such as the ill-fated Sunningdale Agreement of December 1973. The comparison is pertinent since the Good Friday Agreement is often compared to Sunningdale; indeed, the 1998 settlement has been dubbed in some quarters 'Sunningdale Mark Two' or, in Seamus Mallon's striking phrase, 'Sunningdale for slow learners'. The similarities in terms of the provisions for power sharing and an Irish dimension are obvious. But the enormous advantage that the Good Friday Agreement enjoys over its predecessor is its legitimacy. Sunningdale never secured the popular mandate it needed to survive. Yet in some respects appearances are a little deceptive.

The outcome of the referendum in Northern Ireland was in reality less decisive than it appeared at first sight. Catholics constituting about 43 per cent of the electorate had voted virtually unanimously for the Agreement, while Protestants were almost equally divided between 'yes' and 'no' voters. That, at least, could be inferred from exit polls that had been conducted for newspapers. No official breakdown of the voting by polling district was made available. Further, among 'yes' voters it was apparent that widely differing interpretations of the Agreement prevailed. The main pro-Agreement Unionist party, the Ulster Unionist Party, conspicuously ran its own campaign, keeping its distance from the non-party 'yes' campaign. It also seemed that Sinn Féin's enthusiasm for the Good Friday Agreement stemmed from a tactical presumption that it would prove transitional to its objective of a united Ireland. The deal as such had so little appeal to Sinn Féin that it declined to issue a leaflet giving its views of the Agreement even though it was entitled to the free delivery of such a leaflet to every household in Northern Ireland. Perhaps surprisingly that did not deter its own supporters from turning out and voting 'yes' in overwhelming numbers. Admittedly, it might be argued that nationalist enthusiasm for the Agreement had been stimulated during the campaign by the rhetoric of its Unionist opponents who portrayed it as a slippery slope to a united Ireland. However, as this was not the prime basis of the 'no' campaign, it cannot be the whole explanation for the massive turnout of Catholic voters for the Agreement.

The extent of Protestant division over the Agreement became clearer following the elections to the Northern Ireland Assembly on 25 June 1998. Of parties that won representation in the Assembly, the pro-Agreement Unionist parties (the Ulster Unionist Party and the Progressive Unionist Party) won a total of 31 seats to 28 seats for anti-Agreement Unionists (the Democratic Unionist Party, the UK Unionist Party and three independent Unionists). The Agreement provides that key decisions of the Assembly are taken on a cross-community basis so that they need either the parallel consent of both Unionists and nationalists or a weighted majority of 60 per cent with at least 40 per cent of Unionists and of nationalists voting for the proposal. In short, Unionist opponents of the Agreement are close to being in a position to block decisions of the Assembly, especially as three of the members of the Ulster Unionist Party elected to the Assembly campaigned against the Agreement in the referendum and therefore cannot be relied upon to give consistent support to their leader, David Trimble.

However, it is possible to overstate the difficulties that opposition to the Agreement has presented to its implementation. In fact, it is remarkable how little opposition there has been to the constitutional provisions of the Agreement. This can be interpreted in a variety of ways. One is that its complex compromises enable it to be read as either legitimising partition or as providing a pathway to an eventual united Ireland. Admittedly, such uncertainty does not derive from the provisions of the Agreement alone; it is also a product of uncertainty over demographic trends.

Thus, the substantial narrowing of the gap in the numbers of Protestants and Catholics and the large increase in the nationalist share of the vote in elections (45 per cent in the elections for the European Parliament in 1999 exceeding most estimates of the proportion of Catholics in the electorate) have created expectations that a nationalist majority might emerge at some time in the future. This is reflected in the Agreement itself which provides for the holding of a referendum, should a majority for a united Ireland appear likely to be achieved. Further, the mechanisms in the Agreement for protecting the identity of the nationalist minority could equally in future be used to protect that of a Unionist minority. Of course, it is perfectly possible, and some demographers would currently even argue probable, that a nationalist majority will not arise.

Another way that the lack of opposition to the Agreement's constitutional provisions might be interpreted is as indicating that for nationalists equality within Northern Ireland matters as much as, if not more than, whether there will be a united Ireland at some time in the future. To put it another way, the main objection of Catholics to partition has been that it resulted in their subordination as a community, not the existence *per se* of two jurisdictions on the island of Ireland. After all, the Troubles arose not from Catholic mobilisation behind traditional anti-partitionist demands, but out of the conflict that occurred when they demanded civil rights. Finally, it is also possible to see the relative lack of contention over the Agreement's constitutional provision as incompatible calculations by Unionists and republicans that they will be so able to influence the actual workings of the Agreement as to transform it into an arrangement that serves their ends. This is slightly different from simply interpreting the Agreement differently, since it presupposes the need to take active steps to effect the way the Agreement is implemented.

In practice, both opposition to the Agreement and the difficulties which its implementation has encountered have revolved round the issues of force and violence and the provisions of the Agreement in relation to security in all its aspects. This reflects the extent to which violence had become, after nearly three decades of inter-communal conflict, not just a symptom of sectarian divisions, but a major cause in itself of the polarisation of the society. The fundamental difficulty is that, while it is utterly unrealistic to expect the threat of violence to disappear overnight in a deeply divided society like Northern Ireland, it is also obviously impossible for the political authorities to be seen to condone intimidation, the maintenance of paramilitary arsenals or the violation of human rights, whether by the security forces or by paramilitaries, even though they are virtually the inevitable consequence of the existence of a force field in which the threat of violence has not vanished. Of course, the consistent aim of the authorities has to be movement towards a society free of any of these manifestations of conflict, yet it is also obvious that in a deeply divided society, progress towards this objective is only likely to take place on the basis on a step-by-step approach. This particularly applies to the decommissioning of paramilitary arsenals.

While it drew on a long-standing republican physical-force tradition, the Provisional IRA came into existence in 1969 in large part to defend Catholic areas from loyalist mobs and because of the perceived failure of the existing leadership of the republican movement to respond to this threat, as was underlined by the derisive slogan that appeared on Belfast walls at the time, 'IRA = I Ran Away'. This has made the issue of decommissioning a sensitive one for the current leadership of the republican movement. The Agreement commits the parties to 'use any influence they may have, to achieve the decommissioning of all paramilitary arms within two years following endorsement in referendums North and South of the agreement and in the context of the implementation of the overall settlement'.[1] Interpretation of these words has varied from there being an absolute commitment to complete decommissioning by May 2000 to a mere aspiration that such decommissioning should take place. Adherents of the former interpretation have inferred, at least since the elections to the Assembly, that to meet the deadline substantial decommissioning should already have begun. This was the justification for the Unionist stance that Sinn Féin should not be included in the Executive before guns had been handed in. Adherents of the latter interpretation saw this Unionist stance as itself a serious breach of the Agreement. The problem was compounded by the way that the issue was connected to important asymmetries.

The first of these was that only one political party linked to a paramilitary organisation had secured representation in the Executive and that was Sinn Féin. Hence the question of exclusion from the Executive over decommissioning arose only in relation to Sinn Féin. The fear of nationalists was that Unionists were using the issue of decommissioning as a pretext for Sinn Féin's exclusion so that they would be able to dominate the institutions of devolved government in Northern Ireland. The second of these was that Unionism was divided in its attitude towards the Agreement, whereas nationalists appeared far more united behind the Agreement's equality agenda. This led to a Unionist fear that, unless Sinn Féin was excluded, the Executive would tilt in its operation towards the nationalists because of Unionist divisions. The effect of these two asymmetries was a nationalist disbelief in Unionist willingness to share power with Sinn Féin and a corresponding Unionist disbelief that the SDLP would ever agree to the exclusion of Sinn Féin, except perhaps on a very temporary basis, regardless of the activities of the Provisional IRA.

These calculations explain why what seemed to outside opinion simply a matter of sequencing between the formation of the Executive and the start of decommissioning should have created an impasse that threatened the very survival of the Agreement. It took all of George Mitchell's skill as a mediator, as well as his legendary patience, to secure an agreement between the Ulster Unionist Party and Sinn Féin over decommissioning. This involved a carefully choreographed series of steps by each side which enabled Trimble to set aside as a condition for the formation of the Executive that the Provisional IRA should have put some weapons out of use and to undertake to persuade his party to accept such a course of action. Mitchell succeeded where the two governments had failed in March/April and then in June/July 1999, in part, because the parties recognised that the failure of his review might spell the end of the Agreement and, in part, because he was prepared to give the parties the time to arrive at their own deal. Mitchell's review lasted eleven weeks and to begin with was marked by recriminations among the parties that suggested that it would be no more successful than previous attempts to resolve the issue. Progress started to be made when both the Ulster Unionist Party and Sinn Féin negotiators accepted that both parties wished the Agreement to survive and that their different stances on decommissioning were not motivated by a desire to destroy the Agreement.

Another factor in the outcome of the Mitchell review was the exclusion of the media from the process, enabling the parties to focus on the problem at hand without being distracted by extraneous developments or unhelpful editorialising. Thus, while both the *Belfast Telegraph* and *The Irish Times* waxed lyrical over the success of the completed review, during it they took up self-righteous stances that were totally incompatible with the possibility of agreement on the vexed question of decommissioning. In the June/July set of negotiations Unionists had been encouraged to reject the two governments' proposals by the opportunistic stance of the British Conservative Opposition. It did not hesitate to exploit the issue for partisan political purposes, in sharp contrast to the supportive attitude towards government policy adopted by the Labour Party when John Major was in power and facing difficulties in setting up inclusive negotiations. Even since the Mitchell review, the party's Northern Ireland spokesman, Andrew MacKay, has continued to cast doubt on the commitment of the pro-Agreement paramilitaries to peace by highlighting the continuance of forms of violence and intimidation, as if removing the threat of violence in a deeply divided society was a simple matter of throwing a switch. The shrill demand of Conservative politicians and commentators during the summer of 1999 that the Provisional IRA should surrender all its weapons according to an inflexible, pre-set timetable, while loyalist paramilitary groups opposed to the peace process continued a low level campaign of violence against Catholics, showed both little appreciation of the problem of violence in Northern Ireland and scant concern for understandable fears of the minority. Even after the success of the Mitchell review and the devolution of powers to the Northern Ireland Executive, the issue of decommissioning remains a threat to the survival of settlement.

Lurking underneath the issues of security and violence is the question of Northern Ireland's legitimacy as a political entity. International opinion has always been sympathetic to the nationalist position that the island should never have been partitioned. Indeed, it is unlikely that the reception for the Good Friday Agreement would have been so favourable, had it not been read as designed ultimately to deliver a united Ireland. One of the ironies of international assumptions about the Agreement is the consequent admiration for the Ulster Unionist leader, David Trimble, in the false belief that he has brought about Unionist acceptance of an inevitable end to partition. That this grossly exaggerates the significance of the Agreement's Irish dimension in the form of cross-border bodies and cooperation, in practice, has mattered little. The problem for republican critics of the Agreement is that their strictures on the partitionist implications of the Agreement have not been believed abroad, while inside Ireland peace and equality are higher priorities than unity, even for most of Sinn Féin's supporters. Admittedly, the objective of unity does remain important to both leaders and ordinary members of the Provisional IRA, which explains in part the organisation's reluctance to accord legitimacy to Northern Ireland by endorsing the Good Friday Agreement, except in the most conditional terms.

Both this and the Provisional IRA's unwillingness to declare that the war is over have been significant factors in fuelling Unionist distrust of republican intentions. By the same token Unionist reluctance to acknowledge that Unionist hegemony in the past did not amount to democratic rule is a factor that disturbs nationalists, not least because of its implications for how Unionists intend to approach the future governance of Northern Ireland. In general, Unionists and Protestants have found it more difficult to face up to the implications of Northern Ireland's sectarian divisions for the legitimacy of government in the province than have nationalists and Catholics. The emotive cry that concessions to the minority are nothing but the appeasement of terrorism still carries considerable weight among Unionists, though it has been undermined to a considerable extent by the increasing experience of power sharing at a local level. This has largely been a product of demographic change that has forced cooperation on reluctant Unionists in many areas of the province, but the change in grassroots Unionist attitudes that this has brought about should not be underestimated. Thus, in the failed negotiations in June/July 1999 on the formation of the Executive, it was apparent that, had Trimble wished to accede to the government's proposals, he would almost certainly have been able to secure the support of a majority of Unionists for such a stance. He was not the prisoner of Unionist public opinion. However, it seems that Trimble calculated that July was simply the wrong time for such a gamble. His judgement on this point can hardly be criticised considering that he was able to deliver his party successfully to a compromise in November 1999.

It is somewhat paradoxical that a settlement which has made possible the establishment of a fully legitimate government in Northern Ireland for the first time in its history and thus possesses the potential to ensure the long-term survival of Northern Ireland as a political entity should have faced greater opposition from Unionists, who have always insisted on the legitimacy of partition, than from nationalists, who have always rejected its legitimacy. The paradox is partly to be explained by Unionist and nationalist calculations as to the alternative to this settlement. In particular, it would seem that some Unionists either believe that the Good Friday Agreement is incapable of delivering more than a temporary truce or prefer to live with the continuation of the conflict rather than seeing their opponents politically empowered. Yet the weight of international opinion in favour of a united Ireland cannot be discounted altogether. It might ultimately exercise some influence on the parties in the context of the operation of the Agreement, though arguably much less than would be the case if the peace process broke down. What can safely be concluded, nevertheless, is that the success of the Agreement presents the only foreseeable alternative to Irish unity which is capable of bringing about the closure of the Irish Question.

The difficulties that the implementation of the Good Friday Agreement has encountered have understandably tended to direct attention away from the capacity of the Agreement to provide a model for the resolution of ethnic conflicts in other parts of the world. Yet the precedent it has set for the development of cross-border institutions to accommodate the national identity of a minority is relevant in many parts of the world, as is the British-Irish Council with its provision for relations among different levels of government, including the national, contrary to Westphalian notions of sovereignty. A weakness is that these developments do not as yet have much basis in the declarations of the international community on self-determination and the rights of minorities. *Ad hoc* response to crisis has marked the international community's reaction to events in the Balkans and there is the danger that, in the absence of global consensus on the interpretation of international norms, power politics will dominate outcomes and the innovative potential of the approach taken in the Good Friday Agreement as a model for other settlements will be lost.

Note

1 See section on Decommissioning in the Belfast Agreement, Appendix 2.

Appendices

APPENDIX 1

Chronology of Northern Ireland
from war to peace

1968 5 October – clashes between civil rights demonstrators and the police in Londonderry/Derry after protest march is banned by the minister of home affairs, William Craig. This event is often taken to mark the start of Northern Ireland's Troubles.

1969 14 August – British troops deployed in Northern Ireland in aid of the civil power. 28 December – Announcement of the formation of the Provisional Irish Republic Army (IRA).

1971 9 August – Introduction of internment (detention without trial). September – Formation of the Ulster Defence Association (UDA).

1972 30 January – fourteen civil rights demonstrators killed by the Parachute Regiment in Londonderry/Derry. 24 March – Direct Rule from Westminster imposed on Northern Ireland.

1973 9 December – Sunningdale Agreement under which parties to share power in a new devolved government in Northern Ireland agree to establish a Council of Ireland to provide Irish dimension to the political settlement.

1974 28 May – Collapse of power sharing Executive following general strike organised by the Ulster Workers Council.

1981 Hunger strikes at the Maze prison.

1984 New Ireland Forum

1985 15 November – Signature of the Anglo-Irish Agreement under which the British government undertook to consult the government of the Republic of Ireland on its policies in Northern Ireland.

1988 14 October – Talks in Duisburg, West Germany among representatives of the Ulster Unionist Party (UUP), the Democratic Unionist Party (DUP), the Social Democratic and Labour Party (SDLP) and the Alliance Party of Northern Ireland.

1990 9 November – The secretary of state for Northern Ireland, Peter Brooke, declares that Britain has no selfish strategic or economic interest in Northern Ireland.

1991 26 March – The terms of agreement among the province's constitutional parties to enter into talks on the future of Northern Ireland announced by Peter Brooke.

1992 17 February – Launch of Sinn Féin publication, *Towards a Lasting Peace in Ireland*.
10 April – Provisional IRA bombs in the City of London the day after the British general election cause massive damage.
10 November – Brooke/Mayhew talks among the constitutional parties end in deadlock.

1993 24 April – John Hume, leader of the SDLP, and Gerry Adams, president of Sinn Féin, issue first joint statement.
15 December – British and Irish governments issue *Joint Declaration*.

1994 31 August – Provisional IRA proclaims ceasefire.
13 October – Combined Loyalist Military Command proclaims ceasefire.

1995 22 February – Launch of *Framework Documents* by British and Irish governments.
7 March – Decommissioning of some weapons set as condition for Sinn Féin's entry into all-party talks by the secretary of state for Northern Ireland, Sir Patrick Mayhew.
30 November – Bill Clinton visits Northern Ireland.

1996 24 January – Publication of the Report of the International Body (on decommissioning).
9 February – Provisional IRA ends ceasefire with the bombing of Canary Wharf in London.
30 May – Elections for Northern Ireland forum.
10 June – Start of multi-party negotiations.

1997 20 July – Resumption of Provisional IRA ceasefire.

1998 12 January – British and Irish governments issue document, *Propositions of Heads of Agreement*.
10 April – Good Friday Agreement announced at conclusion of talks among the eight parties participating in the multi-party negotiations.
22 May – Referenda in Northern Ireland and the Republic of Ireland massively endorse Good Friday Agreement.
25 June – Elections to Northern Ireland Assembly.
15 August – twenty-nine people are killed in Omagh by bomb placed by dissident Republican group, the Real IRA.

1999 15 March – Human rights lawyer, Rosemary Nelson, assassinated by loyalists.
2 July – British and Irish governments issue joint statement intended to provide a way forward on the establishment of the Executive and the decommissioning of weapons. Publication of the report of the Independent International Commission on Decommissioning.
15 July – UUP boycotts formation of the Executive, causing its collapse and resulting in the invocation of the procedures for reviewing the implementation of the Good Friday Agreement. Resignation of Deputy First Minister, Seamus Mallon.
6 September – Start of Mitchell review of the implementation of the Good Friday Agreement.
9 September – Publication of the report of the Patten Commission on policing.

18 November – George Mitchell issues concluding report of his review.

23 November – Award of George Cross to the Royal Ulster Constabulary.

27 November – Ulster Unionist Council supports implementation of the deal agreed between the Ulster Unionist Party and Sinn Féin in the Mitchell review of the implementation of the Agreement, subject to the proviso of a final decision by the Council in February 2000.

29 November – Northern Ireland Assembly votes to annul resignation of Seamus Mallon as Deputy First Minister. Election of Ministers of the Northern Ireland Executive.

2 December – Transfer of powers to devolved institutions in Northern Ireland. First meeting of the Northern Ireland Executive. Anglo-Irish Agreement replaced by new British–Irish Agreement. Amendment of Articles 2 and 3 of the Irish Constitution put into effect.

13 December – Inaugural meeting of the North–South Ministerial Council in Armagh.

17 December – Inaugural meeting of the British–Irish Council in London.

2000 11 February – Suspension of the Executive by the Secretary of State for Northern Ireland, Peter Mandelson, following the failure of the Provisional IRA to start decommissioning of its weapons or to indicate a date by which a start to decommissioning would be made.

25 March – David Trimble defeats South Belfast M.P., the Rev. Martin Smyth, by 457 votes to 348 (57 per cent to 43 per cent) in challenge to his leadership of the Ulster Unionist Party.

5 May – The British and Irish governments issue statement on their proposals to secure the full implementation of the Good Friday Agreement.

6 May – Statement by the Provisional IRA that in the context of the full implementation of the Good Friday Agreement and of the two governments' statement it would initiate a process that would 'completely and verifiably put IRA arms beyond use'. The statement also commits the IRA to permitting the inspection of a number of its arms dumps by third parties as a confidence-building measure.

27 May – Ulster Unionist Council votes to support David Trimble on the issue of re-entering the power-sharing Executive with Sinn Féin by 459 votes to 403 (i.e. by 53 per cent to 47 per cent).

30 May – Restoration of devolution to Northern Ireland.

1 June – Meeting of the Executive.

APPENDIX 2

The Good Friday Agreement (Belfast Agreement), 10 April 1998

The Agreement

Agreement reached in the multi-party negotiations

TABLE OF CONTENTS

ANNEX: Agreement between the Government of the United Kingdom of Great Britain and Northern Ireland and the Government of Ireland.

1. DECLARATION OF SUPPORT

1. We, the participants in the multi-party negotiations, believe that the agreement we have negotiated offers a truly historic opportunity for a new beginning.

2. The tragedies of the past have left a deep and profoundly regrettable legacy of suffering. We must never forget those who have died or been injured, and their families. But we can best honour them through a fresh start, in which we firmly dedicate ourselves to the achievement of reconciliation, tolerance, and mutual trust, and to the protection and vindication of the human rights of all.

3. We are committed to partnership, equality and mutual respect as the basis of relationships within Northern Ireland, between North and South, and between these islands.

4. We reaffirm our total and absolute commitment to exclusively democratic and peaceful means of resolving differences on political issues, and our opposition to any use or threat of force by others for any political purpose, whether in regard to this agreement or otherwise.

5. We acknowledge the substantial differences between our continuing, and equally legitimate, political aspirations. However, we will endeavour to strive in every practical way towards reconciliation and rapprochement within the framework of democratic and agreed arrangements. We pledge that we will, in good faith, work to ensure the success of each and every one of the arrangements to be established under this agreement. It is accepted that all of the institutional and constitutional arrangements – an Assembly in Northern Ireland, a North/South Ministerial Council, implementation bodies, a British–Irish Council and a British–Irish Intergovernmental Conference and any amendments to British Acts of Parliament and the Constitution of Ireland – are interlocking and interdependent and that in particular the functioning of the Assembly and the North/South Council are so closely interrelated that the success of each depends on that of the other.

6. Accordingly, in a spirit of concord, we strongly commend this agreement to the people, North and South, for their approval.

2. CONSTITUTIONAL ISSUES

1. The participants endorse the commitment made by the British and Irish Governments that, in a new British–Irish Agreement replacing the Anglo-Irish Agreement, they will:
    (i) recognise the legitimacy of whatever choice is freely exercised by a majority of the people of Northern Ireland with regard to its status, whether they prefer to continue to support the Union with Great Britain or a sovereign united Ireland;
    (ii) recognise that it is for the people of the island of Ireland alone, by agreement between the two parts respectively and without external impediment, to exercise their right of self-determination on the basis of consent, freely and concurrently given, North and South, to bring about a united Ireland, if that is their wish, accepting that this right must be achieved and exercised with and subject to the agreement and consent of a majority of the people of Northern Ireland;

(iii) acknowledge that while a substantial section of the people in Northern Ireland share the legitimate wish of a majority of the people of the island of Ireland for a united Ireland, the present wish of a majority of the people of Northern Ireland, freely exercised and legitimate, is to maintain the Union and, accordingly, that Northern Ireland's status as part of the United Kingdom reflects and relies upon that wish; and that it would be wrong to make any change in the status of Northern Ireland save with the consent of a majority of its people;

(iv) affirm that if, in the future, the people of the island of Ireland exercise their right of self-determination on the basis set out in sections (i) and (ii) above to bring about a united Ireland, it will be a binding obligation on both Governments to introduce and support in their respective Parliaments legislation to give effect to that wish;

(v) affirm that whatever choice is freely exercised by a majority of the people of Northern Ireland, the power of the sovereign government with jurisdiction there shall be exercised with rigorous impartiality on behalf of all the people in the diversity of their identities and traditions and shall be founded on the principles of full respect for, and equality of, civil, political, social and cultural rights, of freedom from discrimination for all citizens, and of parity of esteem and of just and equal treatment for the identity, ethos, and aspirations of both communities;

(vi) recognise the birthright of all the people of Northern Ireland to identify themselves and be accepted as Irish or British, or both, as they may so choose, and accordingly confirm that their right to hold both British and Irish citizenship is accepted by both Governments and would not be affected by any future change in the status of Northern Ireland.

2.   The participants also note that the two Governments have accordingly undertaken in the context of this comprehensive political agreement, to propose and support changes in, respectively, the Constitution of Ireland and in British legislation relating to the constitutional status of Northern Ireland.

ANNEX A

Draft Clauses/Schedules for Incorporation in British legislation

1.   (1) It is hereby declared that Northern Ireland in its entirety remains part of the United Kingdom and shall not cease to be so without the consent of a majority of the people of Northern Ireland voting in a poll held for the purposes of this section in accordance with Schedule 1.

(2) But if the wish expressed by a majority in such a poll is that Northern Ireland should cease to be part of the United Kingdom and form part of a united Ireland, the Secretary of State shall lay before Parliament such proposals to give effect to that wish as may be agreed between Her Majesty's Government in the United Kingdom and the Government of Ireland.

2.   The Government of Ireland Act 1920 is repealed; and this Act shall have effect notwithstanding any other previous enactment.

SCHEDULE I

Polls for the Purpose of Section 1

1.   The Secretary of State may by order direct the holding of a poll for the purposes of section 1 on a date specified in the order.

2.   Subject to paragraph 3, the Secretary of State shall exercise the power under paragraph 1 if at any time it appears likely to him that a majority of those voting

would express a wish that Northern Ireland should cease to be part of the United Kingdom and form part of a united Ireland.

3. The Secretary of State shall not make an order under paragraph 1 earlier than seven years after the holding of a previous poll under this Schedule.

4. (Remaining paragraphs along the lines of paragraphs 2 and 3 of existing Schedule 1 to 1973 Act.)

ANNEX B

Irish Government draft legislation to amend the Constitution

Add to Article 29 the following sections:

7. 1. The State may consent to be bound by the British–Irish Agreement done at Belfast on the … day of … 1998, hereinafter called the Agreement.

2. Any institution established by or under the Agreement may exercise the powers and functions thereby conferred on it in respect of all or any part of the island of Ireland notwithstanding any other provision of this Constitution conferring a like power or function on any person or any organ of State appointed under or created or established by or under this Constitution. Any power or function conferred on such an institution in relation to the settlement or resolution of disputes or controversies may be in addition to or in substitution for any like power or function conferred by this Constitution on any such person or organ of State as aforesaid.

3. If the Government declare that the State has become obliged, pursuant to the Agreement, to give effect to the amendment of this Constitution referred to therein, then, notwithstanding Article 46 hereof, this Constitution shall be amended as follows:

i. the following Articles shall be substituted for Articles 2 and 3 of the Irish text:

'2. [Irish text to be inserted here]

3. [Irish text to be inserted here]

(ii) the following Articles shall be substituted for Articles 2 and 3 of the English text:

'Article 2

It is the entitlement and birthright of every person born in the island of Ireland, which includes its islands and seas, to be part of the Irish nation. That is also the entitlement of all persons otherwise qualified in accordance with law to be citizens of Ireland. Furthermore, the Irish nation cherishes its special affinity with people of Irish ancestry living abroad who share its cultural identity and heritage.

Article 3

1. It is the firm will of the Irish nation, in harmony and friendship, to unite all the people who share the territory of the island of Ireland, in all the diversity of their identities and traditions, recognising that a united Ireland shall be brought about only by peaceful means with the consent of a majority of the people, democratically expressed, in both jurisdictions in the island. Until then, the laws enacted by the Parliament established by this Constitution shall have the like area and extent of application as the laws enacted by the Parliament that existed immediately before the coming into operation of this Constitution.

2. Institutions with executive powers and functions that are shared between those jurisdictions may be established by their respective responsible authorities for stated purposes and may exercise powers and functions in respect of all or any part of the island.'

iii. the following section shall be added to the Irish text of this Article:

'8. [Irish text to be inserted here]'

and

iv. the following section shall be added to the English text of this Article:

'8. The State may exercise extra-territorial jurisdiction in accordance with the generally recognised principles of international law.'

4. If a declaration under this section is made, this subsection and subsection 3, other than the amendment of this Constitution effected thereby, and subsection 5 of this section shall be omitted from every official text of this Constitution published thereafter, but notwithstanding such omission this section shall continue to have the force of law.

5. If such a declaration is not made within twelve months of this section being added to this Constitution or such longer period as may be provided for by law, this section shall cease to have effect and shall be omitted from every official text of this Constitution published thereafter.

3. STRAND ONE

Democratic Institutions in Northern Ireland

1. This agreement provides for a democratically elected Assembly in Northern Ireland which is inclusive in its membership, capable of exercising executive and legislative authority, and subject to safeguards to protect the rights and interests of all sides of the community.

The Assembly

2. A 108-member Assembly will be elected by PR(STV) from existing Westminster constituencies.

3. The Assembly will exercise full legislative and executive authority in respect of those matters currently within the responsibility of the six Northern Ireland Government Departments, with the possibility of taking on responsibility for other matters as detailed elsewhere in this agreement.

4. The Assembly – operating where appropriate on a cross-community basis – will be the prime source of authority in respect of all devolved responsibilities.

Safeguards

5. There will be safeguards to ensure that all sections of the community can participate and work together successfully in the operation of these institutions and that all sections of the community are protected, including:

    (a) allocations of Committee Chairs, Ministers and Committee membership in proportion to party strengths;

    (b) the European Convention on Human Rights (ECHR) and any Bill of Rights for Northern Ireland supplementing it, which neither the Assembly nor public bodies can infringe, together with a Human Rights Commission;

    (c) arrangements to provide that key decisions and legislation are proofed to ensure that they do not infringe the ECHR and any Bill of Rights for Northern Ireland;

    (d) arrangements to ensure key decisions are taken on a cross-community basis;

    (i) *either* parallel consent, i.e. a majority of those members present and voting, including a majority of the unionist and nationalist designations present and voting;

    (ii) *or* a weighted majority (60%) of members present and voting, including at least 40% of each of the nationalist and unionist designations present and voting.

Key decisions requiring cross-community support will be designated in advance, including election of the Chair of the Assembly, the First Minister and Deputy First Minister, standing orders and budget allocations. In other cases such decisions could be triggered by a petition of concern brought by a significant minority of Assembly members (30/108).

(e) an Equality Commission to monitor a statutory obligation to promote equality of opportunity in specified areas and parity of esteem between the two main communities, and to investigate individual complaints against public bodies.

Operation of the Assembly

6. At their first meeting, members of the Assembly will register a designation of identity – nationalist, unionist or other – for the purposes of measuring cross-community support in Assembly votes under the relevant provisions above.

7. The Chair and Deputy Chair of the Assembly will be elected on a cross-community basis, as set out in paragraph 5(d) above.

8. There will be a Committee for each of the main executive functions of the Northern Ireland Administration. The Chairs and Deputy Chairs of the Assembly Committees will be allocated proportionally, using the d'Hondt system. Membership of the Committees will be in broad proportion to party strengths in the Assembly to ensure that the opportunity of Committee places is available to all members.

9. The Committees will have a scrutiny, policy development and consultation role with respect to the Department with which each is associated, and will have a role in initiation of legislation. They will have the power to:
   - consider and advise on Departmental budgets and Annual Plans in the context of the overall budget allocation;
   - approve relevant secondary legislation and take the Committee stage of relevant primary legislation;
   - call for persons and papers;
   - initiate enquiries and make reports;
   - consider and advise on matters brought to the Committee by its Minister.

10. Standing Committees other than Departmental Committees may be established as may be required from time to time.

11. The Assembly may appoint a special Committee to examine and report on whether a measure or proposal for legislation is in conformity with equality requirements, including the ECHR/Bill of Rights. The Committee shall have the power to call people and papers to assist in its consideration of the matter. The Assembly shall then consider the report of the Committee and can determine the matter in accordance with the cross-community consent procedure.

12. The above special procedure shall be followed when requested by the Executive Committee, or by the relevant Departmental Committee, voting on a cross-community basis.

13. When there is a petition of concern as in 5(d) above, the Assembly shall vote to determine whether the measure may proceed without reference to this special procedure. If this fails to achieve support on a cross-community basis, as in 5(d)(i) above, the special procedure shall be followed.

Executive Authority

14. Executive authority to be discharged on behalf of the Assembly by a First Minister and Deputy First Minister and up to ten Ministers with Departmental responsibilities.

15. The First Minister and Deputy First Minister shall be jointly elected into office by the Assembly voting on a cross-community basis, according to 5(d)(i) above.

16. Following the election of the First Minister and Deputy First Minister, the posts of Ministers will be allocated to parties on the basis of the d'Hondt system by reference to the number of seats each party has in the Assembly.

17. The Ministers will constitute an Executive Committee, which will be convened, and presided over, by the First Minister and Deputy First Minister.

18. The duties of the First Minister and Deputy First Minister will include, inter alia, dealing with and co-ordinating the work of the Executive Committee and the response of the Northern Ireland administration to external relationships.

19. The Executive Committee will provide a forum for the discussion of, and agreement on, issues which cut across the responsibilities of two or more Ministers, for prioritising executive and legislative proposals and for recommending a common position where necessary (e.g. in dealing with external relationships).

20. The Executive Committee will seek to agree each year, and review as necessary, a programme incorporating an agreed budget linked to policies and programmes, subject to approval by the Assembly, after scrutiny in Assembly Committees, on a cross-community basis.

21. A party may decline the opportunity to nominate a person to serve as a Minister or may subsequently change its nominee.

22. All the Northern Ireland Departments will be headed by a Minister. All Ministers will liaise regularly with their respective Committee.

23. As a condition of appointment, Ministers, including the First Minister and Deputy First Minister, will affirm the terms of a Pledge of Office (Annex A) undertaking to discharge effectively and in good faith all the responsibilities attaching to their office.

24. Ministers will have full executive authority in their respective areas of responsibility, within any broad programme agreed by the Executive Committee and endorsed by the Assembly as a whole.

25. An individual may be removed from office following a decision of the Assembly taken on a cross-community basis, if (s)he loses the confidence of the Assembly, voting on a cross-community basis, for failure to meet his or her responsibilities including, inter alia, those set out in the Pledge of Office. Those who hold office should use only democratic, non-violent means, and those who do not should be excluded or removed from office under these provisions.

Legislation

26. The Assembly will have authority to pass primary legislation for Northern Ireland in devolved areas, subject to:
(a) the ECHR and any Bill of Rights for Northern Ireland supplementing it which, if the courts found to be breached, would render the relevant legislation null and void;
(b) decisions by simple majority of members voting, except when decision on a cross-community basis is required;
(c) detailed scrutiny and approval in the relevant Departmental Committee;
(d) mechanisms, based on arrangements proposed for the Scottish Parliament, to ensure suitable co-ordination, and avoid disputes, between the Assembly and the Westminster Parliament;
(e) option of the Assembly seeking to include Northern Ireland provisions in

United Kingdom-wide legislation in the Westminster Parliament, especially on devolved issues where parity is normally maintained (e.g. social security, company law).

27. The Assembly will have authority to legislate in reserved areas with the approval of the Secretary of State and subject to Parliamentary control.

28. Disputes over legislative competence will be decided by the Courts.

29. Legislation could be initiated by an individual, a Committee or a Minister.

Relations with Other Institutions

30. Arrangements to represent the Assembly as a whole, at Summit level and in dealings with other institutions, will be in accordance with paragraph 18, and will be such as to ensure cross-community involvement.

31. Terms will be agreed between appropriate Assembly representatives and the Government of the United Kingdom to ensure effective co-ordination and input by Ministers to national policy-making, including on EU issues.

32. Role of Secretary of State:

(a) to remain responsible for NIO matters not devolved to the Assembly, subject to regular consultation with the Assembly and Ministers;

(b) to approve and lay before the Westminster Parliament any Assembly legislation on reserved matters;

(c) to represent Northern Ireland interests in the United Kingdom Cabinet;

(d) to have the right to attend the Assembly at their invitation.

33. The Westminster Parliament (whose power to make legislation for Northern Ireland would remain unaffected) will:

(a) legislate for non-devolved issues, other than where the Assembly legislates with the approval of the Secretary of State and subject to the control of Parliament;

(b) to legislate as necessary to ensure the United Kingdom's international obligations are met in respect of Northern Ireland;

(c) scrutinise, including through the Northern Ireland Grand and Select Committees, the responsibilities of the Secretary of State.

34. A consultative Civic Forum will be established. It will comprise representatives of the business, trade union and voluntary sectors, and such other sectors as agreed by the First Minister and the Deputy First Minister. It will act as a consultative mechanism on social, economic and cultural issues. The First Minister and the Deputy First Minister will by agreement provide administrative support for the Civic Forum and establish guidelines for the selection of representatives to the Civic Forum.

Transitional Arrangements

35. The Assembly will meet first for the purpose of organisation, without legislative or executive powers, to resolve its standing orders and working practices and make preparations for the effective functioning of the Assembly, the British–Irish Council and the North/South Ministerial Council and associated implementation bodies. In this transitional period, those members of the Assembly serving as shadow Ministers shall affirm their commitment to non-violence and exclusively peaceful and democratic means and their opposition to any use or threat of force by others for any political purpose; to work in good faith to bring the new arrangements into being; and to observe the spirit of the Pledge of Office applying to appointed Ministers.

Review

36. After a specified period there will be a review of these arrangements, including the details of electoral arrangements and of the Assembly's procedures, with a view to agreeing any adjustments necessary in the interests of efficiency and fairness.

ANNEX A

Pledge of Office

To pledge:
(a) to discharge in good faith all the duties of office;
(b) commitment to non-violence and exclusively peaceful and democratic means;
(c) to serve all the people of Northern Ireland equally, and to act in accordance with the general obligations on government to promote equality and prevent discrimination;
(d) to participate with colleagues in the preparation of a programme for government;
(e) to operate within the framework of that programme when agreed within the Executive Committee and endorsed by the Assembly;
(f) to support, and to act in accordance with, all decisions of the Executive Committee and Assembly;
(g) to comply with the Ministerial Code of Conduct.

Code of Conduct

Ministers must at all times:
- observe the highest standards of propriety and regularity involving impartiality, integrity and objectivity in relationship to the stewardship of public funds;
- be accountable to users of services, the community and, through the Assembly, for the activities within their responsibilities, their stewardship of public funds and the extent to which key performance targets and objectives have been met;
- ensure all reasonable requests for information from the Assembly, users of services and individual citizens are complied with; and that Departments and their staff conduct their dealings with the public in an open and responsible way;
- follow the seven principles of public life set out by the Committee on Standards in Public Life;
- comply with this code and with rules relating to the use of public funds;
- operate in a way conducive to promoting good community relations and equality of treatment;
- not use information gained in the course of their service for personal gain; nor seek to use the opportunity of public service to promote their private interests;
- ensure they comply with any rules on the acceptance of gifts and hospitality that might be offered;
- declare any personal or business interests which may conflict with their responsibilities. The Assembly will retain a Register of Interests. Individuals must ensure that any direct or indirect pecuniary interests which members of the public might reasonably think could influence their judgement are listed in the Register of Interests;

4. STRAND TWO

North/South Ministerial Council

1. Under a new British–Irish Agreement dealing with the totality of relationships, and related legislation at Westminster and in the Oireachtas, a North/South Ministerial

Council to be established to bring together those with executive responsibilities in Northern Ireland and the Irish Government, to develop consultation, co-operation and action within the island of Ireland – including through implementation on an all-island and cross-border basis – on matters of mutual interest within the competence of the Administrations, North and South.

2. All Council decisions to be by agreement between the two sides. Northern Ireland to be represented by the First Minister, Deputy First Minister and any relevant Ministers, the Irish Government by the Taoiseach and relevant Ministers, all operating in accordance with the rules for democratic authority and accountability in force in the Northern Ireland Assembly and the Oireachtas respectively. Participation in the Council to be one of the essential responsibilities attaching to relevant posts in the two Administrations. If a holder of a relevant post will not participate normally in the Council, the Taoiseach in the case of the Irish Government and the First and Deputy First Minister in the case of the Northern Ireland Administration to be able to make alternative arrangements.

3. The Council to meet in different formats:
(i) in plenary format twice a year, with Northern Ireland representation led by the First Minister and Deputy First Minister and the Irish Government led by the Taoiseach;
(ii) in specific sectoral formats on a regular and frequent basis with each side represented by the appropriate Minister;
(iii) in an appropriate format to consider institutional or cross-sectoral matters (including in relation to the EU) and to resolve disagreement.

4. Agendas for all meetings to be settled by prior agreement between the two sides, but it will be open to either to propose any matter for consideration or action.

5. The Council:
(i) to exchange information, discuss and consult with a view to co-operating on matters of mutual interest within the competence of both Administrations, North and South;
(ii) to use best endeavours to reach agreement on the adoption of common policies, in areas where there is a mutual cross-border and all-island benefit, and which are within the competence of both Administrations, North and South, making determined efforts to overcome any disagreements;
(iii) to take decisions by agreement on policies for implementation separately in each jurisdiction, in relevant meaningful areas within the competence of both Administrations, North and South;
(iv) to take decisions by agreement on policies and action at an all-island and cross-border level to be implemented by the bodies to be established as set out in paragraphs 8 and 9 below.

6. Each side to be in a position to take decisions in the Council within the defined authority of those attending, through the arrangements in place for co-ordination of executive functions within each jurisdiction. Each side to remain accountable to the Assembly and Oireachtas respectively, whose approval, through the arrangements in place on either side, would be required for decisions beyond the defined authority of those attending.

7. As soon as practically possible after elections to the Northern Ireland Assembly, inaugural meetings will take place of the Assembly, the British–Irish Council and the North/South Ministerial Council in their transitional forms. All three institutions will meet regularly and frequently on this basis during the period

between the elections to the Assembly, and the transfer of powers to the Assembly, in order to establish their modus operandi.

8. During the transitional period between the elections to the Northern Ireland Assembly and the transfer of power to it, representatives of the Northern Ireland transitional Administration and the Irish Government operating in the North/South Ministerial Council will undertake a work programme, in consultation with the British Government, covering at least 12 subject areas, with a view to identifying and agreeing by 31 October 1998 areas where co-operation and implementation for mutual benefit will take place. Such areas may include matters in the list set out in the Annex.

9. As part of the work programme, the Council will identify and agree at least 6 matters for co-operation and implementation in each of the following categories:
   (i) Matters where existing bodies will be the appropriate mechanisms for co-operation in each separate jurisdiction;
   (ii) Matters where the co-operation will take place through agreed implementation bodies on a cross-border or all-island level.

10. The two Governments will make necessary legislative and other enabling preparations to ensure, as an absolute commitment, that these bodies, which have been agreed as a result of the work programme, function at the time of the inception of the British–Irish Agreement and the transfer of powers, with legislative authority for these bodies transferred to the Assembly as soon as possible thereafter. Other arrangements for the agreed co-operation will also commence contemporaneously with the transfer of powers to the Assembly.

11. The implementation bodies will have a clear operational remit. They will implement on an all-island and cross-border basis policies agreed in the Council.

12. Any further development of these arrangements to be by agreement in the Council and with the specific endorsement of the Northern Ireland Assembly and Oireachtas, subject to the extent of the competences and responsibility of the two Administrations.

13. It is understood that the North/South Ministerial Council and the Northern Ireland Assembly are mutually inter-dependent, and that one cannot successfully function without the other.

14. Disagreements within the Council to be addressed in the format described at paragraph 3(iii) above or in the plenary format. By agreement between the two sides, experts could be appointed to consider a particular matter and report.

15. Funding to be provided by the two Administrations on the basis that the Council and the implementation bodies constitute a necessary public function.

16. The Council to be supported by a standing joint Secretariat, staffed by members of the Northern Ireland Civil Service and the Irish Civil Service.

17. The Council to consider the European Union dimension of relevant matters, including the implementation of EU policies and programmes and proposals under consideration in the EU framework. Arrangements to be made to ensure that the views of the Council are taken into account and represented appropriately at relevant EU meetings.

18. The Northern Ireland Assembly and the Oireachtas to consider developing a joint parliamentary forum, bringing together equal numbers from both institutions for discussion of matters of mutual interest and concern.

19. Consideration to be given to the establishment of an independent consultative forum appointed by the two Administrations, representative of civil society, comprising the social partners and other members with expertise in social, cultural, economic and other issues.

Areas for North–South Co-operation and Implementation may include the following:

1. Agriculture – animal and plant health.
2. Education – teacher qualifications and exchanges.
3. Transport – strategic transport planning.
4. Environment – environmental protection, pollution, water quality, and waste management.
5. Waterways – inland waterways.
6. Social Security/Social Welfare – entitlements of cross-border workers and fraud control.
7. Tourism – promotion, marketing, research, and product development.
8. Relevant EU Programmes such as SPPR, INTERREG, Leader II and their successors.
9. Inland Fisheries.
10. Aquaculture and marine matters
11. Health: accident and emergency services and other related cross-border issues.
12. Urban and rural development.

Others to be considered by the shadow North/South Council.

5. STRAND THREE

British–Irish Council

1. A British–Irish Council (BIC) will be established under a new British–Irish Agreement to promote the harmonious and mutually beneficial development of the totality of relationships among the peoples of these islands.
2. Membership of the BIC will comprise representatives of the British and Irish Governments, devolved institutions in Northern Ireland, Scotland and Wales, when established, and, if appropriate, elsewhere in the United Kingdom, together with representatives of the Isle of Man and the Channel Islands.
3. The BIC will meet in different formats: at summit level, twice per year; in specific sectoral formats on a regular basis, with each side represented by the appropriate Minister; in an appropriate format to consider cross-sectoral matters.
4. Representatives of members will operate in accordance with whatever procedures for democratic authority and accountability are in force in their respective elected institutions.
5. The BIC will exchange information, discuss, consult and use best endeavours to reach agreement on co-operation on matters of mutual interest within the competence of the relevant Administrations. Suitable issues for early discussion in the BIC could include transport links, agricultural issues, environmental issues, cultural issues, health issues, education issues and approaches to EU issues. Suitable arrangements to be made for practical co-operation on agreed policies.
6. It will be open to the BIC to agree common policies or common actions. Individual members may opt not to participate in such common policies and common action.
7. The BIC normally will operate by consensus. In relation to decisions on common policies or common actions, including their means of implementation, it will operate by agreement of all members participating in such policies or actions.
8. The members of the BIC, on a basis to be agreed between them, will provide such financial support as it may require.

9. A secretariat for the BIC will be provided by the British and Irish Governments in co-ordination with officials of each of the other members.
10. In addition to the structures provided for under this agreement, it will be open to two or more members to develop bilateral or multilateral arrangements between them. Such arrangements could include, subject to the agreement of the members concerned, mechanisms to enable consultation, co-operation and joint decision-making on matters of mutual interest; and mechanisms to implement any joint decisions they may reach. These arrangements will not require the prior approval of the BIC as a whole and will operate independently of it.
11. The elected institutions of the members will be encouraged to develop interparliamentary links, perhaps building on the British–Irish Interparliamentary Body.
12. The full membership of the BIC will keep under review the workings of the Council, including a formal published review at an appropriate time after the Agreement comes into effect, and will contribute as appropriate to any review of the overall political agreement arising from the multi-party negotiations.

British–Irish Intergovernmental Conference

1. There will be a new British–Irish Agreement dealing with the totality of relationships. It will establish a standing British–Irish Intergovernmental Conference, which will subsume both the Anglo-Irish Intergovernmental Council and the Intergovernmental Conference established under the 1985 Agreement.
2. The Conference will bring together the British and Irish Governments to promote bilateral co-operation at all levels on all matters of mutual interest within the competence of both Governments.
3. The Conference will meet as required at Summit level (Prime Minister and Taoiseach). Otherwise, Governments will be represented by appropriate Ministers. Advisers, including police and security advisers, will attend as appropriate.
4. All decisions will be by agreement between both Governments. The Governments will make determined efforts to resolve disagreements between them. There will be no derogation from the sovereignty of either Government.
5. In recognition of the Irish Government's special interest in Northern Ireland and of the extent to which issues of mutual concern arise in relation to Northern Ireland, there will be regular and frequent meetings of the Conference concerned with non-devolved Northern Ireland matters, on which the Irish Government may put forward views and proposals. These meetings, to be co-chaired by the Minister for Foreign Affairs and the Secretary of State for Northern Ireland, would also deal with all-island and cross-border co-operation on non-devolved issues.
6. Co-operation within the framework of the Conference will include facilitation of co-operation in security matters. The Conference also will address, in particular, the areas of rights, justice, prisons and policing in Northern Ireland (unless and until responsibility is devolved to a Northern Ireland administration) and will intensify co-operation between the two Governments on the all-island or cross-border aspects of these matters.
7. Relevant executive members of the Northern Ireland Administration will be involved in meetings of the Conference, and in the reviews referred to in paragraph 9 below to discuss non-devolved Northern Ireland matters.
8. The Conference will be supported by officials of the British and Irish Governments, including by a standing joint Secretariat of officials dealing with non-devolved Northern Ireland matters.

9. The Conference will keep under review the workings of the new British–Irish Agreement and the machinery and institutions established under it, including a formal published review three years after the Agreement comes into effect. Representatives of the Northern Ireland Administration will be invited to express views to the Conference in this context. The Conference will contribute as appropriate to any review of the overall political agreement arising from the multi-party negotiations but will have no power to override the democratic arrangements set up by this Agreement.

6. RIGHTS, SAFEGUARDS AND EQUALITY OF OPPORTUNITY
Human Rights

1. The parties affirm their commitment to the mutual respect, the civil rights and the religious liberties of everyone in the community. Against the background of the recent history of communal conflict, the parties affirm in particular:
   - the right of free political thought;
   - the right to freedom and expression of religion;
   - the right to pursue democratically national and political aspirations;
   - the right to seek constitutional change by peaceful and legitimate means;
   - the right to freely choose one's place of residence;
   - the right to equal opportunity in all social and economic activity, regardless of class, creed, disability, gender or ethnicity;
   - the right to freedom from sectarian harassment; and
   - the right of women to full and equal political participation.

United Kingdom Legislation

2. The British Government will complete incorporation into Northern Ireland law of the European Convention on Human Rights (ECHR), with direct access to the courts, and remedies for breach of the Convention, including power for the courts to overrule Assembly legislation on grounds of inconsistency.

3. Subject to the outcome of public consultation underway, the British Government intends, as a particular priority, to create a statutory obligation on public authorities in Northern Ireland to carry out all their functions with due regard to the need to promote equality of opportunity in relation to religion and political opinion; gender; race; disability; age; marital status; dependants; and sexual orientation. Public bodies would be required to draw up statutory schemes showing how they would implement this obligation. Such schemes would cover arrangements for policy appraisal, including an assessment of impact on relevant categories, public consultation, public access to information and services, monitoring and timetables.

4. The new Northern Ireland Human Rights Commission (see paragraph 5 below) will be invited to consult and to advise on the scope for defining, in Westminster legislation, rights supplementary to those in the European Convention on Human Rights, to reflect the particular circumstances of Northern Ireland, drawing as appropriate on international instruments and experience. These additional rights to reflect the principles of mutual respect for the identity and ethos of both communities and parity of esteem, and – taken together with the ECHR – to constitute a Bill of Rights for Northern Ireland. Among the issues for consideration by the Commission will be:
   - the formulation of a general obligation on government and public bodies fully to respect, on the basis of equality of treatment, the identity and ethos of both communities in Northern Ireland; and

- a clear formulation of the rights not to be discriminated against and to equality of opportunity in both the public and private sectors.

New Institutions in Northern Ireland

5. A new Northern Ireland Human Rights Commission, with membership from Northern Ireland reflecting the community balance, will be established by Westminster legislation, independent of Government, with an extended and enhanced role beyond that currently exercised by the Standing Advisory Commission on Human Rights, to include keeping under review the adequacy and effectiveness of laws and practices, making recommendations to Government as necessary; providing information and promoting awareness of human rights; considering draft legislation referred to them by the new Assembly; and, in appropriate cases, bringing court proceedings or providing assistance to individuals doing so.

6. Subject to the outcome of public consultation currently underway, the British Government intends a new statutory Equality Commission to replace the Fair Employment Commission, the Equal Opportunities Commission (NI), the Commission for Racial Equality (NI) and the Disability Council. Such a unified Commission will advise on, validate and monitor the statutory obligation and will investigate complaints of default.

7. It would be open to a new Northern Ireland Assembly to consider bringing together its responsibilities for these matters into a dedicated Department of Equality.

8. These improvements will build on existing protections in Westminster legislation in respect of the judiciary, the system of justice and policing.

Comparable Steps by the Irish Government

9. The Irish Government will also take steps to further strengthen the protection of human rights in its jurisdiction. The Government will, taking account of the work of the All-Party Oireachtas Committee on the Constitution and the Report of the Constitution Review Group, bring forward measures to strengthen and underpin the constitutional protection of human rights. These proposals will draw on the European Convention on Human Rights and other international legal instruments in the field of human rights and the question of the incorporation of the ECHR will be further examined in this context. The measures brought forward would ensure at least an equivalent level of protection of human rights as will pertain in Northern Ireland. In addition, the Irish Government will:

- establish a Human Rights Commission with a mandate and remit equivalent to that within Northern Ireland;
- proceed with arrangements as quickly as possible to ratify the Council of Europe Framework Convention on National Minorities (already ratified by the UK);
- implement enhanced employment equality legislation;
- introduce equal status legislation; and
- continue to take further active steps to demonstrate its respect for the different traditions in the island of Ireland.

A Joint Committee

10. It is envisaged that there would be a joint committee of representatives of the two Human Rights Commissions, North and South, as a forum for consideration of human rights issues in the island of Ireland. The joint committee will consider, among other matters, the possibility of establishing a charter, open to signature by all democratic political parties, reflecting and endorsing agreed measures for the protection of the fundamental rights of everyone living in the island of Ireland.

Reconciliation and Victims of Violence

11. The participants believe that it is essential to acknowledge and address the suffering of the victims of violence as a necessary element of reconciliation. They look forward to the results of the work of the Northern Ireland Victims Commission.

12. It is recognised that victims have a right to remember as well as to contribute to a changed society. The achievement of a peaceful and just society would be the true memorial to the victims of violence. The participants particularly recognise that young people from areas affected by the troubles face particular difficulties and will support the development of special community-based initiatives based on international best practice. The provision of services that are supportive and sensitive to the needs of victims will also be a critical element and that support will need to be channelled through both statutory and community-based voluntary organisations facilitating locally-based self-help and support networks. This will require the allocation of sufficient resources, including statutory funding as necessary, to meet the needs of victims and to provide for community-based support programmes.

13. The participants recognise and value the work being done by many organisations to develop reconciliation and mutual understanding and respect between and within communities and traditions, in Northern Ireland and between North and South, and they see such work as having a vital role in consolidating peace and political agreement. Accordingly, they pledge their continuing support to such organisations and will positively examine the case for enhanced financial assistance for the work of reconciliation. An essential aspect of the reconciliation process is the promotion of a culture of tolerance at every level of society, including initiatives to facilitate and encourage integrated education and mixed housing.

Economic, Social and Cultural Issues

1. Pending the devolution of powers to a new Northern Ireland Assembly, the British Government will pursue broad policies for sustained economic growth and stability in Northern Ireland and for promoting social inclusion, including in particular community development and the advancement of women in public life.

2. Subject to the public consultation currently under way, the British Government will make rapid progress with:

(i) a new regional development strategy for Northern Ireland, for consideration in due course by the Assembly, tackling the problems of a divided society and social cohesion in urban, rural and border areas, protecting and enhancing the environment, producing new approaches to transport issues, strengthening the physical infrastructure of the region, developing the advantages and resources of rural areas and rejuvenating major urban centres;

(ii) a new economic development strategy for Northern Ireland, for consideration in due course by the Assembly, which would provide for short and medium term economic planning linked as appropriate to the regional development strategy; and

(iii) measures on employment equality included in the recent White Paper ('Partnership for Equality') and covering the extension and strengthening of anti-discrimination legislation, a review of the national security aspects of the present fair employment legislation at the earliest possible time, a new more focused Targeting Social Need initiative and a range of measures aimed at combating unemployment and progressively eliminating the differential in unemployment rates between the two communities by targeting objective need.

3. All participants recognise the importance of respect, understanding and tolerance in relation to linguistic diversity, including in Northern Ireland, the Irish language, Ulster-Scots and the languages of the various ethnic communities, all of which are part of the cultural wealth of the island of Ireland.

4. In the context of active consideration currently being given to the UK signing the Council of Europe Charter for Regional or Minority Languages, the British Government will in particular in relation to the Irish language, where appropriate and where people so desire it:
   - take resolute action to promote the language;
   - facilitate and encourage the use of the language in speech and writing in public and private life where there is appropriate demand;
   - seek to remove, where possible, restrictions which would discourage or work against the maintenance or development of the language;
   - make provision for liaising with the Irish language community, representing their views to public authorities and investigating complaints;
   - place a statutory duty on the Department of Education to encourage and facilitate Irish medium education in line with current provision for integrated education;
   - explore urgently with the relevant British authorities, and in co-operation with the Irish broadcasting authorities, the scope for achieving more widespread availability of Teilifis na Gaeilige in Northern Ireland;
   - seek more effective ways to encourage and provide financial support for Irish language film and television production in Northern Ireland; and
   - encourage the parties to secure agreement that this commitment will be sustained by a new Assembly in a way which takes account of the desires and sensitivities of the community.

5. All participants acknowledge the sensitivity of the use of symbols and emblems for public purposes, and the need in particular in creating the new institutions to ensure that such symbols and emblems are used in a manner which promotes mutual respect rather than division. Arrangements will be made to monitor this issue and consider what action might be required.

7. DECOMMISSIONING

1. Participants recall their agreement in the Procedural Motion adopted on 24 September 1997 'that the resolution of the decommissioning issue is an indispensable part of the process of negotiation', and also recall the provisions of paragraph 25 of Strand 1 above.

2. They note the progress made by the Independent International Commission on Decommissioning and the Governments in developing schemes which can represent a workable basis for achieving the decommissioning of illegally-held arms in the possession of paramilitary groups.

3. All participants accordingly reaffirm their commitment to the total disarmament of all paramilitary organisations. They also confirm their intention to continue to work constructively and in good faith with the Independent Commission, and to use any influence they may have, to achieve the decommissioning of all paramilitary arms within two years following endorsement in referendums North and South of the agreement and in the context of the implementation of the overall settlement.

4. The Independent Commission will monitor, review and verify progress on decommissioning of illegal arms, and will report to both Governments at regular intervals.

6. Both Governments will take all necessary steps to facilitate the decommissioning process to include bringing the relevant schemes into force by the end of June.

8. SECURITY

1. The participants note that the development of a peaceful environment on the basis of this agreement can and should mean a normalisation of security arrangements and practices.

2. The British Government will make progress towards the objective of as early a return as possible to normal security arrangements in Northern Ireland, consistent with the level of threat and with a published overall strategy, dealing with:
   (i) the reduction of the numbers and role of the Armed Forces deployed in Northern Ireland to levels compatible with a normal peaceful society;
   (ii) the removal of security installations;
   (iii) the removal of emergency powers in Northern Ireland; and
   (iv) other measures appropriate to and compatible with a normal peaceful society.

3. The Secretary of State will consult regularly on progress, and the response to any continuing paramilitary activity, with the Irish Government and the political parties, as appropriate.

4. The British Government will continue its consultation on firearms regulation and control on the basis of the document published on 2 April 1998.

5. The Irish Government will initiate a wide-ranging review of the Offences Against the State Acts 1939-85 with a view to both reform and dispensing with those elements no longer required as circumstances permit.

9. POLICING AND JUSTICE

1. The participants recognise that policing is a central issue in any society. They equally recognise that Northern Ireland's history of deep divisions has made it highly emotive, with great hurt suffered and sacrifices made by many individuals and their families, including those in the RUC and other public servants. They believe that the agreement provides the opportunity for a new beginning to policing in Northern Ireland with a police service capable of attracting and sustaining support from the community as a whole. They also believe that this agreement offers a unique opportunity to bring about a new political dispensation which will recognise the full and equal legitimacy and worth of the identities, senses of allegiance and ethos of all sections of the community in Northern Ireland. They consider that this opportunity should inform and underpin the development of a police service representative in terms of the make-up of the community as a whole and which, in a peaceful environment, should be routinely unarmed.

2. The participants believe it essential that policing structures and arrangements are such that the police service is professional, effective and efficient, fair and impartial, free from partisan political control; accountable, both under the law for its actions and to the community it serves; representative of the society it polices, and operates within a coherent and co-operative criminal justice system, which conforms with human rights norms. The participants also believe that those structures and arrangements must be capable of maintaining law and order including responding effectively to crime and to any terrorist threat and to public order problems. A police service which cannot do so will fail to win public confidence and acceptance. They believe that any such structures and arrangements should be capable of delivering a policing service, in constructive and inclusive partnerships with the community at

all levels, and with the maximum delegation of authority and responsibility, consistent with the foregoing principles. These arrangements should be based on principles of protection of human rights and professional integrity and should be unambiguously accepted and actively supported by the entire community.

3. An independent Commission will be established to make recommendations for future policing arrangements in Northern Ireland including means of encouraging widespread community support for these arrangements within the agreed framework of principles reflected in the paragraphs above and in accordance with the terms of reference at Annex A. The Commission will be broadly representative with expert and international representation among its membership and will be asked to consult widely and to report no later than Summer 1999.

4. The participants believe that the aims of the criminal justice system are to:
   - deliver a fair and impartial system of justice to the community;
   - be responsive to the community's concerns, and encouraging community involvement where appropriate;
   - have the confidence of all parts of the community; and
   - deliver justice efficiently and effectively.

5. There will be a parallel wide-ranging review of criminal justice (other than policing and those aspects of the system relating to the emergency legislation) to be carried out by the British Government through a mechanism with an independent element, in consultation with the political parties and others. The review will commence as soon as possible, will include wide consultation, and a report will be made to the Secretary of State no later than Autumn 1999. Terms of Reference are attached at Annex B.

6. Implementation of the recommendations arising from both reviews will be discussed with the political parties and with the Irish Government.

7. The participants also note that the British Government remains ready in principle, with the broad support of the political parties, and after consultation, as appropriate, with the Irish Government, in the context of ongoing implementation of the relevant recommendations, to devolve responsibility for policing and justice issues.

ANNEX A

Commission on Policing for Northern Ireland

TERMS OF REFERENCE

Taking account of the principles on policing as set out in the agreement, the Commission will inquire into policing in Northern Ireland and, on the basis of its findings, bring forward proposals for future policing structures and arrangements, including means of encouraging widespread community support for those arrangements.

Its proposals on policing should be designed to ensure that policing arrangements, including composition, recruitment, training, culture, ethos and symbols, are such that in a new approach Northern Ireland has a police service that can enjoy widespread support from, and is seen as an integral part of, the community as a whole.

Its proposals should include recommendations covering any issues such as retraining, job placement and educational and professional development required in the transition to policing in a peaceful society.

Its proposals should also be designed to ensure that:
- the police service is structured, managed and resourced so that it can be effective in discharging its full range of functions (including proposals on any necessary arrangements for the transition to policing in a normal peaceful society);
- the police service is delivered in constructive and inclusive partnerships with the community at all levels with the maximum delegation of authority and responsibility;
- the legislative and constitutional framework requires the impartial discharge of policing functions and conforms with internationally accepted norms in relation to policing standards;
- the police operate within a clear framework of accountability to the law and the community they serve, so:
  * they are constrained by, accountable to and act only within the law;
  * their powers and procedures, like the law they enforce, are clearly established and publicly available;
  * there are open, accessible and independent means of investigating and adjudicating upon complaints against the police;
  * there are clearly established arrangements enabling local people, and their political representatives, to articulate their views and concerns about policing and to establish publicly policing priorities and influence policing policies, subject to safeguards to ensure police impartiality and freedom from partisan political control;
  * there are arrangements for accountability and for the effective, efficient and economic use of resources in achieving policing objectives;
  * there are means to ensure independent professional scrutiny and inspection of the police service to ensure that proper professional standards are maintained;
- the scope for structured co-operation with the Garda Siochana and other police forces is addressed; and
- the management of public order events which can impose exceptional demands on policing resources is also addressed.

The Commission should focus on policing issues, but if it identifies other aspects of the criminal justice system relevant to its work on policing, including the role of the police in prosecution, then it should draw the attention of the Government to those matters.

The Commission should consult widely, including with non-governmental expert organisations, and through such focus groups as they consider it appropriate to establish.

The Government proposes to establish the Commission as soon as possible, with the aim of it starting work as soon as possible and publishing its final report by Summer 1999.

ANNEX B

Review of the Criminal Justice System

TERMS OF REFERENCE

Taking account of the aims of the criminal justice system as set out in the Agreement, the review will address the structure, management and resourcing of publicly funded elements of the criminal justice system and will bring forward proposals for future criminal justice arrangements (other than policing and those aspects of the system relating to emergency legislation, which the Government is considering separately) covering such issues as:

- the arrangements for making appointments to the judiciary and magistracy, and safeguards for protecting their independence;
- the arrangements for the organisation and supervision of the prosecution process, and for safeguarding its independence;
- measures to improve the responsiveness and accountability of, and any lay participation in the criminal justice system;
- mechanisms for addressing law reform;
- the scope for structured co-operation between the criminal justice agencies on both parts of the island; and
- the structure and organisation of criminal justice functions that might be devolved to an Assembly, including the possibility of establishing a Department of Justice, while safeguarding the essential independence of many of the key functions in this area.

The Government proposes to commence the review as soon as possible, consulting with the political parties and others, including non-governmental expert organisations. The review will be completed by Autumn 1999.

10. PRISONERS

1. Both Governments will put in place mechanisms to provide for an accelerated programme for the release of prisoners, including transferred prisoners, convicted of scheduled offences in Northern Ireland or, in the case of those sentenced outside Northern Ireland, similar offences (referred to hereafter as qualifying prisoners). Any such arrangements will protect the rights of individual prisoners under national and international law.
2. Prisoners affiliated to organisations which have not established or are not maintaining a complete and unequivocal ceasefire will not benefit from the arrangements. The situation in this regard will be kept under review.
3. Both Governments will complete a review process within a fixed time frame and set prospective release dates for all qualifying prisoners. The review process would provide for the advance of the release dates of qualifying prisoners while allowing account to be taken of the seriousness of the offences for which the person was convicted and the need to protect the community. In addition, the intention would be that should the circumstances allow it, any qualifying prisoners who remained in custody two years after the commencement of the scheme would be released at that point.
4. The Governments will seek to enact the appropriate legislation to give effect to these arrangements by the end of June 1998.
5. The Governments continue to recognise the importance of measures to facilitate the reintegration of prisoners into the community by providing support both prior to and after release, including assistance directed towards availing of employment opportunities, re-training and/or re-skilling, and further education.

11. VALIDATION, IMPLEMENTATION AND REVIEW

Validation and Implementation

1. The two Governments will as soon as possible sign a new British–Irish Agreement replacing the 1985 Anglo-Irish Agreement, embodying understandings on constitutional issues and affirming their solemn commitment to support and, where appropriate, implement the agreement reached by the participants in the negotiations which shall be annexed to the British–Irish Agreement.
2. Each Government will organise a referendum on 22 May 1998. Subject to Parliamentary approval, a consultative referendum in Northern Ireland, organised under

the terms of the Northern Ireland (Entry to Negotiations, etc.) Act 1996, will address the question: 'Do you support the agreement reached in the multi-party talks on Northern Ireland and set out in Command Paper 3883?'. The Irish Government will introduce and support in the Oireachtas a Bill to amend the Constitution as described in paragraph 2 of the section 'Constitutional Issues' and in Annex B, as follows: (a) to amend Articles 2 and 3 as described in paragraph 8.1 in Annex B above and (b) to amend Article 29 to permit the Government to ratify the new British–Irish Agreement. On passage by the Oireachtas, the Bill will be put to referendum.

3.   If majorities of those voting in each of the referendums support this agreement, the Governments will then introduce and support, in their respective Parliaments, such legislation as may be necessary to give effect to all aspects of this agreement, and will take whatever ancillary steps as may be required including the holding of elections on 25 June, subject to parliamentary approval, to the Assembly, which would meet initially in a 'shadow' mode. The establishment of the North–South Ministerial Council, implementation bodies, the British–Irish Council and the British–Irish Intergovernmental Conference and the assumption by the Assembly of its legislative and executive powers will take place at the same time on the entry into force of the British–Irish Agreement.

4.   In the interim, aspects of the implementation of the multi-party agreement will be reviewed at meetings of those parties relevant in the particular case (taking into account, once Assembly elections have been held, the results of those elections), under the chairmanship of the British Government or the two Governments, as may be appropriate; and representatives of the two Governments and all relevant parties may meet under independent chairmanship to review implementation of the agreement as a whole.

Review Procedures following Implementation

5.   Each institution may, at any time, review any problems that may arise in its operation and, where no other institution is affected, take remedial action in consultation as necessary with the relevant Government or Governments. It will be for each institution to determine its own procedures for review.

6.   If there are difficulties in the operation of a particular institution, which have implications for another institution, they may review their operations separately and jointly and agree on remedial action to be taken under their respective authorities.

7.   If difficulties arise which require remedial action across the range of institutions, or otherwise require amendment of the British–Irish Agreement or relevant legislation, the process of review will fall to the two Governments in consultation with the parties in the Assembly. Each Government will be responsible for action in its own jurisdiction.

8.   Notwithstanding the above, each institution will publish an annual report on its operations. In addition, the two Governments and the parties in the Assembly will convene a conference 4 years after the agreement comes into effect, to review and report on its operation.

AGREEMENT BETWEEN THE GOVERNMENT OF
THE UNITED KINGDOM OF GREAT BRITAIN
AND NORTHERN IRELAND
AND THE GOVERNMENT OF IRELAND

The British and Irish Governments:

Welcoming the strong commitment to the Agreement reached on 10th April 1998 by themselves and other participants in the multi-party talks and set out in Annex 1 to this Agreement (hereinafter 'the Multi-Party Agreement');

Considering that the Multi-Party Agreement offers an opportunity for a new beginning in relationships within Northern Ireland, within the island of Ireland and between the peoples of these islands;

Wishing to develop still further the unique relationship between their peoples and the close co-operation between their countries as friendly neighbours and as partners in the European Union;

Reaffirming their total commitment to the principles of democracy and non-violence which have been fundamental to the multi-party talks;

Reaffirming their commitment to the principles of partnership, equality and mutual respect and to the protection of civil, political, social, economic and cultural rights in their respective jurisdictions;

Have agreed as follows:

ARTICLE 1

The two Governments:

(i) recognise the legitimacy of whatever choice is freely exercised by a majority of the people of Northern Ireland with regard to its status, whether they prefer to continue to support the Union with Great Britain or a sovereign united Ireland;

(ii) recognise that it is for the people of the island of Ireland alone, by agreement between the two parts respectively and without external impediment, to exercise their right of self-determination on the basis of consent, freely and concurrently given, North and South, to bring about a united Ireland, if that is their wish, accepting that this right must be achieved and exercised with and subject to the agreement and consent of a majority of the people of Northern Ireland;

(iii) acknowledge that while a substantial section of the people in Northern Ireland share the legitimate wish of a majority of the people of the island of Ireland for a united Ireland, the present wish of a majority of the people of Northern Ireland, freely exercised and legitimate, is to maintain the Union and accordingly, that Northern Ireland's status as part of the United Kingdom reflects and relies upon that wish; and that it would be wrong to make any change in the status of Northern Ireland save with the consent of a majority of its people;

(iv) affirm that, if in the future, the people of the island of Ireland exercise their right of self-determination on the basis set out in sections (i) and (ii) above to bring about a united Ireland, it will be a binding obligation on both Governments to introduce and support in their respective Parliaments legislation to give effect to that wish;

(v) affirm that whatever choice is freely exercised by a majority of the people of Northern Ireland, the power of the sovereign government with jurisdiction there shall be exercised with rigorous impartiality on behalf of all the people in the diversity of their identities and traditions and shall be founded on the principles of full respect for, and equality of, civil, political, social and cultural rights, of freedom from discrimination for all citizens, and of parity of esteem and of just and equal treatment for the identity, ethos and aspirations of both communities;

(vi) recognise the birthright of all the people of Northern Ireland to identify themselves and be accepted as Irish or British, or both, as they may so choose, and accordingly confirm that their right to hold both British and Irish citizenship is accepted by both Governments and would not be affected by any future change in the status of Northern Ireland.

ARTICLE 2

The two Governments affirm their solemn commitment to support, and where appropriate implement, the provisions of the Multi-Party Agreement. In particular there shall be established in accordance with the provisions of the Multi-Party Agreement immediately on the entry into force of this Agreement, the following institutions:

(i) a North/South Ministerial Council;

(ii) the implementation bodies referred to in paragraph 9 (ii) of the section entitled 'Strand Two' of the Multi-Party Agreement;

(iii) a British–Irish Council;

(iv) a British–Irish Intergovernmental Conference.

ARTICLE 3

(1) This Agreement shall replace the Agreement between the British and Irish Governments done at Hillsborough on 15th November 1985 which shall cease to have effect on entry into force of this Agreement.

(2) The Intergovernmental Conference established by Article 2 of the aforementioned Agreement done on 15th November 1985 shall cease to exist on entry into force of this Agreement.

ARTICLE 4

(1) It shall be a requirement for entry into force of this Agreement that:

(a) British legislation shall have been enacted for the purpose of implementing the provisions of Annex A to the section entitled 'Constitutional Issues' of the Multi-Party Agreement;

(b) the amendments to the Constitution of Ireland set out in Annex B to the section entitled 'Constitutional Issues' of the Multi-Party Agreement shall have been approved by Referendum;

(c) such legislation shall have been enacted as may be required to establish the institutions referred to in Article 2 of this Agreement.

(2) Each Government shall notify the other in writing of the completion, so far as it is concerned, of the requirements for entry into force of this Agreement. This Agreement shall enter into force on the date of the receipt of the later of the two notifications.

(3) Immediately on entry into force of this Agreement, the Irish Government shall ensure that the amendments to the Constitution of Ireland set out in Annex B to the section entitled 'Constitutional Issues' of the Multi-Party Agreement take effect.

In witness thereof the undersigned, being duly authorised thereto by the respective Governments, have signed this Agreement.

Done in two originals at Belfast on the 10th day of April 1998.

For the Government
of the United Kingdom of
Great Britain and Northern Ireland
For the Government
of Ireland

ANNEX 1

The Agreement Reached
in the Multi-Party Talks

ANNEX 2

Declaration on the Provisions of
Paragraph (vi) of Article 1
In Relationship to Citizenship

The British and Irish Governments declare that it is their joint understanding that the term 'the people of Northern Ireland' in paragraph (vi) of Article 1 of this Agreement means, for the purposes of giving effect to this provision, all persons born in Northern Ireland and having, at the time of their birth, at least one parent who is a British citizen, an Irish citizen or is otherwise entitled to reside in Northern Ireland without any restriction on their period of residence.

'Towards a Lasting Peace', Sinn Féin Document, 1992

(extract)

ARMED STRUGGLE

Armed struggle has, throughout history and in all parts of the globe, been seen as a legitimate component of peoples' resistance to foreign oppression. In Ireland, it was armed struggle which created the conditions for the removal of British jurisdiction over the 26 Counties and the emergence of a separate (if truncated) Irish state.

However, armed struggle is recognised by republicans to be an option of last resort when all other avenues to pursue freedom have been attempted and suppressed.

It must be recognised that there has been no consistent constitutional strategy to pursue a national democracy in Ireland. Certainly, there has been no consistent and principled strategy advanced during the last 20 years of continuous conflict.

Objective evaluations of the armed struggle, including those of the British government, recognise that its history to date indicates that it is likely to be sustained for the foreseeable future.

In these circumstances there is an onus on those who proclaim that the armed struggle is counter-productive to advance a credible alternative. Such an alternative would be welcomed across the island but nowhere more than in the oppressed nationalist areas of the Six Counties which have borne the brunt of British rule since partition and particularly for over 20 years past. The development of such an alternative would be welcomed by Sinn Féin.

APPENDIX 4

Joint Declaration on Peace (Downing Street Declaration), 15 December 1993

1. The Taoiseach, Mr. Albert Reynolds, TD and the Prime Minister, the Rt. Hon. John Major MP, acknowledge that the most urgent and important issue facing the people of Ireland, North and South, and the British and Irish Governments together, is to remove the conflict, to overcome the legacy of history and to heal the divisions which have resulted, recognising the absence of a lasting and satisfactory settlement of relationships between the peoples of both islands has contributed to continuing tragedy and suffering. They believe that the development of an agreed framework for peace, which has been discussed between them since early last year, and which is based on a number of key principles articulated by the two Governments over the past 20 years, together with adaptation of other widely accepted principles, provides the starting point of a peace process designed to culminate in a political settlement.

2. The Taoiseach and the Prime Minister are convinced of the inestimable value to both their peoples, and particularly for the next generation, of healing divisions in Ireland and of ending a conflict which has been so manifestly to the detriment of all. Both recognise that the ending of divisions can come about only through the agreement and co-operation of the people, North and South, representing both traditions in Ireland. They therefore make a solemn commitment to promote co-operation at all levels on the basis of the fundamental principles, undertakings, obligations under international agreements, to which they have jointly committed themselves, and the guarantees which each Government has given and now reaffirms, including Northern Ireland's statutory constitutional guarantee. It is their aim to foster agreement and reconciliation, leading to a new political framework founded on consent and encompassing arrangements within Northern Ireland, for the whole island, and between these islands.

3. They also consider that the development of Europe will, of itself, require new approaches to serve interests common to both parts of the island of Ireland, and to Ireland and the United Kingdom as partners in the European Union.

4. The Prime Minister, on behalf of the British Government, reaffirms that they will uphold the democratic wish of the greater number of the people of Northern Ireland on the issue of whether they prefer to support the Union or a sovereign united Ireland. On this basis, he reiterates, on the behalf of the British Government, that they have no selfish strategic or economic interest in Northern Ireland. Their primary interest is to see peace, stability and reconciliation established by agreement among all the people inhabit the island, and they will work together with the Irish Government to achieve such an agreement, which will embrace the totality of relationships. The role of the British Government will be to encourage, facilitate and enable the achievement of such agreement over a period through a process of dialogue and co-operation based on full respect for the rights and identities of both traditions in Ireland. They accept that such agreement may, as of right, take the form of agreed structures for the island as a whole, including a united Ireland achieved by peaceful means on the following basis. The British Government agree that it is for the people of the island of Ireland alone, by agreement between the two parts respectively, to exercise their right of self-determination on the basis of consent, freely and concurrently given, North and South, to bring about a united Ireland, if that is their wish. They reaffirm as a binding obligation that they will, for their part, introduce the necessary legislation to give effect to this, or equally to any measure of agreement on future relationships in Ireland which the people living in Ireland may themselves freely so determine without external impediment. They believe that the people of Britain would wish, in friendship to all sides, to enable the people of Ireland to reach agreement on how they may live together in harmony and in partnership, with respect for their diverse traditions, and with full recognition of the special links and the unique relationship which exist between the peoples of Britain and Ireland. The Taoiseach, on behalf of the Irish Government, considers that the lessons of Irish history, and especially of Northern Ireland, show that stability and well-being will not be found under any political system which is refused allegiance or rejected on grounds of identity by a significant minority of those governed by it. For this reason, it would be wrong to attempt to impose a united Ireland, in the absence of the freely given consent of the majority of the people of Northern Ireland. He accepts, on behalf of the Irish Government, that the democratic right of self-determination by the people of Ireland as a whole must be achieved and exercised with and subject to the agreement and consent of a majority of the people of Northern Ireland and must, consistent with justice and equity, respect the democratic dignity and the civil rights and religious liberties of both communities, including: – the right of free political thought; – the right of freedom and expression of religion; – the right to pursue democratically national and political aspirations; – the right to seek constitutional change by peaceful and legitimate means; – the right to live wherever one chooses without hindrance; – the right to equal opportunity in all social and economic activity, regardless of class, creed, sex or colour. These would be reflected in any future political and constitutional arrangements emerging from a new and more broadly based agreement.

5. The Taoiseach however recognises the genuine difficulties and barriers to building relationships of trust either within or beyond Northern Ireland, from which both traditions suffer. He will work to create a new era of trust, in which suspicion of the motives and actions of others is removed on the part of either community. He considers that the future of the island depends on the nature of the relationship

between the two main traditions that inhabit it. Every effort must be made to build a new series of trust between those communities. In recognition of the fears of the Unionist community and as a token of his willingness to make a political contribution to the building up of that necessary trust, the Taoiseach will examine with his colleagues any elements in the democratic life and organisation of the Irish State that can be represented to the Irish Government in the course of political dialogue as a real and substantial threat to their way of life and ethos, or that can be represented as not being fully consistent with a modern democratic and pluralist society, and undertakes to examine any possible ways of removing such obstacles. Such an examination would of course have due regard to the desire to preserve those inherited values that are largely shared throughout the island or that belong to the cultural and historical roots of the people of this island in all their diversity. The Taoiseach hopes that over time a meeting of hearts and minds will develop, which will bring all the people of Ireland together, and will work towards that objective, but he pledges in the meantime that as a result of the efforts that will be made to build mutual confidence no Northern Unionist should ever have a fear in future that this ideal will be pursued either by threat or coercion.

6. Both Governments accept that Irish unity would be achieved only by those who favour this outcome persuading those who do not, peacefully and without coercion or violence, and that, if in the future a majority of the people of Northern Ireland are so persuaded, both Governments will support and give legislative effect to their wish. But, notwithstanding the solemn affirmation by both Governments in the Anglo-Irish Agreement that any change in the status of Northern Ireland, would only come about with a consent of the majority of the people of Northern Ireland, the Taoiseach also recognises the continuing uncertainties and misgivings which dominate so much of Northern Unionist attitudes towards the rest of Ireland. He believes that we stand at a stage of our history when the genuine feelings of all traditions in the North must be recognised and acknowledged. He appeals to both traditions at this time to grasp the opportunity for a fresh start and a new beginning, which could hold such promise for all our lives and the generations to come. He asks the people of Northern Ireland to look on the people of the Republic as friends, who share their grief and shame over all the suffering of the last quarter of a century, and who wants to develop the best possible relationship with them, a relationship in which trust and new understanding can flourish and grow. The Taoiseach also acknowledges the presence in the *Constitution of the Republic* of elements which are deeply resented by Northern Unionists, but which at the same time reflect hopes and ideals which lie deep in the hearts of many Irish men and women North and South. But as we move towards a new era of understanding in which new relationships of trust may grow and bring peace to the island of Ireland, the Taoiseach believes that the time has come to consider together how best the hopes and identities of all can be expressed in more balanced ways, which no longer engender division and the lack of trust to which he has referred. He confirms that, in the event of an overall settlement, the Irish Government will, as part of a balanced constitutional accommodation, put forward and support proposals for change in the *Irish Constitution* which would fully reflect the principle of consent in Northern Ireland.

7. The Taoiseach recognises the need to engage in dialogue which would address the honesty and integrity the fears of all traditions. But that dialogue, both within the North and between the people and their representatives of both parts of Ireland, must be entered into with an acknowledgment that the future security and welfare

of the people of the island will depend on an open, frank and balanced approach to all the problems which for too long have caused division.

8. The British and Irish Governments will seek, along with the Northern Ireland constitutional parties through a process of political dialogue, to create institutions and structures which, while respecting the diversity of the people of Ireland, would enable them to work together in all areas of common interest. This will help over a period to build the trust necessary to end past divisions, leading to an agreed and peaceful future. Such structures would, of course, include institutional recognition of the special links that exist between the peoples of Britain and Ireland as part of the totality of relationships, while taking account of newly forged links with the rest of Europe.

9. The British and Irish Governments reiterate that the achievement of peace must involve a permanent end to the use of, or support for, paramilitary violence. They confirm that, in these circumstances, democratically mandated parties which establish a commitment to exclusively peaceful methods and which have shown that they abide by the democratic process, are free to participate fully in democratic politics and to join in dialogue in due course between the Governments and the political parties on the way ahead.

10. The Irish Government would make their own arrangements within their jurisdiction to enable democratic parties to consult together and share in dialogue about the political future. The Taoiseach's intention is that these arrangements could include the establishment, in consultation with other parties, of a Forum for Peace and Reconciliation to make recommendations on ways in which agreement and trust between both traditions can be promoted and established.

11. The Taoiseach and the Prime Minister are determined to build on the fervent wish of both their peoples to see old fears and anomalies replaced by a climate of peace. They believe the framework they have set out offers the people of Ireland, North and South, whatever their tradition, the basis to agree that from now on their differences can be negotiated and resolved exclusively by peaceful political means. They appeal to all concerned to grasp the opportunity for a new departure. That step would compromise no position or principle, nor prejudice the future of either community. On the contrary, it would be an incomparable gain for all. It would break decisively the cycle of violence and the intolerable suffering it entails for the people of these islands, particularly for both communities in Northern Ireland. It would allow the process of economic and social co-operation on the island to realise its full potential for prosperity and mutual understanding. It would transform the prospects for building on the progress already made in the Talks process, involving the two Governments and the constitutional parties in Northern Ireland. The Taoiseach and the Prime Minister believe that these arrangements offer an opportunity to lay the foundation for a more peaceful and harmonious future, devoid of the violence and bitter divisions which have scarred the past generation. They commit themselves and their Governments to continue to work together, unremittingly, towards that objective.

APPENDIX 5

A personal message from Rt Hon. Sir Patrick Mayhew, December 1993

A PERSONAL MESSAGE FROM
RT HON SIR PATRICK MAYHEW, QC, MP
Secretary of State for Northern Ireland

The Prime Minister and the Taoiseach made a Joint Declaration on 15 December. Because of the importance of its message, I have tried to make it as widely available as possible, through this booklet. I am also taking this opportunity to set out some of the key features of the Declaration.

The Declaration, which complements and underpins the Talks process and the search for a comprehensive political settlement, has been made following discussions between the two Governments, since early last year, on a framework for peace. It challenges those who use or support violence to stop now.

The Declaration sets out constitutional principles and political realities which safeguard the vital interests of both sides of the community in Northern Ireland. It reflects the beliefs of both Governments, but compromises the principles of neither. It makes no prejudgements.

The text both reiterates Northern Ireland's statutory constitutional guarantee and reaffirms that the British Government will uphold the democratic wish of a greater number of the people of Northern Ireland, on the issue on whether they prefer to support the Union or a sovereign united Ireland. On this basis the British Government reiterates that they have no selfish strategic or economic interest in Northern Ireland. They agree that it is for the people of the island of Ireland alone, by agreement between the two parts respectively, to exercise their right of self-determination on the basis of consent, freely and concurrently given, North and South, to bring about a united Ireland, if that is their wish.

For their part, the Irish Government accept that it would be wrong to attempt to impose a united Ireland, in the absence of the freely given consent of a majority of the people of Northern Ireland and that the democratic right of self-determination by the people of Ireland as a whole must be achieved and exercised with and subject to the agreement and consent of a majority of Northern Ireland.

In short, the consent of a majority of the people in Northern Ireland is required before any constitutional change could come about.

The Irish Government also confirm that in the event of an overall settlement, they will, as part of a balanced constitutional accommodation, put forward and support proposals for change in the Irish Constitution, which would fully reflect the principle of consent in Northern Ireland.

The Declaration reinforces the firm foundation for future political development, on the same three stranded basis that the main constitutional parties in Northern Ireland and the two Governments have already accepted. Both Governments reiterate that, following a cessation of violence, democratically mandated parties which establish a commitment to exclusively peaceful methods, and which have shown that they abide by the democratic process, are free to participate fully in democratic politics and to join in dialogue in due course between Governments and the political parties on the way ahead.

The Joint Declaration represents a sound platform for the Talks process and a realistic core for lasting peace. It shows the British and Irish Governments working together; for democracy and against violence. As such, I commend it to you.

The TUAS* Document circulated by the republican leadership, summer 1994

The briefing paper of April deals with strategic objectives and events to that date in more detail than this paper. However, a brief summary is helpful. Our goals have not changed. A united 32-county democratic socialist Republic.

The main strategic objectives to move us towards that goal can be summarised thus. To construct an Irish nationalist consensus with international support on the basis of the dynamic contained in the Irish peace initiative. This should aim for:

a   The strongest possible political consensus between the Dublin government, Sinn Féin and the SDLP.
b   A common position on practical measures moving us towards our goal.
c   A common nationalist negotiation position.
d   An international dimension in aid of the consensus (mostly U.S.A. and E.U.).

The strategic objectives come from prolonged debate but are based on a straightforward logic: that republicans at this time and on their own do not have the strength to achieve the end goal. The struggle needs strengthening; most obviously from other nationalist constituencies led by SDLP, Dublin government and the emerging Irish-American lobby, with additional support from other parties in E.U. rowing in behind and accelerating the momentum created.

The aim of any such consensus is to create a dynamic which can:

1   Effect [sic] the domestic and international perception of the republican position, i.e. as one which is reasonable.
2   To develop a northern nationalist consensus on the basis of constitutional change.
3   To develop an Irish national consensus on the same basis.
4   To develop Irish-America as a significant player in support of the above.
5   To develop a broader and deeper Irish nationalist consensus at grassroots level.
6   To develop and mobilise an anti~imperialist Irish peace movement.
7   To expose the British government and the unionists as the intransigent parties.
8   To heighten the contradictions between British unionist and 'Ulster Loyalism'.
9   To assist the development of whatever potential exists in Britain to create a mood/climate/party/movement for peace.

* It is understood this stands for 'Tactical Use of Armed Struggle'

10 To maintain the political cohesion and organisational integrity of Sinn Féin so as to remain an effective political force.

Present British intentions are the subject of much debate and varied opinion. However, what can be said is that sometime preceding the Downing Street Declaration of December '93 a deal was done with the U.U.P. to keep the Conservatives in power. This becomes an obstacle to movement.

The D.S.D. (Downing Street Declaration) does not hold a solution. Republicans are not prepared to wait around for the Brits to change, but as always we are prepared to force their hand. It is nonetheless important to note that there has been no recent dialogue between the Brit government and Republican representatives since November '93. The republican position is that if the Brits want to talk they should do it through normal political channels.

At the end of the April briefing it states: 'Our (strategic) objectives should guide all our actions. Given that these are our guidelines we must now look at what our options are and what initiatives we can undertake.'

After prolonged discussion and assessment the Leadership decided that if it could get agreement with the Dublin government, the SDLP and the Irish-American lobby on basic republican principles which would be enough to create the dynamic that would considerably advance the struggle, then it would be prepared to use the TUAS option.

We attempted to reach such a consensus on a set of principles which can be summarised briefly thus;

1   Partition has failed.
2   Structures must be changed.
3   No internal settlement within 6 counties
4   British rule breaches the principle of N.S.D. [national self-determination].
5   The Irish as a whole have the right to N.S.D. without external impediment.
6   It is up to the Dublin/London governments with all parties to bring about N.S.D. in the shortest time possible.
7   The unionists have no veto over discussions involved or their outcome.
8   A solution requires political and constitutional change.
9   An agreed united and independent Ireland is what republicans desire. However an agreed Ireland needs the allegiance of varied traditions to be viable.

Contact with the other parties involved have been in that context. There are of course differences of opinion on how a number of these principles are interpreted or applied.

In particular: on British rule breaching the principle of N.S.D.; on the absolute right of the Irish to N.S.D. without external impediment; or interpretation of what veto and consent mean; on the issue of timescales.

Nevertheless, differences aside, the leadership believes there is enough in common to create a substantial political momentum which will considerably advance the struggle at this time. Some substantial contribution factors which point towards now being the right time for an initiative are:

•   Hume is the only SDLP person on the horizon strong enough to face the challenge.
•   Dublin's coalition is the strongest government in 25 years or more.
•   Reynolds has no historical baggage to hinder him and knows how popular such a consensus would be among grassroots.
•   There is potentially a very powerful Irish-American lobby not in hock to any particular party in Ireland or Britain.

- Clinton is perhaps the first U.S. President in decades to be substantially influenced by such a lobby.
- At this time the British government is the least popular in the E.U. with other E.U. members.

It is the first time in 25 years that all the major Irish nationalist parties are rowing in roughly the same direction. These combined circumstances are unlikely to gel again in the foreseeable future.

The leadership has now decided that there is enough agreement to proceed with the Tuas option. It has been stated from the outset that this is a risky strategy. Its success will depend greatly on workload. All activists must be pro-active. Those who continue their present work need to double effect. If you find yourself idle help in another field.

Tuas has been part of every other struggle in the world this century. It is vital that activists realise the struggle is not over. Another front has opened up and we should have the confidence and put in the effort to succeed on that front. We have the ability to carry on indefinitely. We should be trying to double the pressure on the British.

For various reasons, which include the sensitivity of discussions up to this point, communication up and down the organisation has been patchy. Since we are now entering a more public aspect to the initiative communication should be a less encumbered matter and therefore more regular than before.

APPENDIX 7

IRA Ceasefire Statement, 31 August 1994

IRISH REPUBLICAN ARMY (IRA) CEASEFIRE STATEMENT
31 August 1994

Recognising the potential of the current situation and in order to enhance the democratic process and underlying our definitive commitment to its success, the leadership of the IRA have decided that as of midnight, August 31, there will be a complete cessation of military operations. All our units have been instructed accordingly.

At this crossroads the leadership of the IRA salutes and commends our volunteers, other activists, our supporters and the political prisoners who have sustained the struggle against all odds for the past 25 years. Your courage, determination and sacrifice have demonstrated that the freedom and the desire for peace based on a just and lasting settlement cannot be crushed. We remember all those who have died for Irish freedom and we reiterate our commitment to our republican objectives. Our struggle has seen many gains and advances made by nationalists and for the democratic position.

We believe that an opportunity to secure a just and lasting settlement has been created. We are therefore entering into a new situation in a spirit of determination and confidence, determined that the injustices which created this conflict will be removed and confident in the strength and justice of our struggle to achieve this.

We note that the Downing Street Declaration is not a solution, nor was it presented as such by its authors. A solution will only be found as a result of inclusive negotiations. Others, not the least the British government have a duty to face up to their responsibilities. It is our desire to significantly contribute to the creation of a climate which will encourage this. We urge everyone to approach this new situation with energy, determination and patience.

APPENDIX 8

Combined Loyalist Military Command (CLMC) Ceasefire Statement, 13 October 1994

After a widespread consultative process initiated by representations from the Ulster Democratic and Progressive Unionist Parties, and after having received confirmation and guarantees in relation to Northern Ireland's constitutional position within the United Kingdom, as well as other assurances, and, in the belief that the democratically expressed wishes of the greater number of people in Northern Ireland will be respected and upheld, the CLMC will universally cease all operational hostilities as from 12 midnight on Thursday 13th October 1994.

The permanence of our ceasefire will be completely dependant upon the continued cessation of all nationalist/republican violence, the sole responsibility for a return to War lies with them.

In the genuine hope that this peace will be permanent, we take the opportunity to pay homage to all our Fighters, Commandos and Volunteers who paid the supreme sacrifice. They did not die in vain. The Union is safe.

To our physically and mentally wounded who have served Ulster so unselfishly, we wish a speedy recovery, and to the relatives of these men and women, we pledge our continued moral and practical support.

To our prisoners who have undergone so much deprivation and degradation with great courage and forbearance, we solemnly promise to leave no stone unturned to secure their freedom.

To our serving officers, NCOs and personnel, we extend our eternal gratitude for their obedience of orders, for their ingenuity, resilience and good humour in the most trying of circumstances, and, we commend them for their courageous fortitude and unshakeable faith over the long years of armed confrontation.

In all sincerity, we offer to the loved ones of all innocent victims over the past twenty years, abject and true remorse. No words of ours will compensate for the intolerable suffering they have undergone during the conflict.

Let us firmly resolve to respect our differing views of freedom, culture and aspiration and never again permit our political circumstances to degenerate into bloody warfare.

We are on the threshold of a new and exciting beginning with our battles in future being political battles, fought on the side of honest, decency and democracy against the negativity of mistrust, misunderstanding and malevolence, so that, together, we can bring forth a wholesome society in which our children, and their children, will know the meaning of true peace.

A New Framework for Agreement 1995

(extract)

A NEW FRAMEWORK FOR AGREEMENT

A shared understanding between
the British and Irish Governments
to assist discussion and negotiation involving
the Northern Ireland parties

North/South Institutions

24. Both Governments consider that new institutions should be created to cater adequately for present and future political, social and economic inter-connections on the island of Ireland, enabling representatives of the main traditions, North and South, to enter agreed dynamic, new, co-operative and constructive relationships.

25. Both Governments agree that these institutions should include a North/South body involving Heads of Department on both sides and duly established and maintained by legislation in both sovereign Parliaments. This body would bring together these Heads of Department representing the Irish Government and new democratic institutions in Northern Ireland, to discharge or oversee delegated executive, harmonising or consultative functions, as appropriate, over a range of matters which the two Governments designate in the first instance in agreement with the parties or which the two administrations, North and South, subsequently agree to designate. It is envisaged that, in determining functions to be discharged or overseen by the North/South body, whether by executive action, harmonisation or consultation, account will be taken of:

(i) the common interest in a given matter on the part of both parts of the island; or
(ii) the mutual advantage of addressing a matter together; or
(iii) the mutual benefit which may derive from it being administered by the North/South body; or
(iv) the achievement of economies of scale and the avoidance of unnecessary duplication of effort.

In relevant posts in each of the two administrations participation in the North/South body would be a duty of service. Both Governments believe that the legislation should provide for a clear institutional identity and purpose for the North/South body. It would also establish the body's terms of reference, legal status and arrangements for political, legal, administrative and financial accountability. The North/South body could operate through, or oversee, a range of functionally-related subsidiary bodies or other entities established to administer designated functions on an all-island or cross-border basis.

26. Specific arrangements would need to be developed to apply to EU matters. Any EU matter relevant to the competence of either administration could be raised for consideration in the North/South body. Across all designated matters and in accordance with the delegated functions, both Governments agree that the body will have an important role, with their support and co-operation and in consultation with them, in developing on a continuing basis an agreed approach for the whole island in respect of the challenges and opportunities of the European Union. In respect of matters designated at the executive level, which would include all EC programmes and initiatives to be implemented on a cross-border or island-wide basis in Ireland, the body itself would be responsible, subject to the Treaty obligations of each Government, for the implementation and management of EC policies and programmes on a joint basis. This would include the preparation, in consultation with the two Governments, of joint submissions under EC programmes and initiatives and their joint monitoring and implementation, although individual projects could be implemented either jointly or separately.

27. Both Governments envisage regular and frequent meetings of the North/South body:
   • to discharge the functions agreed for it in relation to a range of matters designated for treatment on an all-Ireland or cross-border basis;
   • to oversee the work of subsidiary bodies.

28. The two Governments envisage that legislation in the sovereign Parliaments should designate those functions which should, from the outset, be discharged or overseen by the North/South body; and they will seek agreement on these, as on other features of North/South arrangements, in discussion with the relevant political parties in Northern Ireland. It would also be open to the North/South body to recommend to the respective administrations and legislatures for their consideration that new functions should be designated to be discharged or overseen by that body; and to recommend that matters already designated should be moved on the scale between consultation, harmonisation and executive action. Within those responsibilities transferred to new institutions in Northern Ireland, the British Government have no limits of their own to impose on the nature and extent of functions which could be agreed for designation at the outset or, subsequently, between the Irish Government and the Northern Ireland administration. Both Governments expect that significant responsibilities, including meaningful functions at executive level, will be a feature of such agreement. The British Government believe that, in principle, any function devolved to the institutions in Northern Ireland could be so designated, subject to any necessary savings in respect of the British Government's powers and duties, for example to ensure compliance with EU and international obligations. The Irish Government also expect to designate a comparable range of functions.

29. Although both Governments envisage that representatives of North and South in the body could raise for discussion any matter of interest to either side which falls within the competence of either administration, it is envisaged, as already

mentioned, that its designated functions would fall into three broad categories:

consultative: the North/South body would be a forum where the two sides would consult on any aspect of designated matters on which either side wished to hold consultations. Both sides would share a duty to exchange information and to consult about existing and future policy, though there would be no formal requirement that agreement would be reached or that policy would be harmonised or implemented jointly, but the development of mutual understanding or common or agreed positions would be the general goal;

harmonising: in respect of these designated responsibilities there would be, in addition to the duty to exchange information and to consult on the formulation of policy, an obligation on both sides to use their best endeavours to reach agreement on a common policy and to make determined efforts to overcome any obstacles in the way of that objective, even though its implementation might be undertaken by the two administrations separately;

executive: in the case of these designated responsibilities the North/South body would itself be directly responsible for the establishment of an agreed policy and for its implementation on a joint basis. It would however be open to the body, where appropriate, to agree that the implementation of the agreed policy would be undertaken either by existing bodies, acting in an agency capacity, whether jointly or separately, North and South, or by new bodies specifically created and mandated for this purpose.

30. In this light, both Governments are continuing to give consideration to the range of functions that might, with the agreement of the parties, be designated at the outset and accordingly they will be ready to make proposals in that regard in future discussions with the relevant Northern Ireland parties.

31. By way of illustration, it is intended that these proposals would include at the executive level a range of functions, clearly defined in scope, from within the following broad categories:

- sectors involving a natural or physical all-Ireland framework;
- EC programmes and initiatives;
- marketing and promotion activities abroad;
- culture and heritage.

32. Again, by way of illustration, the Governments would make proposals at the harmonising level for a broader range of functions, clearly defined in scope (including, as appropriate, relevant EU aspects), from within the following categories:

aspects of
- agriculture and fisheries;
- industrial development;
- consumer affairs;
- transport;
- energy;
- trade;
- health;
- social welfare;
- education; and
- economic policy.

33. By way of example, the category of agriculture and fisheries might include

agricultural and fisheries research, training and advisory services, and animal welfare; health might include co-operative ventures in medical, paramedical and nursing training, cross-border provision of hospital services and major emergency/ accident planning; and education might include mutual recognition of teacher qualifications, co-operative ventures in higher education, in teacher training, in education for mutual understanding and in education for specialised needs.

34. The Governments also expect that a wide range of functions would be designated at the consultative level.

35. Both Governments envisage that all decisions within the body would be by agreement between the two sides. The Heads of Department on each side would operate within the overall terms of reference mandated by legislation in the two sovereign Parliaments. They would exercise their powers in accordance with the rules for democratic authority and accountability for this function in force in the Oireachtas and in new institutions in Northern Ireland. The operation of the North/South body's functions would be subject to regular scrutiny in agreed political institutions in Northern Ireland and the Oireachtas respectively.

36. Both Governments expect that there would be a Parliamentary Forum, with representatives from agreed political institutions in Northern Ireland and members of the Oireachtas, to consider a wide range of matters of mutual interest.

37. Both Governments envisage that the framework would include administrative support staffed jointly by members of the Northern Ireland Civil Service and the Irish Civil Service. They also envisage that both administrations will need to arrange finance for the North/South body and its agencies on the basis that these constitute a necessary public function.

38. Both Governments envisage that this new framework should serve to help heal the divisions among the communities on the island of Ireland; provide a forum for acknowledging the respective identities and requirements of the two major traditions; express and enlarge the mutual acceptance of the validity of those traditions; and promote understanding and agreement among the people and institutions in both parts of the island. The remit of the body should be dynamic, enabling progressive extension by agreement of its functions to new areas. Its role should develop to keep pace with the growth of harmonisation and with greater integration between the two economies.

The Mitchell Principles, January 1996

(extract)

THE MITCHELL PRINCIPLES

Extract from Report of the International Body on Arms Decommissioning:
Principles of Democracy and Non-Violence, January 1996

20. Accordingly, we recommend that the parties to such negotiations affirm their total and absolute commitment:

   a To democratic and exclusively peaceful means of resolving political issues;
   b To the total disarmament of all paramilitary organizations;
   c To agree that such disarmament must be verifiable to the satisfaction of an independent commission;
   d To renounce for themselves, and to oppose any effort by others, to use force, or threaten to use force, to influence the course or the outcome of all-party negotiations;
   e To agree to abide by the terms of any agreement reached in all-party negotiations and to resort to democratic and exclusively peaceful methods in trying to alter any aspect of that outcome with which they may disagree; and
   f To urge that 'punishment' killings and beatings stop and to take effective steps to prevent such actions.

21. We join the Governments, religious leaders and many others in condemning 'punishment' killings and beatings. They contribute to the fear that those who have used violence to pursue political objectives in the past will do so again in the future. Such actions have no place in a lawful society.

APPENDIX 11

IRA Ceasefire Statement, 19 July 1997

TEXT OF THE IRA CEASEFIRE STATEMENT

19 July 1997

On August 31, 1994 the leadership of Oglaigh na hEireann (IRA) announced their complete cessation of military operations as our contribution to the search for lasting peace.

After 17 months of cessation in which the British government and the unionists blocked any possibility of real or inclusive negotiations, we reluctantly abandoned the cessation.

The IRA is committed to ending British rule in Ireland. It is the root cause of divisions and conflict in our country. We want a permanent peace and therefore we are prepared to enhance the search for a democratic peace settlement through real and inclusive negotiations.

So having assessed the current political situation, the leadership of Oglaigh na hEireann are announcing a complete cessation of military operations from 12 midday on Sunday 20 July, 1997.

We have ordered the unequivocal restoration of the ceasefire of August 1994. All IRA units have been instructed accordingly.

APPENDIX 12

'Propositions on Heads of Agreement' issued by British and Irish governments, 12 January 1998

'PROPOSITIONS ON HEADS OF AGREEMENT' 12 JANUARY 1998

[The following is the full text of the document entitled
'Propositions on Heads of Agreement' issued by the British and Irish governments]

Balanced constitutional change, based on commitment to the principle of consent in all its aspects by both British and Irish governments, to include both changes to the Irish Constitution and to British constitutional legislation.

Democratically-elected institutions in Northern Ireland, to include a Northern Ireland assembly, elected by a system of proportional representation, exercising devolved executive and legislative responsibility over at least the responsibilities of the six Northern Ireland departments and with provisions to ensure that all sections of the community can participate and work together successfully in the operation of these institutions and that all sections of the community are protected.

A new British–Irish agreement to replace the existing Anglo-Irish Agreement and help establish close co-operation and enhance relationships, embracing:

- An intergovernmental council to deal with the totality of relationships, to include representatives of the British and Irish governments, the Northern Ireland administration and the devolved institutions in Scot land and Wales, with meetings twice a year at summit level.
- A North–South ministerial council to bring together those with executive responsibilities in Northern Ireland and the Irish Government in particular areas. Each side will consult, co-operate and take decisions on matters of mutual interest within the mandate of, and accountable to, the Northern Ireland assembly and the Oireachtas respectively. All decisions will be by agreement between the two sides, North and South.
- Suitable implementation bodies and mechanisms for policies agreed by the North–South council in meaningful areas and at an all-island level.
- Standing intergovernmental machinery between the Irish and British governments, covering issues of mutual interest, including non-devolved issues for Northern Ireland, when representatives of the Northern Ireland administration would be involved.

Provision to safeguard the rights of both communities in Northern Ireland, through arrangements for the comprehensive protection of fundamental human, civil, political, social, economic and cultural rights, including a Bill of Rights for Northern Ireland supplementing the provisions of the European Convention and to achieve full respect for the principles of equity of treatment and freedom from discrimination, and the cultural identity and ethos of both communities. Appropriate steps to ensure an equivalent level of protection in the Republic.

Effective and practical measures to establish and consolidate an acceptable peaceful society, dealing with issues such as prisoners, security in all its aspects, policing and decommissioning of weapons.

The Hillsborough Statement, 1 April 1999

TEXT OF THE DECLARATION
ISSUED BY BRITISH AND IRISH GOVERNMENTS
1 April 1999
(The Hillsborough Statement)

The following is the text of the declaration issued by the Taoiseach, Mr Ahern, and the British Prime Minister, Mr Blair, at Hillsborough Castle yesterday

Working draft, 1 April Declaration

It is now one year since the Good Friday Agreement was concluded. Last May it was emphatically endorsed by the people, North and South, and as such it now represents their democratic will.

The Agreement, in its own words, offers a truly historic opportunity for a new beginning. It gives us a chance, in this generation, to transcend the bitter legacy of the past and to transform relationships within Northern Ireland, between North and South, and between these islands.

All parties firmly believe that the violence we have all lived through must be put behind us. Never again should we or our children have to suffer the consequences of conflict. It must be brought to a permanent end. In partnership together we want to ensure a future free from conflict.

The realisation of that future places a heavy obligation on us all, individually and collectively. The implementation in full of the Agreement is inevitably a lengthy and complex process, involving continuing effort and commitment on all our parts.

It is encouraging and important that, even though much remains to be done, very substantial progress has already been made in turning the promise of the Agreement into a reality. We must not forget or underplay how far we have come.

Balanced changes to both the Irish Constitution and to British constitutional legislation based on the principle of consent, have been approved and are now ready to take effect.

The Northern Ireland Assembly was elected last June and has since been preparing for devolution. The international agreement signed in Dublin on 8 March provides for the establishment of the North–South ministerial council and implementation bodies, the British–Irish Council and the British–Irish Intergovernmental Conference.

The Northern Ireland Human Rights Commission has been established and its members appointed, and the new Equality Commission has been legislated for. Comparable steps by the Irish Government are well under way.

The needs of victims of violence, and their families, including those of the disappeared, are being addressed in both jurisdictions, though we acknowledge that for many their pain and suffering will never end.

The commitments in the Agreement in relation to economic, social and cultural issues, including as regards the Irish language, are being carried forward, though much of this work is inevitably long term.

Steps have been taken towards normalisation of security arrangements and practices, while the Commission on Policing for Northern Ireland and the review of criminal justice are both well advanced in their vital work.

Numerous prisoners, in both jurisdictions, have benefited from mechanisms providing for their accelerated release.

Against this background there is agreement among all parties that decommissioning is not a precondition but is an obligation deriving from their commitment in the Agreement, and that it should take place within the time-scale envisaged in the Agreement, and through the efforts of the Independent International Commission on Decommissioning.

Sinn Féin have acknowledged these obligations but are unable to indicate the time-scale on which decommissioning will begin. They do not regard the Agreement as imposing any requirement to make a start before the establishment of the new institutions.

The UUP do not wish to move to the establishment of the new institutions without some evident progress with decommissioning.

It would be a tragedy if this difference of view about timing and the sequence of events prevented the implementation of the Agreement from advancing.

We believe that decommissioning will only happen against a background where implementation is actively moving forward. Continued progress in establishing the new institutions will in itself create confidence. On the other hand, it is understandable that those who take the next steps in implementation should seek to be assured that these steps are not irrevocable if, in the event, no progress is made with decommissioning.

We therefore propose the following way forward.

On [date to be set] nominations will be made under the d'Hondt procedure of those to take up office as ministers when powers are devolved.

At a date to be proposed by the Independent International Commission on Decommissioning but not later than [one month after nomination date] a collective act of reconciliation will take place. This will see some arms put beyond use on a voluntary basis, in a manner which will be verified by the Independent International Commission on Decommissioning, and further moves on normalisation and demilitarisation in recognition of the changed situation on security.

In addition to the arrangements in respect of military material, there will at all times be ceremonies of remembrance of all victims of violence, to which representatives of all parties and the two governments, and all churches, will be invited.

Around the time of the act of reconciliation, powers will be devolved and the British–Irish Agreement will enter into force.

The following institutions will then be established: the NorthSouth Ministerial

Council, the North–South Implementation Bodies, the British–Irish Council and the British–Irish Intergovernmental Conference.

By [one month after nomination date], the Independent International Commission on Decommissioning will make a report on progress. It is understood by all that the successful implementation of the Agreement will be achieved if these steps are taken within the proposed time-scales; if they are not taken, the nominations mentioned above will fall to be confirmed by the Assembly.

APPENDIX 14

'The Way Forward' Joint Statement by British and Irish governments at Stormont, 2 July 1999

'THE WAY FORWARD' JOIN STATEMENT

BY THE IRISH AND BRITISH GOVERNMENTS AT STORMONT

ON 2 JULY 1999

After five days of discussion, the British and Irish Governments have put to all the parties a way forward to establish an inclusive Executive, and to decommission arms.

These discussions have been difficult. But as they conclude, the peace process is very much alive, and on track.

The Good Friday Agreement presents the best chance of peace and prosperity in decades.

It is clear from our discussions that nobody wants to throw that opportunity away.

We believe that unionist and nationalist opinion will see that our approach meets their concerns, and will support it accordingly.

The way forward is as follows:

1. All parties reaffirm the three principles agreed on 25 June

    - an inclusive Executive exercising devolved powers;
    - decommissioning of all paramilitary arms by May 2000;
    - decommissioning to be carried out in a manner determined by the International Commission on Decommissioning.

2. The D'Hondt procedure to nominate Ministers to be run on 15 July.
3. The Devolution Order to be laid before the British Parliament on 16 July to take effect on 18 July. Within the period specified by the de Chastelain Commission, the Commission will confirm the start to the process of decommissioning, that start to be defined as in their report of 2 July.
4. As described in their report today, the commission will have urgent discussions with the groups' points of contact. The commission will specify that actual decommissioning is to start within a specified time. They will report progress in September and December 1999, and in May 2000.

5. A 'failsafe' clause: the governments undertake that, in accordance with the review provisions of the agreement, if commitments under the agreement are not met, either in relation to decommissioning or to devolution, they will automatically, and with immediate effect, suspend the operation of the institutions set up by the agreement.

In relation to decommissioning, this action will be taken on receipt of a report at any time that the commitments now being entered into, or steps which are subsequently laid down by the commission are not fulfilled, in accordance with the Good Friday agreement. The British government will legislate to this effect.

All parties have fought very hard to ensure their basic concerns have been met. This means that we are now closer than ever to a fulfilling the promise of the Good Friday agreement:

- a government for Northern Ireland in which the two traditions work together in a devolved administration;
- new North–South and British–Irish institutions;
- the decommissioning of paramilitary arms;
- constitutional change;
- equality, justice, human rights and the normalisation of Northern Ireland society.

All sides have legislative safeguards to ensure that commitments entered into are met. This is an historic opportunity. Now is the time to seize it.

APPENDIX 15

Statement issued by the IRA, 21 July 1999

STATEMENT ISSUED BY THE IRA

21 July 1999

The argument that the present political process can deliver real and meaningful change has been significantly undermined by the course of events over the past 15 months.

This culminated in the failure last week to establish the political institutions set out in the Good Friday agreement.

The agreement has failed to deliver tangible progress and its potential for doing so has substantially diminished in recent months.

The credibility and motivation of unionist leaders who signed up to the agreement is clearly open to question. They have repeatedly reneged on the commitments they made in signing the agreement and successfully blocked the implementation of its institutional aspects.

It is clearly their intention to continue their obstructionist tactics indefinitely. There is irrefutable evidence that the unionist political leadership remains, at this time, opposed to a democratic peace settlement.

Recent events at Stormont cannot obscure the fact that the primary responsibility for the developing political crisis rests squarely with the British government. They have once again demonstrated a lack of political will to confront the unionist veto.

Over the past five years we have called and maintained two prolonged cessations of military operations to enhance the peace process and underline our definitive commitment to its success. We have contributed in a meaningful way to the creation of a climate which would facilitate the search for a durable settlement.

The first of these cessations floundered on the demand by the Conservative government for an IRA surrender. Those who demand the decommissioning of IRA weapons lend themselves, in the current political context, inadvertently or otherwise, to the failed agenda which seeks the defeat of the IRA. The British government have the power to change that context and should do so.

It remains our view that the roots of conflict in our country lie in British involvement in Irish affairs. Responsibility for repairing the damage to the argument that the present political process can deliver real change rests primarily with the British government.

APPENDIX 16

Statement by Senator George Mitchell concluding the Review of the Northern Ireland Peace Process, 18 November 1999

STATEMENT BY SENATOR GEORGE MITCHELL CONCLUDING THE REVIEW OF THE NORTHERN IRELAND PEACE PROCESS, 18 NOVEMBER 1999

I indicated in my last statement on 15 November that I expected to be in a position to issue a concluding report on the review soon after the publication of the assessment on the Independent International Commission on Decommissioning (IICD) and of the parties' positions on the issues which we have been considering together in the review.

Those steps have now been taken. Together they represent a set of extremely positive developments.

I welcome the statements from the parties, which should further build mutual confidence in each other's commitment to the full implementation of the Good Friday Agreement and to the three principles as agreed on 25 June, namely:

- An inclusive executive exercising devolved powers.
- Decommissioning of all paramilitary arms by May 2000.
- Decommissioning to be carried out in a manner determined by the IICD.

I also welcome the IICD assessment of how it can best achieve the mandate under the agreement. I share its conclusion that:

Decommissioning is by definition a voluntary act and cannot be imposed. To bring decommissioning about, the Commission will need the co-operation and support of the political parties, using all the influence they have, together with the wholehearted commitment of paramilitary organisations.

While decommissioning is an essential element of the agreement, the context in which it can be achieved is the overall implementation of that agreement. All participants have a collective responsibility in this regard.

In response to the IICD assessment, the parties have made clear that the IICD is the agreed mechanism for achieving decommissioning, under the terms of the Good Friday Agreement.

In the light of these and other encouraging developments, including the proposed appointment of authorised representatives of paramilitary organisations to the IICD, I believe that a basis now exists for devolution to occur, for the institutions to be established, and for decommissioning to take place as soon as possible.

Devolution should take effect, then the executive should meet, and then the paramilitary groups should appoint their authorised representatives, all on the same day, in that order.

I hereby recommend to the governments and the parties that they make the necessary arrangements to proceed, and call on them to do so without delay. That completes the review, and with it my role in this process. I conclude with some personal comments.

Not long ago, the Ulster Unionists and Sinn Féin did not speak directly. In the early weeks of the review, their exchanges were harsh and filled with recrimination. But gradually, as one of them put it, 'trust crept in'.

It may not be trust yet, but it is an important start, and the discussions did become serious and meaningful.

For that credit goes to the leaders, David Trimble and Sir Reg Empey; and Gerry Adams and Martin McGuinness. They, and the other leaders of their parties, set aside their hostility for the good of their society.

The Social Democratic and Labour Party, led by John Hume and Seamus Mallon, provided crucial insight and involvement. It will play an important role in the executive.

The leaders of the other pro-agreement parties were strongly supportive: Sean Neeson and Seamus Close of Alliance, David Ervine and Billy Hutchinson of the Progressive Unionist Party, Monica McWilliams and Jane Morrice of the Northern Ireland Women's Coalition, and Gary McMichael and David Adams of the Ulster Democratic Party; and all of their colleagues.

They and their parties were essential to the Good Friday Agreement. They are indispensable to its full implementation. It cannot and will not be done without them.

The prime ministers of the United Kingdom and Ireland, Tony Blair and Bertie Ahern, and President Clinton, played important roles in this effort, as did Mo Mowlam, David Andrews and Liz O'Donnell.

The new Secretary of State, Peter Mandelson, is a strong and effective leader who, in a short time, has had an enormous positive impact.

I also would like to recognise two superb officials, Bill Jeffrey for the British, and Dermot Gallagher for the Irish. With their colleagues, they provided me with invaluable assistance, for which they have my gratitude.

As a result of all of these efforts, neither side will get all it wanted and both will endure severe political pain.

But there is no other way forward. Prolonging the stalemate will leave this society uncertain and vulnerable.

If this process succeeds, the real winners will be the people, who want their political leaders to work out their differences through democratic dialogue.

I have been involved in this effort for nearly five years. I cannot say that I've enjoyed every minute of it.

But while on occasion it has been difficult, it has also been one of the most meaningful times of my life.

I am totally committed to the cause of peace and reconciliation in Northern Ireland.

Admiration

And I can say that the longer I've been here the more I have come to admire and like and believe in the people.

They are energetic and productive, warm and generous. I have been treated here as though I were at home.

In a sense I am at home, because my emotions and a part of my heart will be here forever, even though I will not always be physically present.

My thanks to you ladies and gentlemen of the press for your courtesy, to the prime minister and taoiseach for inviting me to take part in this process, to the party leaders with whom I have spent these past few months and who I respect for their courage, and, finally, to the people for their warmth and hospitality.

I hope to return often, in other capacities. My fervent prayer is that it will be to a society in which hope and opportunity are alive and where a durable peace, tolerance and mutual respect are not distant dreams, but rather are the reality of daily life for all of the people.

Index